TOWARDS REVOLUTION
Volume I

ALSO BY JOHN GERASSI

The Great Fear in Latin America
The Boys of Boise
Venceremos! (Editor)
North Vietnam: A Documentary
Latin American Radicalism (Co-editor)

TOWARDS REVOLUTION

Volume I

CHINA, INDIA, ASIA,
THE MIDDLE EAST, AFRICA

Selected, edited and introduced by
JOHN GERASSI

WEIDENFELD AND NICOLSON
5 WINSLEY STREET LONDON W1

Casebound SBN 297 00148 5
Paperback SBN 0 297 00351 8

Printed in Great Britain by
Willmer Brothers Limited, Birkenhead

To Huey P. Newton and Charles Garry

If there is no struggle, there is no progress.
Those who profess to favour freedom, and yet
depreciate agitation, are men who want crops
without plowing up the ground. They want rain
without thunder and lightning. They want the
ocean without the awful roar of its many waters.
Power concedes nothing without demand.

Frederick Douglass

Revolution is the larva of civilization.

Victor Hugo

CONTENTS

Contents

A*

Acknowledgements

Though the idea for this work was born shortly after the first conference of the Tricontinental organization in January 1966, it did not really take shape until after three events that have become crucial in my life: my trip to North Vietnam over Christmas–New Year 1966–7, my attendance at the first conference of the Organization of Latin American Solidarity in Havana in the summer of 1967, and my friendship with Huey Newton, whom I used to visit regularly in the Alemeda County jail in 1968. From the Vietnamese I learned what peoples' solidarity is all about; from the OLAS delegates, many of whom had come directly from the guerrilla struggles of Latin America, I realized that only through such solidarity will man ever stop exploiting man; and from Huey Newton I understood that individual fulfilment is meaningful only when it is felt in and through such solidarity.

The Vietnamese and the Cubans and Latin American delegates to OLAS helped me obtain material for this book. Huey gave me invaluable insight into the Black Liberation Movement and dictated an article exclusively for this book. Many others, too, helped to track down needed documents, among them Bernardo Garcia, Karen Wald, Torregian Sotere, the staff of the Hoover Institute at Stanford, Beverly Axelrod and Anatole Anton in the Bay Area; Malcolm Caldwell, Farris Glubb, Russell Stetler, Antonio Cisneros, Peter Buckman, Ruth First, Basil Davidson in London; staff members of the North American Congress on Latin America (NACLA), Liberation News Service (LNS), Elizabeth Sutherland Martinez, the *Guardian*, the Free School (University) in New York. Advice from and discussion and/or arguments with Irving Louis and Danielle Horowitz, Pat Bell, Reies Tijerina, David Horowitz, Herbert Marcuse, Carlos Romeo, Roberto Fernandez Retamar, Ralph Miliband, William Pomeroy, Jerry Rubin, Jean Pierre Vigier, Jean-Paul Sartre, Simone de Beauvoir, Sharon Krebs, Ricardo Romo, Danny Schechter, Ed Vickery, Sol Yurick, Carl Oglesby, Sean Gervasi, Steve Weissman, Julio Alvarez del Vayo, David and Barbara Stone, David Hilliard, Fred Goff, Mike Locker, John Levin, Margaret Leahy, Fred Gardner, Todd Gitlin, Carol Cina, Jane Alpert, Bobby Seale, Stokeley

Acknowledgements

Carmichael, Marcel Nidergang, Pito Colon, Chuck Bradley, D. F. Fleming, Bob Ockene, Keith Lampe, Jean Ripert, Jean Conilh, Fawwaz Trabulsi, Pamela Copp, Howard Senzel, Joe Berke, Paul Dufeu, Diane Gerros, George Gourevitch and especially Charles Garry and students at San Francisco Stage College helped me in my focus.

Besides the translators credited herein, I would like to thank the typists, proof-readers and researchers who gave so much of their time to make this work possible, among them Lesley Churchill, Shirley Ward, Mara Sabinson, Sara Carter, Ruth Nelson, Camille Alonso, John Taylor, Johnny McGuigan, and Peter, Simon and Collin. Helena Bradley in Berkeley, Sue LeGrand, Jenny James and especially, Heather Musgrove in London made up the real collective that got this book together.

Finally, I would like to thank all the unnamed revolutionaries in Asia, Africa, and America who took time out to answer my queries and requests. I can only hope that this collection will help make clear the reason and the cause for their actions and commitment.

Foreword: The Future is Revolution

Every now and then throughout history, lines harden, myths crumble, contradictions crystallize. From contradiction emerges confrontation, and from confrontation eventually surges progress. All over the world today, confrontation is developing into a way of life. The division between master and slave, exploiter and exploited, alienating and alienated, robot and rebel is becoming clearer. In the decades to come, familiar concepts will be discarded, systems will be smashed, empires will be destroyed. Once again, the future is revolution.

Human progress, whether we like it or not, has always come about as a result of confrontation—and revolution. From gods to kings, from plutocracies to technocracies, change has been generated by people, men and women who drew the line, who shouted 'enough!' and made their stand. No power has ever been too strong, no class too thorough, no elite too shrewd, no army too invulnerable permanently to suppress the desire for redress by ordinary people.

Inevitably, at each stage, that general desire has been manipulated—channelled, sidetracked, mis-routed, betrayed—by the few. And also inevitably, each step forward has been paid for in astronomical human costs. The curve of progress is nowhere a straight vertical. Rather it is a jagged, broken line. But its overall path is firmly upwards.

At each climactic confrontation the slogans have varied. But not the cause, not the often-unstated ideals. Whether the rebellions were against autocratic rulers who treated men as animals, or against dehumanized organizations who counted men as numbers, or simply against men whose privileges denied the necessities of other men, the goal of rebels has always been the same: freedom.

It is said that the word—freedom—means many things to many people. Certainly it is often used to justify its opposite. To cite an obvious example, in Vietnam, US forces have destroyed innumerable freedoms that the people cherished, while claiming the right to do so in freedom's name ('I'll make you free even if I have to wreck your country to do it'). But the word is just as full of force and content today as it was when the Indians resisted the invading Puritans, when the canudos revolted against their landlords and when Spartacus rose against Rome.

Freedom is not the right to say or do anything you want that does not infringe on the freedom of others. Freedom means having the material and psychological *power* to say or do that thing. Freedom is the real possibility of being relevant, of being meaningful, of being total. No man who is poor when another is rich is free. No man who does not exert control, equal to all other men, over his courts, police, government or army is free. No country which is financially, militarily or geopolitically dependent on another is free. To talk about freedom of the press when only the rich control the media, to herald free enterprise when health (hospitals, doctors, medicine, etc.) costs money, to cherish free courts when lawyers, bail, appeals, etc., require wealth—in general to hail a society as free when money is the means by which one buys one's free choice is a travesty.

Obviously, no society is completely free—and probably never will be. But some come closer to the great ideal than others. And in history, mankind has been appproximating bit by bit all along. That *is* history: man's struggle to be free. Most historians, of course, view it as the movement of forces, sometimes very abstract, and analyse events as if occurring somehow independently of people. Names, dates, places—that is the foodstuff of history books, while people tend to be merely cannon fodder. If one does scrutinize, say, a particular battle, it is perfectly true that the superiority of the fire power of one army over the other, the quality of leadership, the economic resources of the opposing sides, and so on, will explain the battle's outcome much more succinctly than, perhaps, the fact that the cannon fodder on one side believed themselves to be fighting for something more meaningful than what the other side was fighting for.

But on the long run and in the long view, what changes man's relationship to man (though perhaps not their countries' borders) is precisely that fodder. If today, you and I are relatively freer than were our grandparents it is because the gladiators refused to kill each other, because individual believers refused to buy through tithes their place in heaven, because the bourgeoisie of Paris wanted as much say in the affairs of France as the Bourbons, because farmers in New England did not want to be ruled by red-coated foreigners, because the workers of St Petersburg went hungry once too often, because the Wobblies in the USA wanted to own their mines and factories.

Human progress is never initiated by governments. They merely reflect the will and desire of the ruling classes. Progress is won *from* governments as a result of struggle—strikes, demonstrations, rebellions, insurrections. If a particular government figure or bureaucracy enacts laws that do bring about some progress, it is only because the upsurge from below, the outcry of the fodder, has frightened the ruling class enough to allow concessions—for its own survival.

Depending on that strength from below, the ruling class either crushes dissent (reaction), gives into some demands and incorporates reforms which do not change the fundamental structure (liberalism) or is overthrown (revolution). When reforms are not enough to satisfy the discontent, the ruling class inevitably resorts to reaction, inevitable precisely because the reforms demanded require the ruling class to commit class suicide. It is as if we demanded that all cars produced be indestructible, unpolluting and cheap (all technologically feasible). General Motors, Ford, the oil and the insurance companies would obviously object. They're in business to make profits, which they use to maintain their life style. If people's demands grew louder, they might try a few reforms: more padding, better seat belts, a special carburettor which cuts down pollution and a policy of recalling cars to fix major defects at their expense (all of which they've done, or are doing). But suppose we still weren't satisfied—you and me and all the other fodder—and our discontent grew to the point that we were willing to seize General Motors, burn down the insurance companies (and the banks who finance the operations)? Then what? Well, Ford or General Motors bosses are certainly not going to give up their yachts and planes and villas in eight countries, nor the control they exercise through their wealth over every institution in the land. They'll tell their representatives (the government) to put an end to the dissent and the government will then try to jail or kill us. Our only alternative is revolution.

The first of us to try will fail. Revolution is a long process. Before every success lie scores of failures. Sometimes so many of us fail that in our generation the spirit will die altogether. It won't start again until the next. But it will eventually succeed. Russia's Decembrists didn't get very far in the last century, but without them there would have been no 1905 revolution. That one failed too, but it set the stage for the success of 1917. Likewise in China, the revolutionaries almost got wiped out in 1927. The few who survived started literally from the bottom again—and didn't win until 1949. The Cuban revolution of 1895 seized power in 1959. The Algerian 'war' lasted only seven years, but the rebellions started more than a century before, and without them the FLN's victory would not have been possible. As Che Guevara once put it: 'It does not matter what the results of today's struggles are. It does not matter, as far as the final result is concerned, whether one movement or another is momentarily defeated. What is definitive is the determination to fight (which matures from day to day), the awareness of the need for revolutionary change, and the certainty that the latter is possible.'[1]

The awareness of the need for revolutionary change certainly does exist throughout the world today. In varying degrees, to be sure, and against various Establishments (ruling elites). The Czech youth, for example, considers the Soviet Russian Establishment its main enemy, because it controls the puppets who rule in Prague. The rebels of Angola, Mozambique and Guiné-Bissau are fighting against Portugal, which occupies these lands as colonies. The leaders of the rebels are perfectly aware that behind Portugal is the USA which furnishes it with the arms, planes, napalm and money to wage the war. But the immediate enemy is nevertheless Portugal. In South Africa and Zimbabwe, the revolutionary forces know that without the connivance, support, trade and aid of international (mostly US) capitalists, the apartheid regimes would have a harder time profiting from their vicious rule. But they cannot ignore, even if they do not talk about it, that Russia and other so-called communist countries of Eastern Europe also trade and benefit from these racist governments. In Guyana and Trinidad, in the Persian Gulf and Malayan Peninsula, as well as the USA, which owns most of the countries' resources, the enemy is also Great Britain, which constantly intervenes (inevitably prodded by the USA) in the countries' affairs in order to maintain the semi-feudalistic capitalist structure. In Martinique, Guadeloupe, Réunion and Chad, the villain is France.

Whatever the enemy, the fight is to the finish. For once begun, it cannot stop. As revolutionaries say: 'In revolution, one either wins or dies.'

John Gerassi
1 May 1970

Overview Part 1:

PEASANTS AND PARTISANS

As a pragmatist, Lenin believed that the only way a revolution could come about in Europe in his time was by the creation of a revolutionary organization. That organization had to be tight, well-trained, loyal to its central committee, dedicated—and narrow, not only for ideological reasons (hence purges and sectariarist splits* were to be encouraged during its formative years) but also for security. 'The more we *confine* the membership of such an organization to people who are professionally engaged in revolutionary activity and who have been professionally trained in the art of combating the political police, the more difficult will it be to unearth the organization.'[2] And clearly, by training Lenin did not mean just study groups or trade-union infiltration. He meant action. 'Let the squads begin to train for immediate operations,' he wrote after the 1905 massacre, 'some can undertake to assassinate a spy or blow up a police station, others can attack a bank to expropriate funds for an insurrection. Let every squad learn, if only by beating up police'[3] (precisely the tactics of black revolutionary movements and the Weathermen in the USA).

Besides training and agitation (propaganda) among the masses, Lenin also strongly advocated infiltration and agitation in the state armies. In *The Proletarian Revolution and the Renegade Kautsky*, Lenin said:

Not a single great revolution has ever taken place, or ever can take place, without the 'disorganization' of the army. For the army is the most ossified instrument for supporting the old regime, the most hardened bulwark of bourgeois discipline, buttressing up the rule of capital, and preserving and fostering among the working people the servile spirit of submission and subjection to capital. Counter-revolution has never tolerated, and never could tolerate, armed workers side by side with the army.[4]

* And from 1902 when his vanguard organ, the paper *Iskra* (Spark), was barely functioning well, Lenin ruthlessly manipulated splits in order to weed out from the organization those he considered weak or unreliable.

Lenin's aim was to set up dual power before the revolution: the state above, and below, workers' power (what today would be called people's power, black power, brown power, etc. When the Black Panthers in the USA began establishing their breakfast programme*, they were in effect spreading this dual power—which is why they were so viciously repressed). But when all is said and done, Lenin's primary advice for revolutionaries was simple: 'de l'audace, de l'audace, encore de l'audace.'[5]†

Audacity is precisely what characterized best Mao Tse-tung and the Chinese revolutionaries. But they also had an equal portion of tenacity. Thus when it appeared to all and sundry that they were beaten, they merely retreated, started anew and gradually reassaulted their enemies, wiping them out more than twenty years later. Unlike the Russians, the Chinese communists did not win through general insurrection. Nor did they focus their attention on the cities, as did the Bolsheviks. Instead they fought in the countryside, establishing not dual power but separate power, that is, areas where they were in complete control, and then kept expanding those areas until they surrounded and strangled the cities. To do so they had to fight a civil war. But then so did the Bolsheviks, after they had seized power in central Russia.

Neither the Bolsheviks nor the Chinese communists shunned such conflagration. Both knew it was inevitable. As Lenin had said in 1906, more than a decade before he was proved correct:

The enemies of our revolution among the people are few in number, but as the struggle grows more acute they become more and more organized and receive the support of the reactionary strata of the bourgeoisie. It is therefore absolutely natural and inevitable that in such a period, a period of nationwide political strikes, an uprising cannot assume the old form of individual acts restricted to a very short time and to a very small area. It is absolutely natural and inevitable that the uprising should assume the higher and more complex form of a prolonged civil war embracing the whole country, i.e. an armed struggle between two sections of the people.[6]

In fact, civil war has always accompanied revolution, whatever its ideology. It happened in France in 1789–93, for example, and

---

* The Panthers try to feed some 100,000 ghetto kids every morning.

† Actually the slogan, often quoted by Engels, was transformed somewhat in the retranslation of Danton's original shout: 'De l'audace, encore de l'audace, toujours de l'audace' (roughly translated: 'audacity, more audacitys, always audacity').

also in the USA in 1776–80, when far more settlers, proportionally, left America in hatred of George Washington than from Cuba because of Fidel.

At first, the Chinese Communist revolution stuck faithfully to the Leninist programme. The CP loyally cooperated with the bourgeois-military regime of Chiang Kai-shek (who had taken over as titular head of the Chinese Republic when Sun Yat-sen died in 1925), and focused most of its activities among the proletarians of the major cities. Receiving Russian aid, Chiang successfully defeated one warlord after another as he marched north on his 'great unification' drive. But it was the workers, led by their dynamic and dashing leader Chou En-lai, who seized Shanghai. Chou then agreed to turn over the city to Chiang and his Kuomintang (Nationalist Party), which the Russians viewed somewhat as the equivalent to their own provisional government. But Chiang was far worse than Kerensky. In April 1927, as Chiang's forces occupied Shanghai, they immediately set upon their allies, slaughtering thousands of workers and every communist they could find. (Chou was tipped off by a friend at the last minute; Mao himself was captured but managed to dive into a long patch of high grass and escape—only 200 yards away from the wall where he would have been shot.)

After Chiang's double-cross, Mao, who was then not the top leader in the CP, led a peasant revolt. When it failed, he was repudiated as an adventurer by his Party comrades. Undaunted, he took his 1,000 weary, beaten, surviving peasants into the mountains of Chingkangshan along the border of Hunan and Kiangsi provinces and began to wage guerrilla warfare. In April 1928 he was joined by Chu Teh, a conscience-ridden Chiang general, and the 2,000 men he had managed to lead out of the Kuomintang army. Together they established their first liberated area, where landlords were executed or exiled, land was given to peasants, corruption was eliminated, taxes lowered and collected fairly, etc. In his report to the Central Committee, Mao said:

China is the only country in the world today where one or more small areas under Red political power have emerged in the midst of a White regime which encircles them. We find on analysis that one reason for this phenomenon lies in the incessant splits and wars within China's comprador and landlord classes. So long as these splits and wars continue, it is possible for an armed independent regime of workers and peasants to survive and grow. In addition, its survival and growth require the following conditions: (1) a sound base, (2) a sound Party organization, (3) a fairly strong Red Army, (4) terrain favourable to military operations, and (5) economic resources sufficient for sustenance.[7]

Incredibly, however, Mao continued to honour the alliance with the Kuomintang as Russia demanded—except, of course, when attacked. In the same report, he explained his reasons:

We fully agree with the Communist International's resolution on China. There is no doubt that China is still at the stage of the bourgeois-democratic revolution. The programme for a thorough democratic revolution in China comprises, externally, the overthrow of imperialism* so as to achieve complete national liberation, and, internally, the elimination of the power and influence of the comprador class in the cities, the completion of the agrarian revolution in order to abolish feudal relations in the villages, and the overthrow of the government of the warlords. We must go through such a democratic revolution before we can lay a real foundation for the transition to socialism. In the past year we have fought in many places and are keenly aware that the revolutionary tide is on the ebb in the country as a whole. While Red political power has been established in a few small areas, in the country as a whole the people lack the ordinary democratic rights, the workers, the peasants, and even the bourgeois democrats do not have freedom of speech or assembly, and the worst crime is to join the Communist Party. Wherever the Red Army goes, the masses are cold and aloof, and only after our propaganda do they slowly move into action. Whatever enemy units we face, there are hardly any cases of mutiny or desertion, to our side, and we have to fight it out. This holds even for the enemy's Sixth Army which recruited the greatest number of 'rebels' after the May 21st Incident.† We have an acute sense of our isolation which we keep hoping will end. Only by launching a political and economic struggle for democracy, which will also involve the urban petty bourgeoisie, can we turn the revolution into a seething tide that will surge through the country.[8]

Progress in the urban areas was much slower, however. Yet, despite the fact that every city uprising was crushed, the Chinese CP, obedient to the Russian experience, insisted that the revolution

---

* China was still totally dominated economically by the great powers (England, France, Japan, USA), and often military, politically, culturally and by the police as well. As late as 1905 a sign in a Shanghai park said: 'Dogs and Chinese not allowed.'

† On 21 May 1927 a counter-revolutionary coup in Changsha, Hunan, led to vast peasant massacres. Many of the surviving peasants were then drafted into the Sixth Army. Changsha was Mao's home town; his first wife and her younger sister died in that massacre.

must be waged by workers, not peasants, and refused to earmark any aid to the Mao–Chu enclave. Mao, whose solid peasant background gave him faith in his people, tried gently to persuade the Central Committee. In a letter to party cadres, entitled *A Single Spark Can Start a Prairie Fire,* he wrote: 'It would be wrong to abandon the struggle in the cities, but in our opinion it would also be wrong for any of our Party members to fear the growth of peasant strength lest it would outstrip the workers' strength and harm the revolution.' It is then also that Mao issued his famous guerrilla warfare slogan: '... the enemy advances, we retreat; the enemy camps, we harass; the enemy tires, we attack; the enemy retreats, we pursue.'[9]

These tactics did not please the CP hierarchy. In 1932 it abandoned its Shanghai underground for the safety of Mao's liberated area, which was now in southern Kiangsi. By then Mao and Chu were firmly established; they had defeated sixteen out of the thirty-three divisions Chiang sent against them in his 'annihilation campaign'. Nevertheless, the CP theorists insisted that Mao's policy of quick withdrawals was bound to alienate the farmers left behind, and forced him to alter his tactics. With his mobility gone and Chiang attacking in strength (even when invading Japanese seized Manchuria and prepared to assault China proper), Mao, who still had the complete loyalty of the communist field commanders, decided to leave Kiangsi for northern Yenan—a forced march of 6,000 miles, as far as from the tip of South Africa to Glasgow. In the process he took over complete control of the Political Bureau of the Party's Central Committee and in December 1935 became top policy formation leader.

It is then that Mao called for a united front with his enemies, Chiang's Kuomintang, to fight the Japanese—who had invaded China itself.

If our government [said Mao] has hitherto been based on the alliance of the workers, the peasants and the urban petty bourgeoisie, from now on it must be so transformed as to include also the members of all other classes who are willing to take part in the national revolution ... it may include those who are interested only in the national revolution and not in the agrarian revolution, and even, if they so desire, those who may oppose Japanese imperialism and its running dogs, though they are not opposed to the European and US imperialists because of their close ties with the latter.... In 1927 ... the revolutionary united front had no mainstay, no strong revolutionary armed forces. . . . Today things are different. Now we have a strong Communist Party and a strong Red Army, and we also have the bare areas of the Red Army. Not only are the Communist Party and the Red Army serving as the initiator of a national united front against Japan today, but in the future too they will inevitably become the powerful mainstay of China's anti-Japanese government and army, capable of preventing the Japanese imperialists and Chaing Kai-shek from carrying through their policy of disrupting this united front.[10]

The alliance was brittle. In 1936 Chiang was kidnapped by rebellious Kuomintang officers and handed to the communists. Under orders from Moscow, he was released—but only after promising to send his troops against the Japanese, not the Reds. Instead, Chiang held his troops back, letting the Red Army do most of the fighting. By 1937 Mao ruled 30,000 square miles and two million people. By 1939 the Eighth Route and the New Fourth Armies, which had been welded into steel by Chu Teh, quadrupled the Red-liberated areas. It was then that Mao wrote *The Chinese Revolution and the Chinese Communist Party*[11] as a textbook for CP cadre-formation schools. It is this text which elevated Mao's two-stage revolution from a tactic (means) to a strategy (principle). First, said Mao, organize a solid communist apparatus. Then, develop a Red Army under the direction of the apparatus. Next, launch a patriotic or democratic war against foreign imperialists. Only when this has been brought to a successful conclusion, undertake the next stage—the socialist revolution. This means that the war will be very prolonged ('protracted', to use his word). It must be fought primarily in the rural areas: because the imperialists always control the cities; because guerrilla warfare needs mobility possible only in an extensive territory; because the economy always disfavours the rural population; and because the counter-revolutionary camp is disunited outside its cities (in Vietnam later, for example, some US militarists wanted only to hold the enclaves, others constantly to launch find-destroy-withdraw operations, and still others to occupy and pacify the whole country). But Mao also warned that unless the CP had strong links within the cities the rural apparatus would easily become isolated. City work was to remain important. But in the cities, the proletariat cannot win alone. It must, therefore, enter into alliance with every anti-imperialist force. The united front must be prepared to join the legal (elections, trade union, etc.) struggle and win over the national bourgeoisie. Thus the first stage of revolution must be anti-imperialist (i.e. anti-foreign capital) but not anti-capitalist (i.e. not anti-national capital).

Mao's strategy worked perfectly. Though Chiang's rested troops attacked Mao's war-worn armies immediately after Japan had been put to rout, the country's moral support went solidly to the communists. Chiang was forced to use his troops to quell disorders in the cities, and could no longer control inflation. Within four years, despite massive US aid, arms and advisers, the Kuomintang was smashed. Mao and his men, their clothes in tatters but their spirit elated, entered into Peking in March 1949. Immediately Mao went into stage two of the revolution, and by 1951 China was communist.

To the Chinese it was then clear that by following their model the people of any imperialized country could do as well. Marshal Lin Piao, Mao's heir-designate, saw in the Chinese experience a world-scale model; in each underdeveloped country (especially in Asia), he said, communists should organize the peasants, lead a protracted people's war, surround and strangle the cities, the bastions of imperialism. In September 1965 Lin Piao wrote an article commemorating the twentieth anniversary of Japan's defeat. Published in *Renmin Ribae* (People's Daily), it soon became known the world over as the 'Lin Piao theory' for people's war and revolution in the underdeveloped world through the 'strangulation of the cities'. Of fundamental importance to all Maoists, it not only explained how people's war was to be fought—stressing the need for united anti-imperialist fronts, that is, for alliance with the national bourgeoisies—but also emphasized the subordination of the military to the political. 'During the anti-Japanese war our army staunchly performed three tasks, fighting, mass work, and production,' he said. 'It was at the same time a fighting force, a political work force and a production corps. Everywhere it went, it did propaganda work among the masses, organized and armed them and helped them set up revolutionary political power.... The essence of a people's army is that politics is the commander. Political work is the lifeline of our army.'

Then, generalizing broadly, he added:

The countryside and the countryside alone can provide the revolutionary bases from which the revolutionaries can go forward to final victory. Taking the entire globe, if North America and Western Europe can be called the cities of the World then Asia, Africa and Latin America constitute the rural areas of the world . . . in this stage of revolution, imperialism and its lackeys are the principal enemy; it is necessary to rally all anti-imperialist patriotic forces, including the national bourgeoisie. . . . It is very harmful to confuse the two stages, that is, the national-democratic and the socialist revolutions.*

Just as the Russian model failed in the early days of the Chinese revolution, so the Chinese model failed in other Asian countries afterwards. To be sure, the Chinese model was not adhered to strictly and confirmed Maoists can point to these divergencies as reasons for their failure. And some of the divergencies were outstanding. In Indonesia, for example, the Indonesian Communist Party on the one hand made an absolute fetish of its alliance with President Sukarno and his forces (the national bourgeoisie), while on the other, though PKI boss D. N. Aidit swore faithfully to Peking, it never developed liberated areas, never launched a Red Army, never prepared its cadre for protracted struggle. It was thus caught totally off guard by the October 1965 military–CIA coup. The result: 700,000 communists dead.

In the Philippines, the Communist Party (PKP†) was faithful to Moscow, not Peking, yet developed a formidable military guerrilla apparatus, the Huks, first to fight against Japan, then against the US neo-colonialized Philippine government. Today the Huks are totally divorced from the PKP and their struggle has certainly been protracted. Yet, although they are spreading, the Chinese pattern is not being repeated.

The fundamental difference between China and the Philippines is that the latter is not occupied by foreign imperialists. Mao and Chu could and did successfully wage a patriotic war because of the Japanese invaders. They could and did appeal to all non-imperialist sectors of the population, *inside the cities* as well as out, to rally to their cause. The Huks cannot. Hence they are restricted to rural areas. Since the PKP now repudiates them and since they have no urban apparatus, their protracted war remains isolated. No matter how successful they are in the countryside, Manila and the other major cities can ignore them. Obviously, some *additional* tactic has

---

* See below, p. 70. 'Lin Piao theory' of revolution is still applied wherever the revolutionaries are Maoist.

† Partedi Komunista ng Pilipinas.

to be devised, or else the Chinese model is deficient in neo-colonialized countries.

In Burma, the revolutionaries are totally committed to Mao's thought. There, too, they have been waging armed struggle—for some twenty-two years of the Communist Party's thirty years of existence. In 1945 the CPB was one of the leading parties. In 1948 the civil war began. By 1950 the communists controlled most of the rural areas and almost every town and city except Rangoon, the capital. Then the government—first U Nu, then Ne Win—launched a series of counter-attacks. Well planned and well armed (by the British and the USA, which secretly gave the army modern weapons[12] and napalm[13]), the government offensive regained much of the ground. In 1965, however, the communists increased their activity in thirty-one of Burma's fifty-odd provinces. Then on 24 September 1968 Thakhin Than Tun, the Party's chairman, was killed, and once again the CPB's fate seemed to ebb—despite considerable successes carried by Burma's minorities, the Kachins, Shans, Karens and Kayas, who also oppose the government and are allied to the communists. A year later the guerrillas, led by Thakin Ba Thein Tin, seemed to be gaining once again, though the minority armies appeared to be dormant.[14]

Subjectively the seesaw can probably be explained by Party errors, failed alliances, wrong tactics. Objectively, the explanation may again be that Burma is not under foreign invasion, and the 'White Flag' Communist Party (as it is called, since the Red Flag CP refers to the smaller Trotskyist Party) does not maintain an independent machinery in Rangoon proper. Or else, not enough propaganda had been carried out among the peasants to insure the guerrillas of infallible intelligence and local support, which Mao and Chu always had before launching military operations. They obtained such support by immediately carrying out an agrarian reform in the areas they controlled. But in order to enforce such reforms, they had to hold the area first.

In China, the circle was breakable simply because of its size: the communists could seize a remote area—in Kiangsi or Yenan—and hold it long enough to restructure its social relations before any government invasion. Indeed the necessity of holding liberated areas was always fundamental to Chinese communist tacticians; as early as 1935 they insisted on it as a matter of strategy (principle).[15] But in such a relatively small country as Burma the military can easily attack the guerrillas long before they have established their administrative power. In fact, with helicopter warfare a normal aspect of counter-insurgency today, even space is no guarantee; government troops can descend into the remotest jungle back country within hours. In such cases, perhaps the only remedy is to propagandize the peasants without reforms—through social clubs, Party cell study groups, charity food programmes, teachers, doctors, veterinarians, agronomists, lawyers, etc. But then, the two-stage revolution is out of the question, as the general line of the revolution must be tied to local problems, and in the cases described, foreign troops are not present.

In Vietnam, Laos, Cambodia, Puerto Rico, Panama, Palestine, the Arab Gulf, Eritrea, Chad, the Portuguese-colonized areas of Africa, the apartheid countries of Africa, a patriotic or national war against the foreigners—the USA, England, Israel, France, Portugal or the white ruling minorities—can catch the enthusiasm of the population. But in technically unoccupied countries, places like Burma, India, Ghana, Congo—Kinshasa, most of Latin America, etc., where the domination by foreigners is indirect—through control of the economy and the local repressive forces—peoples' war cannot operate in two stages. Even if the local army, police and para-military goon squads are trained, financed and directed by USA or British 'advisers', the identifiable enemy is not the foreigners but the national profiteers—the oligarchy or comprador class. The revolutionaries' propaganda, hence, must be directly socialist. In fact, a case can be made that unless the revolution is socialistic from the start today, neo-colonial takeovers will generally follow stage one anyway, especially where the anti-imperialist liberation struggle is not very protracted or mostly peaceful—viz. most of 'independent' black Africa. But to prepare the revolution by preaching socialism usually means to create a tight Party organization first, precisely the role played by most Moscow-oriented Communist Party structures. Otherwise, it means using the revolutionary intellectuals (i.e. petty bourgeois) as an advance guard, expecting them to commit class suicide before the revolution. A difficult task.

Yet Amilcar Cabral apparently succeeded in doing that in Portuguese Guinea. A brilliant agronomist, one of his country's four blacks with an advanced university degree, Cabral began his political work with an agricultural census taken for the colonial administration (1952–4). In 1956, with five other 'petty bourgeois' intellectuals, as he calls himself, he launched the African Independence Party of Guiné and Cape Verde (PAIGC). For the next three years their focus was internal Party development. Cabral himself led the group in serious analyses of the forces and classes of his country, concluding that neither the peasants nor the proletariat (virtually non-existent) could act as the revolutionary vanguard.[16] That role was left up to his own class, the petty bourgeoisie. From 1959, Cabral and his petty bourgeois comrades fanned out across their small country (15,500 square miles, roughly the size of Switzerland, with 800,000 inhabitants) and intensively propagandized for reforms, changes, civil rights, equality. Whenever the Portuguese reacted with repression the PAIGC men then drove home the theme of counter-violence and war of liberation. Meanwhile, volunteers were being moulded into the People's Revolutionary Armed Forces (FARP) in the neighbouring Republic of Guinea.

Repressions hardened, massacres increased. Still Cabral waited. He wanted the people to be ready, to be thirsting to fight. He wanted them so aware of the colonialist violence that, as Fanon said, they would be perfectly decided to 'embody history' in each of their own persons in order to surge 'into the forbidden quarters'.[17] Cabral had to achieve what the Vietnam National Liberation Front's Nguyen van Tien once said was primordial: '... that people themselves discover the need for armed struggle. As for guns, those you can always find.'[18] When his people were that ready, Cabral launched the offensive—during the night of 30 June–1 July 1962. Today, as I write, the PAIGC has liberated two-thirds of the countryside—despite the 40,000 Portuguese troops armed with the most modern of NATO (US) weapons, planes, bombs and napalm.

From the very first, Cabral characterized the armed struggle as much more than an anti-colonial war. Chaliand reports that even in the bush, Cabral always plugged for socialism. For example, in a pep talk to illiterate guerrillas about to go into combat, he said: 'If we wage this struggle just to chase out the Portuguese, the struggle is not worth it. We fight for that, yes, but also so no one may exploit anyone else, white or black.... We fight to build. Not the work of individuals, but of all, together....'*[19] In Havana, Milan and Paris, but especially deep inside his own territory, Cabral repeatedly hammered away at the PAIGC's ultimate goals:

* Editor's translation.

African unity, socialism, a new society. Nevertheless, as original and astute a socialist thinker and leader as he is, the struggle he waged was first and foremost against the Portuguese invaders. In the minds of his people the enemy was there—in the flesh, active, repressive. The PAIGC was hence fighting a two-stage revolution, eloquently displaying its merit in a war where the enemy, proportional to the population, had deployed more strength and fire power than even in Vietnam.

Cabral's originality lies in the way he adapted the Chinese model to modern times, substituting a form of elitist indoctrination for the initial liberated zones, guiding his own class comrades to commit class suicide, and never forgetting that there is no such thing as a general class analysis, only particular analyses, anchored to specific times and places. Modification of the Chinese or PAIGC model seems to be working in Palestine, Angola, Mozambique, Eritrea (where the invaders are the Ethiopian troops of pro-US Haile Selassie), Dhufat and the Persian Gulf, in the Sino-Tibetan regions of India where such dominated minorities as the Ahoms, Nagas and Mizos fight Indian 'pacification' troops using napalm and strategic hamlets. But where neo-colonialism is entrenched—in Kenya, Congo—Kinshasa, the Cameroons, Morocco—the wars of liberation are flagging.* Another model for revolution is needed.

Cuba has tried to furnish that model. It is called the *foco*. The word means a centre or a nucleus (*foyer* in French) of guerrilla operations rather than a base. Indeed, it is used precisely in contradistinction to base or liberated area, and refers to the unit of men fighting in a particular province or area rather than stationed in a

---

* Eritrea, given as a trust to Emperor Haile Selassie after the Second World War was totally annexed by him on 13 November 1962, and he then tried to 'integrate' its mostly Moslem population (3,000,000 people) by imposing his language (Ahmaric) and religion (Coptic) with US and Israeli guns, in exchange for naval (Massawa and Assab), airforce (Asmara) and tracking (Kagnew) bases (which Israel and the US jointly control); the Eritrean Liberation Front (ELF) has been fighting Selassie through its Eritrean Liberation Army (ELA) since 1965. In north eastern India, the Ahams, Nagas and Mizos have been at war against India more or less since 1947; for years their arms came from Pakistan but today they are getting Chinese aid. The Cameroons, run by a pro-French neo-colonialist regime, are now the scene of some of black Africa's most bitter fighting, but the National Liberation Army (ALNC) does not seem able to augment its liberated areas; on 15 March 1966 one of Africa's most notable economists and political scientists, Afana Osende, who organized the Union of the Peoples of Cameroon (UPC) of which the ALNC is the fighting arm, was killed in battle.[20] Two other great African intellectuals who led the UPC and were murdered, apparently by the French, were Reuben Um Nyobe and Felix Moumié.

specific place. The word first came into use in Cuba where the Fidelistas established a *foco* in the Sierra Maestra mountain range of Oriente Province, and from there directed the revolutionary war against the Cuban dictator, Fulgencio Batista. Regis Debray, in his *Revolution in the Revolution?*, thinks of *foco* as a force rather than centre. The way to overthrow capitalist power in Latin America, he says, is 'by means of the more or less slow building up, through guerrilla warfare carried out in suitably chosen rural zones, of a *mobile strategic force,** nucleus of a people's army and of a future socialist state.'[21] The *foco*, then, is thought of operationally rather than descriptively; it leads to the creation of a people's army. It is the *motor* to the revolution. Basically, this revolutionary theory claims that in most countries of the imperialized world, and certainly in Latin America, the objective conditions for revolution already exist. What is needed are subjective conditions—leadership, revolutionary fervour, faith and hope. In such a situation, a few dedicated armed men, by establishing a *foco* in the countryside, can prove their tenacity and dedication through combat much faster and much more convincingly than through normal or usual propaganda-agitation means. After the peasants become convinced that this *foco* is serious, they will join it and it will grow into a people's army.

Actually, the *foco* theory entails a deeper analysis, which has in fact been carried out by Debray, Guevara, Castro, Armando Hart, Carlos Romeo and others.[22] It goes like this. Because of the role played by Russia's Comintern and indeed because of half a century of habit, revolution has fallen into the domain of Communist Parties. These Parties have always followed, if not the dictates,† certainly the suggestions of the theoreticians inside the Kremlin. Those theoreticians seem convinced today that capitalism's internal contradictions are so acute that it must crack by itself if brought into open, unrepressive world competition with socialist economies and if liberal bourgeois democracies allow free development of mass organizations. Because of the economic competition, hence the demand for an ever-increasing labour force, and because the general awareness of peoples generates constant social demands, such a development is inevitable. Communists are therefore advised to concentrate their organizational efforts on the urban proletariat—

* Debray's italics.
† Castro once referred to such Parties as an 'international mafia'[23]

which is in keeping with Leninist principles that communism can only be established by a dictatorship of the proletariat.

The *foco* theorists reject both the traditional CP's analysis and their methods. Capitalism is dynamic, not static, they say. It can constantly integrate workers into its structure at a high enough rate to perpetuate the myth of class mobility. What it cannot do, because that doesn't pay, is develop the infrastructure in rural areas. Schools, roads, electricity and housing in places thinly populated do not bring profits. Hence the rural population is doomed to remain marginal or outside the money economy altogether. Capitalist agrarian reform (buying and distributing the lands of owners who have become urban entrepreneurs anyway) cannot solve the problems of the rural peoples, because simply owning the land is not enough. Farmers must have access to markets (roads and transportation), modernity (refrigeration, hence electricity and training, hence schooling) and a certain economic flexibility (capital) to vary crops or survive disasters both natural (drought, storms, unseasonal cold, etc.) and commercial (sharp fluctuation in commodity prices). No capitalist system can solve these needs in the underdeveloped world, unless it totally mechanizes agriculture and forces the rural population into the urban centres—a plan once proposed by Lauchlin Currie, one of FDR's ex-brain trusters, in Colombia in 1962.[24] But if that were to happen, the huge demand for jobs and the massive development of workers' organizations would swamp the industrial bourgeoisie, forcing the government to intervene so extensively that socialism would take over by default—a fate that bourgeoisie, which controls the government, wants to avoid at all costs. The contradictions between rural and urban areas are hence insoluble.

But capitalism, especially foreign (i.e. imperialism), is perfectly disposed never to solve that contradiction. It can pursue its goals without caring about the countryside at all. It can slowly increase production in the urban centres, turn them into high-consuming areas (such as Saigon, Caracas, Rio de Janeiro, Lima, Buenos Aires, Casablanca, Nairobi, Manila, Rangoon, Singapore, etc.) where demand for its manufactured goods constantly rises. It can reinvest its capital, in fact import more capital, and see it grow. It can aid education, communication and transportation via welfare imperialism. It can even help develop a so-called middle sector, which will be tied through holding companies to the capitalist–oligarchy partnership. And should labour agitation spread threateningly, it can always accede to union demands, catching back its profit margin through its control of prices, finances, export–import and inflation.

Precisely because of this spiral, say the *foco* theorists, the CP is caught in an 'economist' well. It must constantly agitate for trade-union demands and, since it keeps winning them, must try to keep up to itself lest it loses its hold on the workers now accustomed to fighting for bread-and-butter issues only. As the CP develops into a Fabian society, so does labour — and vice versa. The next step in the process is elections, positions of responsibility, an occasional judge-ship, and finally a big, respectable Party, like in France and Italy. In those countries, though they are thoroughly disciplined, the com-munists cannot even envisage seizing power except through the ballot — where in fact they could take over with half their force. Thus an urbanized traditional Communist Party not only abandons its revolutionarism, it actually becomes counter-revolutionary: its stake is identified with the game. It is part of the Establishment.

While playing the established game of elections and trade unionism in the cities,* some Latin American Communist Parties did send organizers into the countryside. This was especially true in Bolivia, where the miners of Camiri had a long tradition of mili-tant action, and in Colombia where the peasants of such almost totally isolated areas as Manquetalia, Riochiquito, El Pato and Guayabero lived completely divorced from the civilization of Bogotá. In both countries, the communist policy was to solidify these workers into self-defence communities (so vast were the Colombian areas that they became known as 'independent repub-lics'). In Bolivia, where rapid progress was registered after the na-tional bourgeois revolution of 1952, the communists were Trotsky-ists.† In Colombia, the CP was traditional and it formulated its self-defence policy as early as October 1949. Yet in 1964 and 1965 these self-defence communities were totally wiped out; many of the Colombian communists escaped, but only to become mobile

---

* Which, of course, was in accord with Lenin's teaching.[25]

† In Peru's Convencion Valley, Hugo Blanco, a Trotskyist official, rapidly and successfully organized peasant unions. His goal was dual power.[26] The next stage was to be seizing power, at least in the valley. Presumably, after that, the area was to become a self-defence enclave–except that the military swooped down on the valley before he ever established dual power, and destroyed the Trotskyist apparatus. Blanco was condemned to 25 years, and is still in jail.

guerillas.* As a result, no revolutionary group today advocates self-defence warfare. Most communists insist on the legal struggle only. But even if they do practise armed struggle, their warriors are subservient to the Party. The guerrillas are under orders of city-based elites. Hence, say the *foco* theorists, they become tools in a political chess game waged by fat functionaries stretched out in carpeted offices amidst of the hustle-bustle of asphalt alleys and acid addicts, high-rise hangars and high-ball hangovers.

A revolutionary, says Castro, is not necessarily Marxist–Leninist. But he is necessarily someone who fights. To be in the vanguard, he must thus embody both political and military leadership. That means he has to be in the field, where the action is. Communists who direct 'revolutionary' operations from city offices lose contact with the masses, with the very people they supposedly fight for. Revolutionaries who practise what they preach learn in the process what they are truly fighting for.

The first law of guerrilla life [writes Debray] is that no one survives alone. The group's interest is the interest of each one, and vice versa. To live and conquer is to live and conquer all together. If a single combatant lags behind a marching column it affects the speed and security of the entire column. In the rear is the enemy : impossible to leave the comrade behind or send him home. It is up to everyone, then, to share the burden, lighten his knapsack or cartridge-case, and help him all the way. Under these conditions class psychology melts like snow under the summer sun, undermining the ideology of the same stratum. Where else could such an encounter, such an alliance, take place? By the same token, the only conceivable line for a guerrilla group to adopt is the mass line; it can live only with their support, in daily contact with them. Bureaucratic faint-heartedness becomes irrelevant. Is this not the best education for a future socialist leader or cadre? Revolutionaries make revolutionary civil wars; but to an even greater extent it is revolutionary civil war that makes revolutionaries.[28]

Everyone learns from revolutionary civil war. Fidel Castro is no exception. From the Sierra Maestra he wrote:

---

* The communist guerrillas are still fighting in Colombia, but not on self-defence basis. They are now called the Armed Revolutionary Forces of Columbia (FARC). For a fascinating account of the 1964 government offensive and the description of day-to-day fighting from the communist side, see the book by Jacobo Arenas,[27] member of the executive committee of the Columbia CP and current chief-of-staff of the FARC, who fought in Marquetalia and Riochiquito (he also lets Manuel Marulanda, known as *Tirofijo*, or 'Sure Shot', a member of the Central Committee of the CC and current FARC commander-in-chief, talk extensively)

Here the word 'people', which is often utilized in a vague and confused sense, becomes a living, wonderful and dazzling reality. *Now* I know who the people are: I see them in that invincible force that surrounds us everywhere, I see them in the bands of 30 or 40 men, lighting their way with lanterns, who descend the muddy slopes at two or three in the morning, with 30 kilos on their backs, in order to supply us with food. Who has organized them so wonderfully? Where did they acquire so much ability, astuteness, courage, self-sacrifice? No one knows! It is almost a mystery! They organize themselves all alone, spontaneously! When weary animals drop to the ground, unable to go further, men appear from all directions and carry the goods. Force cannot defeat them. It would be necessary to kill them all, to the last peasant, and that is impossible; this the dictatorship cannot do; the people are aware of it and are daily more aware of their own growing strength.*

* From Fidel Castro's last letter to Frank País, written in the Sierra Maestra, 21 July 1957. The same wonderment is expressed today in the letters of Turcios, Douglas Bravo, Camilo Torres, and others. Of course this does not mean that it is easy to obtain peasant support immediately; but when it is obtained, it performs wonders. Fidel wrote the letter after eight months in the Sierra and after having escaped betrayal by several peasants.'[29]

INTRODUCTION

In the modern era, Russia's October Revolution was the first to establish a 'people's democracy'. It did so, basically, via general insurrection. The Eastern European revolutionaries who seized power after the Second World War relied mostly on the Soviet Red Army. As such theirs was not a revolution, even if it did lead to the Soviet-style regimes (perhaps one reason why the people of Eastern Europe, non-participants in their 'revolutionary' process, are far from satisfied with their imposed way of life). Since then, every successful restructuring socialist revolution has come about after some form of guerrilla warfare—China, Vietnam, Algeria, Cuba (and perhaps Southern Yemen).

True, other governments claim to be carrying out social revolution—in Syria, Iraq, Egypt, Sudan. But these 'revolutionary' governments are in power as a result of a military coup; the people are not armed and do not participate in the decision-making process. As a possible consequence—some would insist a direct consequence— the restructuring of society inside these countries, whatever their governments' foreign policies and ideological rhetoric, is not revolutionary. If that is so, it is another argument in the thesis that a direct relation exists between people's war and people's democracy, between arming the people and genuine socialism. Thus, many modern revolutionaries today claim that the main strategic weapon, as well as the ideological prerequisite, for a sweeping total revolution is guerrilla warfare—or people's war.

Old-style revolutionaries, however, often tend to disagree. Some insist that guerrilla war is only one, and not necessarily the most important, means of seizing revolutionary power. Soviet Communists, for example, are convinced that capitalism's inherent contradictions must necessarily lead to its own destruction if allowed to compete freely on an economic and propaganda level with totally planned Communist societies (as exists, they say, in the Soviet Union). Hence, they espouse and proselytize the so-called peaceful coexistence line.

Some such 'communists' who call themselves revolutionaries even believe that a revolution can be achieved by playing according to the rules imposed by their capitalist enemies. They point out that all revolutions which have succeeded since the Second World War have been in the occupied underdeveloped world, that part of the globe economically, politically, culturally and militarily exploited and dominated by affluent capitalist nations. Since those poor lands are now relatively free of occupiers, guerrilla warfare, insurrection, even general political strikes tend to alienate rather than politicize the people, who have been fooled into believing that they are masters of their own political fates.

Whatever the viewpoint, the fact is that only in those countries— of the underdeveloped world—where the people have taken up arms has the revolution been victorious (though the converse has not necessarily been true). Understandably then, guerrilla warfare remains the most discussed subject among revolutionaries. It seems appropriate, therefore, that this book begin with an analysis of guerrilla warfare by Lenin, who, after all, is recognized by all contemporary revolutionaries, whether they consider themselves Marxist–Leninists or not, as their greatest mentor.

Contrary to most Marxist–Leninists of today, Lenin was rarely dogmatic. He was perfectly willing to admit, and does in the text that follows, that there are all sorts of forms of revolutionary struggle which neither he nor his comrades have yet imagined. Nor was he ever opposed to spontaneous revolutionary acts, as are those old-leftists today who condemn the 'New Left'. He did insist, however, that a spontaneous act, say a local rebellion, that is not quickly organized is bound to fail. But those he would condemn for such a failure would not be the rebels but his own trained party cadremen who would have been incapable of recognizing the needs of those who rebelled. A popular rebellion can never be wrong, Lenin said, for it is conditions which cause people to say no—and mean it with guns or rocks. Likewise, the eruption of a guerrilla war is brought about by the conditions under which people live, and hence cannot be criticized, only aided and guided.

The one fundamental truth— or dogma—that Lenin always upheld was that a revolutionary seizes power, he doesn't win it in a poker game, in an election, or by default. His task is to overturn a ruling class, not chase an individual out of a palace. And no ruling class ever willingly releases its grip on the machinery of a state in

B*

which and from which it profits. That is not to say that, tactically, a revolutionary cannot at times use peaceful means to advance his cause. But the actual revolution is the seizure, consolidation and expansion of power—out of the hands of the haves (the bourgeoisie and up) and into the hands of the have-nots (the proletariat, peasants, petty bourgeois intellectuals and down). That can only be done through force, which entails a civil war. Thus, 'a Marxist cannot regard civil war, or guerrilla warfare, which is one of its forms, as abnormal'.

Many of Lenin's contemporary comrades criticized guerrilla warfare as alienating, too polarizing and adventuristic, as apt to disorganize the 'movement', get out of hand or be defeated, thus to set the revolution back—arguments used by Soviet communists today to condemn Latin American guerrilla fighters. Lenin's answer: 'It is not guerrilla actions which disorganize the movement, but weakness of a party which is incapable of taking such actions under its control' and 'every military action in any war to a certain extent disorganizes the ranks of the fighters. But this does not mean that one must not fight. It means that one must learn to fight. That is all.'

*The question of guerrilla action is one that greatly interests our Party and the mass of the workers. We have dealt with this question in passing several times, and now we propose to give the more complete statement of our views we have promised.

Let us begin from the beginning. What are the fundamental demands which every Marxist should make of an examination of the question of forms of struggle? In the first place, Marxism differs from all primitive forms of socialism by not binding the movement to any one particular form of struggle. It recognizes the most varied forms of struggle; and it does not 'concoct' them, but only generalizes, organizes, gives conscious expression to those forms of

* V. I. Lenin: Guerrilla Warfare. Article dated 30 September 1906 originally published in Lenin's newspaper *Proletary* No. 5 (13 October 1906). English version in V. I. Lenin, *Collected Works*, Volume Eleven (June 1906–1907), (Moscow, Foreign Languages Publishing House, 1962).

struggle of the revolutionary classes which arise of themselves in the course of the movement. Absolutely hostile to all abstract formulas and to all doctrinaire recipes, Marxism demands an attentive attitude to the mass struggle in progress, which, as the movement develops, as the class-consciousness of the masses grows, as economic and political crises become acute, continually gives rise to new and more varied methods of defence and attack. Marxism, therefore, positively does not reject any form of struggle. Under no circumstances does Marxism confine itself to the forms of struggle possible and in existence at the given moment only, recognizing as it does that new forms of struggle, unknown to the participants of the given period, inevitably arise as the given social situation changes. In this respect Marxism learns, if we may so express it, from mass practice, and makes no claim whatever to teach the masses forms of struggle invented by 'systematizers' in the seclusion of their studies. We know—said Kautsky, for instance, when examining the forms of social revolution—that the coming crisis will introduce new forms of struggle that we are now unable to foresee.

In the second place, Marxism demands an absolutely historical examination of the question of the forms of struggle. To treat this question apart from the concrete historical situation betrays a failure to understand the rudiments of dialectical materialism. At different stages of economic evolution, depending on differences in political, national-cultural, living and other conditions, different forms of struggle come to the fore and become the principal forms of struggle; and in connection with this, the secondary, auxiliary forms of struggle undergo change in their turn. To attempt to answer yes or no to the question whether any particular means of struggle should be used, without making a detailed examination of the concrete situation of the given movement at the given stage of its development, means completely to abandon the Marxist position.

These are the two principal theoretical propositions by which we must be guided. The history of Marxism in Western Europe provides an infinite number of examples corroborating what has been said. European Social Democracy at the present time regards parliamentarism and the trade union movement as the principal forms of struggle; it recognized insurrection in the past, and is quite prepared to recognize it, should conditions change, in the future—despite the opinion of bourgeois liberals like the Russian Cadets and the

Bezzaglavtsi.* Social Democracy in the seventies rejected the general strike as a social panacea, as a means of overthrowing the bourgeoisie at one stroke by non-political means—but Social Democracy fully recognizes the mass political strike (especially after the experience of Russia in 1905) as one of the methods of struggle essential under certain conditions.† Social Democracy recognized street barricade fighting in the forties, rejected it for definite reasons at the end of the nineteenth century, and expressed complete readiness to revise the latter view and to admit the expediency of barricade fighting after the experience of Moscow, which, in the words of K. Kautsky, initiated new tactics of barricade fighting.

Having established the general Marxist propositions, let us turn to the Russian revolution. Let us recall the historical development of the forms of struggle it produced. First there were the economic strikes of workers (1896–1900), then the political demonstrations of workers and students (1901–2), peasant revolts (1902), the beginning of mass political strikes variously combined with demonstrations (Rostov 1902, the strikes in the summer of 1903, 9 January, 1905),‡ the all-Russian political strike accompanied by local cases of barricade fighting (October 1905), mass barricade fighting and armed uprising (December 1905), the peaceful parliamentary struggle (April–June 1906), partial military revolts (June 1905–July 1906) and partial peasant revolts (autumn 1905–autumn 1906).

Such is the state of affairs in the autumn of 1906 as concerns forms of struggle in general. The 'retaliatory' form of struggle adopted by the autocracy is the Black-Hundred pogrom, from Kishinev in the spring of 1903 to Sedlets in the autumn of 1906.§ All through this period the organization of Black-Hundred pogroms and the beating up of Jews, students, revolutionaries and class-conscious workers continued to progress and perfect itself, combining the violence of the Black-Hundred troops with the violence of hired ruffians, going

---

* Those affiliated with *Bes Zaglavia* (*Without Title*) magazine, published in 1906 by moderate socialists who sympathized with the left-wing of the Constitutional Democrats (Cadets)—ed.

† The general strike of August 1905 was absolute by October, forcing the government to issue the 'October Manifesto' and pretend to form a semi-constitutional regime—ed.

‡ 'Bloody Sunday', the trigger to the 1905 revolution—ed.

§ The Black Hundreds, right-wing terrorists organized by the secret police, were sent by the tsarist regime against the Jews on the assumption that Russia's revolutionaries were all Jews and thus "retaliatory" pogroms would frighten the revolutionaries into abandoning their agitation—ed.

as far as the use of artillery in villages and towns and merging with punitive expeditions, punitive trains and so forth.

Such is the principal background of the picture. Against this background there stands out—unquestionably as something partial, secondary and auxiliary—the phenomenon to the study and assessment of which the present article is devoted. What is this phenomenon? What are its forms? What are its causes? When did it arise and how far has it spread? What is its significance in the general course of the revolution? What is its relation to the struggle of the working class organized and led by Social Democracy? Such are the questions which we must now proceed to examine after having sketched the general background of the picture.

The phenomenon in which we are interested is the armed struggle. It is conducted by individuals and by small groups. Some belong to revolutionary organizations, while others (the majority in certain parts of Russia) do not belong to any revolutionary organization. Armed struggle pursues two different aims, which must be strictly distinguished: in the first place, this struggle aims as assassinating individuals, chiefs and subordinates in the army and police; in the second place, it aims at the confiscation of monetary funds both from the government and from private persons. The confiscated funds go partly into the treasury of the Party, partly for the special purpose of arming and preparing for an uprising, and partly for the maintenance of persons engaged in the struggle we are describing. The big expropriations (such as the Caucasian, involving over 200,000 roubles, and the Moscow, involving 875,000 roubles) went in fact first and foremost to revolutionary parties—small expropriations go mostly, and sometimes entirely, to the maintenance of the 'expropriators'. This form of struggle undoubtedly became widely developed and extensive only in 1906, i.e., after the December uprising. The intensification of the political crisis to the point of an armed struggle and, in particular, the intensification of poverty, hunger and unemployment in town and country, was one of the important causes of the struggle we are describing. This form of struggle was adopted as the preferable and even exclusive form of social struggle by the vagabond elements of the population, the lumpen proletariat and anarchist groups. Declaration of martial law, mobilization of fresh troops, Black-Hundred pogroms (Sedlets), and military courts must be regarded as the 'retaliatory' form of struggle adopted by the autocracy.

The usual appraisal of the struggle we are describing is that it is anarchism, Blanquism, the old terrorism, the acts of individuals isolated from the masses, which demoralize the workers, repel wide strata of the population, disorganize the movement and injure the revolution. Examples in support of this appraisal can easily be found in the events reported every day in the newspapers.

But are such examples convincing? In order to test this, let us take a locality where the form of struggle we are examining is most developed—the Lettish Territory. This is the way *Novoya Vremya** (in its issues of 9 and 12 September) complains of the activities of the Lettish Social Democrats. The Lettish Social-Democratic Labour Party (a section of the Russian Social-Democratic Labour Party) regularly issues its paper in 30,000 copies. The announcement columns publish lists of spies whom it is the duty of every decent person to exterminate. People who assist the police are proclaimed 'enemies of the revolution', liable to execution and, moreover, to confiscation of property. The public is instructed to give money to the Social Democratic Party only against signed and stamped receipt. In the Party's latest report, showing a total income of 48,000 roubles for the year, there figures a sum of 5,600 roubles contributed by the Libau branch for arms which was obtained by expropriation. Naturally, *Novoya Vremya* rages and fumes against this 'revolutionary law', against this 'terror government'.

Nobody will be so bold as to call these activities of the Lettish Social Democrats anarchism, Blanquism or terrorism. But why? Because here we have a clear connection between the new form of struggle and the uprising which broke out in December and which is again brewing. This connection is not so perceptible in the case of Russia as a whole, but it exists. The fact that 'guerrilla' warfare became widespread precisely after December, and its connection with the accentuation not only of the economic crisis but also of the political crisis is beyond dispute. The old Russian terrorism was an affair of the intellectual conspirator; today as a general rule guerrilla warfare is waged by the worker combatant, or simply by the unemployed worker. Blanquism and anarchism easily occur to the minds of people who have a weakness for stereotype; but under the circumstance of an uprising, which are so apparent in the

---

* *Novoya Vremya* was a leading conservative newspaper of the day. The Lettish guerrillas, extremely well organized, operated in the Baltic states—ed.

Lettish Territory, the inappropriateness of such trite labels is only too obvious.

The example of the Letts clearly demonstrates how incorrect, unscientific and unhistorical is the practice so very common among us of analyzing guerrilla warfare without reference to the circumstances of an uprising. These circumstances must be borne in mind, we must reflect on the peculiar features of an intermediate period between big acts of insurrection, we must realize what forms of struggle inevitably arise under such circumstances, and not try to shirk the issue by a collection of words learned by rote, such as are used equally by the Cadets and the *Novoya Vremya*-ites : anarchism, robbery, hooliganism!

It is said that guerrilla acts disorganize our work. Let us apply this argument to the situation that has existed since December 1905, to the period of Black-Hundred pogroms and martial law. What disorganizes the movement more in such a period: the absence of resistance or organized guerrilla warfare? Compare the centre of Russia with her western borders, with Poland and the Lettish Territory. It is unquestionable that guerrilla warfare is far more widespread and far more developed in the western border regions. And it is equally unquestionable that the revolutionary movement in general, and the Social-Democratic movement in particular, are more disorganized in central Russia than in the western border regions. Of course, it would not enter our heads to conclude from this that the Polish and Lettish Social-Democratic movements are less disorganized thanks to guerrilla warfare. No. The only conclusion that can be drawn is that guerrilla warfare is not to blame for the state of disorganization of the Social-Democratic working-class movement in Russia in 1906.

Allusion is often made in this respect to the peculiarities of national conditions. But this allusion very clearly betrays the weakness of the current argument. If it is a matter of national conditions then it is not a matter of anarchism, Blanquism or terrorism—sins that are common to Russia as a whole and even to the Russians especially—but of something else. Analyze this something concretely, gentlemen! You will find that national oppression or antagonism explain nothing, because they have always existed in the western regions, whereas guerrilla warfare has been engendered only by the present historical period. There are many places where there is national oppression and antagonism, but no guerrilla struggle, which sometimes develops where there is no national oppression whatever. A concrete analysis of the question will show that it is not a matter of national oppression, but of conditions of insurrection. Guerrilla warfare is an inevitable form of struggle at a time when the mass movement has actually reached the point of an uprising and when fairly large intervals occur between the 'big engagements' in the civil war.

It is not guerrilla actions which disorganize the movement, but the weakness of a party which is incapable of taking such actions under its control. That is why the anathemas which we Russians usually hurl against guerrilla actions go hand in hand with secret, casual, unorganized guerrilla actions which really do disorganize the Party. Being incapable of understanding what historical conditions give rise to this struggle, we are incapable of neutralizing its deleterious aspects. Yet the struggle is going on. It is engendered by powerful economic and political causes. It is not in our power to eliminate these causes or to eliminate this struggle. Our complaints against guerrilla warfare are complaints against our Party weakness in the matter of an uprising.

What we have said about disorganization also applies to demoralization. It is not guerrilla warfare which demoralizes, but unorganized, irregular, non-Party guerrilla acts. We shall not rid ourselves one least bit of this most unquestionable demoralization by condemning and cursing guerrilla actions, for condemnations and curses are absolutely incapable of putting a stop to a phenomenon which has been engendered by profound economic and political causes. It may be objected that if we are incapable of putting a stop to an abnormal and demoralizing phenomenon, this is no reason why the Party should adopt abnormal and demoralizing methods of struggle. But such an objection would be a purely bourgeois-liberal and not a Marxist objection, because a Marxist cannot regard civil war, or guerrilla warfare, which is one of its forms, as abnormal and demoralizing in general. A Marxist bases himself on the class struggle, and not social peace. In certain periods of acute economic and political crises the class struggle ripens into a direct civil war, i.e. into an armed struggle between two sections of the people. In such periods a Marxist is obliged to take the stand of civil war. Any moral condemnation of civil war would be absolutely impermissible from the standpoint of Marxism.

In a period of civil war the ideal party of the proletariat is a

fighting party. This is absolutely incontrovertible. We are quite prepared to grant that it is possible to argue and prove the inexpediency
from the standpoint of civil war of particular forms of civil war
at any particular moment. We fully admit criticism of diverse forms
of civil war from the standpoint of military expediency and absolutely
agree that in this question it is the Social Democratic practical
workers in each particular locality who must have the final say. But
we absolutely demand in the name of the principles of Marxism
that an analysis of the conditions of civil war should not be evaded
by hackneyed and stereotyped talk about anarchism, Blanquism and
terrorism, and that senseless methods of guerrilla activity adopted
by some organization or other of the Polish Socialist Party at some
moment or other should not be used as a bogey when discussing the
question of the participation of the Social-Democratic Party as such
in guerrilla warfare in general.

The argument that guerrilla warfare disorganizes the movement
must be regarded critically. Every new form of struggle, accompanied
as it is by new dangers and new sacrifices, inevitably 'disorganizes'
organizations which are unprepared for this new form of struggle.
Our old propagandist circles were disorganized by recourse to
methods of agitation. Our committees were subsequently disorganized
by recourse to demonstrations. Every military action in any war to
a certain extent disorganizes the ranks of the fighters. But this does
not mean that one must not fight. It means that one must learn to
fight. That is all.

When I see Social Democrats proudly and smugly declaring 'we
are not anarchists, thieves, robbers, we are superior to all this, we
reject guerrilla warfare'—I ask myself: Do these people realize what
they are saying? Armed clashes and conflicts between the Black-
Hundred government and the population are taking place all over
the country. This is an absolutely inevitable phenomenon at the
present stage of development of the revolution. The population is
spontaneously and in an unorganized way—and for that very reason
often in unfortunate and undesirable forms—reacting to this
phenomenon also by armed conflicts and attacks. I can understand
us refraining from Party leadership of this spontaneous struggle in a
particular place or at a particular time because of the weakness
and unpreparedness of our organization. I realize that this question
must be settled by the local practical workers, and that the remoulding of weak and unprepared organizations is no easy matter. But

when I see a Social-Democratic theoretician or publicist not displaying regret over this unpreparedness, but rather a proud smugness and a self-exalted tendency to repeat phrases learned by rote in early youth about anarchism, Blanquism and terrorism, I am hurt by this degradation of the most revolutionary doctrine in the world.

It is said that guerrilla warfare brings the class-conscious proletarians into close association with degraded, drunken riff-raff. That is true. But it only means that the party of the proletariat can never regard guerrilla warfare as the only, or even as the chief, method of struggle; it means that this method must be subordinated to other methods, that it must be commensurate with the chief methods of warfare, and must be ennobled by the enlightening and organizing influence of socialism. And without this latter condition, all, positively all, methods of struggle in bourgeois society bring the proletariat into close association with the various non-proletarian strata above and below it and, if left to the spontaneous course of events, become frayed, corrupted and prostituted. Strikes, if left to the spontaneous course of events, become corrupted into 'alliances'—agreements between the workers and the masters against the consumers. Parliament becomes corrupted into a brothel, where a gang of bourgeois politicians barter wholesale and retail 'national freedom', 'liberalism', 'democracy', 'republicanism', 'anti-clericalism', 'socialism' and all other wares in demand. A newspaper becomes corrupted into a public pimp, into a means of corrupting the masses, of pandering to the low instincts of the mob, and so on and so forth. Social Democracy knows of no universal methods of struggle, such as would shut off the proletariat by a Chinese wall from the strata standing slightly above or slightly below it. At different periods, Social Democracy applies different methods, always qualifying the choice of them by strictly defined ideological and organizational conditions.*

* The Bolshevik Social Democrats are often accused of a frivolous passion for guerrilla actions. It would therefore not be amiss to recall that in the draft resolution on guerrilla actions (*Partiiniye Izvestia*, No. 2, and Lenin's report on the Congress), the section of the Bolsheviks who defend guerrilla actions suggested the following conditions for their recognition: 'expropriations' of private property were not to be permitted under any circumstances; 'expropriations' of government property were not to be recommended but only allowed, provided that they were controlled by the Party and their proceeds used for the needs of an uprising. Guerrilla acts in the form of terrorism were to be recommended against brutal government officials and active members of the Black Hundreds, but on conditions that 1) the Sentiments of the masses be taken into account: 2) the conditions of the

The forms of struggle in the Russian revolution are distinguished by their colossal variety compared with the bourgeoisie revolutions in Europe. Kautsky partly foretold this in 1902 when he said that the future revolution (with the exception perhaps of Russia, he added) might be not so much a struggle of the people against the government as a struggle between two sections of the people. In Russia we undoubtedly see a wider development of this latter struggle than in the bourgeois revolutions in the west. The enemies of our revolution among the people are few in number, but as the struggle grows more acute they become more and more organized and receive the support of the reactionary strata of the bourgeoisie. It is therefore absolutely natural and inevitable that in such a period, a period of nationwide political strikes, an uprising cannot assume the old form of individual acts restricted to a very short time and to a very small area. It is absolutely natural and inevitable that the uprising should assume the higher and more complex form of a prolonged civil war embracing the whole country, i.e., an armed struggle between two sections of the people. Such a war cannot be conceived otherwise than as a series of a few big engagements at comparatively long intervals and a large number of small encounters during these intervals. That being so—and it is undoubtedly so—the Social Democrats must absolutely make it their duty to create organizations best adapted to lead the masses in these big engagements and, as far as possible, in these small encounters as well. In a period when the class struggle has become accentuated to the point of civil war, Social Democrats must make it their duty not only to participate but also to play the leading role in this civil war. The Social Democrats must train and prepare their organizations to be really able to act as a belligerent side which does not miss a single opportunity of inflicting damage on the enemy's forces.

This is a difficult task, there is no denying. It cannot be accomplished at once. Just as the whole people are being retrained and are

working-class movement in the given locality be reckoned with, and 3) care be taken that the forces of the proletariat should not be frittered away. The practical difference between this draft and the resolution which was adopted at the Unity Congress lies exclusively in the fact that 'expropriations' of government property are not allowed. [Lenin's note].

The Unity Congress Lenin refers to here was the Fourth Congress of the Russian Social-Democratic Workers Party held in Stockholm in April and May 1906. In September the Moscow Bolshevik Party Committee came out in favour of 'offensive tactics' and issued a general call for 'partisan war'. Lenin favoured this militant line—ed.

learning to fight in the course of the civil war, so our organizations must be trained, must be reconstructed in conformity with the lessons of experience to be equal to this task.

We have not the slightest intention of foisting on practical workers any artificial form of struggle, or even of deciding from our armchair what part any particular form of guerrilla warfare should play in the general course of the civil war in Russia. We are far from the thought of regarding a concrete assessment of particular guerrilla actions as indicative of a trend in Social Democracy. But we do regard it as our duty to help as far as possible to arrive at a correct theoretical assessment of the new forms of struggle engendered by practical life. We do regard it as our duty relentlessly to combat stereotypes and prejudices which hamper the class-conscious workers in correctly presenting a new and difficult problem and in correctly approaching its solution.

Editor's Personal note

The writers included in this work are all comrades. They may not agree with each other on tactics or even strategy, but they have all put their lives at the service of man's liberation. Some died before I read their works. Others may die before you read them. Not one talks very much about future society; they were or are too busy fighting against this oppressive one to worry much about the next. Each continues to influence. Not many write well; they were or are men of action, not stylists. (Except for Lenin, each entry herein has been condensed, but accurately and only to eliminate repetition.) They are revolutionaries; men who always found audacity because they had faith—not in systems or causes or philosophies (though that, too, sometimes), but faith in men.

CHINA

No contemporary revolutionaries have done more to popularize the concept of people's war than the Chinese communists. And with the most convincing reason possible: in China, it worked. It is too easy, however, to forget the price for such victory. In 1927, after years of hard struggle to help establish the Chinese Republic (1911) under the weak liberal patriarch, Sun Yat-sen, and formidable sacrifices to help crush vicious regional warlords (especially in 1926 in the north), the communists were suddenly attacked by their long-time ally, Chiang Kai-shek, head of the Kuomintang (Nationalist) Party. Literally thousands, some say as many as 50,000, communists were arrested, tortured and murdered as Chiang tried to consolidate his power over all of China. He almost succeeded. Surviving communists, having fled in all directions, had to reassemble and begin anew.

Inevitably, they were depressed, pessimistic, even defeatist. They challenged their theories, questioned their analysis, distrusted their own experiences. Most—but not all. One optimist was Mao Tsetung, the self educated peasant's son from Hunan who had attended the 1921 conspirators' meeting in the girls' school of the French Legation, where the Chinese Communist Party was born. Despite his antipathy for Sun Yat-sen, Mao had followed Leninist 'principles' to work with the bourgeois government (in order to create a communist base first) until Sun died in 1925; then, again despite his suspicion of Chiang as a glorified warlord, had stuck to dogma and doubled as a Kuomintang agent—even after Chiang's first purge of communists in 1926. Mao was caught in 1927 but managed to escape barely 200 yards away from the wall where he would have been shot. On Party orders he then organized a peasant uprising, was defeated and repudiated by his Party bosses as a 'military adventurer'. Undaunted, he led his 1,000-odd raggle-taggle survivors to the southern mountains between Hunan and Kiangsi and launched what would turn out to be the Red Army—without a single machine gun. By 1930, already, in effect, the true leader of the reorganized underground Communist Party, he wrote a letter to communist cadremen exhorting them to action. Known today as 'A Single Spark Can Start a Prairie Fire', the letter–article clearly explained that the Chinese revolution would have to proceed through 'prolonged and tangled' guerrilla warfare, based on peasants establishing Liberated Areas first in remote townships, then in districts, then in counties. He explained how the many contradictions—between classes and among the imperialist powers controlling China's main cities—had to lead to eventual communist victory. 'All China is littered with dry faggots which will soon be aflame,' he wrote. He went on to list all the 'objective' conditions why a peasant army fighting in its own territory (specifically in Kiangsi) could endure a massive enemy onslaught, spelled out the basis for the strangulation theory (later known as the Lin Piao theory) and detailed the way to form Red guards, Red militiamen and Red soldiers.

In this task he was helped by his faithful friend and comrade, Chu Teh, a former military school-trained Chiang officer totally addicted to opium who had decided to reform himself (sailing back and forth on a British steamer where no drugs were available, he had often collapsed from insupportable cravings but came ashore cured) and joined the Communist Party. Strong but easygoing, Chu was a master military technician and did more than any other man, save perhaps Mao, to build the famous Eighth Route and New Fourth armies which eventually defeated the Japanese in China and then Chiang's Kuomintang Army in 1949. How to build such an army, a people's army, how to train it from the outset for the revolutionary seizure of power, and how to use it constructively for the consolidation of the revolution are the themes Chu Teh develops in the second article in this section.

All of Mao's and Chu's talents, however, could not stop Chiang's endless supply of troops, money (from England) and advisers (mostly German) in the early thirties. What was worse was that Mao's Russian advisers insisted that flexibility and mobility demoralized peasants when left alone to face the Kuomintang and thus lost Mao's troops their greatest asset. And so, in 1934, Mao and Chu, who had both lost their wives in actual combat, decided to abandon Kiangsi. Thus began the famous long march: 90,000 men, women and children, on foot, carrying not just guns and bullets, but printing presses, paper, scrap iron and farming machinery, marching six thousand miles across China, like twice across America, from

New York to San Francisco and back, all the while attacked by fresh rested troops, tanks and planes. Mao, feverish most of the march, never let up, and each night he would find the time to read by the light of a small lantern he kept in his knapsack one of the score of books he lugged with him. Lin Piao, suffering from heart trouble, would often fall behind, then desperately catch up. Chou En-lai, bleeding from both feet for four months, never missed a battle. And so for the others. Yet on and on they went, crossing eighteen mountain ranges, twenty-four rivers and ten different warlord armies. The battles they fought along the way could fill every page of this volume. And when at last they reached their destination, the north-west province of Shensi, near the Mongolian border, safe from Kuomintang attacks, they numbered barely 6,000—and with new recruits picked up along the way counted in.

Yet, almost at once, they started again. They established a Liberated Area, carried out an agrarian reform, regrouped into two armies—the Eighth and New Fourth—and went on the offensive. Simultaneously, Mao issued his familiar call for a united China. Japan was menacing, he said; all Chinese should unite to fight as one. Incredibly, he was again willing to make an alliance with Chiang's Kuomintang. Once attacked by Japan, Chiang agreed, and Mao sent his troops against the Invaders—while Chiang, predictably, attacked the communists. This time Mao's troops were not caught by surprise; they either retreated from Chiang's forces or fought them off. But by and large the communists stuck to the alliance, and Mao kept proclaiming his faith in a United Front and in the Patriotic War. In fact, he was following his old dictum: first consolidate the base, then destroy the enemy. In China from 1937 to 1945 that meant first fight the Japanese, organize more and more liberated areas, spread the agrarian reform, politicize the masses— all under the slogan of fighting the foreign aggressor. It was Mao's 'Revolution in Two Stages', as he explained in 1939, the first article in this section.

In actual combat, his tactics were also the same: 'The enemy advances, we retreat; the enemy camps, we harass; the enemy tires, we attack; the enemy retreats, we pursue.' And everywhere the Red armies went they politicized. Where landlords were ousted for collaboration with the enemy, land was distributed to the peasants who worked it. Where the landlords remained loyal, rents were lowered. Revolutionary medical men treated the population. Teachers

taught the children. Engineers or agronomists solved local agricultural problems. If a harvest was due, both soldiers and officers
pitched in. If a region had been depleted, both soldiers and officers
shared their rations. _Never, in a Red army, was an officer better off
than a soldier, and never were either better off than the people._ It
was inevitable that by 1945 the Chinese communists controlled most
of the north-west and 95 million people. The Red Army was now
500,000 strong, but weary from having borne all the major fighting
against the Japanese. Chiang's forces, on the other hand, numbered
two million and they had been held back from the Sino-Japanese
war in order to attack the communists. And so, despite a new Mao–
Chiang pact signed in Chungking in 1945, Chiang immediately attacked Yenan.

But it was too late. Mao was ready. Once again he resorted to
guerrilla warfare, then to surrounding the cities, then to strangling
the cities one by one. Lin Piao, in his speech on people's war (the
third article herein), explains why Chiang could not win—and in
1949 he and his Kuomintang were chased out of the Chinese main-
land despite all the massive aid that they had received from both the
USA and Russia (which dealt with China, not Mao, during the
Second World War).

Out of the Chinese communists' incredible revolutionary experience, their leaders—Mao, Lin Piao, Chou En-lai—have drawn
iron-firm lessons. One is, that without a people's war no revolution
can succeed. Another is that a people's war must be divided into
two stages, patriotic then socialist, national then class. That means
that revolutionaries can and must work with the national bourgeoisie, at least during the first phase. After that, Mao has said in
'Democratic Dictatorship' (30 June 1949), 'the people have a powerful state apparatus in their hands—there is no need to fear rebellion by the national bourgeoisie'—a conclusion that a great many
revolutionaries in Latin America, Africa and even Asia will firmly
challenge. Still another tenet which the Chinese uphold is that
guerrilla warfare must be waged from the countryside until the
cities are isolated: first, because the imperialists control the cities;
second, because the urban and rural economies are so uneven that
the peasants feel little relationship to the cities; and third, because
the counter-revolutionary camp is much more disunited in the
countryside (but Mao insists that armed struggle cannot win unless
it is coordinated with other forms of struggle, including legal, and

he stresses the fact that unless the Party has strong ties in the cities, the guerrilla forces can be totally isolated).

On a world scale, says Lin Piao in 'People's War', the cities are the capitalist strongholds of Europe and North America while the countryside is the underdeveloped world. Though he does not use the slogan 'Create two, three . . . many Vietnams', made famous by Che Guevara, he spells out the same concept—convinced that the USA cannot sustain many people's wars all over the world, especially if they are waged simultaneously. And finally, as Chou En-lai succinctly states in his 'Four Point Statement' (the fourth article in this section), the Chinese have learned that a dedicated, politicized, armed people—the result of a people's war—cannot be defeated. Hence, there is no reason to fear even such a technological titan as the USA. In the last analysis, say the Chinese, wars are won by people, not machines.

I Mao Tse-tung: *Revolution in Two Stages*[30]

Developing along the same lines as many other nations of the world, the Chinese people (here we refer mainly to the Hans) went through many thousands of years of life in classless primitive communes. Some four thousand years have gone by since the collapse of these primitive communes and the transition to class society, which took the form first of slave and then of feudal society. Throughout the history of Chinese civilization its agriculture and handicrafts have been renowned for their high level of development; there have been many great thinkers, scientists, inventors, statesmen, soldiers, men of letters and artists, and we have a rich store of classical works. The compass was invented in China very long ago. The art of paper-making was discovered as early as 1,800 years ago. Block-printing was invented 1,300 years ago, and movable type 800 years ago. The use of gunpowder was known to the Chinese before the Europeans. Thus China has one of the oldest civilizations in the world; she has a recorded history of nearly four thousand years.*

* The compass was first invented in the third century B.C., used in the first century B.C. and all Chinese navigators seemed to rely on it by the twelfth century; gunpowder, invented in the ninth century, was used to fire cannon in the eleventh —ed.

The Chinese nation is known throughout the world not only for its industriousness and stamina, but also for its ardent love of freedom and its rich revolutionary traditions. The history of the Han people, for instance, demonstrates that the Chinese never submit to tyrannical rule but invariably use revolutionary means to overthrow or change it. In the thousands of years of Han history, there have been hundreds of peasant uprisings, great and small, against the dark rule of the landlords and nobility. And most dynastic changes came about as a result of such peasant uprisings. All the nationalities of China have resisted foreign oppression and have invariably resorted to rebellion to shake it off. They favour a union on the basis of equality but are against the oppression of one nationality by another. During the thousands of years of recorded history, the Chinese nation has given birth to many national heroes and revolutionary leaders. Thus the Chinese nation has a glorious revolutionary tradition and a splendid historical heritage.

Although China is a great nation and although she is a vast country with an immense population, a long history, a rich revolutionary tradition and a splendid historical heritage, her economic, political and cultural development was sluggish for a long time after the transition from slave to feudal society. This feudal society, beginning with the Chou and Ching Dynasties, lasted about three thousand years.

The main features of the economic and political system of China's feudal era were as follows:

1. A self-sufficient natural economy predominated. The peasants produced for themselves not only agricultural products but most of the handicraft articles they needed. What the landlords and the nobility exacted from them in the form of land rent was also chiefly for private enjoyment and not for exchange. Although exchange developed as time went on, it did not play a decisive role in the economy as a whole.

2. The feudal ruling class composed of landlords, the nobility and the emperor owned most of the land, while the peasants had very little or none at all. The peasants tilled the land of the landlords, the nobility and the royal family with their own farm implements and had to turn over to them for their private enjoyment 40, 50, 60, 70, or even 80 per cent or more of the crop. In effect the peasants were still serfs.

3. Not only did the landlords, the nobility and the royal family live

*C**

on rent extorted from the peasants, but the landlord state also exacted tribute, taxes and corvée services from them to support a horde of government officials and an army which was used mainly for their repression.

4. The feudal landlord state was the organ of power protecting this system of feudal exploitation. While the feudal state was torn apart into rival principalities in the period before the Ching Dynasty, it became autocratic and centralized after the first Ching emperor unified China, though some feudal separatism remained. The emperor reigned supreme in the feudal state, appointing officials in charge of the armed forces, the law courts, the treasury and state granaries in all parts of the country and relying on the landed gentry as the mainstay of the entire system of feudal rule.

It was under such feudal economic exploitation and political oppression that the Chinese peasants lived like slaves, in poverty and suffering, through the ages. Under the bondage of feudalism they had no freedom of person. The landlord had the right to beat, abuse or even kill them at will, and they had no political rights whatsoever. The extreme poverty and backwardness of the peasants resulting from ruthless landlord exploitation and oppression is the basic reason why Chinese society remained at the same stage of socio-economic development for several thousand years.

The principal contradiction in feudal society was between the peasantry and the landlord class.

The peasants and the handicraft workers were the basic classes which created the wealth and culture of this society.

The ruthless economic exploitation and political oppression of the Chinese peasants forced them into numerous uprisings against landlord rule. There were hundreds of uprisings, great and small, all of them peasant revolts or peasant revolutionary wars. The scale of peasant uprisings and peasant wars in Chinese history has no parallel anywhere else. The class struggles of the peasants, the peasant uprisings and peasant wars constituted the real motive force to historical development in Chinese feudal society. For each of the major peasant uprisings and wars dealt a blow to the feudal regime of the time, and hence more or less furthered the growth of the social productive forces. However, since neither new productive forces, nor new regulations of production, nor new class forces, nor any advanced political party existed in those days, the peasant uprisings and wars did not have correct leadership such as the proletariat and the Communist Party provide today; every peasant revolution failed, and the peasantry was invariably used by the landlords and the nobility, either during or after the revolution, as a lever for bringing about dynastic change. Therefore, although some social progress was made after each great peasant revolutionary struggle, the feudal economic relations and political system remained basically unchanged.

It is only in the last hundred years that a change of a different order has taken place. As China's feudal society had developed a commodity economy, and so carried within itself the seeds of capitalism, China would of herself have developed slowly into a capitalist society even without the impact of foreign capitalism. Penetration by foreign capitalism accelerated this process. Foreign capitalism played an important part in the disintegration of China's social economy; on the one hand, it undermined the foundations of her self-sufficient natural economy and wrecked the handicraft industry both in the cities and in the peasants' homes; and on the other, it hastened the growth of a commodity economy in town and country.

Apart from its disintegrating effects on the foundations of China's feudal economy, this state of affairs gave rise to certain objective conditions and possibilities for the development of capitalist production in China. For the destruction of the natural economy created a commodity market for capitalism while the bankruptcy of large numbers of peasants and handicraftsmen provided it with a labour market.

In fact, some merchants, landlords and bureaucrats began investing in modern industry as far back as sixty years ago, in the latter part of the nineteenth century, under the stimulus of foreign capitalism and because of certain cracks in the feudal economic structure. About forty years ago, at the turn of the century, China's national capitalism took its first steps forward. Then about twenty years ago, during the first imperialist world war, China's national industry expanded, chiefly in textiles and flour milling, because the imperialist countries in Europe and America were preoccupied with the war and temporarily relaxed their oppression of China.

The history of the emergence and development of national capitalism is at the same time the history of the emergence and development of the Chinese bourgeoisie and proletariat. Just as a section of the merchants, landlords and bureaucrats were precursors of the Chinese bourgeoisie, so a section of the peasants and handicraft workers were the precursors of the Chinese proletariat. As distinct social classes, the Chinese bourgeoisie and proletariat are new-born and never existed before in Chinese history. They have evolved into new social classes from the womb of feudal society. They are twins born of China's old (feudal) society, at once linked to each other and antagonistic to each other. However, the Chinese proletariat emerged and grew simultaneously not only with the Chinese national bourgeoisie but also with the enterprises directly operated by the imperialists in China. Hence, a very large section of the Chinese proletariat is older and more experienced than the Chinese bourgeoisie, and is therefore a greater and more broadly based social force.

However, the emergence and development of capitalism is only one aspect of the change that has taken place since the imperialist penetration of China. There is another concomitant and obstructive aspect, namely, the collusion of imperialism with the Chinese feudal forces to arrest the development of Chinese capitalism.

It is certainly not the purpose of the imperialist powers invading China to transform feudal China into capitalist China. On the contrary, their purpose is to transform China into their own semi-colony or colony. To this end the imperialist powers have used and continue to use military, political, economic and cultural means of oppression, as follows:

1. The imperialist powers have waged many wars of aggression against China, for instance, the Opium War launched by Britain in 1840, the war launched by the Anglo-French allied forces in 1857, the Sino-French War of 1884, the Sino-Japanese War of 1894, and the war launched by the allied forces of the eight powers in 1900. After defeating China in war, they not only occupied many neighbouring countries formerly under her protection, but seized or 'leased' parts of her territory. For instance, Japan occupied Taiwan and the Penghu Islands and 'leased' the port of Lushun; Britain seized Hong Kong and France 'leased' Kwangchowwan. In addition to annexing territory, they exacted huge indemnities. Thus heavy blows were struck at China's huge feudal empire.*

---

* From 1856 to 1860 Britain and France jointly waged war against China, with the United States and tsarist Russia supporting them from the side-lines. The government of the Ching Dynasty was then devoting all its energies to suppressing peasant revolutions and adopted a policy of passive resistance towards the foreigners. The Anglo-French forces occupied such major cities as Canton, Tientsin and

2. The imperialist powers have forced China to sign numerous un-equal treaties by which they have acquired the right to station land and sea forces and exercise consular jurisdiction in China, and they have carved up the whole country into imperialist spheres of influence.

3. The imperialist powers have gained control of all the important trading ports in China by these unequal treaties and have marked off areas in many of these ports as concessions under their direct administration. They have also gained control of China's customs, foreign trade and communications (sea, land, inland water and air). Thus they have been able to dump their goods in China, turn her into a market for their industrial products, and at the same time subordinate her agriculture to their imperialist needs.

4. The imperialist powers operate many enterprises in both light and heavy industry in China in order to utilize her raw materials and cheap labour on the spot, and they thereby directly exert economic pressure on China's national industry and obstruct the development of her productive forces.

5. The imperialist powers monopolize China's banking and finance by extending loans to the Chinese government and establishing banks in China. Thus they have not only overwhelmed China's national capitalism in commodity competition; they have also se-cured a stranglehold on her banking and finance.

6. The imperialist powers have established a network of comprador and merchant-usurer exploitation right across China, from the trad-ing ports to the remote hinterland, and have created a comprador and merchant-usurer class in their service, so as to facilitate their

Peking, plundered and burned down the Yuan Ming Yuan palace in Peking and forced the Ching government to conclude the Treaties of Tientsin and Peking. Their main provisions included the opening of all major ports, and the granting to foreigners of special privileges for travel, missionary activities and inland navigation of China's interior. In 1882–3 the French invaded the northern part of Indochina. In 1884–5 they extended their war to the Chinese provinces of Kwangsi, Taiwan, Fukien and Chekiang. The Sino-Japanese War of 1894 was started by the Japanese bent on conquering Korea. In 1900 eight imperialist powers–Britain, the United States, Germany, France, tsarist Russia, Japan, Italy and Austria–sent a joint force to attack China to suppress a popular rebellion against the Ching dynasty. The allied forces captured Taku and occupied Tientsin and Peking. In 1901 the Ching government concluded a treaty with the eight imperialist countries; its main provisions were that China had to pay those countries the huge sum of 450 million taels of silver as war reparations and grant them the special privilege of stationing troops in Peking and in the area from Peking to Tientsin and Shanhaikuan–ed.

exploitation of the masses of the Chinese peasantry and other sections of the people.

7. The imperialist powers have made the feudal landlord class as well as the comprador class the main props of their rule in China.

8. The imperialist powers supply the reactionary government with large quantities of munitions and a host of military advisers, in order to keep the warlords fighting among themselves and to suppress the Chinese people.

9. Furthermore, the imperialist powers have never slackened their efforts to poison the minds of the Chinese people. This is their policy of cultural aggression. And it is carried out through missionary work, through establishing hospitals and schools, publishing newspapers and inducing Chinese students to study abroad. Their aim is to train intellectuals who will serve their interests and to dupe the people.

10. Since 18 September 1931 the large-scale invasion of Japanese imperialism has turned a big chunk of semi-colonial China into a Japanese colony.

It is thus clear that in their aggression against China the imperialist powers have on the one hand hastened the disintegration of feudal society, and the growth of elements of capitalism, thereby transforming a feudal into a semi-feudal society, and on the other imposed their ruthless rule on China, reducing an independent country to a semi-colonial and colonial country.

Taking both these aspects together, we can see that China's colonial, semi-colonial and semi-feudal society possesses the following characteristics :

1. The foundations of the self-sufficient natural economy of feudal times have been destroyed, but the exploitation of the peasantry by the landlord class, which is the basis of the system of feudal exploitation, not only remains intact but, linked as it is with exploitation by comprador and usurer capital, clearly dominates China's social and economic life.

2. National capitalism has developed to a certain extent and has played a considerable part in China's political and cultural life, but it has not become the principal pattern in China's social economy; it is flabby and is mostly associated with foreign imperialism and domestic feudalism in varying degrees.

3. The autocratic rule of the emperors and nobility has been overthrown, and in its place there has arisen first the warlord-bureaucrat

rule of the landlord class and then the joint dictatorship of the land-lord class and the big bourgeoisie. In the occupied areas there is the rule of Japanese imperialism and its puppets.

4. Imperialism controls not only China's vital financial and eco-nomic arteries but also her political and military power. In the occupied areas everything is in the hands of the Japanese.

5. China's economic, political and cultural development is very un-even, because she has been under the complete or partial domination of many imperialist powers, because she has actually been in a state of disunity for a long time, and because her territory is immense.

6. Under the twofold oppression of imperialism and feudalism, and especially as a result of the large-scale invasion of Japanese imperia-lism, the Chinese people, and particularly the peasants, have be-come more and more impoverished and have even been pauperized in large numbers, living in hunger and cold and without any poli-tical rights. The poverty and lack of freedom among the Chinese people are on a scale seldom found elsewhere.

The contradiction between imperialism and the Chinese nation and the contradiction between feudalism and the great masses of the people are the basic contradictions in modern Chinese society. Of course, there are others, such as the contradiction between the bourgeoisie and the proletariat and the contradictions within the reactionary ruling classes themselves. But the contradiction between imperialism and the Chinese nation is the principal one. These contradictions and their intensification must inevitably result in the incessant growth of revolutionary movements.* The great revolu-tions in modern and contemporary China have emerged and grown on the basis of the basic contradictions.

Only when we grasp the nature of Chinese society will we be able clearly to understand the targets, tasks, motive forces and character

* Among these, the most important recent rebellions included the Revolution of 1911, led by Sun Yat-sen, which overthrew the Ching Dynasty and established the Chinese Republic; the 30 May Movement, a nation-wide series of protests against British Police massacres in Shanghai, which were also savagely put down by the British and thus made the Chinese consciously anti-imperialist; the 'revolu-tionary army' 1926 expedition against brutal northern warlords which gained its communist leadership vast popular support but failed when the CP's ally, Chiang Kai-shek, double-crossed the communists and slaughtered thousand of them; and the Agrarian Revolutionary War (1927–37) when the Red Army established power in many rural areas. Known as the Second Revolutionary Civil War, it was curtailed when the CP again entered into a pact with Chiang's Kuomintang (Nationalist) Party to fight the Japanese invaders–ed.

of the Chinese revolution and its perspectives and future transition. A clear understanding of the nature of Chinese society, that is, of Chinese conditions, is therefore the key to a clear understanding of all the problems of the revolution.

Since the nature of present-day Chinese society is colonial, semi-colonial and semi-feudal, what are the chief targets or enemies at this stage of the Chinese revolution?

They are imperialism and feudalism, the bourgeoisie of the imperialist countries and the landlord class of our country. For it is these two that are the chief oppressors, the chief obstacles to the progress of Chinese society at the present stage. The two collude with each other in oppressing the Chinese people, and imperialism is the foremost and most ferocious enemy of the Chinese people, because national oppression by imperialism is the more onerous.

The Chinese bourgeoisie, which is also a victim of imperialist oppression, once led or played a principal role in revolutionary struggles such as the revolution of 1911, and has participated in revolutionary struggles such as the northern expedition and the present War of Resistance against Japan. In the long period from 1927 to 1937, however, its upper stratum, namely the section represented by the reactionary clique within the Kuomintang, collaborated with imperialism, formed a reactionary alliance with the landlord class, betrayed the friends who had helped it—the Communist Party, the proletariat, the peasantry and other sections of the petty bourgeoisie—betrayed the Chinese revolution and brought about its defeat. At that time, therefore, the revolutionary people and the revolutionary political party (the Communist Party) could not but regard these bourgeois elements as one of the targets of the revolution. In the War of Resistance a section of the big landlord class and the big bourgeoisie, represented by Wang Ching-wei, has turned traitor and deserted to the enemy. Consequently, the anti-Japanese people cannot but regard these big bourgeois elements who have betrayed our national interests as one of the targets of the revolution.

It is evident, then, that the enemies of the Chinese revolution are very powerful. They include not only powerful imperialists and powerful feudal forces, but also, at times, the bourgeois reactionaries who collaborate with the imperialist and feudal forces to oppose the people. Therefore, it is wrong to underestimate the strength of the enemies of the revolutionary Chinese people.

In the face of such enemies, the Chinese revolution cannot be other than protracted and ruthless. With such powerful enemies, the revolutionary forces cannot be built up and tempered into a power capable of crushing them except over a long period of time. With enemies who so ruthlessly suppress the Chinese revolution, the revolutionary forces cannot hold their own positions, let alone capture those of the enemy, unless they steel themselves and display their tenacity to the full.

In the face of such enemies, the principal means or form of the Chinese revolution must be armed struggle, not peaceful struggle. For our enemies have made peaceful activity impossible for the Chinese people and have deprived them of all political freedom and democratic rights. In the face of such enemies, there arises the question of revolutionary base areas. Since China's key cities have long been occupied by the powerful imperialists and their reactionary Chinese allies, it is imperative for the revolutionary ranks to turn the backward villages into advanced, consolidated base areas, into great military, political, economic and cultural bastions of the revolution from which to fight their vicious enemies who are using the cities for attacks on the rural districts, and in this way gradually to achieve the complete victory of the revolution through protracted fighting; it is imperative for them to do so if they do not wish to compromise with imperialism and its lackeys but are determined to fight on, and if they intend to build up and temper their forces, and avoid decisive battles with a powerful enemy while their own strength is inadequate. Such being the case, victory in the Chinese revolution can be won first in the rural areas, and this is possible because China's economic development is uneven (her economy not being a unified capitalist economy), because her territory is extensive (which gives the revolutionary forces room to manoeuvre), because the counter-revolutionary camp is disunited and full of contradictions, and because the struggle of the peasants who are the main force in the revolution is led by the Communist Party, the party of the proletariat; but, on the other hand, these very circumstances make the revolution uneven and render the task of winning complete victory protracted and arduous. Clearly then the protracted revolutionary struggle in the revolutionary base areas consists mainly in peasant guerrilla warfare led by the Chinese Communist Party. Therefore, it is wrong to ignore the necessity of using rural districts as revolutionary base areas, to neglect painstaking work among the peasants, and to neglect guerrilla warfare.

However, stressing armed struggle does not mean abandoning other forms of struggle; on the contrary, armed struggle cannot succeed unless coordinated with other forms of struggle. And stressing the work in the rural base areas does not mean abandoning our work in the cities and in the other vast rural areas which are still under the enemy's rule; on the contrary, without the work in the cities and in these other rural areas, our own rural base areas would be isolated and the revolution would suffer defeat. However, the final objective of the revolution is the capture of the cities, the enemy's main bases, and this objective cannot be achieved without adequate work in the cities.

It is thus clear that the revolution cannot triumph either in the rural areas or in the cities without the destruction of the enemy's army, his chief weapon against the people. Therefore, besides annihilating the enemy's troops in battle, there is the important task of disintegrating them.

It is also clear that the Communist Party must not be impetuous and adventurist in its propaganda and organizational work in the urban and rural areas, which have been occupied by the enemy and dominated by the forces of reaction and darkness for a long time, but that it must have well-selected cadres working underground, must accumulate strength and bide its time there. In leading the people in struggle against the enemy, the Party must adopt the tactics of advancing step by step slowly and surely, keeping to the principle of waging struggles on just grounds, to our advantage, and with restraint, and making use of such open forms of activity as are permitted by law, decree and social custom; empty clamour and reckless action can never lead to success.

Unless imperialist rule is overthrown, the rule of the feudal landlord class cannot be terminated, because imperialism is its main support. Conversely, unless help is given to the peasants in their struggle to overthrow the feudal landlord class, it will be impossible to build powerful revolutionary contingents to overthrow imperialist rule, because the feudal landlord class is the main social base of imperialist rule in China and the peasantry is the main force in the Chinese revolution. Therefore the two fundamental tasks, the national revolution and the democratic revolution, are at once distinct and united.

In fact, the two revolutionary tasks are already linked, since the main immediate task of the national revolution is to resist the Japanese imperialist invaders and since the democratic revolution must be accomplished in order to win the war. It is wrong to regard the national revolution and the democratic revolution as two entirely different stages of the revolution.

Since Chinese society is colonial, semi-colonial and semi-feudal, since the targets of the revolution are mainly foreign imperialist rule and domestic feudalism, and since its tasks are to overthrow these two oppressors, which of the various classes and strata in Chinese society constitute the forces capable of fighting them? This is the question of the motive forces of the Chinese revolution at the present stage. A clear understanding of this question is indispensable to a correct solution of the problem of the basic tactics of the Chinese revolution.

What classes are there in present-day Chinese society? There are the landlord class and the bourgeoisie, the landlord class and the upper stratum of the bourgeoisie constituting the ruling classes in Chinese society. And there are the proletariat, the peasantry, and the different sections of the petty bourgeoisie other than the peasantry, all of which are still the subject classes in vast areas of China.

(1) The Landlord Class

The landlord class forms the main social base for imperialist rule in China; it is a class which uses the feudal system to exploit and oppress the peasants, obstructs China's political, economic and cultural development and plays no progressive role whatsoever. Therefore, the landlords, as a class, are a target and not a motive force of the revolution.

In the present War of Resistance a section of the big landlords, along with one section of the big bourgeoisie (the capitulationists), has surrendered to the Japanese aggressors and turned traitor, while another section of the big landlords, along with another section of the big bourgeoisie (the die-hards), is increasingly wavering even though it is still in the anti-Japanese camp. But a good many of the enlightened gentry who are middle and small landlords and who have some capitalist colouration display some enthusiasm for the war, and we should unite with them in the common fight against Japan.

(2) The Bourgeoisie

There is a distinction between the comprador big bourgeoisie and the national bourgeoisie.

The comprador big bourgeoisie is a class which directly serves the capitalists of the imperialist countries and is nurtured by them; countless ties link it closely with the feudal forces in the country-side. Therefore, it is a target of the Chinese revolution and never in the history of the revolution has it been a motive force. However, different sections of the comprador big bourgeoisie owe allegiance to different imperialist powers, so that when the contradictions among the latter become very acute and the revolution is directed mainly against one particular imperialist power, it becomes possible for the sections of the comprador class which serve other imperialist groupings to join the current anti-imperialist front to a certain extent and for a certain period. But they will turn against the Chinese revolution the moment their masters do.

The national bourgeoisie is a class with a dual character. On the one hand, it is oppressed by imperialism and fettered by feudalism and consequently is in contradiction with both of them. In this respect it constitutes one of the revolutionary forces. In the course of the Chinese revolution it has displayed a certain enthusiasm for fighting imperialism and the governments of bureaucrats and war-lords.

But, on the other hand, it lacks the courage to oppose imperialism and feudalism thoroughly because it is economically and politically flabby and still has economic ties with imperialism and feudalism. This emerges very clearly when the people's revolutionary forces grow powerful.

It follows from the dual character of the national bourgeoisie that, at certain times and to a certain extent, it can take part in the revolution against imperialism and the governments of bureaucrats and warlords and can become a revolutionary force, but that at other times there is the danger of its following the comprador big bourgeoisie and acting as its accomplice in counter-revolution.

The national bourgeoisie in China, which is mainly the middle bourgeoisie, has never really held political power but has been restricted by the reactionary policies of the big landlord class and big bourgeoisie which are in power, although it followed them in opposing the revolution in the period from 1927 to 1931. In the present war, it differs not only from the capitulationists of the big landlord class and big bourgeoisie but also from the big bourgeois die-hards, and so far has been a fairly good ally of ours. Therefore, it is absolutely necessary to have a prudent policy towards the national bourgeoisie.

(3) The Different Sections of the Petty Bourgeoisie other than the Peasantry

The petty bourgeoisie, other than the peasantry, consists of the vast numbers of intellectuals, small tradesmen, handicraftsmen and professional people. Their status somewhat resembles that of the middle peasants: they all suffer under the oppression of imperialism, feudalism and the big bourgeoisie, and they are being driven ever nearer to bankruptcy or destitution. Hence these sections of the petty bourgeoisie constitute one of the motive forces of the revolution and are a reliable ally of the proletariat. Only under the leadership of the proletariat can they achieve their liberation.

The intellectuals and student youth do not constitute a separate class or stratum. In present-day China most of them may be placed in the petty-bourgeois category, judging by their family origin, their living conditions and their political outlook. Their numbers have grown considerably during the past few decades. Apart from that section of the intellectuals which has associated itself with the imperialists and the big bourgeoisie and works for them against the people, most intellectuals and students are oppressed by imperialism, feudalism and the big bourgeoisie, and live in fear of unemployment or of having to discontinue their studies. Therefore, they tend to be quite revolutionary. They are more or less equipped with bourgeois scientific knowledge, have a keen political sense and often play a vanguard role or serve as a link with the masses in the present stage of the revolution. In particular, the large numbers of more or less impoverished intellectuals can join hands with the workers and peasants in supporting or participating in the revolution. In China, it was among the intellectuals and young students that Marxist–Leninist ideology was first widely disseminated and accepted. The revolutionary forces cannot be successfully organized and revolutionary work cannot be successfully conducted without the participation of revolutionary intellectuals. But the intellectuals often tend to be subjective and individualistic, impractical in their thinking and irresolute in action until they have thrown themselves heart and soul into mass revolutionary struggles, or made up their minds to serve the interests of the masses and become one with them. Hence although the mass of revolutionary intellectuals in China can play a vanguard role or serve as a link with the masses, not all of them will remain revolutionaries to the end. Some will drop out of the revolutionary ranks at critical moments and become passive, while a few may even become enemies of the revolution. The intellectuals can overcome their shortcomings only in mass struggles over a long period.

The small tradesmen, generally, run small shops and employ few or no assistants. They live under the threat of bankruptcy as a result of exploitation by imperialism, the big bourgeoisie and the usurers. Handicraftsmen are very numerous. They possess their own means of production and hire no workers, or only one or two apprentices or helpers. Their position is similar to that of the middle peasants. Professional people, including doctors, do not exploit other people, or do so only to a slight degree. Their position is similar to that of the handicraftsmen. These sections of the petty bourgeoisie make up a vast multitude of people whom we must win over and whose interests we must protect because in general they can support or join the revolution and are good allies. Their weakness is that some of them are easily influenced by the bourgeoisie; consequently, we must carry on revolutionary propaganda and organizational work among them.

(4) The Peasantry

The peasantry constitutes approximately eighty per cent of China's total population and is the main force in her national economy today. A sharp process of polarization is taking place among the peasantry.

First, the rich peasants. They form about five per cent of the rural population (or about ten per cent together with the landlords) and constitute the rural bourgeoisie. Most of the rich peasants in China are semi-feudal in character, since they let a part of their land, practise usury and ruthlessly exploit the farm labourers. But they generally engage in labour themselves and in this sense are part of the peasantry. The rich-peasant form of production will remain useful for a definite period. Generally speaking, they might make some contribution to the anti-imperialist struggle of the peasant masses and stay neutral in the agrarian revolutionary struggle against the landlords. Therefore we should not regard the rich peasants as belonging to the same class as the landlords and should not prematurely adopt a policy of liquidating the rich peasantry.

Second, the middle peasants. They form about twenty per cent of China's rural population. They are economically self-supporting (they may have something to lay aside when the crops are good, and occasionally hire some labour or lend small sums of money at interest); and generally they do not exploit others but are exploited by imperialism, the landlord class and the bourgeoisie. They have no political rights. Some of them do not have enough land, and only a section (the well-to-do middle peasants) have some surplus land. Not only can the middle peasants join the anti-imperialist revolution and the agrarian revolution, but they can also accept socialism. Therefore the whole middle peasantry can be a reliable ally of the proletariat and is an important motive force of the revolution. The positive or negative attitude of the middle peasants is one of the factors determining victory or defeat in the revolution, and this is especially true after the agrarian revolution when they become the majority of the rural population.

Third, the poor peasants. The poor peasants in China, together with the farm labourers, form about seventy per cent of the rural population. They are the broad peasant masses with no land or insufficient land, the semi-proletariat of the countryside, the biggest motive force of the Chinese revolution, the natural and most reliable ally of the proletariat and the main contingent of China's revolutionary forces. Only under the leadership of the proletariat can the poor and middle peasants achieve their liberation, and only by forming a firm alliance with the poor and middle peasants can the proletariat lead the revolution to victory. Otherwise neither is possible. The term 'peasantry' refers mainly to the poor and middle peasants.

(5) The Proletariat

Among the Chinese proletariat, the modern industrial workers number from 2,500,000 to 3,000,000; the workers in small-scale industry and in handicrafts and the shop assistants in the cities total about 12,000,000, and in addition there are great numbers of rural proletariats (the farm labourers) and other propertyless people in the cities and the countryside.

In addition to the basic qualities it shares with the proletariat everywhere—its association with the most advanced form of economy, its strong sense of organization and discipline and its lack of private means of production—the Chinese proletariat has many other outstanding qualities.

First, the Chinese proletariat is more resolute and thoroughgoing in revolutionary struggle than any other class—because it is subjected to a threefold oppression (imperialist, bourgeois, and feudal) which is marked by a severity and cruelty seldom found in other countries. Since there is no economic basis for social reformism in colonial and semi-colonial China as there is in Europe, the whole proletariat, with the exception of a few scabs, is most revolutionary.

Second, from the moment it appeared on the revolutionary scene, the Chinese proletariat came under the leadership of its own revolutionary party—the Communist Party of China—and became the most politically conscious class in Chinese society.

Third, because the Chinese proletariat by origin is largely made up of bankrupted peasants, it has natural ties with the peasant masses, which facilitates its forming a close alliance with them.

Therefore, in spite of certain unavoidable weaknesses—for instance, its smallness (as compared with the peasantry), its youth (as compared with the proletariat in the capitalist countries) and its low educational level (as compared with the bourgeoisie)—the Chinese proletariat is nonetheless the basic motive force of the Chinese revolution. Unless it is led by the proletariat, the Chinese revolution cannot possibly succeed. To take an example from the past, the revolution of 1911 miscarried because the proletariat did not consciously participate in it and the Communist Party was not yet in existence. More recently, the revolution of 1924–7 achieved great success for a time because the proletariat consciously participated and exercised leadership and the Communist Party was already in existence; it ended in defeat because the big bourgeoisie betrayed its alliance with the proletariat and abandoned the common revolutionary programme and also because the Chinese proletariat and its political party did not yet have enough revolutionary experience. Now take the present anti-Japanese war—because the proletariat and the Communist Party are exercising leadership in the Anti-Japanese National United Front, the whole nation has been united and the great War of Resistance has been launched and is being resolutely pursued.

The Chinese proletariat should understand that although it is the class with the highest political consciousness and sense of organization, it cannot win victory by its own strength alone. In order to win, it must unite, according to varying circumstances, with all classes and strata that can take part in the revolution, and must organize a revolutionary united front. Among all the classes in Chinese society, the peasantry is a firm ally of the working class, the urban petty bourgeoisie is a reliable ally, and the national bourgeoisie is an ally in certain periods and to a certain extent. This is one of the fundamental laws established by China's modern revolutionary history.

(6) The Vagrants

China's status as a colony and semi-colony has given rise to a multitude of rural and urban unemployed. Denied proper means of making a living, many of them are forced to resort to illegitimate ones, hence the robbers, gangsters, beggars and prostitutes and the numerous people who live on superstitious practices. This social stratum is unstable; while some are apt to be bought over by the reactionary forces, others may join the revolution. These people lack constructive qualities and are given to destruction rather than construction; after joining the revolution, they become a source of roving-rebel and anarchist ideology in the revolutionary ranks. Therefore, we should know how to remould them and guard against their destructiveness.

We have now gained an understanding of the nature of Chinese society, i.e., of the specific conditions in China; this understanding is the essential prerequisite for solving all China's revolutionary problems. We are also clear about the targets, the tasks and the motive forces of the Chinese revolution; these are basic issues at the present stage of the revolution and arise from the special nature of Chinese society, i.e., from China's specific conditions. Understanding all this, we can now understand another basic issue of the revolution at the present stage, i.e. the character of the Chinese revolution.

Since Chinese society is colonial, semi-colonial and semi-feudal, since the principal enemies of the Chinese revolution are imperialism and feudalism, since the tasks of the revolution are to overthrow these two enemies by means of a national and democratic revolution in which the bourgeoisie sometimes takes part, and since the edge of the revolution is directed against imperialism and feudalism and not against capitalism and capitalist private property in general even if the big bourgeoisie betrays the revolution and becomes its enemy—since all this is true, the character of the Chinese revolution at the present stage is not proletarian-socialist but bourgeois-democratic.

However, in present-day China the bourgeois-democratic revolution is no longer of the old general type, which is now obsolete, but one of a new special type. We call this type the new democratic revolution and it is developing in all other colonial and semi-colonial countries as well as in China. The new democratic revolution is part of the world proletarian-socialist revolution, for it resolutely opposes imperialism, i.e., international capitalism. Politically, it strives for the joint dictatorship of the revolutionary classes over the imperialists, traitors and reactionaries, and opposes the transformation of Chinese society into a society under bourgeois dictatorship. Economically, it aims at the nationalization of all the big enterprises and capital of the imperialists, traitors and reactionaries, and the distribution among the peasants of the land held by the landlords, while preserving private capitalist enterprise in general and not eliminating the rich-peasant economy. Thus, the new type of democratic revolution clears the way for capitalism on the one hand and creates the prerequisites for socialism on the other. The present stage of the Chinese revolution is a stage of transition between the abolition of the colonial, semi-colonial and semi-feudal society and the establishment of a socialist society, i.e., it is a process of new democratic revolution. This process, begun only after the First World War and the Russian October Revolution, started in China with the 4 May Movement of 1919.* A new democratic

---

* The 4 May Movement was an anti-imperialist and anti-feudal revolutionary movement which began on 4 May 1919. In the first half of that year, the victors of the First World War, i.e. Britain, France, the United States, Japan, Italy and other imperialist countries, met in Paris to divide the spoils and decided that Japan should take over all the privileges previously enjoyed by Germany in Shantung Province, China. The students of Peking were the first to show determined opposition to this scheme, holding rallies and demonstrations on 4 May. The northern warlord government arrested more than thirty students in an effort to suppress this opposition. In protest, the students of Peking went on strike and large numbers of students in other parts of the country responded. On 3 June the northern warlord government started arresting students in Peking *en masse*, and within two days about

revolution is an anti-imperialist and anti-feudal revolution of the broad masses of the people under the leadership of the proletariat. Chinese society can advance to socialism only through such a revolution; there is no other way.

The new democratic revolution is vastly different from the democratic revolutions of Europe and America in that it results not in a dictatorship of the bourgeoisie but in a dictatorship of the united front of all the revolutionary classes under the leadership of the proletariat. In the present War of Resistance, the anti-Japanese democratic political power established in the base areas which are under the leadership of the Communist Party is the political power of the Anti-Japanese National United Front; this is neither a bourgeois nor a proletarian one-class dictatorship, but a joint dictatorship, of the revolutionary classes under the leadership of the proletariat. All who stand for resistance to Japan and for democracy are entitled to share in this political power, regardless of their party affiliations.

The new democratic revolution also differs from a socialist revolution in that it overthrows the rule of the imperialists, traitors, and reactionaries in China but does not destroy any section of capitalism which is capable of contributing to the anti-imperialist, anti-feudal struggle.

There can be no doubt that the ultimate perspective of the Chinese revolution is not capitalism but socialism and communism, since China's bourgeois-democratic revolution at the present stage is not of the old general type but is a democratic revolution of a new special type—a new democratic revolution—and since it is taking place in the new international environment of the 1930s and 40s characterized by the rise of socialism and the decline of capitalism, in the period of the Second World War and the era of revolution.

However, it is not at all surprising but entirely to be expected that

a thousand were taken into custody. This aroused still greater indignation throughout the country. From 5 June onwards the workers of Shanghai and many other cities went on strike and the merchants in these places shut their shops. Thus, what was at first a patriotic movement consisting mainly of intellectuals rapidly developed into a national patriotic movement embracing the proletariat, the urban petty bourgeoisie and the bourgeoisie. And along with the growth of this patriotic movement, the new cultural movement which had begun before 4 May as a movement against feudalism and for the promotion of science and democracy grew into a vigorous and powerful revolutionary cultural movement whose main current was the propagation of Marxism–Leninism Mao.

a capitalist economy will develop to a certain extent within Chinese society with the sweeping away of the obstacles to the development of capitalism after the victory of the revolution, since the purpose of the Chinese revolution at the present stage is to change the existing colonial, semi-colonial and semi-feudal state of society, i.e., to strive for the completion of the new democratic revolution. A certain degree of capitalist development will be an inevitable result of the victory of the democratic revolution in economically backward China. But that will be only one aspect of the outcome of the Chinese revolution and not the whole picture. The whole picture will show the development of socialist as well as capitalist factors. What will the socialist factors be? The increasing relative importance of the proletariat and the Communist Party among the political forces in the country; leadership by the proletariat and the Communist Party which the peasantry, intelligentsia and the urban petty bourgeoisie already accept or are likely to accept; and the state sector of the economy owned by the democratic republic, and the cooperative sector of the economy owned by the working people. All these will be socialist factors. With the addition of a favourable international environment, these factors render it highly probable that China's bourgeois-democratic revolution will ultimately avoid a capitalist future and enjoy a socialist future.

Some immature Communists think that our task is confined to the present democratic revolution and does not include the future socialist revolution, or that the present revolution or the agrarian revolution is actually a socialist revolution. It must be emphatically pointed out that these views are wrong. Every Communist ought to know that, taken as a whole, the Chinese revolutionary movement led by the Communist Party embraces the two stages, i.e., the democratic and the socialist revolutions, which are two essentially different revolutionary processes, and that the second process can be carried through only after the first has been completed. The democratic revolution is the necessary preparation for the socialist revolution, and the socialist revolution is the inevitable sequel to the democratic revolution.

II Chu Teh: *The Revolutionary Army** [31]

There are two kinds of armies, now as in the past. One kind organizes, arms and trains the people to protect the interests of the
people and serve the people. The other also organizes, arms and
trains the people; but it does so to protect the interests of the few —
the big landlords, the big compradors and big bankers — and to
oppress, exploit and enslave the people.

The people's army, for the very reason that it is closely united
with the people, can effectively protect the country against foreign
invasions, and, inside the country, can safeguard the people's rights
to democracy and freedom. The army of the big landlords and
bourgeoisie, for the reason that it is divorced from the people, is
bound to be powerless to defend the country: it vacillates, becomes
defeatist, and may even betray its trust (to the extent of becoming
a puppet army). Moreover, it undermines and suppresses the democratic liberties of the people.

The people's army practises democracy within its own ranks.
Officers and men are as one. It is democratic in relation to the
people: people and army are as one. The army of the big landlords
and bourgeoisie imposes within its own ranks a system of oppression
and double-dealing. If that were not the case, it could not order its
officers and men, the vast majority of whom come from the people,
to act against the people. The recruiting system of an army of big
landlords and bourgeoisie must necessarily be against the wishes of
the people : without compulsion, nobody would join. Those who join
our army come of their own free will because they want to resist
Japanese aggression, save their country and build up a China with a
system of new democracy. Some of them are Communists. The
majority are not. The English Route and New Fourth Armies,†
just because they have this close contact with the people, have an
inexhaustible supply of manpower.

When in the future a coalition government and a joint supreme
command are set up, a system of obligatory military service will
possibly be adopted. But any such system will be radically different
from the vicious conscription system of the Kuomintang govern-

* The thesis he develops here, though applied to the anti-Japanese struggle and
post-Second World War civil war, is still upheld as valid by the contemporary
Chinese leadership, which still includes Chuh Teh himself–ed.

† The two main Red Army forces during the Second World War, which went on
to defeat the forces of Chiang Kai-shek's Kuomintang (Nationalist Party)–ed.

ment, because it will be built on a voluntary basis, a basis of persuasion.

An army not based on, and in fact antagonistic to, the people maintains itself by exploitation of the people, and consequently by exploitation of the soldiers as well! But the method of a people's army is one based on love for the people, and consequently love for the soldiers, too. The latter is the method practised by the Eighth Route and New Fourth Armies.

Starting from the exploitation of the people and the soldiers, the reactionary clique in the Kuomintang employs various schemes to extort military funds from the people on the pretext that 'the state should maintain the troops'. Not satisfied with extorting money at home, it turns to foreign countries for loans in the name of the state. And when funds for military purposes are collected, the Kuomintang reactionaries pocket the money by 'padding the payroll' and other devices. Embezzlement is rife among officers from top to bottom. The higher the officer's rank, the more he can appropriate for himself.

Our soldiers are armed peasants in uniform. Our army is a collection of ordinary people under arms and in uniform. They want to wear clothes, to eat, drink, rest and work just like the common people. Their main material needs are clothing, food, housing and transport. Their spiritual need is education.

The material upkeep of our army follows the principle that it shall not become too heavy a burden on the people, otherwise a conflict of interests will be created between army and people. If the people's life is made hard, army life will become hard too. Its strength to fight the enemy will be sapped. When a situation develops requiring expansion of the army, it must be expanded without excessively increasing the burden on the people. When we run into difficult times, as we did in 1942, the principle we work on is to take into consideration the interests of both army and people: we reduce the number of troops, raise their quality, and simplify government administration in the enemy rear. Our treatment of the whole army is based on the principle of equal treatment for officers and men. The officers set an example by taking the rough with the smooth, along with their men. Only those who have the interests of their men at heart, who take into account what they have to put up with, and who do not stand aloof from the rank and file, can be considered good officers. We have in recent years introduced a completely new principle into the maintenance of the army, by enabling it, in intervals between periods of fighting and training, to engage in productive work, and, in so doing, help to meet the material needs of the army and lighten the burden on the people. For the army this new contribution is something extremely important. Experience gained in the border region from the army's participation in productive work shows that, in the absence of fighting, we can in the first year become partly self-supporting, in the second, half self-supporting, and in the third, wholly so. In areas where fighting is going on, the army may, by taking part in such work, become partly or half self-supporting. Personal participation of commanders in this productive work is an important means of drawing the army in, too. Whenever the army takes part in production, the people's burden is lightened, the ties between army and people become closer, army life becomes richer, the army becomes more close-knit, training is more effective, fighting spirit is enhanced; and an inexhaustible source of funds to maintain the army is tapped.

As regards special treatment for the families of fighting men and care of disabled or demobilized soldiers, we have taken a number of new measures in recent years. Besides getting their neighbours to plough the land of such families, giving them pensions and other assistance, we are helping soldiers' families to go in for production so that they can become economically independent. Indeed, many heroes of labour have emerged from among them, and they are not doing so badly. Every Liberated Area should endeavour to do this work well and see that they live comfortably.

The method used by an army not based on the people, one in fact antagonistic to them, is to treat soldiers as slaves, whereas the method used by a people's army is to treat them as politically conscious fighters. The big landlords and bourgeoisie organize and arm people so as to have an army to use against the people. That, of course, is no easy matter; and that is why an army of this kind resorts to all sorts of barbarities in leading its troops. The policy of the reactionaries is to keep soldiers in a state of ignorance, applying the maxim that 'the most valuable quality in generals is wisdom, in soldiers ignorance'.* For if soldiers were wise they would not act against the people. So the reactionaries devise a set of military

* In my days as a drafted GI, the maxim we were told a million times was 'Yours not to question why, yours is to do and die'–ed.

codes, military orders and discipline, on the basis of which they impose a ruthless system of dictatorship and absolute obedience. Those who fail to toe the line are punished, those who do, get promotion and grow rich! On the one hand the reactionaries use threats, on the other they dangle baits. What this means is that they do not regard their subordinates and soldiers as individual human beings, but bully and cow them, through this rotten system of absolute obedience, into allowing dictators to use the army just as they think fit.

We regard officers and men alike as individual human beings on an equal footing. The only difference between them is in matters of duty. No officers are allowed to oppress the men, no senior officers to oppress their juniors. Our soldiers join the army to serve the people, not the officers. We call for extremely strict discipline, both in military affairs and in relations with the people; but this kind of discipline is based on political understanding, and observed by officers and men alike without exception.

The method employed in training an army not founded on the people but actually antagonistic to them is based on ignorance and compulsion; whereas the method used in training a people's army is based on political understanding and voluntary acceptance. The first thing in training an army is to train the mind of the soldier. There will be no spirit of initiative in an army whose political understanding is low, which does not know what it is fighting for. In that case no amount of training will get results. Courage without political understanding is brute bravery. Conscious courage resulting from political awareness is real courage. To heighten political understanding and military knowledge a certain educational level is essential.

The political understanding of our army is high, and that is why it is unconquerable. As a result of our fight in recent years against tendencies to be dogmatic or formalistic, political training has become more practical and advanced. Both officers and men have systematically improved their military knowledge, and a considerable advance has been made in the study and application of strategy and tactics. With regard to all-round education, while we could show some results right from the start, we have done much better in recent years. As far as cultivation of mind goes, we have for the past year or so given our troops training for various productive occupations as well as political and general education.* Such training for production not only helps the campaign to secure greater output, but also fosters a sound attitude towards labour and prevents our men from becoming scoundrels in uniform or loafers. When the war is over they will still be useful members of society.

Fighting involves hand-to-hand combat, a matching of strength. Physical training, therefore, is important. Building physical strength demands, first of all, a full stomach and warm clothing. Next comes training in technique and tactics. In the past there was a tendency in our army to pooh-pooh the idea of physical strength and technique. It was regarded as enough for the army to have political awareness. This is quite wrong. During the last couple of winters we carried out training on a large scale. In some areas this developed into military training for the whole people. Our regular troops have improved enormously, and large numbers of the militia have now learned how to lay mines. To have done so much is pretty significant.

In recent years we have worked out a new method of training troops by replacing the 'officer line', which gave officers and instructors sole control of conduct of training from above, with the 'mass line' on a basis of cooperation between officers and men. In our army we have introduced a new educational method, one of improving ourselves through both teaching and learning. The officers teach the men and the men teach the officers. The officers teach each other. Those who are intellectuals and those who are of worker or peasant origin help and learn from each other. We place a high value on the lectures on special technical skills given by our officers or military experts. At the same time officers must not overlook the fact that every one of the hundreds or thousands of men under their command has his own strong points, that in our army there are highly skilled men from every trade. Officers should not be too proud to learn from them. We have changed the attitude of officers from one of conceit and superiority to one of untiringly learning from others and teaching others. In short, the classrooms and drill grounds which the men used to fear have been turned into places where military skill and knowledge are cultivated and tempered.

---

* It should also be pointed out that we owe a great deal of the success of cultivation of mind in our army to the many intellectuals and young men of good education who have joined it–Chu Teh.

D

The whole atmosphere is different, interest has been heightened, and the barracks have been turned into schools.

There are two different methods of carrying on a war. An army not based on, and, in fact, hostile to the people, is necessarily limited to cut-and-dried rules and formulas. But a people's army uses methods of extreme flexibility and constantly adapts itself to the situation. Because the army of the big landlords and bourgeoisie oppresses the people and receives no help from them, because there is no community of interest between officers and men, such an army cannot, when engaged in war, rely on the initiative and morale of its junior officers and men. This makes it very difficult to wage a war with such an army. The higher command issues orders based entirely on preconceived, cut-and-dried rules, without weighing enemy strength against its own and disregarding special conditions of time and place. Consequently such orders are utterly impracticable. When a unit receives orders which cannot be carried out, it makes a false report to the higher command. Both superiors and subordinates try to pull the wool over each others' eyes.

Whenever we are fighting we are helped everywhere by the people. Since the organization of the militia and the starting of tunnel-digging and mine-laying movements, the scale and importance of the help the people have given us are incalculable. Within the army itself, because it has a high degree of political understanding and because there is mutual understanding and a feeling of solidarity between officers and men, everyone knows where he stands and can act on his own initiative. Having a single aim, the fighters are mobile and swift; they can fight bravely.

Our policy in conducting the war may be summed up like this. Whether we join battle depends on the weapons we possess, the kind of enemy we have to cope with, and the time and place of the engagement. It means, too, that battle has to be planned and fought on the basis of our own equipment, the strength of the enemy, and taking into account the factors of time and place. This new method of conducting war is both practical and materialist. I use these words advisedly. Many a military expert, in China and abroad, both nowadays and formerly, failed disastrously in this respect. And some of our comrades who held 'leftist' ideas in the past failed to understand just this point. Earlier on, when the only weapons at our disposal were rifles, spears and big swords, we simply had to study conditions, make up our minds and determine our tactics accordingly. We didn't talk in high faluting terms about tactics of a mechanized army. When we passed from the period of civil war to that of the anti-Japanese war, when the enemy we had to face was the Japanese army, we did not content ourselves with sticking to experience gained in the civil war period. On the basis of that experience we made the changes and improvements necessary. We made up our minds and determined our tactics through a thorough study of the situation of the enemy. And of course, on the battle front of the liberated areas we have to map out tactics applicable to the time and place of a battle front of this kind. Alongside these general rules for conducting war goes a special feature — the unity between army and people. On the one hand, the fight waged by the army serves to help the various struggles in which the people are engaged; and on the other, the people's efforts — political, economic, cultural and military, as well as disruption of the enemy lines of communication — serve to help the army wage war. This coordination in all spheres between army and people is thoroughly carried out on the battle fronts, in every campaign and in every battle. This is the new method of making war which we have worked out in the course of the people's war.

Officers, men and people have one constant endeavour; to seek to attack the enemy in every possible way. Consequently, even if, once in a while, orders are impracticable or belated, no harm is done, because lower units are able to adapt themselves to circumstances, and judge and act independently. That is why we are winning all along the line.

Now a word on military theory. Whenever this subject is discussed, some people like to show off with a series of high-sounding military academy lectures, or quote at length from the military history of one country or another. What they say is all very profound, but unfortunately their theories are not necessarily of practical value to the Chinese people. Undoubtedly we must absorb the military theories and experience of all countries. We ought to learn from them. It will be bad for us if we do not. What we must not do is to apply such theories and experience mechanically; we must not accept them as immutable dogmas. The northern expedition, the agrarian revolutionary war and the eight years of the anti-Japanese war have given birth to a correct military science which, as events prove, best suits the needs of the Chinese people. It is a military science which combines theory with practice, and which has led to three basic principles: to avoid rashness in attack; to avoid conservatism in defence; and to resist any tendency to run in panic from the enemy when withdrawing from a point. These basic principles are bound up with the close fighting unity between army and people; and because of this unity they can be applied.

Our political work sets out: (1) to raise the political understanding of officers and men, to inspire them with love for their country and their people, and to fire them with a desire to re-educate themselves; (2) to bring about unity between friendly army units; (3) to cement the unity between army and people, so as to make the people more politically aware, to safeguard the country and democracy, and to help spread education and culture among the people; (4) to demoralize the Japanese and puppet troops by political and psychological means so as to sap their fighting strength; and (5) to consolidate and raise the fighting strength of our army, to guarantee the carrying out of orders, and to help the army itself make an intensive study of politics, military matters, general education and production. These five aspects of our political work are interrelated and complementary to one another.

For several years the most difficult problem we have been up against on the battle fronts of the liberated areas is that of obtaining equipment and military supplies. We are solving it in several ways. First, we arm ourselves with weapons seized from the enemy. For several years now we have relied on this method of strengthening our forces and maintaining our fighting power. Second, we make use of materials obtainable locally. The abundance of coal and iron and metal obtained from dismantled railway tracks in northern China have greatly facilitated our manufacture of arms; and this is how the greater part of the militia forces have been able to extend the tactics of mine-laying. Third, we have set up small-scale ordnance factories by assembling odds and ends of equipment captured from the Japanese and puppet troops. Fourth, these factories, which often became the target of enemy 'mopping-up' campaigns, must be dispersed and camouflaged. Greater armed protection must be provided for them so that ammunition can be uninterruptedly produced to supply the front. As far as medical supplies go, we have adopted the principle of using both Chinese herbal medicines and Western medicines. We manufacture only a small part of the medicines we use, the main source of supply being seizure from the enemy and purchase.

The armed forces in the liberated areas fall into three categories: the main forces, local forces, and self-defence militia forces. The main job of the militia and self-defence forces is to protect their own villages while carrying on with their regular work. By protecting homes and defending themselves they are, wherever they may be, fighting the war against Japan in conjunction with other districts and the whole of the liberated areas. Local and national tasks in this war go hand in hand. In the whole history of our armies there have never been militia forces on such a scale in the liberated areas, and the very fact that we have learned to organize such a militia speaks volumes. For once the militia is organized it can fight either in co-ordination with the regular army or on its own. It has done a fine job in protecting the people so that they could push ahead and produce more; and the recovery of many positions behind the enemy lines owes a great deal to the success of the militia in tying down the enemy. For weapons, the militia use chiefly land-mines. Besides these they have some rifles, hand-grenades and sundry primitive weapons, including improvised grenade-throwers. To solve the problem of securing arms by their own efforts, in many places the militia reclaim plots of land and use the money raised by the sale of produce to buy arms. In many localities the militia of other areas. Here we see the militia starting to turn into regular local forces. Moreover, the militia and local self-defence forces take an active part in production : they are both fighters and producers, both a military and a labour force. That is something that radically changes the former face of the countryside. The local forces occupy a place midway between the main forces and the militia. They are responsible for the defence of one or several counties. They are responsible not only for the comparatively important military task of launching counter-'mopping-up' campaigns, but for looking after the immediate interests of the people; for example, giving protec-tion to the local people at the time of harvest or sowing, besides fighting flood, drought and other hazards of nature. The men who form these local forces naturally love the locality where they were born, where they grew up and where their forefathers are buried. That makes it possible for us to strengthen such forces so that they can act as local garrisons in the War of Resistance. Then, as each local force, in carrying out this task, becomes tempered and strong, it gets more like and more on the level of a main force. Sometimes the main forces are concentrated. At other times they are dispersed, and then it is necessary for them to join with local and militia forces to add to their strength and attack the enemy with greater weight. Working in unity with each other, the main, local and militia forces become an organic whole. When circumstances are critical, we can act on the principle of dispersing the main forces and mingling them with the masses to our advantage. On the other hand, when the situation favours the expansion of our work, the militia and local forces can, in certain conditions, come together to cooperate with the main forces, or actually become part of the main forces themselves so as to fulfil the more important tasks called for by such expansion. By such measures our people's armies have created a militia of over two million men to serve as their support and reserve. That is one of the reasons why they can withstand protracted warfare. This is an enormous step forward in the process of building up our military forces in the Liberated Areas.

III   Lin Piao: *People's War**[32]

In the summer of 1937 Japanese imperialism unleashed its all-out war of aggression against China. The nation-wide War of Resistance thus broke out. Could the War of Resistance be victorious? And how was victory to be won?

Japan was a powerful imperialist country. But Japanese imperialism was in its era of decline and doom. The war it had unleashed was a war of aggression, a war that was retrogressive and barbarous; it was deficient in manpower and material resources and could not stand a protracted war; it was engaged in an unjust cause and therefore had meagre support internationally. China, on the other hand, was a weak semi-colonial and semi-feudal country. But she was in her era of progress. She was fighting a war against aggres-

* Originally the transcription of a speech, the article was meant to commemorate the twentieth anniversary of Japan's defeat in China by the Red Army, but quickly became known as the 'Lin Piao Theory' of revolution in the underdeveloped world through 'strangulation of the cities'. The author, a veteran of the famous Long March and numerous guerrilla battles, was at the time of writing Vice-Chairman of the Central Committee of the Communist Party of China, Vice-Premier of the State Council and Minister of Defence. At the Ninth Congress of the Communist Party, held in Peking in April 1969, Lin Piao was designated Mao's successor as Chairman–ed.

sion, a war that was progressive and just; she had sufficient manpower and material resources to sustain a protracted war; internationally, China enjoyed extensive sympathy and support.

China's War of Resistance would be protracted, and prolonged efforts would be needed gradually to weaken the enemy's forces and expand our own, so that the enemy would change from being strong to being weak and we would change from being weak to being strong and accumulate sufficient strength finally to defeat him through three stages: namely, the strategic defensive, the strategic stalemate and the strategic offensive. The protracted war was also a process of mobilizing, organizing and arming the people. It was only by mobilizing the entire people to fight a people's war that the War of Resistance could be persevered in and the Japanese aggressors defeated.

In order to turn the anti-Japanese war into a genuine people's war, our Party firmly relied on the broadest masses of the people, united with all the anti-Japanese forces that could be united, and consolidated and expanded the Anti-Japanese National United Front. The basic line of our Party was boldly to arouse the masses of the people and expand the people's forces so that, under the leadership of the Party, they could defeat the aggressors and build a new China.

In order to win a people's war, it is imperative to build the broadest possible united front and formulate a series of policies which will ensure the fullest mobilization of the basic masses as well as the unity of all the forces than can be united.

The Anti-Japanese National United Front embraced all the anti-Japanese classes and strata. These classes and strata shared a common interest in fighting Japan, an interest which formed the basis of their unity. But they differed in the degree of their firmness in resisting Japan, and there were class contradictions and conflicts of interest among them. Hence the inevitable class struggle within the united front.

The workers, the peasants, and the urban petty bourgeoisie firmly demanded that the War of Resistance should be carried through to the end; they were the main force in the fight against Japanese aggression and constituted the basic masses who demanded unity and progress.

The bourgeoisie was divided into the national and the comprador bourgeoisie. The national bourgeoisie formed the majority of the bourgeoisie; it was rather flabby, often vacillated and had contradictions with the workers, but it also had a certain degree of readiness to oppose imperialism and was one of our allies in the War of Resistance. The comprador bourgeoisie was the bureaucrat-capitalist class, which was very small in number but occupied the ruling position in China. Its members attached themselves to different imperialist powers, some of them being pro-Japanese and others pro-British and pro-American. The pro-Japanese section of the comprador bourgeoisie were the capitulators, the overt and covert traitors. The pro-British and pro-American section of this class favoured resistance to Japan to a certain extent, but they were not firm in their resistance and very much wished to compromise with Japan, and by their nature they were opposed to the Communist Party and the people.

The landlords fell into different categories; there were the big, the middle and the small landlords. Some of the big landlords became traitors, while others favoured resistance but vacillated a great deal. Many of the middle and small landlords had the desire to resist, but there were contradictions between them and the peasants.

In the face of these complicated class relationships, our Party's policy regarding work within the united front was one of both alliance and struggle. This is to say, its policy was to unite with all the anti-Japanese classes and strata, try to win over even those who could be only vacillating and temporary allies, and adopt appropriate policies to adjust the relations among these classes and strata so that they all served the general cause of resisting Japan. At the same time, we had to maintain our Party's principle of independence and initiative, make the bold arousing of the masses and expansion of the people's forces the centre of gravity in our work, and wage the necessary struggles against all activities harmful to resistance, unity and progress.

Our Party made a series of adjustments in its policies in order to unite all the anti-Japanese parties and groups, including the Kuomintang, and all the anti-Japanese strata in a joint fight against the foe.

The government of the Shensi-Kansu-Ningsia revolutionary base area was renamed the Government of the Shensi-Kansu-Ningsia Special Region of the Republic of China. Our Workers' and Peasants' Red Army was redesignated the Eighth Route Army and the New Fourth Army of the National Revolutionary Army. Our land policy, the policy of confiscating the land of the landlords, was changed to one of reducing rent and interest. In our own base areas we shared power with non-Communists, drawing in those representatives of the petty bourgeoisie, the national bourgeoisie and the enlightened gentry and those members of the Kuomintang who stood for resistance to Japan and did not oppose the Communist Party. In accordance with the principles of the Anti-Japanese National United Front, we also made necessary and appropriate changes in our policies relating to the economy, taxation, labour and wages, anti-espionage, people's rights, culture and education, etc.

While making these policy adjustments, we maintained the independence of the Communist Party, the people's army and the base areas. We also insisted that the Kuomintang should institute a general mobilization, reform the government apparatus, introduce democracy, improve the people's livelihood, arm the people, and carry out a total war of resistance. We waged a resolute struggle against the Kuomintang's passive resistance to Japan and active opposition to the Communist Party, against its suppression of the people's resistance movement and its treacherous activities for compromise and capitulation. The lessons learned at the cost of blood helped to sober many of our comrades and increase their ability to distinguish the correct line which included:

1. All people favouring resistance (that is, all the anti-Japanese workers, peasants, soldiers, students and intellectuals, and businessmen) were to unite and form the Anti-Japanese National United Front.

2. Within the united front, our policy was to be one of independence and initiative, i.e. both unity and independence were necessary.

3. As far as the military strategy was concerned, our policy was to be guerrilla warfare waged independently and with the initiative in our own hands, within the framework of a unified strategy; guerrilla warfare was to be basic, but no chance of waging mobile warfare was to be lost when the conditions were favourable.

4. In the struggle against the anti-Communist die-hards headed by Chiang Kai-shek, our policy was to make use of contradictions, win over the many, oppose the few and destroy our enemies one by one,

*D**

and to wage struggles on just grounds, to our advantage, and with restraint.

5. In the Japanese-occupied and Kuomintang areas our policy was, on the one hand, to develop the united front to the greatest possible extent and, on the other, to have selected cadres working underground. With regard to the forms of organization and struggle, our policy was to assign selected cadres to work under cover for a long period, so as to accumulate strength and bide our time.

6. As regards the alignment of the various classes within the country, our basic policy was to develop the progressive forces, win over the middle forces and isolate the anti-Communist die-hard forces.

7. As for the anti-Communist die-hards, we followed a revolutionary dual policy of uniting with them, in so far as they were still capable of bringing themselves to resist Japan, and of struggling against and isolating them, in so far as they were determined to oppose the Communist Party.

8. With respect to the landlords and the bourgeoisie—even the big landlords and big bourgeoisie—it was necessary to analyse each case and draw distinctions. On the basis of these distinctions we were to formulate different policies so as to achieve our aim of uniting with all the forces that could be united.

History shows that when confronted by ruthless imperialist aggression, a Communist Party must hold aloft the national banner and, using the weapon of the united front, rally around itself the masses and the patriotic and anti-imperialist people who form more than ninety per cent of a country's population, so as to mobilize all positive factors, unite with all the forces that can be united and isolate to the maximum the common enemy of the whole nation. If we abandon the national banner, and thus isolate ourselves, it is out of the question to exercise leadership and develop the people's revolutionary cause, and this in reality amounts to helping the enemy and bringing defeat on ourselves.

History shows that within the united front the Communist Party must maintain its ideological, political and organizational independence, adhere to the principle of independence and initiative, and insist on its leading role. Since there are class differences among the various classes in the united front, the Party must have a correct policy in order to develop the progressive forces, win over the middle forces and oppose the die-hard forces.

History shows that during the national-democratic revolution there must be two kinds of alliance within this united front: first, the worker-peasant alliance and, second, the alliance of the working people with the bourgeoisie and other non-working people. The worker-peasant alliance is the foundation of the united front. Whether the working class can gain leadership of the national-democratic revolution depends on whether it can lead the broad masses of the peasants in struggle and rally them around itself. Only when the working class gains leadership of the peasants, and only on the basis of the worker-peasant alliance, is it possible to establish the second alliance, form a broad united front and wage a people's war victoriously. Otherwise everything that is done is unreliable, like castles in the air or so much empty talk.

The peasantry constituted more than eighty per cent of the entire population of semi-colonial and semi-feudal China. They were subjected to the three-fold oppression and exploitation of imperialism, feudalism and bureaucrat-capitalism, and they were eager for resistance against Japan and for revolution. It was essential to rely mainly on the peasants if the people's war was to be won.

In the period of the War of Resistance against Japan, the peasants were the most reliable and the most numerous ally of the proletariat and constituted the main force of resistance. The peasants were the main source of manpower for China's armies. The funds and the supplies needed for a protracted war came chiefly from the peasants. The War of Resistance against Japan was in essence a peasant revolutionary war led by our Party. By arousing and organizing the peasant masses and integrating them with the proletariat, our Party created a powerful force capable of defeating the strongest enemy. To rely on the peasants, build rural base areas and use the countryside to encircle and finally capture the cities— such was the way to victory in the Chinese revolution.

During the War of Resistance against Japan, the Japanese imperialist forces occupied many of China's big cities and the main lines of communication, but owing to the shortage of troops they were unable to occupy the vast countryside, which remained the vulnerable sector of the enemy's rule. Consequently, the possibility of building rural base areas became even greater. Shortly after the beginning of the War of Resistance, when the Japanese forces surged into China's hinterland and the Kuomintang forces crumbled and fled in one defeat after another, the Eighth Route and New Fourth Armies boldly drove into the areas behind the enemy lines in small contingents and established base areas throughout the countryside. During the eight years of the war, we established nineteen anti-Japanese base areas in northern, central and southern China. With the exception of the big cities and the main lines of communication, the vast territory in the enemy's rear was in the hands of the people.

In the anti-Japanese base areas, we carried out democratic reforms, improved the livelihood of the people, and mobilized and organized the peasant masses. Organs of anti-Japanese democratic political power were established on an extensive scale and the masses of the people enjoyed the democratic right to run their own affairs; at the same time we carried out the policies of 'a reasonable burden' and 'the reduction of rent and interest', which weakened the feudal system of exploitation and improved the people's livelihood. As a result, the enthusiasm of the peasant masses was deeply aroused, while the various anti-Japanese strata were given due consideration and were thus united. In formulating our policies for the base areas, we also took care that these policies should facilitate our work in the enemy-occupied areas.

In the enemy-occupied cities and villages, we combined legal with illegal struggle, united the basic masses and all patriots, and divided and disintegrated the political power of the enemy and his puppets so as to prepare ourselves to attack the enemy from within in co-ordination with operations from without when conditions were ripe.

The base areas established by our Party became the centre of gravity in the Chinese people's struggle to resist Japan and save the country. Relying on these bases, our Party expanded and strengthened the people's revolutionary forces, persevered in the protracted war and eventually won the War of Resistance against Japan.

Naturally, it was impossible for the development of the revolutionary base areas to be plain sailing all the time. They constituted a tremendous threat to the enemy and were bound to be attacked. Therefore, their development was a tortuous process of expansion, contraction and then renewed expansion. Between 1937 and 1940 the population in the anti-Japanese base areas grew to 100,000,000. But in 1941–2 the Japanese imperialists used the major part of their invading forces to launch frantic attacks on our base areas and wrought havoc. Meanwhile, the Kuomintang, too, encircled these base areas, blockaded them and went so far as to attack them. So by 1942 the anti-Japanese base areas had contracted and their population was down to less than 50,000,000. After this setback, the army and the people in the base areas were tempered and grew stronger. From 1943 onwards our base areas were gradually restored and expanded, and by 1945 the population had grown to 160,000,000. Taking the entire course of the Chinese revolution into account, our revolutionary base areas went through even more ups and downs, and they weathered a great many tests before the small, separate base areas, expanding in a series of waves, gradually developed into extensive and contiguous base areas. In these base areas, we built the Party, ran the organs of state power, built the people's armed forces and set up mass organizations; we engaged in industry and agriculture and operated cultural, educational and all other undertakings necessary for the independent existence of a separate region. Our base areas were in fact a state in miniature. And with the steady expansion of our work in the base areas, our Party established a powerful people's army, trained cadres for various kinds of work, accumulated experience in many fields and built up both the material and the moral strength that provided favourable conditions for nation-wide victory.

The revolutionary base areas established in the War of Resistance later became the springboards for the People's War of Liberation, in which the Chinese people defeated the Kuomintang reactionaries. In the War of Liberation we continued the policy of first encircling the cities from the countryside and then capturing the cities, and thus won the nation-wide victory.

The special feature of the Chinese revolution was armed revolution against armed counter-revolution. The main form of struggle was war and the main form of organization was the army which was under the absolute leadership of the Chinese Communist Party, while all the other forms of organization and struggle led by our Party were coordinated, directly or indirectly, with the war.

During the First Revolutionary Civil War, many fine Party comrades took an active part in the armed revolutionary struggle. But our Party was then still in its infancy and did not have a clear understanding of this special feature of the Chinese revolution. It was only after the First Revolutionary Civil War, only after the Kuomintang had betrayed the revolution, massacred large numbers of Communists and destroyed all the revolutionary mass organizations, that our Party reached a clearer understanding of the supreme importance of organizing revolutionary armed forces and of studying the strategy and tactics of revolutionary war, and created the Workers' and Peasants' Red Army, the first people's army under the leadership of the Communist Party of China.

At the start of the War of Resistance against Japan, the people's army led by the Chinese Communist Party had only a little over forty thousand men. The Kuomintang reactionaries attempted to restrict, weaken and destroy this people's army in every conceivable way. Comrade Mao Tse-tung pointed out that, in these circumstances, in order to sustain the War of Resistance and defeat the Japanese aggressors, it was imperative greatly to expand and consolidate the Eighth Route and New Fourth Armies and all the guerrilla units led by our Party. The whole Party should give close attention to war and study military affairs. Every Party member should be ready at all times to take up arms and go to the front.

Our people's army steadily expanded in the struggle, so that by the end of the war it was already a million strong, and there was also a militia of over two million. That was why we were able to engage nearly two-thirds of the Japanese forces of aggression and ninety-five per cent of the puppet troops and to become the main force in the War of Resistance against Japan. While resisting the Japanese invading forces, we repulsed three large-scale anti-Communist onslaughts launched by the Kuomintang reactionaries in 1939, 1941 and 1943, and smashed their countless 'friction-mongering' activities.

During the anti-Japanese war our army staunchly performed three tasks — fighting, mass work, and production; it was at the same time a fighting force, a political work force and a production corps. Everywhere it went, it did propaganda work among the masses, organized and armed them and helped them set up revolutionary political power. Our armymen strictly observed the Three Main Rules of Discipline and the Eight Points for Attention,* carried

* The Three Main Rules of Discipline and the Eight Points for Attention were drawn up by Comrade Mao Tse-tung for the Chinese Workers' and Peasants' Red Army during the Agrarian Revolutionary War and were later adopted as rules of discipline by the Eighth Route Army and the New Fourth Army and the present People's Liberation Army. As these rules varied slightly in content in the army units of different areas, the General Headquarters of the Chinese People's Liberation Army in October 1947 issued a standard version as follows:

The Three Main Rules of Discipline:
(1) Obey orders in all your actions.
(2) Do not take a single needle or piece of thread from the masses.
(3) Turn in everything captured.

out campaigns to 'support the government and cherish the people', and did good deeds for the people everywhere. They also made use of every possibility to engage in production themselves so as to overcome economic difficulties, better their own livelihood and lighten the people's burden.

The essence of building a people's army is that politics is the commander. Political work is the lifeline of our army. True, a people's army must pay attention to the constant improvement of its weapons and equipment and its military technique, but in its fighting it does not rely purely on weapons and technique, it relies mainly on politics, on the proletarian revolutionary consciousness and courage of the commanders and fighters, on the support and backing of the masses.

During the War of Resistance against Japan, Comrade Mao Tse-tung raised guerrilla warfare to the level of strategy, because guerrilla warfare is the only way to mobilize and apply the whole strength of the people against the enemy, the only way to expand our forces in the course of the war, deplete and weaken the enemy, gradually change the balance of forces between the enemy and ourselves, switch from guerrilla to mobile warfare, and finally defeat the enemy.

In the initial period of the Second Revolutionary Civil War, Comrade Mao Tse-tung enumerated the basic tactics of guerrilla warfare as follows: 'The enemy advances, we retreat; the enemy camps, we harass; the enemy tires, we attack; the enemy retreats, we pursue.'[33]

In the later period of the War of Resistance against Japan and during the Third Revolutionary Civil War we switched our strategy from that of guerrilla warfare as the primary form of fighting to that of mobile warfare in the light of the changes in the balance of forces between the enemy and ourselves. By the middle, and especially the later, period of the Third Revolutionary Civil War, our

The Eight Points for Attention:

(1) Speak politely.
(2) Pay fairly for what you buy.
(3) Return everything you borrow.
(4) Pay for everything you damage.
(5) Do not hit or swear at people.
(6) Do not damage crops.
(7) Do not take liberties with women.
(8) Do not ill-treat captives.

–Lin Piao

operations had developed into large-scale mobile warfare, including the storming of big cities.

War of annihilation is the fundamental guiding principle of our military operations. This guiding principle should be put into effect regardless of whether mobile or guerrilla warfare is the primary form of fighting. It is true that in guerrilla warfare much should be done to disrupt and harass the enemy, but it is still necessary actively to advocate and fight battles of annihilation whenever conditions are favourable. In mobile warfare superior forces must be concentrated in every battle so that the enemy forces can be wiped out one by one. Comrade Mao Tse-tung has pointed out:

> A battle in which the enemy is routed is not basically decisive in a contest with a foe of great strength. A battle of annihilation, on the other hand, produces a great and immediate impact on any enemy. Injuring all of a man's ten fingers is not as effective as chopping off one, and routing ten enemy divisions is not as effective as annihilating one of them.[34]

In order to annihilate the enemy, we must adopt the policy of luring him in deep and abandon some cities and districts of our own accord in a planned way, so as to let him in. It is only after letting the enemy in that the people can take part in the war in various ways and that the power of a people's war can be fully exerted. It is only after letting the enemy in that he can be compelled to divide up his forces, take on heavy burdens and commit mistakes. In other words, we must let the enemy become elated, stretch out all his ten fingers and become hopelessly bogged down. Thus, we can concentrate superior forces to destroy the enemy forces one by one, to eat them up mouthful by mouthful. Only by wiping out the enemy's effective strength can cities and localities be finally held or seized. We are firmly against dividing up our forces to defend all positions and putting up resistance at every place for fear that our territory might be lost and our pots and pans smashed, since this can neither wipe out the enemy forces nor hold cities or localities. It is opportunism if one won't fight when one can win. It is adventurism if one insists on fighting when one can't win. Fighting is the pivot of all our strategy and tactics. It is because of the necessity of fighting that we admit the necessity of moving away. The sole purpose of moving away is to fight and bring about the final and complete destruction of the enemy. This strategy and these tactics can be applied only when one relies on the broad masses of the people, and such application brings the superiority of people's war into full play. However superior he may be in technical equipment and whatever tricks he may resort to, the enemy will find himself in the passive position of having to receive blows, and the initiative will always be in our hands.

During the War of Resistance against Japan, our Party maintained that China should rely mainly on her own strength while at the same time trying to get as much foreign assistance as possible. Our Party held that it was possible to exploit the contradictions between US–British imperialism and Japanese imperialism, but that no reliance could be placed on the former. In fact, the US–British imperialists repeatedly plotted to bring about a 'Far Eastern Munich' in order to arrive at a compromise with Japanese imperialism at China's expense, and for a considerable period of time* they provided the Japanese aggressors with war materials. In helping China during that period, the US imperialists harboured the sinister design of turning China into a colony of their own.

The Kuomintang government gave the Eighth Route and New Fourth Armies some small allowance in the initial stage of the anti-Japanese war, but gave them not a single penny later. The Liberated Areas faced great difficulties as a result of the Japanese imperialists' savage attacks and brutal 'mopping-up' campaigns, of the Kuomintang's military encirclement and economic blockade and of natural calamities. The difficulties were particularly great in the years 1941 and 1942, when we were very short of food and clothing.

Difficulties are not invincible monsters. If everyone cooperates and fights them, they will be overcome. The Kuomintang reactionaries thought that it could starve us to death by cutting off allowances and imposing an economic blockade, but in fact it helped us by stimulating us to rely on our own efforts to surmount our difficulties. While launching the great campaign for production, we applied the policy of 'better troops and simpler administration' and economized in the use of manpower and material resources; thus we not only surmounted the severe material difficulties and successfully met the crisis, but lightened the people's burden, improved their livelihood and laid the material foundations for victory in the anti-Japanese war.

The problem of military equipment was solved mainly by relying on the capture of arms from the enemy, though we did turn out some weapons too. Chiang Kai-shek, the Japanese imperialists and

* Prior to 7 December 1941–ed.

the US imperialists have all been our 'chiefs of transportation corps'. The arsenals of the imperialists always provide the oppressed peoples and nations with arms.

In order to make a revolution and to fight a people's war and be victorious, it is imperative to adhere to the policy of self-reliance, rely on the strength of the masses in one's own country and prepare to carry on the fight independently even when all material aid from outside is cut off. If one does not operate by one's own efforts, does not independently ponder and solve the problems of the revolution in one's own country and does not rely on the strength of the masses, but leans wholly on foreign aid — even though this be aid from socialist countries which persist in revolution — no victory can be won, or be consolidated even if it is won.

The Chinese revolution is a continuation of the great October Revolution. The road of the October Revolution is the common road for all people's revolutions. The Chinese revolution and the October Revolution have in common the following basic characteristics : (1) Both were led by the working class with a Marxist–Leninist party as its nucleus. (2) Both were based on the worker-peasant alliance. (3) In both cases state power was seized through violent revolution and the dictatorship of the proletariat was established. (4) In both cases the socialist system was built after victory in the revolution. (5) Both were component parts of the proletarian world revolution.

Naturally the Chinese revolution had its own peculiar characteristics. The October Revolution took place in imperialist Russia, but the Chinese revolution broke out in a semi-colonial and semi-feudal country. The former was a proletarian socialist revolution, while the latter developed into a socialist revolution after the complete victory of the new democratic revolution. The October Revolution began with armed uprisings in the cities and then spread to the countryside, while the Chinese revolution won nation-wide victory through the encirclement of the cities from the rural areas and the final capture of the cities.

The people's war led by the Chinese Communist Party, comprising the War of Resistance and the Revolutionary Civil Wars, lasted for twenty-two years. It constitutes the most drawn-out* and most

---

* By 1969 the Vietnamese revolution, which began in 1945 (though the Vietnamese fought the Japanese during the Second World War much as did the Chinese), had become the longest—ed.

complex people's war led by the proletariat in modern history, and it has been the richest in experiences.

In the last analysis, the Marxist–Leninist theory of proletarian revolution is the theory of the seizure of state power by revolutionary violence, the theory of countering war against the people by people's war. As Marx so aptly put it : 'Force is the midwife of every old society pregnant with a new one.' It was on the basis of the lessons derived from the people's wars in China that Comrade Mao Tse-tung, using the simplest and the most vivid language, advanced the famous thesis that 'political power grows out of the barrel of a gun'.

War is the product of imperialism and the system of exploitation of man by man. Lenin said that 'war is always and everywhere begun by the exploiters themselves, by the ruling and oppressing classes'.[35] So long as imperialism and the system of exploitation of man exist, the imperialists and reactionaries will invariably rely on armed force to maintain their reactionary rule and impose war on the oppressed nations and peoples. This is an objective law independent of man's will.*

In the world today, all the imperialists, headed by the United States and their lackeys, without exception, are strengthening their state machinery, and especially their armed forces. US imperialism, in particular, is carrying out armed aggression and suppression everywhere.

In the last analysis, whether one dares to wage a tit-for-tat struggle against armed aggression and suppression by the imperialists and their lackeys, whether one dares to fight a people's war against them, means whether one dares to embark on revolution. The history of people's war in China and other countries provides conclusive evidence that the growth of the people's revolutionary forces from weak and small beginnings into strong and large forces is a universal law of development of class struggle, a universal law of development of people's war. A people's war inevitably meets with many difficulties, with ups and downs and setbacks in the course of its development, but no force can alter its general trend towards inevitable triumph.

* Modern analysts would disagree, pointing to India as an example of a neocolonialized (i.e., imperialist dominated) country. Lin Piao would probably answer that the US could not possibly control India's economy (its lack of agrarian reform, its capitalist structure, etc.) unless its might was militarily as well as economically so powerful–ed.

The establishment of rural revolutionary base areas and the encirclement of the cities from the countryside is of outstanding and universal practical importance for the present revolutionary struggles of all the oppressed nations and peoples in Asia, Africa and Latin America against imperialism and its lackeys.

The basic political and economic conditions in many of these countries have many similarities to those that prevailed in old China. As in China, the peasant is extremely important in these regions. In committing aggression against these countries, the imperialists usually begin by seizing big cities and the main lines of communication, but they are unable to bring the vast countryside completely under their control. The countryside and the countryside alone, can provide the broad areas in which the revolutionaries can manoeuvre freely. The countryside and the countryside alone, can provide the revolutionary bases from which the revolutionaries can go forward to final victory.

Taking the entire globe, if North America and Western Europe can be called 'the cities of the world', then Asia, Africa and Latin America constitute 'the rural areas of the world'.* Since the Second World War, the proletarian revolutionary movement has for various reasons been temporarily held back in the North American and West European capitalist countries, while the people's revolutionary movement in Asia, Africa and Latin America has been growing vigorously. In a sense, the contemporary world revolution also presents a picture of the encirclement of cities by the rural areas. In the final analysis, the whole cause of world revolution hinges on the revolutionary struggles of the Asian, African and Latin American peoples who make up the overwhelming majority of the world's population. The socialist countries should regard it as their internationalist duty to support the people's revolutionary struggles in Asia, Africa and Latin America.

The experience of the Chinese revolution shows that the tasks of the national-democratic revolution can be fulfilled only through long and tortuous struggles. In this stage of revolution, imperialism and its lackeys are the principal enemy; it is necessary to rally all anti-imperialist patriotic forces, including the national bourgeoisie and all patriotic personages. All those patriotic personages from among the bourgeoisie and other exploiting classes who join the

---

* Many revolutionary communists today would include Russia and Eastern Europe among the 'cities'–ed.

anti-imperialist struggle play a progressive historical role; they are not tolerated by imperialism but welcomed by the proletariat. It is very harmful to confuse the two stages, that is, the national-democratic and the socialist revolutions. The Chinese revolution provides a successful lesson for making a thoroughgoing national-democratic revolution under the leadership of the proletariat; it likewise provides a successful lesson for the timely transition from the national-democratic revolution to the socialist revolution under the leadership of the proletariat.

Since the Second World War, US imperialism has stepped into the shoes of German, Italian and Japanese fascism and has been trying to build a great American empire by dominating and enslaving the whole world. It is the most rabid aggressor in human history and the most ferocious common enemy of the people of the world. Every people or country in the world that wants revolution, independence and peace cannot but direct the spearheads of its struggle against US imperialism.

Just as the Japanese imperialists' policy of subjugating China made it possible for the Chinese people to form the broadest possible united front against them, so the US imperialists' policy of seeking world domination makes it possible for the people throughout the world to unite all the forces that can be united and form the broadest possible united front for a converging attack on US imperialism.

At present, the main battlefield of the fierce struggle between the people of the world on the one side and US imperialism and its lackeys on the other is the vast area of Asia, Africa and Latin America. In the world as a whole, this is the area where the people suffer worst from imperialist oppression and where imperialist rule is most vulnerable. Since the Second World War, revolutionary storms have been rising in this area, and today they have become the most important force directly pounding US imperialism. The contradiction between the revolutionary peoples of Asia, Africa and Latin America and the imperialists headed by the United States is the principal contradiction in the contemporary world. The development of this contradiction is promoting the struggle of the people of the whole world against US imperialism and its lackeys.

Since the Second World War, people's war has increasingly demonstrated its power in Asia, Africa and Latin America. The peoples of China, Korea, Vietnam, Laos, Cuba, Indonesia, Algeria and other countries have waged people's wars against the imperialists and their lackeys and won great victories. The classes leading these people's wars may vary, and so may the breadth and depth of mass mobilization and the extent of victory, but the victories in these people's wars have very much weakened and pinned down the forces of imperialism. Today, the conditions are more favourable than ever before for the waging of people's wars by the revolutionary peoples of Asia, Africa and Latin America against US imperialism.

US imperialism is stronger, but also more vulnerable, than any imperialism of the past. It sets itself against the people of the whole world, including the people of the United States. Its human, military, material and financial resources are far from sufficient for the realization of its ambition of dominating the whole world. It has further weakened itself by occupying so many places in the world, overreaching itself, stretching its fingers out wide and dispersing its strength, with its rear so far away and its supply lines so long. When committing aggression in a foreign country, it can only employ part of its forces, which are sent to fight an unjust war far from their native land and therefore have a low morale. The people subjected to its aggression are having a trial of strength with US imperialism neither in Washington nor New York, neither in Honolulu nor Florida, but are fighting for independence and freedom on their own soil. Once they are mobilized on a broad scale, they will have inexhaustible strength.

The struggles waged by the different peoples against US imperialism reinforce each other and merge into a torrential world-wide tide of opposition to US imperialism. The more successful the development of people's war in a given region, the larger the number of US imperialist forces that can be pinned down and depleted there. When the US aggressors are hard pressed in one place, they have no alternative but to loosen their grip on others. Therefore, the conditions become more favourable for the people elsewhere to wage struggles against US imperialism and its lackeys.

Everything is divisible. And so is the colossus of US imperialism. It can be split up and defeated. The peoples of Asia, Africa, Latin America and other regions can destroy it piece by piece, some striking at its head and others at its feet. That is why the greatest fear of US imperialism is that people's wars will be launched in different parts of the world, and particularly in Asia, Africa and Latin America, and why it regards people's war as a mortal danger.

Nuclear weapons cannot save US imperialism from its doom. Nuclear weapons cannot be used lightly. US imperialism has been condemned by the people of the whole world for its towering crime of dropping two atom bombs on Japan. If it uses nuclear weapons again, it will become isolated in the extreme. Moreover, the US monopoly of nuclear weapons has long been broken; US imperialism has these weapons, but others have them too. If it threatens other countries with nuclear weapons, US imperialism will expose its own country to the same threat. For this reason, it will meet with strong opposition not only from the people elsewhere but also inevitably from the people in its own country.

However highly developed modern weapons and technical equipment may be and however complicated the methods of modern warfare, in the final analysis the outcome of a war will be decided by the sustained fighting of the ground forces, by the fighting at close quarters on battlefields, by the political consciousness of the men, by their courage and spirit of sacrifice. Here the weak points of US imperialism will be completely laid bare, while the superiority of the revolutionary people will be brought into full play. The reactionary troops of US imperialism cannot possibly be endowed with the courage and the spirit of sacrifice possessed by the revolutionary people. The spiritual atom bomb which the revolutionary people possess is a far more powerful and useful weapon than the physical atom bomb.

Vietnam is the most convincing current example of a victim of aggression defeating US imperialism by a people's war. The United States has made South Vietnam a testing ground for the suppression of people's war. It has carried on this experiment for many years, and everybody can now see that the US aggressors are unable to find a way of coping with people's war. They are deeply worried that their defeat in Vietnam will lead to a chain reaction. They are expanding the war in an attempt to save themselves from defeat. But the more they expand the war, the greater will be the chain reaction. The more they escalate the war, the heavier will be their failure and the more disastrous their defeat. The people in other parts of the world will see still more clearly that US imperialism can be defeated, and that what the Vietnamese people can do, they can do too.

The fundamental reason why the Khrushchev revisionists are opposed to people's war is that they have no faith in the masses and are afraid of US imperialism, of war and of revolution. Like all other opportunists, they are blind to the power of the masses and do not believe that the revolutionary people are capable of defeating imperialism. They submit to the nuclear blackmail of the US imperialists and are afraid that, if the oppressed peoples and nations rise up to fight people's wars or the people of socialist countries repulse US imperialist aggression, US imperialism will become incensed, they themselves will become involved and their fond dream of Soviet–US cooperation to dominate the world will be spoiled.

Ever since Lenin led the great October Revolution to victory, the experience of innumerable revolutionary wars has borne out the truth that a revolutionary people who rise up with only their bare hands at the outset finally succeed in defeating the ruling classes who are armed to the teeth. The poorly armed have defeated the better armed. People's armed forces, beginning with only primitive swords, spears, rifles and hand-grenades, have in the end defeated the imperialist forces armed with modern aeroplanes, tanks, heavy artillery and atom bombs. Guerrilla forces have ultimately defeated regular armies. 'Amateurs' who were never trained in any military schools have eventually defeated 'professionals' graduated from military academies.

The Khrushchev revisionists insist that a nation without nuclear weapons is incapable of defeating an enemy with nuclear weapons, whatever methods of fighting it may adopt. This is tantamount to saying that anyone without nuclear weapons is destined to come to grief, destined to be bullied and annihilated, and must either capitulate to the enemy when confronted with his nuclear weapons or come under the 'protection' of some other nuclear power and submit to its beck and call. The Khrushchev revisionists assert that nuclear weapons and strategic rocket units are decisive while conventional forces are insignificant. They have staked the whole future of their country on nuclear weapons and are engaged in a nuclear gamble with US imperialism, with which they are trying to strike a political deal. Their theory of military strategy is the theory that nuclear weapons decide everything. Their line in army building is the bourgeois line which ignores the human factor and sees only the material factor and which regards technique as everything and politics as nothing.

The Khrushchev revisionists maintain that a single spark in any part of the globe may touch off a nuclear conflagration and bring destruction to mankind. If this were true, our planet would have been destroyed time and time again. There have been wars of national liberation throughout the twenty years since the Second World War. But has any single one of them developed into a world war? Isn't it true that the US imperialists' plans for a world war have been upset precisely thanks to the wars of national liberation in Asia, Africa and Latin America? By contrast, those who have done their utmost to stamp out the 'sparks' of people's war have in fact encouraged US imperialism in its aggressions and wars.

The Khrushchev revisionists claim that if their general line of 'peaceful coexistence, peaceful transition and peaceful competition' is followed, the oppressed will be liberated and 'a world without weapons, without armed forces and without wars' will come into being. But the inexorable fact is that imperialism and reaction headed by the United States are zealously priming their war machine and are daily engaged in sanguinary suppression of the revolutionary peoples and in the threat and use of armed force against independent countries. Our attitude towards imperialist wars of aggression has always been clear-cut. First, we are against them, and secondly, we are not afraid of them. We will destroy whoever attacks us. As for revolutionary wars waged by the oppressed nations and peoples, so far from opposing them, we invariably give them firm support and active aid. It has been so in the past, it remains so in the present and, when we grow in strength as time goes on, we will give them still more support and aid in the future. It is sheer daydreaming for anyone to think that, since our revolution has been victorious, our national construction is forging ahead, our national wealth is increasing and our living conditions are improving, we too will lose our revolutionary fighting will, abandon the cause of world revolution and discard Marxism–Leninism and proletarian internationalism. Of course, every revolution in a country stems from the demands of its own people. Only when the people in a country are awakened, mobilized, organized and armed can they overthrow the reactionary rule of imperialism and its lackeys through struggle; their role cannot be replaced or taken over by any people from outside. In this sense, revolution cannot be imported.) But this does not exclude mutual sympathy and support on the part of revolutionary peoples in their struggles against the imperialists and their lackeys. Our support and aid to other revolutionary peoples serves precisely to help their self-reliant struggle.

We are optimistic about the future of the world. We are confident that the people will bring to an end the epoch of wars in human history. All peoples suffering from US imperialist aggression, oppression and plunder, unite! Hold aloft the just banner of people's war and fight for the cause of world peace, national liberation, people's democracy and socialism! Victory will certainly go to the people of the world!

Long live the victory of people's war!

IV Chou En-lai: *Imperialists Beware**[36]

1. China will not take the initiative to provoke a war with the United States. China has not sent any troops to Hawaii; it is the United States that has occupied China's territory of Taiwan province. Nevertheless, China has been making efforts in demanding, through negotiations, that the United States withdraw all its armed forces from Taiwan province and the Taiwan Straits, and she has held talks with the United States for more than ten years, first in Geneva and then in Warsaw, on this question of principle, which admits of no concession whatsoever. All this serves as a very good proof.

2. The Chinese mean what they say. In other words, if any country in Asia, Africa, or elsewhere meets with aggression by the imperialists headed by the United States, the Chinese government and people definitely will give it support and help. Should such just action bring on US aggression against China, we will unhesitatingly rise in resistance and fight to the end.

3. China is prepared. Should the United States impose a war on China, it can be said with certainty that, once in China, the United States will not be able to pull out, however many men it may send over and whatever weapons it may use, nuclear weapons included. Since the fourteen million people of Southern Vietnam can cope

* The author, currently prime minister of China, is an old communist organizer from Shanghai, a Long March veteran and a former foreign minister–ed.

with over 200,000 US troops, the 650,000,000 people of China can undoubtedly cope with ten million of them. No matter how many US aggressor troops may come, they will certainly be annihilated in China.

4. Once the war breaks out, it will have no boundaries. Some US strategists want to bombard China by relying on their air and naval superiority and avoid a ground war. This is wishful thinking. Once the war gets started with air or sea action, it will not be for the United States alone to decide how the war will continue. If you can come from the sky, why can't we fight back on the ground? That is why we say the war will have no boundaries once it breaks out.

INDIA

*No man has done more physical harm to the poor of the world than
Mahatma Gandhi. He may or may not have taught them how to be
happy in poverty, but in the material world he hated so ferociously
he influenced millions to accept as 'good' misery, suffering, disease,
exploitation, and what is generally referred to as 'unnatural' death.
He refused to learn from anyone not 'in touch' with nature, condemned all material progress and told his people, over and over,
that 'Indian civilization is the best'. He condemned sex except for
procreation, and reinforced guilt among his Hindu followers for any
'carnal desire'. He told the Jews that if they offered themselves to
the butcher's knife of Nazi Germany the world would have been
'aroused'. He praised Marshal Pétain for surrendering to Hitler's
storm troopers and appealed to the British to do the same: 'If these
gentlemen choose to occupy your homes, you will vacate them. If
they do not give you free passage out, you will allow yourself, man,
woman and child, to be slaughtered.' And to his own people, who
listened and obeyed, he said that education enslaves, that children
should learn not from books or schools but 'from constant contact
with the parents'. He asked his followers to keep away from doctors,
and medicine: 'Hospitals are the instruments that the devil has been
using for his own purpose, in order to keep his hold on his kingdom,'
he wrote; 'they perpetuate vice, misery and degradation and real
slavery.' The net result has not been the 'independence' of India
(a cynical non-Gandhian elite taking over the state from the
British). Rather it has been that India's Hindu millions have accepted their oppressed existence more than any other people.
Gandhi may have helped save their souls—no mortal can testify to
that—but he certainly did strengthen their oppressors. In brute
material terms, he was an accomplice—in fact, a conspirator—to
the murder of millions of children whose parents, to this day, continue to believe that if they accept their 'fate', that is, their place
in the world, their own souls will be freed (for by what right can*

*they say what's good or bad for the souls of their children?). And
since a revolutionary is he who knows that 'one's place' is determined by man and guns and not gods, it is little wonder that so few
revolutionaries exist among India's teeming millions.*

*The revolutionaries that have long been active are mostly non-
Indian—Nagas, Mizos, Ahoms, and other minorities in north-east
India. Among Indians proper, wars or violence are mostly limited
to racial or religious conflicts. But there are exceptions, and recently some of these exceptions have proved to be so serious that a
people's war can no longer be dismissed as an absurdity. In fact, the
possible germ of such a war exists now among the rebellious peasants
of Terai, in the West Bengal foothills of the Himalayas. There in
1967, at a place called Naxalbari, peasants actually seized arms,
killed local representatives of government authority and jotedars
(rich landowners who do not cultivate their land themselves) and
retreated into the jungle-hills to fight on.*

*At the time both communist parties of India condemned the
rebellion. These two parties had originally split in 1964. The CPI-
Right or Pro-Soviet party opposes all acts of violence. The CPI-
Left or CPI-M(arxist), however, theoretically advocates armed revolution. At least so states its programme, adopted at its seventh All-
Indian party congress in 1964 (both parties held 'All-India' congresses that year). But because the CPI-M, electorally strong in West
Bengal, had entered into a United Front Ministry with bourgeois
parties, the communist leaders, specifically B. T. Ranadive and
Promode Das Gupta, condemned the uprising. They couldn't do so
on ideological grounds; instead they criticized the timing, claiming
that India is 'not yet ripe' for revolution.*

*The article that follows was meant as a refutation of this 'timing'
theory and explains the position of India's 'revolutionary Marxists'
who condemn both the CPI-R and the Maoist CPI-M, although very
pro-Chinese itself. The author's real name has been kept secret,
perhaps because members of this 'revolutionary Marxist' group are
actually involved in the Terai rebellion. Using traditional jargon,
yet as clearly as he can, he tries to prove that the time for revolution in India is now.*

Asit Sen: *Timing the Revolutionary Situation*[37]

It is necessary to understand clearly the meaning of the term 'revolution' in order to ascertain whether the time for revolution has really come. When we say that Darwin revolutionized the zoological science or that Marx ushered in a revolution in the interpretation of human history, the word 'revolution' is used in a certain sense, and signifies that Darwin and Marx brought about fundamental qualitative changes in the realms of zoology and history respectively. In both these subjects all existing theories sprang from an idealist or mechanical materialist world outlook and it was Darwin and Marx who substituted a scientific materialist outlook for the existing idealist and mechanical materialist outlook in their respective fields. Thus the word 'revolution' denotes a fundamental, qualitative change. This, in general, is the meaning of revolution.

In politics we are concerned with social revolution—that is, a qualitative change in the existing social system. In nature everything changes. But it does not happen that a certain thing or phenomenon remains unchanged for a certain period of time and then all of a sudden undergoes a qualitative change. In reality, the changes in things or phenomena take place according to a law, which is that an unceasing process of quantitative changes brings about a qualitative change in them. The development of human society is also guided by this law. But the sphere of social development is a complex thing and so the processes of change, both quantitative and qualitative, in this sphere are also complex. However, complex as they are, they are guided without exception by the basic law of change mentioned above. In other words, a particular social system undergoes a qualitative change only after and as a result of a long process of unceasing quantitative changes. Thus, social revolution is, like any other revolution, the end-result of an unceasing process of changes. That is, the leap of a given social system to a qualitatively higher social system through a victorious social revolution takes place only as a result of a process of quantitative changes which goes on for an entire historical period.

The change in the social system does not, however, occur as a result of 'divine' forces, nor by any directives of human thought. The causes of the change are inherent in the society itself. Every change is also the result of the conflict of two opposing forces. In human society, productive forces and production relations are the two opposing forces.

By productive forces are meant the human labour power and the material implements of labour, i.e., the things by which human labour power is applied profitably. Productive forces are the things that men use to exploit nature in order to satisfy their material and cultural needs.

In struggling against nature, which they must do to satisfy their needs, men inevitably enter into certain relations with one another —and these relations are called production relations, which do not depend on the likes or dislikes of men for their existence. Production relations constitute the real foundation of human society on which is erected a superstructure consisting of such things as politics, social justice, art and literature, philosophy, religion, law, etc. Although these things of the superstructure depend, in the final analysis, on the basis, i.e., production relations and cannot have any existence independent of or separate from that of the basis—yet they can, within limits, act independently and sometimes exert some influence on the basis. Anyway, it is the basis that invariably determines the nature of the superstructure and never the other way round.

As stated before, men enter into certain production relations with one another, that is, live a social life. And these production relations in their turn go on developing the productive forces. But it so happens that a particular form of production relations can help develop the forces of production only up to a certain stage and the reverse process begins after this stage has been reached. In such cases production relations cease to develop the forces of production and gradually begin to impede the process of development of the productive forces. Once that stage is reached no further development of productive forces is possible without bringing about a fundamental change in the production relations, i.e. social structure. When the conflict between the production relations and productive forces in the old social system is thus aggravated, there begins an era of social revolution. In this way the old production relations gradually advance towards their own destruction over an entire period of time and after a certain stage is reached these old relations undergo a qualitative change giving birth to a new social system. Consequent to this revolutionary change in the basis, there begins a revolutionary change in the superstructure. But this change in the superstructure is effected over a much longer period.

It is this basic conflict inside a social system that caused the primitive human society to break up and laid the foundations for a higher social system, namely, the slave society. Later, the same process gave birth to the feudal society, the capitalist society and the socialist society one after the other. While this basic conflict between the production relations and productive forces constitutes the real and root cause that brings about change in social systems, its developments do not always proceed freely and unobstructed.

When this conflict grew acute in primitive society, the existing social order began to break up but it so happened that no element of the superstructure exerted force from above to resist this breaking up. Therefore, there was no necessity for any force to be applied to free the forces of production. In all later forms of society, however, an additional conflict—the class conflict between the exploiters and the exploited—appeared. This happened because the means of production in such societies were owned and controlled by a handful of people. As a result, the unfettered development of the conflict between production relations and the forces of production was weighted down and influenced by the conflict between the classes. This class struggle intruded into the field of social development and got itself imposed upon the basic conflict. And so it became impossible for basic conflict in society to develop freely unless the contradictions between classes were resolved through class struggle. Marx and Engels were expressing this truth when they declared in the beginning of their *Communist Manifesto*: 'The history of all hitherto existing society excepting the primitive Communistic society is the history of class struggles.'

But Marx and Engels did not restrict the real nature and intensity of class conflicts to the statement alone that human history is the history of class struggles. By concretely analysing history they demonstrated how society gets differentiated into two parts—urban and rural; how the necessity of the exploiting classes to preserve the existing social order gives rise to the state power; and how the state power is used to forcibly suppress class struggles. They discovered through an incisive analysis the real role of this state power in a class society and its relation to the entire society and exploded the myths and mystifications created by bourgeois historians around the question of the state. Marx announced this discovery during the lengthy debate at the Second Congress of the Communist League in 1847.

From what has been said above some conclusions can be drawn: (1) social revolution means a qualitative change in the social relations; (2) this qualitative change is nothing but a qualitative change in the relations between classes—that is, the exploiting class is overthrown and its domination is replaced by the domination of the exploited class, which aims ultimately at setting up a classless society; (3) no class can overthrow another class except through intense class struggle; (4) as the state is the organ of maintaining the old class relations by forcible suppression of the class struggle, no social revolution is possible without smashing the old state machinery in the final phase of the class struggle; (5) in order to protect and preserve the fruits of social revolution the exploited class must establish its own state power; (6) the class society determines the nature of state power and not vice versa; so, a new state power can be established only through class struggle. The conflicts between classes can never be abolished by capturing state power from above and by avoiding class struggle.

If we consider social revolution in this broad context, the question 'has the time for revolution come?' will reveal two aspects. First, we shall be faced with the question whether the basic contradiction in social development, namely, the contradiction between the forces of production and production relations, has ripened to the stage of an antagonistic contradiction or not; in other words, whether the existing relations of production are still able to develop the forces of production. If the relations of production have already reached a stage when they act as an impediment instead of as a promoter of the productive forces, then it becomes clear beyond any shadow of doubt that we have arrived at the era of a social revolution. Second, the question arises as to whether the time has come to direct the class struggles with the object of quickening the pace of the social revolution, that is, of hastening to bring about a revolutionary change in class relations. If this be so, we shall have to try to turn the economic struggles into political class struggles as quickly as possible. In other words, the exploited classes must march forward quickly and resolutely to overthrow the exploiting classes by smashing all the legal and political trappings that protect the interests of the exploiters and establish their own political power. Again, as the law and order of the exploiting classes depend, in the final analysis, on the power of the armed forces for their preservation and protection, the exploited classes must, in their march towards establish-

E

ment of political power through class struggle, build up their own armed forces step by step.

Now let us see if we, in India, have entered the phase of revolution. Lenin once remarked, in the course of his criticism of Kautsky, that broadly speaking the era of competitive capitalism ended and the monopolist phase began by 1870. Lenin demonstrated through his analysis that this monopoly capitalism was the economic base of imperialism. That is, capitalism entered the era of imperialism after 1870, which transformed itself gradually into a world system. Lenin established further that imperialism is the highest stage of capitalism and is also the stage of the decay of capitalism, when no further sustained development of the forces of production is possible. Extending this argument further and taking the world as a whole, i.e., as a unit of social system, we may say that the whole world has entered the era of social revolution. This is not to say, however, that revolution will take place simultaneously at all places on the earth and a qualitatively new higher social system will be established in the world at once. Lenin pointed out that owing to the uneven development of capitalism, social revolution will take place in different countries at different times and in different ways. Judged from this point of view it becomes clear that India was already ripe for a social revolution even at the time when she was ruled by the British imperialists. This social revolution had as its objective—the overthrow of foreign imperialism and of native feudalism, which was preserved and protected by the former. But due to the lack of far-sightedness on the part of the exploited classes, that revolution could not succeed and a section of the native bourgeoisie managed, in active collaboration with the imperialists, to make certain changes in the political superstructure and trumpeted these changes as a great social revolution.

From what Lenin taught, every communist knows that the objective conditions for revolution and the necessity to carry it forward quickly to its full consummation are there when both the exploiting and the exploited classes are enmeshed in a nationwide crisis. At a time of such crisis the exploited classes deeply realize from their own living conditions that it is impossible to go on living in the old way. Similarly, the exploiting classes also realize the futility of maintaining their regime of oppression and exploitation in the old way and try to devise ever new methods to maintain the same. To these factors Lenin added one thing more—a revolutionary consciousness which favours the carrying forward of the revolution quickly to complete success. Does this mean, therefore, that the entire toiling people will realize the inevitability of revolution and will begin to act consciously to that end? To this, Lenin replied that what is necessary is that the majority of the working class, at least the majority of the class-conscious and politically active sections of the working class, must come to realize that a revolution is inevitable. When such a consciousness combines with the other objective factors of a revolutionary condition, it becomes necessary to orientate the class struggle quickly towards the objective of bringing about revolutionary changes.

It goes without saying that communists will continue to participate in bourgeois elections, if they are allowed to, till such a revolutionary situation matures. But then, they participate in it only to use it as a means of propagating the necessity of a revolution among the broad masses of the toiling people through their election campaigns, and certainly not to sing the glory of the bourgeois parliamentarism by sending in hundreds of choir-boys. In *'Left-Wing' Communism* Lenin clearly stated that communists never fight the elections to win more seats. Ranadive, who quotes so liberally from *'Left-Wing' Communism,* is however shrewd enough to skip over precisely those portions in the book which have a direct bearing on the discussion of the question of whether the time for revolution has come or not. What else could he do? These are precisely the portions which clearly show the interconnection between the bourgeois elections on the one hand and the forces of revolution on the other, and clearly point out that the primary task before communists is to make the revolution a success and, if they have to participate in the bourgeois elections under special conditions, it is only to facilitate and quicken the achievement of their primary objective. In this alone lies the significance of their participation in bourgeois elections.

Let us now see how we can gauge the situation in our country according to the criteria set by Lenin regarding a revolutionary situation. First, that there is a nationwide crisis today requires no Marxism–Leninism to realize. The toiling people realize from their own experiences how cruel and deep is this crisis. The ruling classes are also sensing the depth of the crisis with their own class consciousness and as such are resorting to new methods to maintain their regime of exploitation. This is finding expression in such

things as exploiting peasants through the new agrarian laws, re-
trenchment of workers in the name of automation and rationalization and attempts to subdue the forces of revolution by opening the
flood-gates of rabid chauvinism.

To all this let us add the factor of revolutionary consciousness,
and see what we have got. The class-conscious and politically active
workers are the vanguard of the working class. Marx and Engels
defined these advanced elements as communists. Lenin defined the
Communist Party as the highest class organization of the toiling
people. Did not this vanguard and its highest class organization in
this country openly admit in its programme adopted at its well-
attended Congress that the revolution is both inevitable and necessary?

The one thing more that, according to Lenin's *'Left-Wing' Communism,* is necessary, is crisis in the government and the increasing
participation by the backward sections of the people in political
activities. Had there been no governmental crisis, no increased participation by the backward sections in political activities, how else
can the fact be explained that eight of the existing state governments were dislodged from power? In other words, the time for
revolution has ripened to such an extent that not only the vanguard
of the working class but even the backward sections of the people
also realize the necessity to break up the existing social order. And
it was because of this that all through 1966 even the backward
sections of the people repeatedly took part in death-defying struggles on various demands and the struggles for economic demands
began to be quickly transformed into political battles. But the backward sections cannot realize on their own the real way in which
they should advance in order to seize political power, and carry the
social revolution through to the victorious end. It is the duty of the
Communist Party, the highest class organization of the vanguard of
the working class, to enlighten them on the way, the manner, in
which they should advance to achieve their goal. The neo-revisionist
leadership of the Communist Party (Maoist) precisely shirked this
duty and for this purpose has artificially raised the bogey that the
time for revolution has not yet come. Thus they have tried to push
the question of revolution back to a position of secondary importance and to raise the question of elections to the position of primary
importance. Instead of clarifying people's minds about the real
connection that exists between the social order and the state

machinery, they have shamelessly tried to capitalize on people's ignorance about it and have assiduously tried to raise false hopes in their minds, by sugar-coated talks and assurances that their living conditions can be bettered, even to a small degree, by replacing the Congress ministers by the so-called progressive ministers. In this way, this neo-revisionist leadership has been trying their utmost to reverse the process of revolutionary mass awakening. Why should they try to do this now? Precisely because a revolutionary situation exists in our country and the masses are waking up to the necessity of making a revolution, these neo-revisionist leaders are so keen on distracting people's attention from revolution and diverting it to the 'blessings' of bourgeois parliamentarism and the game of cabinet-making.

There is further proof to show that these people are shouting 'the time for revolution has not come' precisely for the purpose of hiding from the people the fact that the time for revolution is ripe. Let us remember that on many a previous occasion the people clashed with the police and many a precious life was sacrificed but never before were these people heard raising the bogey of untimeliness. On the contrary, they applauded those clashes in order to strengthen their own positions in the Party and the mass organizations. The reason for this is of course not far to seek. They are fully aware of the fact that in order to make the social revolution thorough-going, the basis of the social order must be smashed and that sporadic clashes with the state power, however valiant, can never achieve that. That is why these agents of the bourgeoisie found nothing to worry over struggles so long as these remained sporadic, and did not think of raising the bogey of untimeliness nor did they care to direct this fighting consciousness towards the main objective of social revolution.

But unfortunately for these men, history is created by the people themselves and not by leaders, however crafty and deceptive they may be. The true representatives of the people, taking lessons from the experience and consciousness of the struggling masses, have to-day revealed before millions of toiling people the path to be taken to make the social revolution completely successful. In the fields and forests of the Terai region they have ushered in a glorious peasant revolution which is the axis of the people's democratic revolution. They have refused to fritter away their revolutionary fighting strength by engaging in sporadic and futile clashes with the state power. Instead, they have started a peasant revolution on correct lines whose main objective is to overthrow the forces of feudalism in the countryside. Their struggle is thus a struggle for land, which, they realize well, can only be successful by using force and never through resort to the legalities or documents of the existing regime. The revolutionary peasants of Terai also realize that what they are up against is not merely the feudal landlords of the countryside, but also the armed might of the state, which protects the interests of the exploiting classes. For this reason, the revolutionary peasants there are getting prepared for an armed struggle and are developing their own armed might in the course of struggles. The essence of seizure of state power is to develop people's own armed power so as to provide an all-round protection for the rights of the people and to maintain decisive control over all matters involving such rights.

The main task of the Indian social revolution at the present stage has for the first time been undertaken at the foot of the Himalayas. It is happening when the time is ripe for revolution in our country. That is why this spark kindled in Terai cannot remain and is not remaining confined to that region alone and is about to kindle a flame that will engulf the entire stretch of West Bengal.

VIETNAM

In non-revolutionary circles, academic debates and the press, it is usual nowadays to talk and even to think of three different 'loyalties' or inspirational source-centres—Moscow, Peking, Havana. Even revolutionaries tend to divide the communist world into three 'loyalty' areas. Basically, what is meant is that such-and-such a movement or individual is morally, materially, politically and/or militarily supported by one of the three revolutionary countries. On an ideological level, the distinction is posited as somewhat more meaningful: (1) the Moscowphile is said to believe that in the long range capitalism cannot sustain economic competition with the communist world and hence sees no reason to risk a world nuclear war for the momentary advantage that might result from some armed confrontation; (2) the Maoist is convinced that only through armed confrontation (though not necessarily conflagration) will capitalism ever be destroyed and that in order to be ready for such armed—people's—war, the masses have to be politically educated first; and (3) the Guevarists, agreeing with the Maoists that people's war is a prerequisite for the seizure of power, insist that fighting is the best politicization process. On a political-tactical level, the distinctions lead to Moscowphiles fostering alliances with liberals and establishing electoral united fronts, Maoists advocating national revolutions in which alliances are maintained with one sector of the exploiting capitalist class enemy known as 'the national bourgeoisie', and Guevarists organizing openly socialist guerrilla groups operating in almost total isolation from the revolutionary or neo-revolutionary forces located in capitalist urban strongholds. In shorthand, these differences are trimmed to such an extent that the Moscowphile is seen as a 'sell-out' or even as a counter-revolutionary, the Maoist as a dogmatic advocate of endless war and the Guevarist as a subjectivist or elitist adventurer.

In reality, such distinctions and differences are much more fluid. While it is true that Moscow-lining communists constantly flee from confrontation (the missile crisis, 1962), refuse to seize power where there is a risk of a strong counter-revolution (France, 1968), actually give technical aid to oligarchies fighting other communists (Colombia), order 'their' men to give up the armed struggle in exchange for legality and the possibility of joining the electoral process (Venezuela) and seem to prefer non-revolutionary 'nationalists' to committed fighters (in 1968, Egypt received twenty times more Russian aid than Vietnam), Moscow nevertheless does help guerrillas in Kurdistan, Palestine, Angola, Mozambique and South Africa and has continued to aid Vietnam (even if not as much as, and proportionately to its wealth, much less than, China). And, more important for Vietnam, it is a fact that Russia's nuclear presence is the only deterrent that stopped John Foster Dulles and his 'massive retaliation' policy from obliterating the Vietnamese with atomic bombs after Dien Bien Phu in 1954.

In its main development, the revolutionary struggle in Vietnam has followed the Chinese example, a protracted people's war against outside imperialist forces and, gradually more defined, their neo-colonialist local partners. It has been mainly a liberation or national revolution, led, as Mao would have it, by the Communist Party vanguard. And it has been a two-stage revolution: all patriots together until the French were driven out, then a socialist transformation in the North; all patriots together until the USA is driven out, then a socialist transformation in the South. The peasants in the countryside were and are the backbone of the revolution, but the workers, petty bourgeoisie and the 'patriotic' elements of the national bourgeoisie are the fundamental partners without which the revolution would risk isolation. All this is very clearly spelled out in all three articles in this section. Yet, the three authors disagree ideologically: Hoc Tap, the theoretical organ of the Vietnamese CP, is Maoist; Le Duan, secretary general of the CP, is Moscowphile; and General Giap, the brilliant military head of the revolution against the French and, it is said, of the war against the USA, is maintaining a Guevarist line—at least in this article.

Actually, the three articles' variances are subtle. Hoc Tap is perhaps the clearest: it completely rejects Russia's fear of atomic war ('nuclear blackmail'), scoffs at alliances with peaceful dissenters ('structural reformists') and does not shrink from the risk of total civil war; on the contrary, following Lenin, sees it as the last stage in people's war. Its definition of violence pulls no punches: revolu-

tionary violence is both necessary and beneficial, it is the only way to win and end counter-revolutionary violence which always causes more suffering, ultimately, than a victorious though bloody civil war —a theme which will be expanded by Fanon and Che Guevara. But the editors of Hoc Tap *are also quite careful to insist that revolutionaries must resort to violence only when the people have been politized, that is when the revolutionary forces include vast sectors of the peasant and worker masses.*

In the first part of his article, Le Duan says fundamentally the same thing, but his emphasis is different. He opposes terrorism (assassination) which, as we have seen, Lenin did not, and he is more concerned than Hoc Tap *about the cities, insisting that a revolution cannot be won without the full participation of the urban workers. Today, all Moscow-lining communists stress this point, partly because traditionally, the communist parties have had more success at organizing or seizing control of unions than peasants and peasant leagues. After all, there isn't much one can promise landless exploited peasants besides land, which is a revolutionary demand. Whereas a union leadership can gain a strong following simply by promising, and obtaining, better working conditions, shorter hours, higher wages—none of which is especially revolutionary. One way of putting the difference, then, would be that one can fool city workers with revolutionary rhetoric and reformist actions but not peasants. Or, to be cynical for a moment, that it is easier to co-opt or Fabianize workers than peasants.*

Proudhon once said that private property was theft, and every social revolutionary, Marxist or not, must agree, for unless private property is abolished, competition will remain the characteristic of how people relate (the relation of productive forces, to use Marxist jargon as Le Duan does so extensively). It follows therefore that a true revolutionary must advocate and eventually fight for a collective society. But Le Duan does not. He wants peasants to join co-operatives, a farming system whereby each peasant owns his own land yet somehow helps both his fellow peasants and the state. But if the peasant does own land, that 'somehow' must then entail some form of material benefit, which leads Le Duan to talk of 'market incentives with education and moral stimulation'. The net result is that the whole countryside must be highly centralized. Like Russian communists, Le Duan ends up with a social structure in which the 'state' is more important than its people. He can then logically

E*

insist that industrialization has priority over agriculture, the city over the country, and the worker over the peasant. Without saying so, he is condemning the Debray–Guevara foco *theory, China's cultural revolution and the whole New Left's concept of decentralization and participatory democracy.*

Not so for General Giap. Perhaps because of his years of day-to-day relationship with guerrilla fighters, who must be decentralized to be efficient (and survive), his class analysis, which at first glance seems quite classical for a Marxist, betrays great trust in ordinary people. What's more, his experience with people's war makes him conclude that warfare builds not only comradeship but also collectivism. It was he, after all, who had to coordinate the movement of thousands of peasants *from hundreds of different localities and scores of distinct ethnic groups to attack the French at Dien Bien Phu. Since 1959, supposedly, he has been doing the same in the South against the USA. During the Têt offensive in 1968, literally thousands of guerrilla units were asked to launch correlated attacks. When one remembers that the NLF (or Viet Cong) operate through semi-autonomous units, each of which expects all their combatants to share in the decision-making process (down to actual discussion of attack plans), such coordination is no minor feat. It is perhaps this attitude towards war and peoples that has made it possible for the NLF to recruit non-communists by the thousands—and for the 'Alliance of National, Democratic and Peace Forces of Vietnam' to join the NLF in combat and in 1969 to join the Provisional Revolutionary Government of South Vietnam. That 'Alliance', set up after the Têt offensive by non-NLF anti-imperialist South Vietnamese, issued a manifesto on 21 April 1968, which insisted that after victory the political regime must be a republic that guarantees 'freedom of speech, freedom of meeting, freedom of organization, freedom to go abroad, etc.... All organs of state power are to be elected by the people through free and fair elections. All people's strata, men and women, all nationalities, all religious communities are to be represented in these organs. All Vietnamese citizens are to be equal in all respects.'*

Of course, the 'Alliance' could be just another 'front' to corral non-communists into the 'nationalist' struggle. But the point remains that the South is decentralized, and that General Giap, who is Commander-in-Chief of the Vietnamese army and Defence Minister of the Democratic Republic of Vietnam, has always worked

*through decentralization to guide his men to victory. Both nation-
ally and internationally he believes that each struggle waged, even
if lost, ups the odds of quicker ultimate victory. Like Che Guevara,
he is convinced that the USA cannot withstand many Vietnams
simultaneously (Giap actually refers to the Dominican Republic almost as if he were saying 'create two, three ... many Santo
Domingos'). Like Che Guevara, he believes that revolutionary practice is the best teacher of revolutionary theory—to the point of stat-
ing that 'revolutionary practice will iron out divergencies among
communists', e.g. Russia and China. And like Che Guevara, finally,
Giap is international in scope. He sees the Vietnamese revolution
as part of the world struggle against imperialism and, hence, that
it is the duty of the Vietnamese to fight not only for a free and
independent Vietnam but also 'to actively contribute' to the struggle
of all peoples, everywhere.*

*But then, on that score, every Vietnamese leader concurs. Ho Chi
Minh, in his testament (written on 10 May 1969 and read by Le
Duan on 9 September 1969 at Ho's funeral), said: 'My ultimate
wish is that our whole party and people will be united in the struggle
for peaceful united independent democratic Vietnam and make a
worthy contribution to the world revolution.' Le Duan himself led
mourners in an oath to carry on Ho's work, promising 'to maintain
the international orientation of the party, contribute to the unity
of socialist peoples and support all revolutionary forces of other
peoples struggling for independence, peace, democracy and socialism'. When I was in North Vietnam during the winter of 1966–7,
I got the feeling that every Vietnamese was indeed an internationalist. Wherever I went during my two thousand mile trip[38] I noticed,
first of all, that the North is quite decentralized and operates on
moral incentives much much more than one would gather from Le
Duan's article; second, that even isolated peasants were aware of
the revolutionary struggles in the rest of Asia, Africa and America;
and third, that all felt as Prime Minister Pham Van Dong told me:
'Right now, we happen to be in the front-lines of the struggle
against imperialism. But it is a struggle of all exploited peoples
everywhere and we consider ourselves just one part of that struggle.
No one will really be totally free until all are.'*

I Hoc Tap: *Peace or Violence?*[39]

How to get state power into the hands of the working class and how to build the state power of the proletariat are the questions of primary concern to every true revolutionary. That is why the method of seizing state power is one of the most important questions communists must study and solve.

The state is the instrument of violence used by the ruling classes to crush all resistance put up by the classes ruled by them. The rulers use troops, policemen, spies, law courts and prisons against the ruled. The exploiting classes in power, on the one hand, are always employing violence to keep down the exploited classes. On the other hand, they use their 'thinkers' to spread pacifism and the theory of 'non-violence' in an effort to cause the exploited to be resigned to their destiny without resorting to violence to resist the exploiting classes in power.

Those who have swallowed the poison of bourgeois pacifism and humanitarianism oppose all kinds of violence. They make no distinction in the class character of the various kinds of violence. To them the violence used by the bourgeoisie to suppress the proletariat and the violence used by the proletariat to resist the bourgeoisie for its own emancipation are one and the same. To the pacifists, every kind of violence is evil. They can do nothing but moan and lament over the death caused by violence. They know nothing about the law of social development. They only see the ugly side of violence and do not understand that despite its ugliness it plays a revolutionary role in history. Marx once said that violence 'is the midwife of every old society pregnant with a new one'.[40]

Today, modern revisionists and Right opportunists in the communist movement and the working-class movement keep wagging their tongues about 'peace', and 'humanitarianism'; they dare not mention the word 'violence'. For them violence is taboo. The fact is that they have negated Marxist–Leninist theory on the role of violence in history.

Communists are not Tolstoyists or the disciples of Gandhi preaching 'non-violence'. Nor do they spread the idea of 'violence for violence' sake'. They are not 'bellicose' and 'bloodthirsty' as the reactionaries always slander them. They simply set forth a fact that violence is a social phenomenon, a result of the exploitation of man by man, a means used by the ruling, exploiting classes to maintain and extend their domination. Communists hold that the working class and other working people—victims of exploitation and domination—must resort to revolutionary violence to crush counter-revolutionary violence, so that they can win their own emancipation and society can advance according to the law of historical development.

The revolutionary cause of the proletariat does not mean ordinary reshuffle of government personnel or a mere cabinet change while the old political and economic order remains intact. The proletarian revolution must not preserve the state machinery (the existing police, gendarmes, armed forces and bureaucratic structure), mainly used to oppress the people, but must crush it and replace it with an entirely new one. The bourgeois revolution does not smash the existing feudal state machinery but takes it over, preserves and perfects it. On the contrary, the proletarian revolution smashes the existing state machinery of the capitalist system. It is a process of bitter struggle in which the bourgeoisie is overthrown, the bourgeois order is destroyed, the properties of the capitalists and landlords are confiscated and the public ownership of the various chief means of production is realized. Smashing the existing state machinery is 'the preliminary condition for every real people's revolution'.[41]

As the reformists see it, there is no difference between the nature of bourgeois democracy and proletarian democracy, there is no swift advance from the capitalist system to the socialist system, and capitalism can evolve gradually into socialism in accordance with the theory of evolution. Modern revisionism, like the revisionism of the early twentieth century, is reformism in essence. Revisionists, in the past, as at present, have made great efforts to sing the praises of the bourgeois parliamentary system. They have made a big fanfare about the entry into socialism through 'parliamentary road'. As a matter of fact democratic rights under the bourgeois parliamentary system are, as Marx put it, nothing more than the rights to decide once every three or six years who of the ruling classes should 'represent' the people in parliament and oppress them. Lenin said: 'Take any parliamentary country, from America to Switzerland, from France to England, Norway and so forth—in these countries the real business of "state" is performed behind the scenes and is carried on by the departments, chancelleries and General Staffs. Parliament itself is given up to talk for the special purpose of fooling the "common people".'[42] Lenin described bourgeois democracy as narrow, emasculated, false and deceptive democracy, the paradise of the rich, but a trap and a deceptive fraud for the exploited and the poor.

The bourgeoisie in power has never voluntarily relinquished state power to the working class. In 'Theses on the Fundamental Tasks of the Second Congress of the Communist International', Lenin pointed out that under the conditions of militarism and imperialism,

The very thought of peacefully subordinating the capitalists to the will of the majority of the exploited, of the peaceful, reformist transition to socialism is not only extreme philistine stupidity, but also downright deception of the workers, the embellishment of capitalist wage slavery, concealment of the truth. . . . Only the violent overthrow of the bourgeoisie, the confiscation of its property, the destruction of the whole of the bourgeois state apparatus from top to bottom – parliamentary, judicial, military, bureaucratic, administrative, municipal, etc., right up to the very wholesale deportation or internment of the most dangerous and stubborn exploiters – putting them under strict surveillance in order to combat inevitable attempts to resist and to restore capitalist slavery – only such measures can ensure the real subordination of the whole class of exploiters.[43]

The process of the proletarian revolutionary movement is, in the final analysis, one of making preparations for the dictatorship of the proletariat (before the seizure of state power), and putting such dictatorship into effect (after seizing power). The proletariat must adopt all forms of struggle, legal and illegal, inside and outside parliament, ranging from strikes, demonstrations, political general strikes up to armed uprisings, the highest form of struggle, so as to overthrow the bourgeois rule and establish the dictatorship of the proletariat. The more the revolutionary movement surges forward, the more frenzied will be the repressions by the ruling bourgeoisie and the more sharp and bitter will be the class struggle. 'Revolution progresses by giving rise to a strong and united counter-revolution, i.e., it compels the enemy to resort to more and more extreme measures of defence and in this way devises ever more powerful means of attack.'[44]

Marx said that 'the weapon of criticism cannot, of course, take the place of criticism with weapons' and that material forces must be overthrown by material forces. Lenin pointed out that in the working-class struggle against the bourgeoisie, it was possible 'at any time to substitute the criticism with weapons for the weapon of criticism'. Lenin, therefore, pointed out the necessity of building up arms for the proletariat and disarming the bourgeoisie, for otherwise it would be impossible for socialism to win. In 'The "Disarmament" Slogan', Lenin wrote: 'Our slogan must be: the arming of the proletariat for the purpose of vanquishing, expropriating and disarming the bourgeoisie.' ... 'An oppressed class which does not strive to learn to use arms, to acquire arms, deserves to be treated like slaves.'[45] Because in every class society the ruling classes possess arms, and it is a fact that the bourgeoisie in power uses them to suppress the working class. Consequently, the working class has no alternative but to take up arms to overthrow its rulers and achieve its own liberation. Lenin also said: 'Only after the proletariat has disarmed the bourgeoisie will it be able, without betraying its world-historical mission, to throw all armaments on the scrap-heap; the proletariat will undoubtedly do this, but only when this condition has been fulfilled, certainly not before.'[46]

Lenin also criticized Plekhanov's view that 'they should not have taken up arms.' In 'Lessons of the Moscow Uprising' he said: 'Nothing could be more short-sighted than Plekhanov's view, seized upon by all the opportunists, that the strike was untimely and should not have been started, and that "they should not have taken up arms." On the contrary, we should have taken to arms more resolutely, energetically and aggressively; we should have explained to the masses that it was impossible to confine things to a peaceful strike and that a fearless and relentless armed fight was necessary.'[47] Lenin taught us the need to spread the idea of armed uprising to the broad masses, and he described armed uprising as a great mass struggle. He regarded recognition of armed uprising as a question of principle for the revolutionaries.

It is not enough to take sides on the question of political slogans; it is also not enough to take sides on the question of an armed uprising. Those who are opposed to it, those who do not prepare for it, must be ruthlessly dismissed from the ranks of the supporters of the revolution, sent packing to its enemies, to the traitors or cowards; for the day is approaching when force of events and the conditions of the struggle will compel us to distinguish between enemies and friends according to this principle.[48]

Of course, communists are very cautious about armed uprising. They regard it as a peculiar form of political struggle with its own specific laws. Communists start an armed uprising only when the opportunity is ripe and when subjective and objective conditions are completely ready, and once it has started they intend to carry it through to the finish. Communists do not propose that arms be used at all times and under all circumstances. If there was a road which would involve less casualties and bloodshed, but which could lead to socialism, they would unhesitatingly take that road. Whether the working class adopts the form of armed struggle or the form of peaceful political struggle does not depend on the subjective desire of the working class but on the extent of resistance by the exploiting classes which first resort to arms to maintain their rule. Since the ruling classes will not surrender state power of their own accord, the working class must use arms to overthrow them.

In the final stage of the Second World War and for a time in the postwar years, because the Soviet Red Army had wiped out the Hitlerite fascists and smashed the fascist state machinery set up by Hitler in the various East European countries, the peoples' regimes led by the working class were established in those countries. With the help of the Soviet Red Army they switched to the tasks of the socialist revolution and the dictatorship of the proletariat after carrying out the work of bourgeois democratic revolution, and so there was no need for an armed uprising. What happened in Czechoslovakia in February 1948 also belongs to this category of revolutionary change. By adopting administrative measures and combining these with mass demonstrations, the Czechoslovak people's regime smashed the plot of the bourgeoisie to foment a cabinet crisis and attempt to restore capitalism, and in this way led the country directly to the road of socialism. Some people are attempting to use the February 1948 event in Czechoslovakia as an example to support their argument for 'peaceful transition'. But this is falsifying history because they separate the February happenings from the liquidation of German fascism by the Soviet Red Army, from the armed uprising and guerrilla warfare of the people in Slovakia in 1944 and the people's general armed uprising in Prague in May 1945. Moreover, in the February 1948 event in Czechoslovakia, the role of revolutionary violence was also embodied in the determined suppression of the bourgeois rebellion by the people's regime, which was in essence a dictatorship of the proletariat, and in the armed demonstration of the Czechoslovak people supporting the administrative measures of the communist-led government.

Since the end of the Second World War, the colonial system of imperialism has been in the process of disintegration. Many nations under the yoke of imperialist enslavement have today achieved national independence. In their fight for national independence, some nations have adopted the form of armed struggle, others have gone through alternate periods of armed struggle and peaceful political struggle or have combined these two forms of struggle in the same period, while still others have attained political independence without armed struggle. Some nations have been able to achieve national independence peacefully because imperialism is steadily declining and a world socialist system has come into existence and is vigorously developing, thus bringing about a change in the balance of forces on a world-wide scale. Confronted with this situation, imperialism is forced to make its choice between two alternatives:

1. To stubbornly resist to the end and eventually be driven out of the colonies, with the result that the colonial nations which have gained complete independence will embark on the path of socialism.

2. To hand over political independence to the native bourgeoisie and in this way to retain its economic interests in the colonies and keep the former colonial nations within the orbit of capitalism.

Many imperialist countries 'wisely' chose the second alternative, and this explains why some former colonial nations have been able to achieve political independence by peaceful means. However, the various nations have a long way to go from arriving at political independence to achieving complete independence and thence going over to socialism. So far, there is not yet a single 'precedent' of peaceful transition to socialism in the world working-class history of revolutionary struggle. Speaking about this possibility, Stalin, in 'The Foundations of Leninism', said :

Of course, in the remote future, if the proletariat is victorious in the principal capitalist countries, and if the present capitalist encirclement is replaced by a socialist encirclement, a 'peaceful' path of development is quite possible for certain capitalist countries, whose capitalists, in view of the 'unfavourable' international situation, will consider it expedient 'voluntarily' to make substantial concessions to the proletariat. But this supposition applies only to a remote possible future.[49]

Today, two-thirds of the world population still live under capitalism. Imperialism is in the process of an advanced development of militarism and bureaucracy. Every capitalist country possesses an enormous state machinery ever ready to suppress the people's revolutionary movement with violence. In these circumstances, the possibility for the proletariat to seize power by peaceful means without launching an armed uprising remains extremely rare.

There are people who claim that as a result of the emergence of nuclear weapons the working class must not seize power by violence but by peaceful means, for revolution by violence will lead to civil war. Because one spark may spread into a conflagration, civil war may lead to a world war which in the present era is bound to develop into a destructive nuclear war. In the circumstances, the only way left for the working class in various countries is to attain state power by peaceful means. And the peaceful means they recommend is the theory of 'structural reform'.

For all their destructive power, nuclear weapons cannot change the law of development of human society. They can only cause certain changes in military strategy and tactics, but never in the strategy and tactics of the working class. Not at all times will a spark develop into a conflagration. This has been proved by the Chinese civil war, by the Korean war, and by the Algerian war. The revolutions of China, Vietnam and Cuba were all revolutions by violence and were all won after the presence of nuclear weapons. It is therefore utterly groundless to assert that the working class should not seize power by violence following the existence of nuclear weapons.

In the face of enemies who are armed to the teeth and are prepared to stamp out revolution at any time by violence, the only way to seize state power is to resort to violence. The possibility of revolution developing peacefully can be realized only when the exploiting classes do not possess a dependable militarist-bureaucratic state machine or at a time when they have lost the will to use this machinery to suppress the revolution although it may still be in their hands. To translate the possibility of the peaceful development of revolution into reality, the working class must possess a mighty force which is equipped with closely knit organization and leadership. That force may be a mass political force, an armed force, or a combination of political and armed forces. Therefore, in striving to make revolution through a peaceful road—the road which involves the least suffering—the working class and its party must vigorously prepare for the seizure of state power by violence. It is only when the working class has organized into a mighty force and firmly taken up arms that it is possible to strive for the peaceful development of the revolution.

Ever since our Party was formed it has applied Marxist–Leninist principles on the strategy and tactics of revolution to the reality of our country. On the one hand, it has stood against the defeatist and capitulationist ideas and against the 'theories' advocating non-rebellion and denouncing the use of arms. On the other hand, it has opposed the idea of organizing 'secret societies' for conspiracies as well as such terrorist activities as assassination of individuals. During the Second World War, the Party particularly stressed the question of seizing state power by armed uprising. The resolution adopted at the seventh session of the Party's Central Committee (November 1940) provided: 'The Party must be prepared to undertake the sacred missions of leading the oppressed nations in Indochina to launch armed rebellion and achieve independence and freedom.' The eighth session of the Party's Central Committee (May 1941) also put forward the task for 'preparing forces at all times', so that 'when the favourable moment arrives, we can, by employing the power already at our disposal, victoriously lead area uprisings one by one in order to pave the way for a large-scale general uprising'.

In August 1945, when Japanese fascism collapsed, our Party led the people throughout the country in starting a timely general armed uprising and seized state power. The August revolution in Vietnam was a revolution by violence, by means of which the state apparatus was established. The August revolution was the result of the prolonged revolutionary struggle and in which the peaceful political struggle of the masses was combined with the launching of local guerrilla war and the work of building bases in the rural areas. The August revolution was the direct result of the armed struggle waged by all the people, mainly the result of combining the activities of professional armed forces with semi-professional armed forces (Liberation Army, guerrilla forces, militia, and self-defence corps, etc.).

The August revolution in Vietnam is different from the Russian October Revolution in that the latter was a general armed uprising, state power was first built in the cities and then in the countryside.

The difference between Vietnam's August revolution and the Chinese revolution is that the Chinese revolution was a prolonged armed struggle, state power was first seized in the countryside, which was used to encircle the cities and finally the cities were liberated.

In the course of decades of protracted and arduous revolutionary movement, our Party has skilfully combined the various kinds of struggles, economic and political, legal and illegal, struggle in the streets and in parliament, armed struggle and peaceful political struggle. During the period of the upsurge of the revolution (1930–1), the Party led the masses in waging blow-for-blow struggles against the enemy. In places where the enemy's power had collapsed (Nghi-an and Ha-tinh) the Party led the people in setting up the state power of the Soviets and training them in administering their own affairs. During the period of the ebbing of the revolution (1932–5), the Party led the people in making a planned withdrawal, establishing secret organizations, and prepared for a new revolutionary upsurge. From 1936 to 1939, by taking advantage of the legitimate conditions brought on by the victory of the French People's Front, the Party launched a movement of open struggle, formed the Democratic Front, led the people in fighting for better living conditions and for democracy and freedom, and for participation in the election campaign and in carrying on a struggle inside parliament. At the end of 1939, the Party again went underground. Utilizing the latent and manifest contradictions existing between the two imperialist countries which then ruled our country, the Party launched guerrilla warfare and set up revolutionary bases. Simultaneously with peaceful political struggle, the form of armed struggle began to appear. This period ended with the general uprising in the August revolution which was the peak of the movement and represented a skilful combination of the two forms of struggle, armed and political. In the more than one year following the August revolution, our Party put emphasis on political struggle so as to consolidate the people's state power and build forces in various spheres, particularly the armed forces. At the same time it carried on armed struggle against the French colonialists staging a come-back and carrying out aggression against the southern part of our country, as well as against the Kuomintang-organized and directed bandits harassing some provinces in the north. From the end of 1946, our Party led the people in waging a nationwide armed struggle against colonialist aggression.

Since 1954, revolution has gone over to the stage of socialism in the northern part of our country. Because state power already was in the hands of the working class during the stage of national-democratic revolution, 'peaceful transition to socialism' has been realized in the north in the past few years. This does not mean that during the stage of the socialist revolution in the north the role of revolutionary violence has ceased to exist. During the stage of the socialist revolution, the people's democratic state has carried out the task of the dictatorship of the proletariat which means using violence to crush counter-revolution.

The struggle being waged by our compatriots in the south at present still falls into the category of the national democratic revolution. They are using revolutionary violence against the counter-revolutionary violence of the US. Of course, to make revolution by violence imposes the necessity of enduring hardship and sacrifices on the part of the broad masses of the people. But this can help shake off at an early date the long suffering and death caused by the brutal oppression and exploitation inflicted by the rulers on a countless number of people. During the general armed uprising in August 1945, only a few score of people were killed throughout the country. On the contrary, as a result of the rule of the Japanese and French fascists, some two million people starved to death in the north from the end of 1944 to the first few months of 1945. History has proved that the extremely heavy losses suffered by the working people from the brutal rule of the exploiting classes cannot be matched by the losses of a revolution, however relentless it may be. The road involving the least suffering for the people is to go in for revolution to overthrow the enemy and win emancipation.

II Le Duan: *Revolutionary Marxism**[50]

In the history of the Vietnamese people's struggle against French colonialism, many patriotic movements followed one upon another, many armed insurrections broke out; some established resistance bases in hardly accessible mountain regions for a long-term struggle,

* The author is secretary general of the Vietnam Workers' Party (the Vietnamese CP)–ed.

as the uprising of Phan Dinh Phung which lasted ten years, or that of Hoang Hoa Tham stretching over nearly thirty years.* However, none of these movements brought the national-liberation cause to success. Their failure was due to many causes, but it clearly proves that revolution must be made by the broad masses, it must be a truly popular movement if it is to succeed.

Right after the founding of the Indochinese Communist Party, a mass revolutionary movement flared up throughout Vietnam, the apex of which being the Nghe An and Ha Tinh Soviets (1930-1). Workers and peasants in these provinces† rose up to overthrow the colonial rule and the local administration of mandarins and despots, setting up worker–peasant power. Though suppressed, the uprising strongly awakened the revolutionary spirit of the entire people and pointed to the immense revolutionary capabilities of the workers and peasants.

From 1936 to 1939, in face of the fascist threat, the Party timely adopted a new orientation, shifting from underground to semi-clandestine and semi-legal activities, ingeniously combining these forms of struggle, even using 'people's councils' and 'colonial councils' to initiate throughout the country a powerful movement against the reactionary colonialists, feudalists and aggressive fascists, for the conquest of democratic freedoms, the improvement of living standards and the safeguard of world peace. This campaign involved millions of people and politically educated broad masses of the workers and peasants, greatly enhancing their patriotism and class consciousness.

After the outbreak of the Second World War and the occupation of Indo-china by the Japanese fascists, the Party shifted its main activities to the countryside; while continuing to build up the political forces of the masses, it created armed forces, started a country-wide patriotic movement and local guerrilla activities against the Japanese and French fascists, and set up the Viet Bac‡ resistance zone and guerrilla bases.

The local insurrections and revolutionary tides started and led by our Party since 1930 were preludes to the August 1945 Revolution which creatively applied Lenin's principles of revolutionary violence

* Phan Dinh led a rebellion against the French from 1885 until he died in 1896. Hoang Hoa Tham's peasant uprising in the North lasted from 1887 until he was murdered by a traitor on 10 February 1913.–ed.

† In Central Vietnam–ed.

‡ Mountain region north of the Red River–ed.

and insurrection to conquer power. The August Revolution aptly combined political struggle with military struggle, local take-over in the countryside with insurrection in the towns, long-term preparation of political and military forces with rapid mobilization of the masses at the favourable moment to overthrow the imperialist and feudal power. It liquidated the colonialist and feudal power, and founded the Democratic Republic of Vietnam, the first worker-peasant state in South-east Asia, ushering in a new era in the history of the country. But, protected by British troops, helped by the American imperialists, the French colonialists then came back and connived with the native reactionary forces to unleash a war of aggression in an attempt to re-establish the colonial and feudal rule.

Under the leadership of the Party, the entire Vietnamese people took to arms and resolutely waged an all-out and protracted war. Relying mainly on their own means, they set up a strong people's army, built up their forces while fighting, consolidated their rear while attacking at the front, waged an armed resistance while gradually implementing democratic reforms then land reform to improve the living conditions of the peasants and boost the potential of the patriotic war in every field. People's war vigorously developed in scope and strength, driving the French Expeditionary Corps to a stalemate then defeat. The glorious victory of Dien Bien Phu brought the resistance war to a successful end, decided the fate of the French colonialists in Indochina and compelled them to sign the Geneva Agreements recognizing Vietnam's independence, sovereignty, unity and territorial integrity.

However, the national-liberation revolution of the Vietnamese people has not yet come to a close. While the completely liberated Northern part has shifted to socialist revolution, the South has to fight on against the aggression of the American imperialists. Indeed, for nearly a quarter of a century US imperialism has been the enemy number one of the Vietnamese people. Having failed in helping the French colonialists to reconquer Vietnam, in prolonging and expanding the Indochina War, the Americans supplanted the French to continue the aggression against South Vietnam with a view to perpetuating the partition of our country, turning South Vietnam into a neo-colony and military base, preparing an offensive against North Vietnam and halting the revolution in South Vietnam and South-east Asia. This is a component of the counter-revolutionary global strategy of US imperialism to check the revolutionary wave storming the bulwark of US-led international imperialism.

The process of the South Vietnamese revolution is one of uniting, organizing and developing all revolutionary and patriotic forces to liberate the South, defend the North, reunify the motherland, safeguard the independence and peace in Vietnam, peace in Southeast Asia and the world. But the August Revolution, like people's revolutions in other countries, have taught the South Vietnamese revolutionaries that any revolution with a marked popular character must use both political and military forces to secure victory. Revolution being the uprising of the oppressed and exploited masses, one must adopt the revolutionary mass viewpoint to understand revolutionary violence which involves two forces—political and military forces—and two forms of struggle—political and armed struggle— and thereby to realize the offensive position of revolution when revolutionary situations are ripe. On the contrary, if one considers revolutionary violence merely from the point of view of armed struggle, and consequently takes into account only the military force of the two sides to appraise the balance of forces between revolution and counter-revolution, mistakes will be inevitable: either one will underestimate the strength of the revolution and dare not mobilize the masses for insurrection, or, once the insurrection has been launched, one will not dare step up the offensive to push ahead the revolution, or, when the armed struggle has been unleashed, one cannot avoid falling back to a defensive strategy.

In 1959–60, when the American imperialists and their henchmen used most barbarous fascist means to sow terror and carry out mass slaughter, the South Vietnamese revolutionaries held that the enemy had sustained a basic political defeat and could no longer rule as in the past, while the people had come to realize more and more clearly that they could no longer live under the enemy's yoke and had to rise up and wage a life-and-death struggle to liberate themselves. Under those circumstances the South Vietnamese people uprose, using mainly political struggle combined with armed struggle, broke the enemy's grip, controlled large rural areas, wrested back power, redistributed land, set up 'self-management committees', made every effort to develop their forces in every field, and launched a widespread people's war to carry on their liberation struggle.

In South Vietnam, as the vast countryside has a natural economy not very dependent on the towns and an almost exclusively peasant population living on agriculture, the aggressors and their henchmen ruling in urban centres cannot establish a strict control over the rural areas. That is why, when conditions are ripe for revolution, the villages constitute the best areas for starting *local insurrections* and destroying the enemy's power apparatus. But victory cannot repose exclusively on the revolutionary forces in the countryside; it is dependent upon revolutionary forces in the towns as well. If the revolutionary upsurge in the countryside some years ago made its impact strongly felt upon the revolutionary movement in the towns, the seething struggle of the urban masses now has created highly favourable conditions for uprisings in the countryside and the extension of people's war. The recent fierce political struggle of the townsfolk has restrained, sometimes slowed down or seriously upset, the military activities of the enemy on the battlefields, thus efficaciously helping the offensive of the revolutionary armed forces; inversely, the military successes on the battle fields, like the repeated attacks by the liberation troops against the enemy's rear bases and his dens in the towns and cities, have accelerated the growth of the urban revolutionary movement. The South's final inevitable victory will be the result of both struggles, united into one mass movement.

In the North, meanwhile, the socialist revolution unfolding since 1954 represents revolutionary processes—revolution in the relations of production, technological revolution, cultural and ideological revolution—aiming at ceaselessly heightening the people's right as collective masters of the whole economy, down to each region and each production unit. *Revolution in the relations of production* was a necessary step of the socialist revolution, for we had first of all to transform the private capitalist industry and trade, and the small individual economy—peasant for the most part—in order to establish socialist relations of production. In the development of the modes of production it is the productive forces which assume the decisive role, but to promote these, appropriate relations of production are needed. The socialist relations of production set up in North Vietnam play a revolutionary part of great importance. They constitute the essential factor which makes it possible for the productive forces to develop and creates social premises to consolidate the dictatorship of the proletariat and further the ideological and cultural revolution. In the initial period of socialist building in which the material and technical bases are still weak, if one knows how to repose on the superiority of the socialist relations of production in order to use properly the labour force brought into play by cooperativization, improve the organization and management of production, gradually ameliorate techniques while enhancing the sense of being collective masters among the people, then one can obtain a higher productivity, boost economic construction and develop production.

In the revolution of relations of production, one must not only transform the relations of ownership of the means of production, but also pay attention to satisfactorily solving the problem of distribution so that in the process of distribution the labouring people realize that they are really masters of social economy. To this end, one must strictly apply the principle of distribution according to work done while ensuring the satisfaction of everybody's basic living requirements in accordance with the development of social production. One must also closely combine the method of material incentives with political education and moral stimulation to heighten the people's ardour in their work. The revolution in the relations of production does not come to an end with the establishment of new ones, but continues throughout the transition period; it must unceasingly consolidate, develop and perfect those relations of production at the same time as proceed with the building of the material and technical bases of socialism and the improvement of economic management.

For a country which advances towards socialism by-passing the stage of capitalist development, the transformation of relations of production is only a first step in the whole revolutionary process. To radically transform the Vietnamese society and firmly set up a socialist mode of production, the key problem is to promote the *technological revolution*. After the establishment of the dictatorship of the proletariat and new relations of production, the technological revolution constitutes the most important motive force to take North Vietnam to socialism. Only by accelerating the tempo of the technological revolution can one bring the productive forces to a high degree of development, create the material bases for the consolidation of the new relations of production and for the building of an advanced culture and science, thereby ensuring victory for socialism.

The advance from a small individual production to large-scale socialist production obviously requires *a new division of labour in the entire society* on modern material and technical bases. This new division of labour is closely related to the three above-mentioned revolutions, particularly to the technological revolution. To push ahead the technological revolution, to improve the instruments of production and provide a new technical equipment to all branches, is to create favourable conditions for a rational division of labour in each branch as well as in the whole economy, which in turn influences and stimulates the technological revolution. The key problem at present is to equip agriculture with a new technique in order to increase its productivity, and apply a rational division of labour in agriculture and in the country's various regions, then on this basis to supply enough manpower for the continuous advance of industry.

In the process of socialist revolution, the establishment of a new mode of production and the building of an economic basis constitute the decisive factor, but from a subjective point of view the impact of man plays a very important role, for it is under the socialist regime that the labouring people make history consciously; moreover, the socialist system alone can liberate man from all social and natural fetters, and restore his genuine value. Indeed, there is a very great leap to make for a waged slave or an owner of a small plot of land to become a collective master of the means of production of the society. This leap requires that the labouring people profoundly understand their role as collective masters and strive to acquire the capacities and virtues needed to be the true masters of the society, of nature and of their own selves. All this shows that the *ideological and cultural revolution* acts also as an important motive force in socialist revolution.

From the ideological point of view, this revolution aims at educating and transforming the various strata of the labouring people in accordance with the requirements of the new social regime, at imbuing them with socialist ethics, with a Marxist–Leninist world outlook and a communist conception of life. From the cultural point of view, its objective is to liquidate illiteracy, raise the knowledge of the labouring people, transform backward customs and habits, and train an intelligentsia of the working class faithful to socialism. In short, the cultural and ideological revolution must on the one hand serve the revolution in the relations of production and the technological revolution, and on the other, form new men possessed of the best revolutionary virtues, the best qualifications for production, a high scientific and technical level, and a fine, rich, healthy cultural and moral life, men capable of continuing and promoting the precious national traditions while eliminating the negative aspects of the regime of small production and of the colonial and feudal society.

The socialist line of economic transformation and construction in North Vietnam is best reflected in two big movements: agricultural cooperativization and socialist industrialization. For lack of a large-scale industry, agricultural cooperativization has to go along with water conservancy and improvement of farming techniques in order to develop a diversified agriculture as *a basis for industrial development*. However, agriculture cannot advance vigorously unless it is impelled by large-scale industry. Therefore, the only way to transform the country's backward agriculture is to build a socialist industry, regarding this task as the central one of the transition period and to give priority to *heavy industry as the corner-stone of the national economy*. In the process of industrialization, one must have a correct orientation by developing both the centrally-run industry and the regional industry, by serving first of all agricultural production and the consolidation of cooperatives, and by ensuring a harmonious development for industry and agriculture so as to make national economy progress vigorously and steadily.

The three above mentioned revolutions constitute the basic content of the socialist revolution in North Vietnam, the steps to be taken by a backward agricultural country in its advance towards socialism. To bring those three revolutions, agricultural cooperativization and social industrialization to success one has to wage a fierce class struggle to solve the problem : who will win between socialism and capitalism? If formerly the struggle for power was the basic content of class struggle, now that power has been conquered, *to carry out those three revolutions constitutes the basic content of class struggle throughout the transition period towards socialism and communism. Those are also the essential tasks of the dictatorship of the proletariat.* To bring the dictatorship of the proletariat into full play the most important decisive problem is unceasingly to enhance and strengthen the leadership of the working class, to build a Marxist–Leninist Party that is staunch, united and closely linked to the masses, to strive to consolidate the worker-peasant alliance, and to rely on the workers and collective peasants as the main force to build socialism.

Socialist transformation of economy has been achieved in the main. Cooperativized agriculture has overcome many trials and proved its superiority over the former individual agriculture. After the first five-year plan (1961–5), the initial bases of heavy industry have been established together with many enterprises of light and regional industry. From 1955 to 1965 industrial production increased by 22 per cent every year and agricultural production by 4.5 per cent; the part of industrial and handicraft production in the national economy rose from 17 to 53 per cent. Education, medical work and culture also made outstanding progress: illiteracy was wiped out, nearly one out of four people went to school, the number of doctors was twenty-five times higher. These initial achievements have brought about a new strength and constitute a source of enthusiasm which stimulates the North Vietnamese people to build a happy life and resolutely defend the socialist regime.

III Vo Nguyen Giap: *War of Liberation*[51]

When US capitalism reached the stage of imperialism, the Western great powers had already divided among themselves almost all the important markets in the world. At the end of the Second World War, when the other imperialist powers had been weakened, the United States became the most powerful and the richest imperialist power. Meanwhile, the world situation was no longer the same: the balance of forces between imperialism and the socialist camp had fundamentally changed; imperialism no longer ruled over the world, nor did it play a decisive role in the development of the world situation. In the new historical conditions, US imperialism, which had a long tradition of expansion through trade, different from the classical policy of aggression through missionaries and gunboats, is all the more compelled to follow the path of neo-colonialism. The countries under its domination enjoy nominal political independence, but in fact are dependent on the United States in the economic, financial, national defence and foreign relations fields.

At the end of the Second World War US imperialism already cast covetous eyes on Vietnam and the other Indochinese countries. In the early fifties, as the situation of the French colonialists was becoming more and more desperate, the US imperialists gradually increased their 'aid' and intervention in the Indochina war. When the war ended with the defeat of the French expeditionary corps, they thought that the opportunity had come for them to take the place of the French colonialists. The images of former colonial rule now belonged to the past. The US imperialists could not, even if they wanted to do it, restore to life the decaying corpse of old colonialism. In 1954, when the defeat of the French colonialists was imminent, the US imperialists envisaged the use of 'national forces', made up of reactionary forces in the country, in an attempt to give more 'dynamism' to the war. And they began to prepare their 'special war' against the South Vietnamese people.

US neo-colonialism used its puppets in South Vietnam as its main tool to carry out its policy of aggression. Neo-colonialism derives its strength on the one hand from the economic and military potential of the metropolitan country, and on the other hand, from the social, economic and political bases of the native reactionary forces. In the South of our country, the puppet regime was set up by the US imperialists at the moment when our people had just won a brilliant victory against imperialism. That is why, since it came into being, it has never shown any vitality, and has borne the seeds of internal contradictions, crisis and war. Its social bases are extremely weak. The feudal landlord class and the comprador bourgeoisie, which had never been very strong under French rule, had become even weaker and more divided in the course of the revolution and the resistance. After peace was restored, they became still more divided, as a result of US-French contradictions.

Under those circumstances, US imperialism used every possible means to set up a relatively stable administration, camouflaged with the labels of 'independence' and 'democracy', in an attempt to rally the reactionary forces and at the same time win over and deceive other strata of the population. With this aim in view, they staged the farce of founding the 'Republic of Vietnam' in order to perpetuate the partition of our country. Their puppets, claiming to have reconquered 'independence' from the French colonialists, proclaimed a 'constitution' with provisions on 'freedom' and 'democracy', and put forth slogans of anti-communism, ordered an 'agrarian reform' and noisily publicized a programme for the 'elimination of vices' and the 'protection of good tradition', etc.

However, the puppet regime could not remain in power if they did not cling to their masters and obey the latters' orders. Outwardly, the 'Republic of Vietnam' has all the usual government organs of internal and external affairs, defence, economy and culture, but all these organs, from the central to local level, are controlled by US 'advisers'. The latter, who enjoy diplomatic privileges, are not under the jurisdiction of the puppet administration, whose civil and penal codes cannot be applied to them. They are directly under the US ambassador's control. It is US imperialism which determines the fundamental line and policies of the South Vietnam regime. Ngo Dinh Diem, fostered by US imperialism, was 'pulled out of Dulles' sleeve' after Dien Bien Phu. The Diem regime, far from springing, as it claimed, from a movement of 'national revolution', was only the result of the replacement of French masters by US masters.

Faced with a popular revolutionary upsurge, the puppet regime had to bluntly oppose the Geneva Agreements. It trampled on the people's most elementary rights and resorted to a most barbarous policy of terror and repression. For these reasons, despite the labels of 'independence' and 'democracy' and certain reforms of a demagogic character, the people immediately saw behind the puppet regime the hideous face of US imperialism which hurriedly built up and trained an army of mercenaries to be used as a tool for the repression of the revolutionary movement, carrying out their perfidious policy of pitting Asians against Asians, Vietnamese against Vietnamese. Besides, US experts have calculated that expenses for an Asian mercenary soldier are twenty-four times less than those required for an American soldier.

The South Vietnam 'national army' is staffed by puppet officers from the rank of general downwards, but this is coupled with a system of military 'advisers' controlling the puppet national defence ministry and extending down to battalion and company level, in the militia as well as the regular forces. US advisers in the puppet army supervise organization, equipment, training and operations. The US imperialists try to camouflage under the labels of 'mutual assistance' and 'self-defence' the participation of their troops in fighting. With a view to turning South Vietnam into a US military base, they have put under their effective control a large number of strategic points, all the main airfields and military ports.

Economic 'aid' is used by the imperialists as a principal means to control South Vietnam's economy. This 'aid' is essentially a way of exporting surplus goods and capital to serve their policy of expansion and war preparation. Three-quarters of the amount of yearly 'aid' derives from the sale of imported goods. The US aid organs completely ignore both the requests of the puppet regime and the needs of the country, and dump into South Vietnam market surplus farm products, luxury goods and also consumer goods that could have been produced locally. Furthermore this aid clearly has a military character. It turns South Vietnam's economy into a war economy, four-fifths of the money being used to cover the military expenses of the puppet regime. This 'aid' makes this regime totally dependent on the US imperialists.

At first the US imperialists, thinking that they could rapidly consolidate the puppet regime and stabilize the political and economic situation in South Vietnam, had prepared the ground for the signing of unequal treaties to open the way to a large-scale penetration of US finance capital. But the situation did not develop as they had expected, and so the money they invested in South Vietnam was insignificant, representing hardly two per cent of the total investments in various branches of the economy. In general, US money was invested in joint enterprises, in a very wily economic penetration. Although present conditions are not favourable to the development of the US sector in the South Vietnam economy, US 'aid' and the creation of counterpart funds have ensured to USOM (United States Operations Mission) complete control over the budget, finances and foreign trade, in fact over the whole economic structure of South Vietnam.

The comprador bourgeoisie in South Vietnam is economically entirely dependent on the imperialists—the French imperialists in former days and the US imperialists in the present time. The comprador bourgeoisie and the feudal landlord class, bound together by many ties, are two reactionary social forces colluding with the imperialists whom they efficiently serve. The comprador bourgeoisie lives on US aid, on trade with imperialist countries, and seeks joint investments with foreign capital. It includes elements from other social classes, such as the big landlords who seek refuge in the larger cities and become bourgeois. Speaking of the comprador bourgeoisie, we should first of all mention the bureaucratic comprador bourgeoisie essentially made up, in former days, of the Ngo Dinh Diem family, and at present of high-ranking puppet officials and officers who use their power to get rich quick through pillage, extortion, graft, embezzlement, hoarding and speculation, and to get hold of key positions in the economy and seize control over all the important branches.

In the new historical conditions, on account of their class character and their desperate situation in face of the victorious revolutionary movement, the pro-US forces in South Vietnam are extremely reactionary and thirst for class revenge. They are also social parasites, divorced from national production and entirely dependent on US dollars. This causes their ranks to shrink further and further, to become more and more heterogeneous and divided by conflicts of interests into rival groups, and cliques tied up with different tendencies in US political, military and intelligence circles. Their position, already not very strong in face of the powerful revolutionary upsurge, has been further weakened and their ranks have become still more divided; consequently, *coups d'état* have succeeded one another and will continue to do so until their final collapse.

Despite its material power, US imperialism has fundamental weaknesses.

1. Economically and militarily, the USA is the most powerful country in the imperialist camp. But faced with the socialist countries, the independent nationalist countries and the revolutionary peoples of the world, its strength is declining further and further. Everywhere now, US imperialism is reduced to the defensive; its forces, scattered all over the world, have proved incapable of saving it from disastrous defeats in continental China, Korea and Cuba.

2. In its aggression against South Vietnam US imperialism has revealed a fundamental weakness: it has been forced to resort to a neo-colonialist policy when important factors for the success of this policy are lacking.

First, it has to try and deceive our people and pose as a 'knight' defender of the independence, sovereignty and freedom of the peoples. But the present conjuncture in the world as well as in South Vietnam is not favourable to such a manoeuvre. Our people, with their high revolutionary consciousness, have long since recognized in US imperialism the enemy number one of the world's peoples. US imperialism unmasked itself by supporting the French colonialists during the Indochina war, a war waged with French blood and US dollars and weapons. It conceived a criminal plan in a vain attempt to save the French expeditionary corps from the

F

Dien Bien Phu disaster. Our people did not wait until 1954 to see in US imperialism an aggressor, and since that date they have even more clearly recognized that it is the enemy number one of the Vietnamese revolution and people.

Second, US imperialism cannot carry out its neo-colonialist policy without a strong support from local reactionary forces, without an outwardly 'independent and democratic' native administration and a 'national' army. But we can affirm that this extremely important, this crucial condition, which decides the fate of neo-colonialism, does not exist in South Vietnam. The reactionary forces, in the first place the most reactionary and pro-US elements of the comprador bourgeoisie and the feudal landlord class, have become extremely weak socially and economically, and completely isolated in the political field. Millions of dollars and hundreds of thousands of tons of arms will not fill this political vacuum. US imperialism will never be capable of creating a stable political regime with even an appearance of independence and democracy. US imperialism is also incapable of building up an army with any fighting spirit; however modern its equipment, the South Vietnam puppet army will never be able to consolidate its sagging morale.

Third, imperialism cannot carry out its neo-colonialist policy without revealing its aggressive nature. Repression of the revolutionary movement must be essentially the work of native reactionary forces, and the war of aggression must be waged mostly with native reactionary armed forces. But a problem arises: what if the puppet forces prove incapable of serving the aims of their masters? The only possible solution is to increase the number of US 'advisers', military personnel and combat troops, and to take part more and more directly in the war of aggression. The United States has been going further and further on this road full of insoluble contradictions.

The South Vietnamese working class, nearly one million strong and concentrated in cities and plantations, constitutes the main production force in important economic enterprises. Having to bear the triple yoke of imperialism, the bourgeois class and the feudal class, it is the most resolute, the most radically revolutionary of all social classes. In the past years the US imperialists and their puppets, using terror and corruption, and through the setting up of reactionary trade union organizations, have been endeavouring to control and divide the ranks of the workers, and to waken their class consciousness and national consciousness. However, the worker movement has been developing gradually and surely, with rich and varied forms of struggle and slogans and increasingly high organization and great solidarity. Fierce struggles regularly broke out in state enterprises under the South Vietnam puppet administration, and in enterprises under US or joint US-local comprador bourgeois management. The worker movement has been growing in intensity, going from small-scale actions to partial and general strikes, from economic claims in the interests of the workers to demands in favour of other sections of the population (such as distribution of land to the peasants, and pay increases for the soldiers) and to political slogans condemning the policy of terror and repression, denouncing the puppet administration and demanding the withdrawal of US imperialism from South Vietnam.

In recent years, the growing strength of the worker movement has resulted in the weakening of the enemy's most vital positions. It has given a strong impulse to the struggle of the labouring masses, particularly the poorer sections of the urban population, and the students in the cities. Born for the majority of families of ruined peasants, the workers, as a class, have many ties with the mass of peasants, and this has greatly facilitated the forming of the worker-peasant alliance basis of the national democratic front—and political work among those of the puppet troops who evince some degree of patriotism, most of them being sprung from the labouring peasantry.

The South Vietnamese peasantry, more than ten million strong, is the largest revolutionary force, and with the working class constitutes the main forces of the revolution. Mostly made up of landless peasants working in hard conditions and living in misery, it has long since evinced a high revolutionary spirit especially since it was placed under the leadership of the vanguard Party of the working class. Together with the latter, it rose up to conquer power, and in the ensuing years it has fought against the enemy to defend the people's power and the tillers' right to land ownership brought about by the revolution. The peasantry has gained rich experience in political and armed struggle, guerrilla warfare, organization of armed forces and the building of resistance villages.

When peace was restored, the US-Diem clique, through a so-called 'agrarian reform', heavy taxation and agricultural credit, robbed the South Vietnamese peasantry of two-thirds of the land it had been given during the resistance. The policies of 'agricultural settlements', 'prosperity zones' and 'strategic hamlets', and the permanent terror, directly and seriously threatened the peasants' lives and property. As a result, until 1959 in the South Vietnam countryside the peasantry was rapidly undergoing a process of differentiation which continues up to the present time in the zones still occupied by the enemy. For the majority of peasants, life has been seriously disrupted; working and living conditions have become unbearable, not only for landpoor and landless peasants, but also for middle peasants and even for the majority of rich peasants. The number of totally or partially unemployed persons in the countryside has been rising rapidly. A large number of peasants have been press-ganged into the puppet army, or herded into 'agricultural settlements' for forced labour; others have had to leave for the towns looking for work.

Faced with the grave danger threatening his fatherland and his own family, the peasant has resolutely taken part in political actions against the enemy and, in recent years, has risen up in a fierce, large-scale revolutionary struggle which has shaken to its foundation and broken up the puppet administration in the countryside. This revolutionary upsurge is in essence an insurrectionary movement of the mass of peasants, in which they carry out successive uprisings, to take over power at the base and reconquer the right to land ownership. A guerrilla war has been started in the rural areas, which has gradually spread to every part of the country, in opposition to the counter-revolutionary war waged by the enemy.

The petty bourgeoisie comprises the mass of small merchants and manufacturers, handicraftsmen, members of the liberal professions, civil servants, intellectuals, college students and school pupils. All these strata of the small bourgeoisie are oppressed and exploited by imperialism, the bureaucratic comprador bourgeoisie and the feudal forces. Their living conditions have been worsening. Animated with fairly strong patriotism, they sympathize with the revolution. They constitute the majority of the population of South Vietnam's towns and cities, which total nearly four million.

The small bourgeoisie's patriotism and political consciousness were heightened by the revolution of August 1945 and the resistance against the French colonialists. With the Northern half of the country completely liberated, the yoke imposed on the South by US imperialism and its puppets only stimulates their patriotism and exacerbates their hatred of the invader. For this reason, the small bourgeoisie constitutes one of the motive forces of the revolution and a sure ally of the working class which is the only leading force capable of helping them advance steadily on the road of the revolution.

In the atmosphere of terror and demagogy created by the US imperialists and their puppets in South Vietnam, a number of persons belonging to the small bourgeoisie, especially its upper strata, have fallen under the influence of reactionary forces and played into the hands of reactionary parties. Others are passive, indifferent or vacillating. However, an increasingly large section of the small bourgeoisie in the cities has shown a growing revolutionary militancy. In many urban centres the struggle movement of college students and school pupils, in coordination with that of the workers and the other poorer sections of the population, is growing in intensity, and on several occasions had a direct aggravating effect on the crisis suffered by the puppet regime in the cities. This movement will certainly play a more and more important role.

The intellectuals, college students and school pupils, though belonging to different social strata, are in general animated with ardent patriotism; only a handful have become lackeys of the enemy, or fallen under their influence. They hate the US imperialists, hate and despise the traitors. During the patriotic war against the French colonialists, they sympathized with the resistance, supported it or joined it. At present, they approve of the political programme of the National Front for Liberation, and large numbers of them are actively taking part in the struggle of the masses in the cities.

The national bourgeoisie, in the South as in the rest of the country, is economically weak, although economic enterprises in South Vietnam are generally more important than in other parts of the country. According to figures which have yet to be ascertained, in 1956 the national bourgeoisie comprised about fifteen thousand persons. Many have gone bankrupt since, and in 1963 only half of the above number were still in business, running a number of precarious enterprises. Oppressed by the imperialists and the feudal class, the national bourgeoisie to some degree evinces an anti-imperialist and anti-feudal spirit.

Following the return of peace, the South Vietnamese national bourgeoisie had expected it would get something from the policy of 'national economic rehabilitation' announced by the US–Diem clique. But US economic and military 'aid' has only aggravated the situation of the South Vietnamese economy, and the national bourgeoisie has found it more and more difficult to engage in industry and commerce. A number of national bourgeoisie joined the ranks of the compradors. As the US imperialists expand their war of aggression in an attempt to enslave our country and impose their control over all branches of the economy, the contradictions between the national bourgeoisie on the one hand and the US imperialists and their puppets on the other have become more acute. The national bourgeoisie is increasingly opposed to US imperialism and its puppets, and more and more favourable to a policy of independence, peace and neutrality. A number of national bourgeois even approve of a gradual advance towards national reunification according to the programme of the NLF. However, on account of its economic and political weakness and the fact that it has not completely severed its ties with the imperialists and their puppets, the national bourgeoisie is not determined to take the road of the revolution.

The national minorities in South Vietnam are more than twenty in number and total over a million persons living in strategically important mountainous regions which constitute two-thirds of the land. In these regions, imperialism pursues a 'divide and rule' policy, pitting the national minorities against one another and against the Kinh.* But the national minorities of South Vietnam as in the rest of the country have long since become conscious of their interests and have foiled the perfidious manoeuvres of the imperialists. Heirs to the national traditions of heroic struggle against foreign invaders, the minority people in South Vietnam greatly contributed to the triumph of the revolution of August 1945 and actively took part in the resistance against the French colonialists. At present, only a handful in the upper strata have been bought over by the enemy; the majority of people believe in the victory of the revolution and are resolutely fighting against the US imperialists and their puppets.

The religions in South Vietnam comprise Buddhism, Christianity, Caodai, Hoahao, etc. Buddhism, practised for many centuries, has no deep influence but has a relatively large number of believers. Christianity is practised by about a million persons. The Caodai religion, a synthetic religion based on Buddhism, has over a million

* Majority people–ed.

believers, mostly poor peasants. Hoahao, which is related to Buddhism, once had nearly a million believers. The religious sects were born and developed at a time when the people's revolutionary struggle was growing in intensity and scope. They have been used to some extent by the French colonialists, then by the US imperialists to further their political aims. But these sects have also suffered from division, restrictions, coercion and repression, and they are more or less opposed to imperialism and its puppets in matters of national, religious and class interests. Under Ngo Dinh Diem's rule, even among the Catholics, there were, besides those who supported the puppet administration, those who were against it. The religious sects are in general heterogeneous in their political tendencies, but, as the majority of believers are labouring people, the progressive tendency has been gaining ground.

To build and enlarge the puppet army, the Saigon administration has had to institute compulsory military service and resort to press-ganging. Owing to the development of the revolutionary war and the repeated victories of the liberation forces, opposition to war is growing in the puppet army. US imperialism is meeting with growing difficulties in the use of this puppet army against the people. Political work among the soldiers of the army enjoys more and more favourable conditions for the eventual building of a united front of workers, peasants, and soldiers to fight against the US imperialists and save the country.

The liberation war of our countrymen in the South will have to face still many difficulties and hardships, but our Southern countrymen and the Liberation Army, with unequalled heroism, have won brilliant successes and created factors of strategic significance to bring about final victory. With the growth of the people's political power and that of the revolutionary armed forces, the liberated zones are continually expanding. The development of the situation in South Vietnam eloquently proves that in a revolutionary struggle, in a revolutionary war, the decisive factor remains the human factor, the political factor, and the decisive force, the force of the popular masses.

The South Vietnamese revolution is an integral part of the world revolution. Each great event in the world has a bearing on our people's struggle; on the other hand, the influence of this struggle on the revolutionary movement in other countries is by no means insignificant. Especially in the present time, the South Vietnamese revolution in particular and the Vietnamese revolution in general are more than ever closely bound to the world situation. All the fundamental contradictions in our time have appeared in Vietnam. The national liberation movement is seething on the Asian, African and Latin American continents, dealing heavy blows to imperialism headed by US imperialism, causing the old colonial system to collapse in big chunks. During the past twenty years, over fifty countries with a population of a billion have conquered political independence in different degrees. Many countries are in full revolution. National, regional and international anti-imperialist fronts have come into being and are being consolidated, with extremely rich and varied forms of struggle.

Africa, only yesterday 'the dark continent', has become the hotbed of anti-imperialist revolution, where many countries are actively struggling against colonialism and neo-colonialism, some of them carrying out an armed struggle. In the twenty countries of Latin America, this 'backyard' of US imperialism, the national liberation movement is developing powerfully. In Asia, the national liberation movement is mounting in a powerful upsurge, especially in Southeast Asia.

The revolutionary struggle for national liberation is directly altering the balance of forces between the socialist and the imperialist camps; it is shaking the rear of imperialism, is a great support for the construction of socialism in the socialist countries, and an active contribution to world peace. It forces imperialism headed by US imperialism to scatter its forces, thus creating in the imperialist chain weak links where revolutionary situations appear which may lead the liberation struggle towards victory. This is an important aid and encouragement to the revolution in the South of our country. To cope with an uprising of the Santo Domingo people alone, the US imperialists had to send there tens of thousands of troops. What would they do when faced with other Santo Domingos?

In this third stage of the general crisis of imperialism, the contradictions among the imperialist countries are becoming ever more acute, as a result of their struggle for markets, which is conditioned by the law of unequal development of the imperialist countries and the narrowing down of territories under their control. The powerful economic growth of the capitalist countries of Western Europe and Japan in the past years more and more restricts the part of US capitalism in the world's industrial production and exports. The West European countries now have more important gold reserves than the United States. A number of countries show a tendency to become independent, to free themselves from US influence. In face of the impetuous development of the world revolutionary movement, the imperialist countries are forced to form alliances, but these alliances by no means exclude competition and contradictions. NATO is deeply divided. SEATO is dangerously cracked, due to opposition by France and Pakistan. CENTO now has only a symbolic character. With regard to a solution to the Vietnam question, conflicts of interests have caused the imperialist countries to hold different views, and the most visible contradiction is that opposing France to the United States.

In the West European countries and in Japan, the large working masses resolutely support the Vietnamese people's just struggle and severely condemn the US imperialists' war of aggression. These great historical changes have created objective conditions which are extremely favourable to the world revolution and to the South Vietnamese revolution. The world revolution follows a complex process of development, a zigzag course, but it continually forges ahead.

Recently, in the ranks of the international communist movement, which is the vanguard force in our time, differences have appeared, but they have only a temporary character and revolutionary practice will certainly iron them out. In face of imperialism, the common enemy, which more and more clearly reveals its aggressive and bellicose nature, the true communists in the world will close their ranks. The communist parties will come out stronger than ever of this struggle for the defence of Marxism–Leninism against modern revisionism, the principal threat to the international communist movement. The imperialists are seeking to exploit the differences in the socialist camp and the international communist movement. In the Vietnam question, the US imperialists are also endeavouring to make full use of these differences. A front of the world's peoples against imperialism headed by US imperialism has come into being, which comprises the socialist countries as the main force, and the oppressed peoples, the working class in capitalist countries and the forces of peace and democracy. This front is developing and being consolidated continuously; it cannot be weakened by any reactionary force.

F*

The position of US imperialism in the world today is no longer what it was at the end of the Second World War. Not only has it not succeeded in achieving world hegemony, but even its supremacy in the capitalist world has been badly shaken. It no longer holds an atomic monopoly and can no longer blackmail the peoples of the world. Today, the Soviet Union has built up a powerful system of defence and holds a leading position in space researches. The People's Republic of China now has its atomic bomb. US imperialism has been forced to change its military strategy, passing from 'massive retaliation', aimed at attacking the socialist camp, to 'flexible response' with the immediate aim of suppressing the national liberation movement, while frantically preparing for a new world war. Everywhere, it has been unmasked as an international gendarme, and this has greatly impaired its political prestige and aroused opposition by all the nations in whose affairs it intervenes. Never has US imperialism found itself so isolated in the world. Lately, it has been forced to ask its allies to help it get out of the South Vietnam quagmire. But, besides some important satellites such as South Korea, Thailand, Taiwan, Australia, and New Zealand, most of its friends give only verbal support or stand aloof. The French government has publicly disapproved of US armed aggression in Indochina and advocates the neutralization of all the countries of South-east Asia. It has withdrawn its delegation from SEATO. French imperialism is the most important buyer of South Vietnamese goods, and French investments at times represent fifty per cent of the total investments in South Vietnam; French property is valued at two billion francs; ninety per cent of the rubber areas and a large number of light industrial enterprises belong to French capitalists. No wonder that such a situation has led to acute contradictions between France and the United States. The governments of Great Britain and Japan, though lately taken in tow by the United States in political matters, have expressed anxiety about US policy of war expansion, which they fear may bring severe defeats to imperialism. Until 1965, the contributions by US satellites in the war of aggression in South Vietnam represented hardly three per cent of the total expenses. The contributions in manpower and equipment have somewhat increased but are still very small. Formerly, when the French expeditionary corps found itself in difficulties, it could expect assistance from the United States. Today, the US imperialists, bogged down in South Vietnam, can expect aid from nobody. If in the Korean war the US imperialists managed to get the support of the majority of UN member countries, today they cannot even use the flag of this organization.

During the first years of the resistance against the French colonialists, our country was surrounded by hostile neighbours. But the liberation war now being waged by the South Vietnamese people enjoys much more favourable conditions. The South is carrying out its struggle at a time when the other half of the country has been liberated, and the neighbouring countries are friendly : Laos is heroically fighting against US imperialism and its puppets, and the Kingdom of Cambodia is resolutely defending its active neutrality. Furthermore, Vietnam as a whole is geographically linked with the mighty socialist camp; she is a close neighbour of China and lies in the heart of the zone of revolutionary tempest in South-east Asia where large masses are rising up in revolutionary struggle and the Marxist–Leninist parties have gained a rich experience in revolutionary leadership. South Vietnam, regarded by US imperialism as the main link in its South-east Asia strategy, is now on the front line of the national liberation movement in this part of the world. And our country as a whole is regarded as the centre of the peoples' revolutionary struggle against US imperialism. Directed against a common enemy, the revolutionary movement now developing in South-east Asia and other parts of the world constitutes an effective support and a great encouragement for the Vietnamese people. On the other hand, our people's *glorious international duty* is to fight resolutely against US imperialism until final victory so as to actively contribute to the defence of peace in Indochina, South-east Asia and the world.

KOREA

Among Asian revolutionaries, the sharpest and, at times, loudest 'Guevarist' is North Korea's Premier, Kim Il Sung. Born Kim Sung Chu in the far north in 1912 and raised in Manchuria, Kim fought with the Chinese communist guerrillas until 1941, then went to Russia and returned to Korea with Russian troops in 1945 as a Soviet army major. Immediately active in the pro-Russian Korean CP, he was instrumental in convincing the pro-Chinese group, known as the New People's Party, to merge with his in 1948. The result was the Korean Workers' Party and Kim was the head of it, becoming also Premier of North Korea. Taking the name of one of Korea's legendary anti-Japanese guerrilla fighters, Kim Il Sung consolidated his position in 1950, purged first the pro-Russian elements out of the Party, then the pro-Chinese. In the 1960s Kim led his country to phenomenal economic success and agricultural self-subsistency, and guided his party into a very militant internationalist yet independent stance. On 5 October 1964 he enthusiastically supported Fidel Castro's call for volunteers to Vietnam. As he does in the following article, he has often criticized Russia's 'modern revisionism' and its peaceful coexistence line, but he has also told China to stop deciding who's right and who's wrong according to pro-Chinese allegiances. 'It is impossible,' Kim has said, 'that any one country can become the "centre of world revolution".'

In the article that follows — a 1965 speech rounded out with a 1966 article for Cuba's Tricontinental *magazine — Kim not only gives a neat, if somewhat pat, résumé of Korea's revolutionary experience but also explains his (and his party's) view of revolutionary activity. That experience, of course, is primarily based on a Chinese-type protracted 'liberation' or 'patriotic' war against a foreign invader (Japan, which seized Korea in 1910). Like Mao, Kim believed then that social revolution proceeded in two stages, first against an outside enemy, then against inside counter-revolutionaries (i.e. the class struggle). For the first, all 'patriots' are partners;*

during the second all class-enemies as well as deviationists, opportu-
nists, revisionists, etc., have to be eliminated. And Kim did just that
—in the North. Because his country was divided, he insisted that
communists consolidate their power first, then move to the offensive,
South or elsewhere. In this sense, he was a strict old-time Leninist,
uncompromising in his addiction to rigid 'democratic centralism',
that is, Party Central Committee leadership. 'Fortify the Party, the
general staff of the revolution,' he says, 'and rally the broad masses
of the people around it.'

But to turn North Korea into an economic miracle, Kim felt
obliged to Koreanize its communism. First of all, he had to get his
people to work as never before, and so established the 'Chollima'
myth or the winged horse meant to symbolize work, and generate
an almost supernatural identification of national pride with indi-
vidual production. Then he fostered a form of national Marxism,
which he called Juche, heralding Korea's 'national peculiarities'.
Fundamentally, Juche simply means that Korea, though struggling
to establish communism, has every right, in fact is obliged, to do so
not according to established Marxist precepts but within national
traditions. In effect, then, Juche is the opposite of dogmatism; as
such, it was only a question of time before Kim lashed out, as he
does here, at the 'worshippers of the great powers'—i.e., Russia and
China. Forced back onto themselves, Korean communists were then
totally dependent on their people, not only materially—North
Korea has received almost no aid from the socialist world since the
Korean War ended—but culturally as well. Hence direct continuous
contact between the leaders and the led became an absolute neces-
sity. And so, Kim developed the 'ri' method, whereby each and
every cadreman, Kim himself included, had to go and live in the
simplest of Korean communities—the ri—at regular intervals. The
ri spirit became a form of renewing the life-line or blood of the
ruling elite. It certainly served to keep the leadership popular and
accessible, and, conversely, taught the leadership to trust the people.
One tangible revolutionary result has been that the Korean CP has
not been afraid to arm its people. Another has been the people's
constantly growing revolutionary consciousness, and, consequently,
its feeling of solidarity with other revolutionaries. Thus, North
Korea has become more and more militant, willing to help not only
South Koreans but also any revolutionary in Asia, (or indeed in the
world) to overthrow the US. Having begun as a Chinese-trained

Moscow-educated 'compromise' communist who benefited very little from Soviet 'internationalism' or Chinese 'solidarity' (after the Korean War), Kim Il Sung ended up a national communist, totally committed to international revolutionary solidarity—a circuitous though not really paradoxical route.

Kim Il Sung: '*Juche*' and Revolutionary Solidarity[52]

The nation-wide March First Uprising in 1919 under the impact of the October Revolution demonstrated the militant patriotic spirit and the revolutionary vigour of the Korean people, but, on the other hand, in its failure it revealed all the limitations and weaknesses of bourgeois nationalism. In the 1920s the working class grew in strength and took an active part in the struggle. Many workers', peasants' and youth organizations appeared and workers' strikes and other forms of mass struggles were unfolded. Then, in 1925, the founding of the Korean Communist Party tried to give new impetus to the development of the working-class, peasant and national-liberation movements. Under its leadership the 10 June Independence Movement took place and mass struggles of the workers and peasants against the Japanese imperialists, landlords and capitalists gained in scope. But in those days communists carried on their activities in difficult conditions in which Japanese imperialism was resorting to severe suppression and the Party itself was suffering from serious weaknesses. Most of the leading posts of the Party were held by the petty-bourgeois careerists; the Party organizations did not take root among the working class and the broad strata of the masses. Worse still, acute factional strife rendered it impossible for the Party to preserve the unity of its ranks. Consequently, it ceased to exist as an organized force three years after its foundation. This shows that the communist movement in Korea was then in the cradle and that the subjective and objective conditions were yet unripe for the movement.

From the late 1920s to the early 1930s the tyranny of Japanese imperialism grew unprecedentedly cruel, depriving the Koreans of every possibility of legal struggle. But such violent suppression was countered by the intensified violent struggle of the workers and peasants.* In this situation it was inevitable that our revolutionary workers and peasants organized and unfolded an armed struggle. Under the leadership of communists our revolutionary army then carried on sanguinary warfare for fifteen long years and, fighting battles shoulder to shoulder with the Chinese People's Army and the Soviet Army to wipe out the Japanese imperialists, won the historic victory of the country's liberation at last.

Thus, the communist movement in Korea grew in scope and strength in the course of the protracted anti-Japanese struggle for national liberation, and in the 1940s it was possible to found our Party on a solid basis even in the complicated circumstances after the country's liberation.

After the 15 August 1945 liberation, however, new, grave difficulties cropped up before the Korean revolution.

The US imperialists occupied South Korea; the reactionaries at home and from abroad flocked there; former lackeys of Japanese imperialism were turned into stooges of US imperialism. We were confronted with the aggressive policy of the US imperialists who were not only opposed to the Korean revolution and the building of a unified independent state by the Korean people but were also seeking to extend their influence to North Korea. Therefore, for the time being, it was inevitable to carry on the Korean communist revolutionary movement in the North and the South separately, under different circumstances and in different forms.

In the North, under the leadership of the Party, our people's power successfully carried out democratic reforms including the land reform and the nationalization of industries with the support and participation of the broad masses of the people. On the basis of the implementation of the democratic reforms, construction in the economic and cultural fields made swift headway and the people's livelihood, too, became stable. At the same time, our Party, in order to defend the gains of the revolution, founded the people's armed forces with the revolutionary cadres fostered and steeled in the course of the long-drawn anti-Japanese armed struggle as the backbone.

In this way the anti-imperialist, anti-feudal democratic revolu-

---

* Among the most violent were the general strike of the Wonsan dockers in 1929, of the workers of the Sinhung Colliery and Pyongyang rubber goods factories in 1930, of the farmers of the Buri Farm in Ryongchon in 1929 and of the peasants in Danchon in 1930 and Yonghung in 1931–ed.

tion was completed in the northern part of Korea in one or two short years following the liberation. As a result, the northern part began to develop as the reliable base of the Korean revolution. It is the decisive guarantee for victory in the revolutionary struggle as well as the construction work to build up the revolutionary force, that is, to fortify the Party, the general staff of the revolution, and rally the broad masses of the people around it. The merging of our Party and the New Democratic Party to form the Workers' Party, a united political party of the labouring masses, was an epochal event in reinforcing our revolutionary forces. As a result of the merger, our Party became a mass political party embracing in its ranks the advanced elements not only of the working class but also of the labouring peasants and the intellectuals serving the working people.*

The war imposed upon us by the US imperialism and its stooges was the sternest trial for our Party and our people. The Korean people and the Korean People's Army, in concert with the Chinese People's Volunteers and enjoying the unanimous support of the peoples of all the socialist countries, waged a heroic struggle to repulse the armed invasion of the enemy and defended the independence of the country and the gains of the revolution. And the US imperialists suffered a miserable military defeat for the first time in the history of the United States. This meant the beginning of a downhill turn for US imperialism. With the serious wound received in this war yet unhealed, the US imperialists have been incessantly running the gauntlet of the revolutionary peoples of the world, and now they are sinking ever deeper into the morass of ruin.

In the postwar period, the socialist revolution and socialist construction became the mature requirements for the socio-economic development in the northern part of Korea. They were urgently needed also for the political and economic reinforcement of our revolutionary base and for the acceleration of the country's unification and the victory of the Korean revolution as a whole.

Following the armistice, therefore, our Party concentrated its efforts, first of all, on rehabilitating the war-ravaged national economy and on stabilizing and improving the livelihood of the people which had deteriorated during the war, while vigorously pushing forward the socialist revolution. The Party put forward the line of

* What he calls here the New Democratic Party was the New People's Party, which was pro-Chinese. The regular Party was Moscowphile—ed.

giving priority to the growth of heavy industry and simultaneously developing light industry and agriculture to decisively reinforce the country's economic basis and ensure a stable livelihood for the people in a short time. Further, the Party's line of actively carrying out the socialist transformation of production relations in parallel with the reconstruction made it possible to recover the productive forces at an early date and open up a broad avenue for their further growth. Industrial and agricultural production were not merely restored to their pre-war levels but raised far above them.

Then the historic December 1956 Plenum of the Party Central Committee gave rise to the unprecedented upsurge of the political and labour zeal of our working people, to a great upsurge in socialist construction and to the great Chollima movement.* Amid such revolutionary upsurge, in 1958 the cooperativization of agriculture and the socialist transformation of private trade and industry were completed. The basis of our own heavy industry with the machine-building industry as its backbone has been created; light industry has also made rapid progress. Our agriculture has been turned into a firm socialist rural economy and is being equipped with new techniques. The problems of food, clothing and housing of the people have been solved in the main, and their material and cultural standards have been improved generally.

In the early post-armistice days the enemy used to prattle that North Korea would be unable to rise to its feet again even in a hundred years. However, our people under the leadership of the Party, in ten years after the war, not only reconstructed the economy on the war debris but also eliminated the centuries-old backwardness and poverty, turned their country into a socialist industrial-agricultural state and built up towns and villages more beautifully than ever.†

* Chollima, the winged horse, symbolizing work, is like a national 'totem' in North Korea, says Charles Meyer. 'There is no other symbol in the whole world which is so dynamic and effective'–ed.

† Joan Robinson, the well-known English economist, visited Korea in October 1964, and reported that, 'Eleven years ago in Pyongyang there was not one stone standing upon another (they reckon that one bomb, of a ton or more, was dropped per head of population). Now a modern city of a million inhabitants stands on two sides of the wide river, with broad tree-lined streets of five-story blocks, public buildings, a stadium, theatres . . . a city without slums.' She added[53] that seventy per cent of villages had electric light in each cottage, that North Korea was 'a nation without poverty [or] illiteracy.' Calling it the 'Korean Miracle', she attributed its success to 'enthusiasm rather than excessive toil'–ed.

The postwar rehabilitation and construction in our country were carried on in the midst of the fierce struggle against the ceaseless subversive activities of the US imperialists and their lackeys and against indescribable economic difficulties and privations. Particularly, as the socialist revolution was carried out on a full scale, class struggle grew very acute. Such struggle unfolding in our society could not but find its reflection within the Party; various opportunist trends raised their heads, against which the Party launched a vigorous struggle. The struggle against factionalism and for strengthening the Party's unity, the struggle against dogmatism and for establishing *Juche,** and the struggle against modern revisionism and for safeguarding the purity of Marxism–Leninism, were the main struggles in the postwar years on the ideological front within the Party.

The composition of our Party was complex due to the fact that the Party itself was young, that it was organized by bringing together the communist groups which had been active separately in different parts of the country and that it developed rapidly into a mass political party after the merger with the New Democratic Party. This is why the Party has always paid the greatest attention to the strengthening of the unit and solidarity of its ranks. We have safeguarded the unity of the Party by reinforcing the core of the Party and tirelessly educating and rallying all the Party members.

The struggle for the unity and cohesion of the Party was unthinkable without the work for establishing *Juche*. Our Party has always held fast to the general prinicples of Marxism–Leninism and at the same time adhered to the creative position of rejecting dogmatism and adopting Marxism–Leninism in conformity with our own historical conditions and national peculiarities. The Party has always maintained the independent position of opposing reliance on others, displaying the spirit of self-reliance and solving its own problems entirely by itself, while constantly strengthening the

* In another speech (to Party Propagandists and Agitators, 28 December 1955) Kim Il Sung defined *Juche* as 'abiding by the principle of solving all problems of the revolution and construction independently in accordance with the actual conditions of one's own country and primarily by one's own efforts. This implies a creative application of Marxism–Leninism and the experience of the international revolutionary movement in keeping with the historic conditions and national peculiarities of one's own country. It also signifies independent solution of one's problems in the revolutionary struggle and construction by displaying the spirit of self-reliance.' Under this *Juche* form of independent Marxism–Leninism, Koreans concentrate intensely on national pride as well as national wrongs or errors.–ed.

solidarity and cooperation with the international revolutionary forces. *Juche* in ideology, independence in politics, self-reliance in economy and self-defence in national defence—these have been the Party's consistent position and line.*

But some obstinate dogmatists infected with flunkeyism towards the great powers continued to obstruct the implementation of the Party's correct lines and policies, doing harm to our work. All the factionalists who appeared in our Party were, without exception, dogmatists and the worshippers of the great powers. They even ignored the history, culture and revolutionary traditions of their own country, not to speak of the actual conditions at home, and thus degenerated into national-nihilists who looked down upon everything that was their own and looked up to everything that was from abroad. They did not have any faith in the strength of their own country, only willing to rely on others in everything.

As modern revisionism was getting rampant in the international communist movement, our fight against factionalism and dogmatism came to be combined with the struggle against the former. In our country revisionists were disseminating first of all illusions about US imperialism, and they tried to divert our Party and people from resolutely fighting against it. They also opposed the socialist revolution in our country, prattling that it was as yet premature; they opposed our Party's line of socialist industrialization, the line of the construction of an independent national economy in particular; and they even brought economic pressure to bear upon us inflicting tremendous losses upon our socialist construction. The aim of the modern revisionists was, in the final analysis, to make our Party betray Marxism–Leninism and revolution, give up the anti-US struggle and take the road of Right capitulationism, following them in their steps.

While the Patriotic War of Liberation was the grimmest struggle against the imperialist aggressive forces and the domestic reactionary forces in the twenty-year history of our Party, the anti-opportunist struggle in the post war period was the most serious struggle against the enemy within the communist movement. Through this struggle our Party was further steeled and strengthened and gained plenty of experiences and lessons. We fortified our

---

* Soviet aid dwindled to insignificant amounts shortly after the Korean War. Joan Robinson reported[54] that North Korea was ninety-three per cent self-sufficient in machine production by 1964–ed.

revolutionary stronghold and opened up a broader highway for our revolution and construction work.

To put the mass line into practice, it is necessary to constantly improve the system and method of Party work on the one hand and, on the other, steadily enhance the level of the political consciousness and ideology of the masses. We carried out a great deal of organizational and ideological work to establish a revolutionary system of work throughout the Party and to help the functionaries rid themselves of bureaucracy and acquire a revolutionary method of work by relying on the masses. The Chongsan-ri spirit and the Chongsan-ri method* signify an embodiment and development of the revolutionary mass line which is a tradition of our Party, in conformity to the new realities of socialist construction. The essentials of the Chongsan-ri method are that the higher organ helps the lower, the superior assists his inferiors and always goes down to work places to have a good grasp of the actual conditions there and to find correct solutions to problems, and gives priority to political work or work with people in all activities to give full pay to the conscious enthusiasm and creative initiative of the masses so as to ensure the fulfilment of revolutionary tasks. This method is not only a powerful method of work enabling us to carry out the immediate revolutionary tasks successfully and substantially, but a powerful method of education that enhances the ideological and political levels and practical ability of the functionaries and revolutionizes the masses.

With the spread of the Chongsan-ri method, a change was brought about in the work of the Party, state and economic organs and the level of leadership of the functionaries in these organs was raised considerably. Since the Chongsan-ri method was accepted by the masses, the work of educating and remoulding the masses became the work of the working people themselves, developing into their mass movement for remoulding ideology. The implementation of the mass line and the generalization of the Chongsan-ri method tended to further enhance the leading role of the Party, expanded and reinforced our revolutionary ranks rapidly and gave a powerful

* A 'ri' is the lowest administrative unit in the countryside. The spirit and method Kim Il Sung is talking about is the now widespread tradition of leaders going to live in such ris periodically in order to learn from the base as well as to maintain contact with the people. Kim himself does so very frequently, in fact worked out Korea's agricultural reorganization plan after spending fifteen days in a remote ri—ed.

impetus to the upswing in socialist construction and the Chollima movement. The Party has done a tremendous work to reinforce the People's Army, arm the entire people and turn the whole country into a fortress, and has thus built up a strong self-defence capable of safeguarding the country and revolution against the encroachment of the enemy.

Our Party always deems the revolution and construction in the northern part of Korea part of the Korean revolution and regards North Korea as the revolutionary base for accomplishing the cause of national liberation throughout the whole of Korea. While steadily pushing forward the revolution and fortifying the revolutionary base in the North, the Party has invariably striven to support the revolutionary struggle of the people in South Korea, liberate it from the yoke of US imperialism and achieve the country's unification. The American imperialists occupying South Korea, taking the place of the Japanese imperialists, have held sway over South Korea as new colonial rulers. Since the first day of their landing in South Korea, they have pursued the aim of reducing it to a colony as well as a military base for establishing their domination over the whole of Korea and for aggression in the Far East and Asia. From this aim have stemmed all the policies the US imperialists have followed in South Korea over the past twenty years.

The US imperialists' rule over South Korea has nothing essentially different from the rule of the Japanese imperialists in the past. The difference, if any, is that whereas Japanese imperialism ruled Korea through a governor-general, today the US imperialists dominate South Korea by the more cunning neo-colonialist method of using the puppet regime as their instrument. The so-called government in South Korea serves as a screen for legalizing the military occupation of US imperialism and covering up its colonial rule, and plays the role of a tool faithfully executing the aggressive policy of US imperialism.

The revolution in South Korea is an anti-imperialist, anti-feudal democratic revolution resulting from the contradictions between the US imperialist aggressive forces and landlords, comprador capitalists and reactionary bureaucrats who are in alliance with them on the one hand, and the workers, peasants, intellectuals, youth and students and people of other social strata in South Korea on the other, and this revolution is an integral part of the Korean revolution as a whole.

Immediately after the surrender of Japanese imperialism, in South Korea, too, as in North Korea, revolutionary potentialities of the masses of the people erupted like a volcano and the patriotic democratic forces grew rapidly. Communists came out from the underground and the Communist Party was organized and began its activities; and the people's committees, the people's organs of political power, were formed all over South Korea. The successive national-salvation struggles included that waged by the miners of the Hwasun coal-mine near Kwangju, the peasant riot on Haui Island in August 1946, the September general strike, the October popular resistance, the 7 February 1948 protest against the 10 May separate elections and the soldiers' mutiny in Ryosu in the same year.* The revolutionary struggle was frustrated temporarily, however, by the infiltration activities of the US imperialists' agents and by factional elements who had wormed their way into the leading body of the Communist Party. By 1949 the Party organizations were completely destroyed. But the patriotic people in South Korea did not stop fighting. The heroic struggle waged by the Masan citizens against the fraudulent 15 March (1960) elections conducted by the Syngman Rhee regime was a signal indicating that the national-salvation struggle of the South Korean people had entered a new stage. In the April Popular Uprising, the people in South Korea toppled the regime of Syngman Rhee, an old-time minion of the US imperialists.

Frightened by this, the US imperialists and their lackeys staged a military coup and tried to stifle the national-salvation struggle of the South Korean people by resorting to fascist suppression. Nevertheless, the patriotic youth, students and people in South Korea have fought heroically against the 'South Korea-Japan talks' in

* The Hwasun coal-miners began by celebrating, on 15 August 1946, the first anniversary of Korea's liberation, went on to protest at US occupation and were finally dispersed by US troops and local police using tanks and killing scores of workers; a few days later, some 700 peasants of Haui attacked the local branch of the New Korea Company, a US-military land exploration agency and were dispersed by gunfire; the September 1946 general strike, started by 40,000 railway workers demanding better living conditions, spread to 400,000 before the US authorities gave in to some of the demands; the October riots mushroomed after the USA fired on 10,000 demonstrators in Taegu, eventually led to the USA declaring a state of siege and firing repeatedly into the up to two million protesters against occupation, killing literally thousands; the 7 February 1948 revolt, launched by students against separate (North-South) elections imposed by the USA through a UN commission, led to a nation-wide protest and fairly successful boycott of the elections–ed.

defiance of the harsh repression by the traitorous Pak Jung Hi clique and are now carrying on their brave struggle for shattering the 'South Korea–Japan agreements'. The series of demonstrations staged in June 1964 and again in August 1965 were anti-imperialist, anti-fascist and for the overthrow of the traitorous clique. The people have come to realize that, so long as the US imperialist colonial domination continues, no solution can be found for any problem by the mere replacement of one US puppet with another, and that the winning of genuine freedom and liberation and the achievement of the country's unification are possible only when the US aggressors are driven out, US imperialist colonial rule is eliminated root and branch and the people seize the political power in their own hands.

The revolution in South Korea has to deal with a strong enemy armed to the teeth, and it still has a tortuous way to go. However, the South Korean people have a tradition of valiant fight against foreign aggressors and internal reaction. And they are not alone in their struggle. They have a powerful revolutionary base in North Korea and enjoy the active support of its people. Our Party and all the people in the North will do everything in their power to support the revolutionary struggle of the people in South Korea and will resolutely fight together with them for the complete liberation and independence of all Korea.

Our Party, always regarding it as the prime internationalist duty for Korean communists and the Korean people to carry out the Korean revolution, makes every effort to promote the development of the international revolutionary movement as a whole.

It is the consistent policy of our Party in international affairs to safeguard the unity of the socialist camp and the solidarity of the international communist movement, to develop the relations of friendship and cooperation with the newly independent countries in Asia, Africa and Latin America, to support the anti-imperialist national-liberation movements of the peoples in these regions and the revolutionary movements of the peoples in all countries, to oppose the imperialist policy of aggression and war and to strive for world peace and the progress of mankind.*

* The following insert is from an article written by Kim Il Sung in 1967.[55] I have included it here because it follows naturally from Kim's 1965 speech while also developing his foreign policy views and commitment to the armed struggle line of the Third World–ed.

In January 1966, the Tricontinental Peoples' Solidarity Organization was founded in Havana. It was an event of very great importance. The aims and ideals of this organization have aroused the sympathy of hundreds of millions of Asian, African and Latin American people and are exerting profound influence on the course of the great changes taking place in the world today. Millions of people in the three continents are fighting for liberation and for the safeguarding of the achievements of the revolution they have already attained. The people who have achieved independence should crush the subversive activities of the foreign imperialists and domestic reactionary forces, tear down their economic footholds, strengthen the revolutionary forces, strive to set up a progressive social system and build an independent national economy and national culture. Only by so doing, can one safeguard the gains of the revolution, achieve the prosperity of the country and the nation and contribute to the common struggle of the peoples of the world over for burying imperialism.

Asia, Africa and Latin America hold seventy-two per cent of the land surface of the globe. These continents are inhabited by more than two-thirds of the world population and endowed with inexhaustible natural wealth. Imperialism grew and fattened by grinding down the peoples of those continents and robbing them of their riches. Still now imperialism is squeezing tens of billions of dollars of profits from these continents every year. The anti-imperialist, anti-colonialist struggle of the peoples of Asia, Africa and Latin America is a sacred liberation struggle of hundreds of millions of oppressed and humiliated people, and, at the same time, a great struggle for cutting the lifeline of world imperialism in these areas. Together with the revolutionary struggle of the international working class for socialism, this struggle is a component of the two major revolutionary forces of our times. These struggles are linked up together in one current which will carry imperialism to its grave.

The imperialists cannot make a gift of independence to colonial peoples. The oppressed peoples can liberate themselves only through their struggle. This is a simple and clear truth confirmed by history. It is necessary to expose the false propaganda of the imperialists and thoroughly dissipate the illusion that the imperialists will give away their position in the colonies and dependent countries with good grace. Where there is oppression, there is resistance. This is the rule. It remains as an inalienable right of the oppressed nations to rise in arms and fight against the aggressors.

It is wrong to avoid the struggle against imperialism under the pretext that, though independence and revoluton are important, peace is still more precious. Genuine peace will not come unless a struggle is waged against the breakers of peace, unless the slave's peace is rejected and the rule of the oppressors is overthrown. We are opposed to the line of compromise with imperialism. At the same time, we cannot tolerate either the practice of only talking big of opposing imperialism, but, indeed, being afraid of fighting against imperialism.

In order to fight against imperialism, it is important first of all to direct the spearhead of attack on US imperialism. There is not a country on the globe whose sovereignty is not violated by US imperialism or which is free from the menace of US imperialist aggression. When Africa and Latin America are not free, Asia cannot enjoy freedom. On the other hand, victory on one front against US imperialism will sap its strength that much, facilitating victory on other fronts. Therefore, it is necessary to form the broadest possible anti-US united front to isolate US imperialism thoroughly, and administer blows to it by united strength everywhere it is engaged in aggression. Only by so doing is it possible to disperse and weaken the force of US imperialism to the last degree and lead the people on every front to beat US imperialism with overwhelming power.

The US imperialists are afraid of the united strength of the revolutionary peoples of the world more than anything else. That is why they are resorting to all kinds of tricks to obstruct the formation of an anti-US united front and have adopted the stratagem of subduing weak and small countries one by one. This stratagem of US imperialism must be thoroughly frustrated. The Asian, African and Latin American countries have differing social systems, and many parties with differing political views exist in these countries. But all these countries and parties, except the stooges of imperialism, have common interests in opposing the imperialist forces of aggression headed by US imperialism. The difference in social systems and political ideals can never be an obstacle to the joint struggle and concerted action against US imperialism. No one must be allowed to split the anti-US united front and refuse joint action, attaching the first importance to his own nation's or party's specific interests.

It is very important in the joint struggle against imperialism to defend the revolution which has already triumphed. It is an internationalist duty of all the revolutionary peoples to fight in defence of the gains of the Cuban revolution. The revolutionary Cuba represents the future of Latin America and its very existence encourages the peoples of this continent in their liberation movement. It is for this very reason that the US imperialists hate and are afraid of so much of this small island country. Today, the Vietnamese people's resistance war of national salvation against the US invasion troops has become the focal point of the anti-imperialist struggle. The US troops are sustaining one defeat after another by the heroic resistance of the Vietnamese people. The Vietnamese people's resistance war proves once again clearly that people who are determined to defend their independence and freedom at whatever sacrifice, and who have the support of the peoples of the whole world, are invincible.

We must neither underestimate nor overestimate the strength of US imperialism. US imperialism can still commit lots more crimes. But US imperialism is on the decline. The Korean War revealed that US imperialism is by no means invulnerable, but can be beaten in fighting. The triumph of the Cuban revolution has proved again this truth under circumstances different from ours. The Vietnamese people's resistance war of national salvation, too, clearly confirms this truth. By fighting in union against the US-led imperialists, the people of Asia, Africa, and Latin America, independent and prosperous, will make a great contribution to world peace and the liberation of mankind.*

To strengthen the international revolutionary forces and vigorously push forward the anti-imperialist struggle of the peoples, we must fight against modern revisionism. The biggest harm of modern revisionism lies in the fact that, scared by the nuclear blackmail of US imperialism, it surrenders to the latter, gives up the struggle against imperialism and compromises with it, restrains and undermines the liberation struggle of the oppressed nations and the exploited peoples. Revisionism still remains the main danger in the international communist movement today.

We are communists fighting against imperialism and for revolution. The unity of the socialist camp and the solidarity of the international communist movement are unthinkable without the anti-

* End of Kim's 1967 article insert.

imperialist struggle. Our Party will develop a common struggle together with the fraternal parties and countries in opposing imperialism headed by US imperialism, and in supporting the revolutionary movement of the peoples, and will, through this struggle, endeavour to strengthen our unity. Our immediate supreme task at the moment is to liberate South Korea. The whole Party and the entire people must oppose all manifestations of indolence and weariness, sharpen vigilance and maintain an unslackening attitude at all times. We should never become the prey of pacifist feelings, and above all must wage a powerful ideological struggle to prevent the penetration into our ranks of the ideological trend of the modern revisionists who are afraid of war. We do not want war but do not fear it.

INDONESIA

As a result of the October 1965 military coup which overthrew President Sukarno, the revolutionary theory and practice of the Indonesian Communist Party have been clearly exposed—and criticized. What emerges is that the CPI (or PKI, for Partai Kommunis Indonesia) was an incredibly dogmatic, elitist and opportunist party obsessed with its own erroneous analysis of conditions, both objective (the class and economic structure) and subjective (the various forces' leaderships). These mistakes were due, in turn, mostly to the fact that the PKI was so Stalinist, and later Maoist, in orientation and allegiance that it stifled every independent or national outlook within its cadre. Incredibly, however, it persistently refused to prepare itself for armed struggle—on the grounds that the 'United National Front' of anti-imperialist forces which it fostered was a growing reality. That 'front' turned out to be totally illusory and the consequences, over the years since 1948, has been the assassination of more than one million communists.

The PKI was launched in 1920 and, almost from the start, its leader, Dipa Nusantara Aidit, repeated the slogans, but rarely the logic, of Russia's revolutionaries. Thus, though the PKI created armed guerrillas during the Second World War to fight the Japanese invaders, it fought only according to Stalin's 'cooperative' wartime policy, that is, in Indonesia's case, under the direction of the Dutch colonialists—with the vague hope that the reward might be 'an independent Indonesia within the Commonwealth of the Dutch Empire'. Never did the PKI even contemplate an agrarian reform or establishing liberated areas during this period, and when the war of liberation began—launched by Sukarno's Nationalist Party —against the Dutch and British colonialists, the PKI again fought bravely but only for independence. Chairman Aidit's concept of two-stage revolution was so liberal that, although many sectors of the national bourgeoisie sided with the enemy, he would brand any Indonesian Communist who opposed the alliance with the 'middle *sectors'* as a left deviationist. As late as 1964, Aidit was still insisting on such an alliance. 'The success and completeness of the leadership of the working class in the revolution,' he wrote in Be a Good and a Better Communist, 'will be determined by the success of the alliance between the workers and the national bourgeoisie.' To talk of socialism or Soviets was unprincipled deviationism, he went on, adding as 'proof' of his argument: 'In his speech to the students at the University of the Peoples of the East on 18 May 1925, Stalin said that this left deviation contained within it the danger of isolating the party from the masses.'

After the 'August 1945 Revolution' ended successfully in 1947 with Indonesian independence, Aidit obeyed Stalin again and ordered his troops to surrender their arms. At that time Indonesia didn't even have a regular army, but the PKI leaders gave the reactionary government the time to create one and in 1948 the 'National Armed Forces', led by the same Abdul Nasution who became co-leader and dictator of the 1965 coup, launched an anticommunist terror campaign in which thousands of communist resistance fighters were massacred. Still, Aidit, his top aide M. H. Lukman and other members of the Central Committee refused to prepare for armed struggle. By 'emphasizing' that 'we are going to make this possibility' of a transition to socialism by peaceful means 'a reality, we can thereby show the people that if violence does occur, it was not started by the communists,' Lukman explained in About the Constitution (1959).

The PKI's fallacious analysis was also grounded in Aidit's absurd reliance on the urban workers as the main revolutionary force. In a country where peasants comprise more than sixty per cent of the population but where the 'proletariat' at most (by including agricultural workers) includes less than twenty per cent, Aidit dogmatically insisted that only the workers could lead 'the masses'. This was partly due to the fact that the PKI leadership was city-based and had relatively little contact with the countryside. More importantly, however, it was based on the proletariat's visible 'politization', a factor which, the Guevarists will say later, has confused revolutionary parties almost everywhere in the underdeveloped world. For though it is true that urban workers join unions and militate constantly for better conditions, it is equally true that they feel more integrated into the capitalist economy than peasants and are easier to buy off, frighten or delude.

All together the fiasco of the Indonesian 'revolution' before 1965 shows that communists cannot and do not always control 'fronts' that they create; that revolutionary principles and practice must never be sacrificed for growth in numbers (from 1945 to 1965, the PKI's membership grew from 19,000 to 3,000,000); that the first of the two-stage revolution is, as Mao himself said, inseparably linked to the second; that the two stages work only when a foreign invader generates a people's war and the revolutionary party uses it to create liberated areas or bases; that no ruling elite ever willingly gives up power to its class enemy; and that the national bourgeoisie and any 'proletarian element' that becomes incorporated into it (such as the armed forces) can never be trusted as an ally. Aidit and the whole PKI's Central Committee violated each and every one of these propositions. Manipulated by the national bourgeoisie, which was in power through President Sukarno, the PKI kept insisting that as long as 'pro-people elements' were in the government and in the army, there was nothing to fear. Shortly before the coup, Aidit stated: 'We will not be provoked. If the army spits in our faces we will wipe it off and smile. We will not retaliate. Time is on our side. We shall win without a struggle.'

On 30 September–1 October 1965, the army did not spit in Aidit's face. It cut it off. Lukman, too, was killed, as were seven other Central Committee men—and anywhere from 300,000 to 1,000,000 communists (700,000 is probably the most accurate figure; se L'Express, Paris 23–29 May 1965). One member of the Central Committee who escaped, as he was in Peking at the time, was Jesuf Aditorop. He has since become head of the PKI—in exile. But all that he seems to have learned from the disaster was that the Party should have been ready for protracted armed struggle. The short passages by Aidit and Aditorop included below are meant simply to acquaint the reader with their thinking. The third article, by a young PKI member with Trotskyist connections, is more serious. It reflects the kind of analysis carried out in 1966 and 1967 in Indonesia proper where communists, having slowly reorganized in clandestinity, are now waging an armed struggle, apparently the beginning of a protracted people's war—without worrying very much about what the surviving PKI leadership is proclaiming from its Peking sanctuary.

I D. N. Aidit: *Fragments*[56]

As we give leadership to the bitter, difficult and protracted struggle of the people, we must adopt tactics of taking the revolutionary struggle of the Indonesian people forward slowly and cautiously, but surely. In the course of carrying out this protracted struggle, we must unceasingly oppose two deviations, the deviations of surrenderism and adventurism, both of which originate from petty bourgeois wavering. Since the enemies of the people make use of all forms of struggle, we too must be skilful at making use of all forms of struggle. We must be skilful at utilizing all forms of open and legal struggle, the forms which are permitted according to law and the regulations, and according to habits and customs in society. The Fourth Plenum of the Central Committee of the CPI drew attention, among other things, to the fact that we 'must be vigilant and must always hold ourselves in readiness and prepare the people in all respects so that the reactionaries will not be able to stand in the way of the people's desire to achieve fundamental social changes peacefully, by parliamentary means'. Of course, the CPI's activities are not confined to parliamentary work alone but also and especially include activities among the masses, the masses of workers, the peasants, the intellectuals and other masses of working people and democratic masses. All these activities, both within and outside Parliament, are aimed at changing the balance of forces between the imperialists, the landlord class and the compradors on the one hand and the forces of the people on the other. In order to attain the objectives of the Party, we must, in making use of these forms of struggle, base ourselves on the principles of justice, advantage and a knowledge of how far we can go.

The CPI Programme states that 'the workers, the peasants, the petty bourgeoisie and the national bourgeoisie must unite in one national front'. The national front is the unification of the progressive and the middle-of-the-road forces. The middle-of-the-road forces are basically the forces of the national bourgeoisie. The CPI Programme also states that the way out of the semi-colonial and semi-feudal situation lies in 'changing the balance of forces between the imperialists, the landlord class and the comprador bourgeoisie on the one hand, and the forces of the people on the other. The way out lies in arousing, mobilizing and organizing the masses, especially the workers and the peasants.' The Fourth Plenum of the

CPI Central Committee (held at the end of July 1956) stated among other things that there are in Indonesian society three forces—the die-hard forces, the middle-of-the-road forces and the progressive forces. It further stated that at the present time the forces of the people, that is the combination between the progressive forces and the middle-of-the-road forces, are striving for the formation of an Indonesian state which is independent in the political and economic spheres.

Although the Indonesian proletariat contains within it certain unavoidable weaknesses, such as for example its smallness in number by comparison with the peasants, its young age by comparison with the proletariat in capitalist countries and the low level of its culture by comparison with the bourgeoisie, it is nevertheless the basic force pushing the Indonesian revolution forward. The Indonesian revolution will not succeed unless it is under the leadership of the Indonesian proletariat. As a recent example, the August Revolution was successful in the beginning because the proletariat more or less consciously took an important part in it, but later on the revolution suffered defeat because the role of the proletariat was pushed into the background and the upper strata of the bourgeoisie betrayed the alliance with the proletariat. Without the proletariat taking an active part, nothing will ever run properly in Indonesian society. This has already been proved and will continue to be proved by history and experience. It must be understood that although the Indonesian proletariat is the class which has the highest political consciousness and organizational understanding, the victory of the revolution can never be achieved without the revolutionary unity under all circumstances with all other revolutionary classes and groups. The proletariat must build up a revolutionary front. Of the classes in society, the peasants are the firmest and most reliable ally of the working class, the urban petty bourgeoisie is a reliable ally, and the national bourgeoisie is an ally under certain circumstances and within certain limits: this is the fundamental law which has already been and is being proved by Indonesia's modern history.

The workers, the peasants, the petty bourgeoisie and the national bourgeoisie are the people, and make up the forces of the revolution, the forces of the united national front.

The CPI Programme has the following to say, among other things: 'Bearing in mind the backwardness of the economy of our country, the CPI is of the opinion that this government (the People's

Democratic government) is not a government of the dictatorship of the proletariat but a government of the dictatorship of the people. This government does not have to carry out socialist changes but democratic changes.' In other words, the character of the Indonesian revolution at the present stage is not a proletarian-socialist revolution but a bourgeois democratic revolution. We can determine the character of our revolution after we understand the specific conditions of Indonesian society which is still semi-colonial and semi-feudal, after knowing that the enemies of the Indonesian revolution at the present time are imperialism and the feudal forces, that the tasks of the Indonesian revolution are to complete the national revolution and the democratic revolution so as to overthrow the two basic enemies (imperialism and feudalism), that the national bourgeoisie can also take part in this revolution and that if the big bourgeoisie betray the revolution and become an enemy of the revolution the direct blows of the revolution must continue to be aimed more at imperialism and feudalism than at capitalism and private ownership of the national capitalists in general.

Since the Indonesian revolution at the present stage is marked by world socialist construction and the disintegration of world capitalism, there can be no doubt that the future of the Indonesian revolution is not capitalism but socialism and communism. Whether we like it or not, whether we agree or not, whether we oppose it or not, this is the perspective for the Indonesian revolution. But do not the perspectives of 'socialism' and 'communism' conflict with the objective of the revolution at the present stage which 'should not carry out socialist changes but democratic changes'? No, there is no conflict. It is indeed so that, seen from one angle, a capitalist economy will develop within certain bounds after the victory of the people's democratic revolution in view of the fact that the obstacles standing in the way of capitalism's growth will have been swept aside. But this is not surprising nor should it be cause for anxiety. The growth within certain bounds of national capitalism is only one aspect of the victory of the Indonesian revolution. Another aspect is that the victory of the democratic revolution will mean the development of *socialist factors*, such as the growing political influence of the proletariat, the growing recognition by the peasants, the intellectuals and other petty-bourgeois elements of the leadership of the proletariat, the growth of state enterprises as well as cooperatives among the peasants, the handicraftsmen, the fisher-

G

men and other sections of the people. All these are socialist factors which provide the guarantee that the future of the Indonesian revolution is socialism and not capitalism.

II Jesuf Aditorop: *Our Mistake*[57]

In drawing lessons from the bitter experiences, it must be pointed out that one of the most important causes of the setback in the revolutionary struggle of our people is the mistake committed by the PKI in appraising the class nature of the state power in Indonesia. In reality, after 1949 when the reactionary Hatta government concluded the Round Table Conference Agreements with the Dutch imperialists, the state of the Republic of Indonesia has become an instrument in the hands of the Indonesian comprador bourgeoisie and landlords to protect the interests of imperialism and to maintain the remnants of feudalism, as well as to suppress the people, especially the workers and the peasants, who wage the struggle against imperialism and feudal vestiges. The revolutionary struggle of the Indonesian people since 1949 had achieved certain results which diminished the anti-democratic character of the bourgeois power. But this by no means altered fundamentally the class nature of this power. The exaggerated assessment of the gains of the revolutionary struggle in this period have given birth to the 'theory' that the state power of the Republic of Indonesia was composed of two aspects, the 'anti-people aspect' and the 'pro-people aspect'. According to this erroneous 'two-aspect theory', the state ceases to be the instrument of suppression in the hands of the ruling classes against other classes but can be made an instrument shared by both the oppressor and the oppressed classes. This 'theory' had led to the illusion that the fundamental change in state power, that is to say the birth of a people's power, could be peacefully accomplished by developing the 'pro-people aspect' and gradually liquidating the 'anti-people aspect'. In practice, this 'theory' had deprived the proletariat of its independence in the united front with the national bourgeoisie, dissolved the interests of the proletariat in a position of tail-end of the national bourgeoisie.

To return the proletariat to the position of leadership in the struggle for emancipation of the Indonesian people, it is absolutely necessary for the PKI to rectify the error of the 'two-aspect theory' and to establish the correct Marxist–Leninist principles on state and revolution. The PKI has stated that: 'the people will come to power only through an armed revolution under the leadership of the working class, to overthrow the power of the comprador bourgeoisie, the bureaucrat-capitalists and the landlords who represent the interests of imperialism and the remnants of feudalism.' At the same time our party has also emphasized that 'the armed struggle to defeat the armed counter-revolution must not be waged in the form of military adventurism, or in the form of a putsch, which is detached from the awakening of the popular masses', and that 'it is the people who will liberate themselves'.

The events in Indonesia have demonstrated the utter bankruptcy of the 'peaceful-road theory' in whatever form, and the danger it has brought to the revolutionary movement. These events have shown with what great sacrifices the proletarian party has to pay, when it harbours even the slightest illusion in the 'peaceful road', and when it abandons the principles of people's war in solving the contradictions between the people and the domestic reactionary classes. This is the most important lesson from the bitter experiences of Indonesia.

III T. Soedarso: *Lesson for the Future**[58]

Reports have appeared with increasing frequency recently, indicating that armed resistance is being mounted by the Indonesian revolutionary forces against the brutal suppressive measures of the Indonesian military-fascist regime. The armed struggle is occurring not only in Central Java, an area considered to be the stronghold of the revolutionary movement, but also in other islands of the republic.

This armed struggle, however, is still uncoordinated. It is still sporadic and anarchistic in nature. It still lacks leadership, either political or military, capable of organizing an armed uprising. It seems that the Communist Party of Indonesia has not recovered from its defeat.

* The author is a young member of the PKI.

It is true, of course, that the future of the Indonesian revolutionary movement has not been destroyed—it cannot be. The movement will rise again in a mightier force that will finally end the system of exploitation of man by man in Indonesia. But it is a fact that it has suffered a serious defeat and setback.

Nevertheless there are some to be found who still do not regard it as a defeat but as a 'blessing in disguise'; since now the line between friend and foe is very clear and the people really know that 'it is not we who resort to violence but the reactionaries'. Such people still maintain that the past policies of the party were quite correct, the recent catastrophe being merely a 'routine' incident in the revolutionary struggle. 'Sacrifices always occur,' they say. Thus these people do not consider it necessary to analyse the previous policies, strategy and tactics of the party; they even argue that it is 'premature' to attempt this or 'it is very dangerous because it can lead to a split in our movement'. Their advice is to 'just continue the struggle in line with the past policy, only with more caution and vigilance'.

This stand is not correct. We must dare to uncover the mistakes of the past that led to this failure. And we must have the courage to make the necessary corrections so that we won't fall into the same fatal errors again. Criticism and self-criticism are necessities for a healthy revolutionary movement.

This was the most fundamental error: the PKI believed that socialism in Indonesia could be achieved by peaceful means. As stated in the constitution of the PKI: 'To achieve its goal, the PKI follows peaceful and democratic ways. This is what is sought by the PKI and what will be consistently pursued.'[59] And the second secretary of the Central Committee of the PKI, M. H. Lukman, explained:

From the theoretical point of view, to affirm the possibility of a transition to socialism by peaceful means signifies affirming the truth that Marxism–Leninism does not point to absolutely the same road for socialism in all countries in different periods and in different international conditions. This also means that we Marxist–Leninists do not bind ourselves to certain forms, methods and roads of completing the revolution, because everything depends on the concrete balance of power among the existing classes, on the quality of the working class organization and its enemy, on the ability of the working class to attract its allies to its side, especially the peasants, and on taking into account the existence of democratic institutions in each country.

In the same speech, Lukman said further:

In accordance with the teachings of Marx and Lenin, namely by taking into account the objective conditions of the world balance of power between the socialist and democratic forces on the one hand, and the imperialist forces on the other, and considering the experiences in the East European countries where the transition to socialism did not occur through a civil war, Comrade Khrushchev at the Twentieth Congress of the CSPU stated the conclusion that in the present situation certain countries have a real possibility of reaching socialism in a peaceful way.[60]

It is therefore understandable why the PKI was unprepared for armed struggle when the crisis came last October. The PKI concentrated activity only on the 'legal' or 'parliamentary democratic' platform. It completely ignored preparations for armed struggle by the workers and peasants under the leadership of the working-class party. This was well-known to the reactionary forces; consequently they launched a quick brutal action to liquidate the revolutionary forces. The only hope for the revolutionary forces was to seek safe retreats, but it was already too late. The toll was very high.

Because of this belief in a peaceful way of achieving socialism, and perhaps especially because of the advice of 'Comrade' Stalin and later 'Comrade' Khrushchev, the leadership of the PKI willingly, if not even faithfully, followed Sukarno's personal leadership and teachings. Sukarno was considered by the party to be a 'pro-people's element' and even the 'great leader of the revolution'. The reactionary forces brutally massacred members of the PKI and other revolutionary forces in the name of Sukarno; yet Second Secretary Njoto still said, 'The PKI recognizes only one head of the state, one supreme commander, one great leader of the revolution—President Sukarno.' Furthermore, 'It is President Sukarno united with the forces of the people who will decide the destiny and future of Indonesia.' In accordance with the 10 October 1965 instructions of the Political Bureau of the Central Committee of the PKI, Njoto continued, all Party members should 'fully support the directives of President Sukarno and pledge themselves to implement these without reserve'. (The 10 October instructions have not been withdrawn to this day.) The party was still seeking to maintain the peaceful road. Njoto said, 'Our party is making every effort in its power to prevent a civil war.'[61]

As for the Indonesian Armed Forces, the PKI held that they constituted forces of the people, since the ranks were made up of the sons of workers and peasants. This viewpoint was maintained even after the '1 October affair', Njoto saying : 'We do not consider the Indonesian National Forces to be like the armies of imperialist countries or the army of India. When you appraise an army, you should study and take into account the history of its formation, its role in the struggle against imperialism and feudalism, its composition which is mainly made up of former poor peasants or workers. It is true that there are still anti-people's elements within the National Forces of Indonesia. This is also true concerning the republic as a whole.' And he stated that 'our party has never had its own army'.[62]

It was argued that it was necessary to follow a policy based on the possibility of a peaceful transition to socialism in order to counteract the propaganda of the reactionary forces; i.e., the propaganda that the communists are 'terrorists', 'monsters', etc. But what was the result? The repudiation of the use of armed struggle in achieving revolutionary goals only demonstrated the weakness of the revolutionary forces in the eyes of the reactionaries and created a feeling of insecurity among the masses.

The propaganda of the reactionaries can be counteracted by explanations and by action. The facts of history constitute the best source to show the people the cruelty and brutality of the reactionaries. For example, the massacre committed by the reactionary Hatta government in 1948; the brutal 'August Razzia' committed by the reactionary Sukiman government in 1951; the brutal armed suppression carried out by the reactionary generals against the peasantry in Sumatra, Java, Sulawesi and other islands; the bombings carried out with planes furnished by the imperialist US and the massacre committed by the reactionary rebels in 1958, etc. Past experience provides the best lessons for teaching the people about the brutality of the reactionaries and the necessity to resist such brutality through armed struggle.

And the propaganda of action is still more important. The people will trust communists and have real confidence in the party if communists genuinely defend their interests and show themselves prepared through sacrifice and armed struggle to safeguard the people from oppression and suppression by the exploiting classes. Communists must demonstrate that they are really cadres of working class and really on the side of the exploited masses; and are not merely pleaders with the 'haves' nor collaborators with the 'good people'.

The Cuban *Granma* was quite correct when it said editorially:

> We are not denying that in a given country, under certain very special conditions, an exception could occur in the future; nevertheless, not one case can be cited of a victorious revolution which has been able to avoid the use of violence, insurrection or armed struggle as fundamental methods. This is a universal experience and the political position of the communist parties must be developed by taking into account what has been learned in the practical experience of revolution and by probing deeply into it.[63]

In the development of the Indonesian revolution, many opportunities arose for the PKI to mobilize the workers and peasants into revolutionary armed forces and to counteract and liquidate the reactionary elements in the 'National Armed Forces of Indonesia'. These opportunities were ignored. For example, during the campaign for the liberation of West Irian from Dutch colonialism, the people were mobilized into voluntary units in anticipation of a clash with the Dutch imperialist forces. This should have been utilized by the Party to mobilize the workers and peasants and to set up bases for armed struggle. The Party did engage in this, but not with the objective of carrying out a socialist revolution. The movement was limited to liberating West Irian and it was disarmed after this aim was achieved.

Again, during the campaign to crush the neo-colonialist regime of 'Malaysia', the Party contributed greatly in mobilizing the masses, but without bringing in the idea of armed struggle for the socialist revolution. Thus the chance slipped by to set up bases for armed revolutionary struggle. Even worse, the Party left the leadership of the voluntary units in the hands of reactionary generals.

Another excellent opportunity came during the campaign for unilateral action to take over the land belonging to the big landowners. This action was led by the PKI. Day by day hundreds of thousands of peasants took part in the action. They faced armed suppression by the feudal forces backed by the reactionary generals. But the party did not organize armed units of the peasants to counter-attack. It left it up to the peasants to organize their own defence on the basis of their own courage and initiative. When this developed into a near revolutionary crisis, with many clashes between the peasants and the reactionary forces, the campaign was stopped. The 'great leader of the revolution' Sukarno had given the order or 'revolutionary command' to stop 'any unilateral action'. He gave the 'command' that 'every conflict or difference should be solved by consultation and agreement'.

In accordance with the appeal from Sukarno in this situation, Aidit proposed the so-called 'NASAKOM Code of Ethics'.* Among other things this laid down the following: 'Among all NASAKOM or MANIPOLIST groups there must be no confrontation. Only consultation to reach agreement.'[64] Blood had been shed by the people, but the action was stopped. As the slogan put it, 'We should have revolutionary patience'.

During the struggle against the Japanese military occupation, the PKI was instructed or 'advised', under Stalin's guidance, to co-operate with the Dutch imperialist government, to carry out 'joint actions' against Japanese imperialism. (This also applied to all the other communist parties, who were told to cooperate with their respective bourgeois governments in fighting against the Axis.) Through such cooperation, the PKI hoped to 'earn' independence for Indonesia at the end of the war. The programme of the PKI as well as the CPN [Communist Party of the Netherlands] called for an 'independent Indonesia within the Commonwealth of the Dutch Empire' as a step toward full independence. This remained a utopian dream. At the end of the war, the Dutch with the backing of the British and US imperialists sent their armed divisions to re-occupy Indonesia. What attitude did the PKI take toward this?

A republic had been proclaimed under the leadership of the bourgeois Sukarno. The masses as a whole were completely ready to defend their newly proclaimed republic. But the PKI still clung to the old programme of establishing Indonesia 'within the Commonwealth of the Dutch Empire'. Thus they followed the line of compromise in face of Dutch aggression. They supported the policy of the reactionary Sjahrir government in signing the Linggadjati Agreement, compromising with Dutch imperialism in 1947.

Then, still worse, the following government under Amir Sjari-fuddin (a PKI leader at the time) signed the so-called 'Renville Agreement'. Under this catastrophic agreement all pockets of the guerrilla forces were to withdraw from Dutch-occupied territory. The reactionary forces used this opportunity to send in reactionary

---

* NASAKOM is an abbreviation for National–Religion–Communism – ed.

armed units (under the command of Nasution, the present co-dictator) to dominate the liberated areas.

Realizing his mistake, Amir Sjarifuddin voluntarily surrendered his government back to Sukarno. This was followed by the formation of the most reactionary government, i.e., the Hatta regime. Under instructions from the US and Dutch imperialists, this government introduced a programme of 'rationalizing' the Indonesian armed forces, which meant liquidating the people's armed units. The Hatta government wanted only 'one type of army'; that is, the so-called 'Indonesian National Armed Forces'.

In 1948, Musso, who was one of the PKI leaders of the twenties and thirties, returned from abroad and called for a 'New Road' for the PKI. Among other things this demanded renunciation of the old policy of compromise. The correction was accepted by the majority of the PKI leaders. But it was too late. Before the PKI could consolidate itself under the new programme, the reactionary Hatta government launched a 'white terror' in the so-called 'Madium Affair'. Thousands of party members and most of the leaders were killed. This affair should have been a salutary lesson for the PKI not to abandon the method of armed struggle. Yet it was not.

When a federal republic was established under the so-called 'Round Table Conference' agreement, the PKI held it best to continue the struggle by 'peaceful democratic' means. Aidit explained this as follows: 'Against this RTC agreement which was signed on 2 November 1949, by Hatta's government under instructions from US imperialism, there were two opposing viewpoints in the party ... the first group wanted to continue armed struggle against the federal republic of the RTC ... while the second, who based their position on revolutionary theory ... wanted to maintain the party's legality'; that is, continue the struggle by 'parliamentary democratic' means.[65] Thus was a beginning provided for the repetition of the old errors.

On the question of the 'Indonesian National Armed Forces', it is not correct to say that they are not 'like the armies of imperialist countries or the army of India'. At the beginning of the August 1945 Revolution there were no regular armed forces. Throughout the islands, the people formed their own armed units for defence against the imperialist aggression. There were many kinds of units. The PKI built a Red Army, and had big influence on the Lasjkar Buruh [Workers' Army], Lasjkar Pesindo [Army of the Socialist

G*

Youth], Lasjkar Rakjat [People's Army] and Tentara Peladjar [Students' Corps].' Following the programme of 'rationalization' under Hatta, most of the irregular armies were liquidated. The most reactionary forces remained. After the RTC Agreement a new 'National Armed Forces' was formed. This was an arithmetic combination of the previous Indonesian 'National Armed Forces' plus the 'Dutch East Indies Troops'. These Dutch Troops (of Indonesian nationality) were much better trained. The remnants of the progressive units within the Indonesian National Armed Forces were subsequently liquidated. Of course, there were still some 'pro-people's' elements within the Indonesian National Armed Forces, but as a whole they belong to the same classification as the 'armies of imperialist countries or the army of India'.

The PKI followed the theory of two stages to the revolution: namely, a national democratic stage followed by a socialist stage.

'To confuse the two stages of the Indonesian revolution and to say that we are already building socialism is demagogic, subjective and reactionary. The national democratic stage constitutes preparation for the socialist stage. The socialist stage cannot be achieved without first completing the national democratic stage.'[66] This was the stand of the PKI. It was said that this national democratic stage constituted in essence a bourgeois democratic stage, but of a new type; namely, one led by the working class.[67]

According to the party's analysis, Indonesia at present still has a semi-colonial and semi-feudal system. And there are 'three forces within Indonesian society; namely, first the die-hards, i.e., the feudalists and compradors who collaborate with the imperialists. This is still a big force, but it is declining. Second, the progressive forces, i.e., the workers, peasants, petty bourgeoisie and revolutionary intellectuals. This force is rather large and is increasing. Third, the middle-of-the-road forces, i.e., the national bourgeoisie and all other patriotic and other anti-colonial forces, including the left group of landowners. This force is rather large. It stands between the reactionary and the progressive forces.'[68]

About the alleged necessity to build a united front with the national bourgeoisie, Aidit said: '... I would like to emphasize once more that although an alliance with the national bourgeoisie is not as important as an alliance with the peasants, *the success and completeness of the leadership of the working class in the revolution will be determined by the success of the alliance between the workers* *and the national bourgeoisie.** Therefore the communists must strive with all their power to preserve and further develop the alliance with the national bourgeoisie.'[69] And anyone in the party who opposed the alliance with the national bourgeoisie was branded a 'left deviationist'.

In reality, following the policy of an alliance between the working class and the national bourgeoisie, the party undermined the alliance between the working class and the peasants. The leadership of the 'United National Front' was never in the hands of the working class or its party, but always in the hands of the national or comprador bourgeoisie. In reality this line led to multi-class collaboration under the leadership of the national bourgeoisie, degenerating into compromises in ideology and in action under cover of the so-called 'musjawarah for mufakat' (consulting to reach agreement).

Full acceptance of the so-called 'Pantja-Sila philosophy'† (a product of the 'genius-like thinking' of Sukarno) is an example of the open ideological compromise reflecting the 'success' of multi-class collaboration. According to Aidit, 'Pantja-Sila is a philosophy for unity.... In Indonesia one finds Catholic philosophy, Islamic philosophy, Buddhist philosophy, Protestant philosophy, Black Magic philosophy, Mystic philosophy ... and Pantja-Sila unites what can be united.'[70] In the same speech he said further: 'The philosophy of Pantja-Sila cannot be separated from the philosophy of Empu Tantular "Bhinneka Tuggal Ika" or "Unity in Diversity". This is very dialectical. "Unity in Diversity"—differences, but in unity.... I do not agree with liquidation of not only these various kinds of philosophy but also political parties. In the second stage of the revolution and the next stages ... because so long as differences remain among us, "Unity in Diversity" and also Pantja-Sila will still be applicable. And in my opinion these differences *will exist forever* ... thus in my opinion Pantja-Sila is also everlasting.'‡ Is such a statement Marxist? Yet Aidit said, 'I accept Pantja-Sila also from the Marxist–Leninist viewpoint.' (In the same speech.)

Similar conclusions hold for the PKI's acceptance of the 'genuine concept' of NASAKOM proposed by the demagogic bourgeois

---

* Author's italics.

† Pantja-Sila is 'Five Principles': belief in a single god, national unity, humanitarianism, democracy and social justice.

‡ Author's italics.

Sukarno. Aidit said, 'Besides *uniting various kinds of classes and groups,* the National Front also unites various kinds of revolutionary ideas ... namely: Islam, Nationalism and Communism. ... In the traditional struggle for national independence in Indonesia, we can find three political streams which were against Dutch colonialism: namely, nationalist, religious and communist political thought. Thus it is natural to say there will be national unity in Indonesia if these three political currents unite within the NASA-KOM cooperation.' And Aidit said, 'This united national front has found its organization : namely, the "National Front".' At the top it is 'headed by President Sukarno himself, who with his vice-presidents reflects the cooperation of NASAKOM ... showing us how deeply rooted is the idea of the national united front among the masses. Now it is our duty to work hard to foster and consolidate it.'[71]

During the struggle against the Dutch colonial power, it is true, there were many political groupings all of which were against the foreign imperialist rulers. But we could also see which were truly revolutionary, which were quasi-revolutionary, and which were opportunist. For example, the PNI [the Indonesian Nationalist Party founded by Sukarno] was clearly bourgeois. Then it degenerated into a vehicle of the national bourgeoisie, bureaucrats, compradors and bribers. Thus during the struggle it always swung opportunistically. And in times of revolutionary crisis it was always on the side of the reactionary forces. A clear example was provided during the 'Madium Affair' in 1948 when it served as the 'vanguard' of the reactionary forces that murdered thousands of communist cadres and revolutionary rank and filers. Sukarno himself at the time issued the challenge : 'Join Sukarno or Musso'.

Again in the recent period (1964), during the campaign for unilateral action in taking over the land belonging to the big landowners, the members of this nationalist party joined in suppressing the peasant movement; and the 'most progressive' leader of this party issued an order to 'stop any unilateral action'. Yet the PNI was considered by the PKI to be its true partner in the NASAKOM cooperation as the representative of the nationalist political stream.

Similarly with the Nadhatul Ulama, an Islamic scholars' party. The NU was very clearly the party of the feudalists and landowners. They used Islam as a cover for their reactionary activities in preserving their landownership and exploitation of the peasants. There is no instance in Indonesian history where this party has played a progressive or revolutionary role. Yet the PKI sought to preserve unity with the NU within the so-called NASAKOM co-operation.

Besides the nationalist and religious parties in the so-called 'National Front' led by Sukarno, there were other reactionary elements, including the generals. Thus the so-called 'National Front' was not a revolutionary front led by the working class. It was not even the united front depicted theoretically in the documents of the PKI; namely, a united front of the working class, peasants, petty bourgeoisie and national bourgeoisie led by the working class. It was clearly collaboration of all classes under the leadership of the demagogic bourgeois Sukarno.

Of course, the PKI cannot and must not struggle alone; the working class must not struggle alone. It needs allies. It should not isolate itself from the masses; but the masses are not the national bourgeoisie! In a country like Indonesia, in which poor peasants constitute more than sixty per cent of the population, peasants are the real ally of the working class. The peasants should become the army of the revolutionary movement led by the working class. Poor city dwellers or the petty bourgeoisie are reserves to be drawn upon.

Towards the national bourgeoisie there should be a cautious and vigilant attitude. The revolutionary movement could and should support the progressive attitudes or actions of the national bourgeoisie, but there should be no class collaboration with the national bourgeoisie, since this can undermine the alliance between the working class and the peasants. The Communist Party should have its own policy based on the demands and experience of the most revolutionary class.

There is, naturally, the influence of Islamic teachings and nationalist thinking among the masses. This should be considered in propaganda work and in enlightening the masses. But it should never mask the class character of the struggle. The masses should be clear that this struggle is a class struggle and not a religious or racial struggle. The struggle is to overthrow the exploiters, to crush and abolish the system of exploitation of man by man. And the masses should even have a very concrete picture in their minds of the true character of the ruling class—the compradors, the bribers, the usurers, the feudalists, the ruling-class apparatus, the reactionary government apparatus, etc. They must be shown how and trained to overthrow these reactionary agencies. Only by such means can the united front among all the oppressed classes be tempered, strengthened and made militant. Not through pleading with the 'national bourgeoisie'.

The PKI's programme calls for making the party 'both a mass party and a cadre party'. In 1952 the membership was only 10,000. In the national conference held that year it was decided 'to expand the membership from 10,000 to 100,000 *within six months*'.*[72] And after the implementation of the first 'Three-Year Plan' (1956-9), the membership increased to 1,500,000. At mid-year 1965 it was reported in the press to have reached 3,000,000. It is an amazing growth. A mass production of communist cadres! Perhaps no precedent exists for this in the history of communist parties. But is it guaranteed that all of these three million members were good revolutionists? Perhaps the CIA agents knew the answer to this better than the members themselves, so that the reactionary forces dared to launch a brutal and massive suppression of the PKI. Of course, the rapid recruitment by the PKI frightened the reactionary forces, but apparently they recognized the fatal weakness of the organization better than did the members of the PKI.

Obviously it is not easy to turn out good revolutionists with mass-production methods. Aidit himself recognized the inherent weakness in this rapid growth and mass production of members. For example, he said:

In the beginning they become party members because they seek protection from the rising revolutionary tide of the peasants. But their cultural level is higher than that of the agricultural workers and poor peasants, therefore within a short time they occupy the chair of leadership in the party and for the time being the peasants grant them their trust. Besides there are cadres who joined the party during the armed struggle in 1945 or even before then, thus in the days before the party had an agrarian programme. At the time they were good cadres; they implemented the party's policy with high spirits against imperialism and took an active part in the campaign to crush the reactionary rebellion. But they are not agrarian cadres.[73]

Yet the slogan still remained, 'Both mass party and cadre party'. The fact is that the real cadres of the party stood at a distance from the mass members of the party. Thus the structure of the party was

* Author's emphasis.

more or less like a mass organization. The cadres did not completely trust the mass members and tended to form many tight, secret rings within the party. The bureaucratic character of the party was thus intensified. And in a time of crisis like last October, the party could do nothing. Instead of issuing instructions on what to do to counteract the brutal massacre initiated by the reactionary forces, the top leadership scurried for safe spots (some of them going to President Sukarno's palace) which they knew about in advance, leaving the mass members in the lurch. Even two months after the disaster there were still many in the rank and file who did not really know what was going on until they were massacred.

Experience shows that it is necessary to build a party of real cadres who have a correct political line, who are actively engaged in political work among the workers and peasants, and who dare to conduct an armed struggle to achieve the goals of the revolution. The party must have a programme 'which reflects the thought and experience of an authentic revolutionary movement, aims at really aiding the highest possible revolutionary activity of the working class, while starting out from its most elementary demands'. There can be no secrecy among the members, since all are cadres, while democratic centralism must rule. Everything is discussed by all members, but all act in unity!

Because of its policy of seeking to achieve socialism by means of a 'parliamentary democratic' struggle and building a false 'united national front', the party concentrated its struggle at the top instead of the bottom. Collaboration at the top was considered to be the best way to inch towards socialism. Activities centred around the 'coalition cabinet' beginning in 1955, then around the 'cooperation cabinet' in 1959, the last one being the 'NASAKOM cabinet' in 1963. The party sought to gain power through 'working together' with its enemies.

Considerable progress was registered throughout this period. The masses were moving towards a revolutionary crisis. But they were not armed—not armed with a correct political line and not armed with real weapons to crush the reactionary ruling class. The peasants were set in motion to take over the land, to smash the domination of the feudalists. But there was no clear political line. And even the land take-overs were stopped because of the 'impending probable' formation of a 'NASAKOM cabinet'.

The party did not protest the banning of strikes in industry because industry was considered to belong to the government, which was almost 'a government of NASAKOM'.

The party did not issue instructions to counteract the military-fascist suppression through armed struggle because 'Sukarno is still at the top', the 'pro-people elements are still in the government'.

The above criticism is not intended to undermine the role of the PKI nor to arouse distrust in Indonesian communism. But the revolutionary movement in Indonesia will be successful only if it learns from past experience, if it learns not to repeat the same mistakes. Only true revolutionists have the courage to correct errors. Criticism and self-criticism constitute the best method of reaching a more correct line. Mistakes are bad, but not to understand the mistakes is worse; and the worst is not to correct a mistake, having recognized it.

The situation is now quite favourable for a new line. People in arms are to be found everywhere. The line between friend and foe is very clear. The brutal character of the reactionary forces is very obvious. The opportunistic character of a bourgeois leader like Sukarno is very clear. Whether the leadership of the party likes it or not, the masses cannot wait out the increasing massacre against them any longer. What is needed now is a politically correct, class-conscious and militant leadership, which will lead an armed struggle to abolish the whole system of exploitation of man by man in Indonesia and establish a workers' state!

PHILIPPINES

Since the beginning of the Second World War the history of the revolutionary movement of the Philippines has been the history of the Huks. Organized mainly by members of the Communist Party (Partodi Komunista ng Pilipinas—PKP) as a patriotic guerrilla force in 1942, the Huks were originally called the 'People's Army to Fight the Japanese' (Hukbo ng Bayan Laban sa Hapon or Hukbalahap). Basically nationalistic in ideology, they were perfectly willing to cooperate with the allies, and always did when asked—despite the fact that the other Philippine wartime guerrilla group, the US-led USAFFE force which General MacArthur left behind when he retreated in 1942, often attacked the Huks even when both were pursued by the Japanese. It was the Huks and not the USA or USAFFE which liberated most of Central Luzon, including Manila. Yet even before the Japanese had been driven off the islands, General MacArthur ordered the Huks to be disarmed, then rounded up and, at times, in some of the most grisly chapters of USA–Philippines relations, massacred. The PKP reacted by ordering Huk partisans to regroup in the jungles—into the Huklong Mapagpagplayang Bayan, the People's Liberation Army.

The postwar Huks' leader was Luis Taruc, a longtime peasant organizer, wartime Huk hero and a member of the Central Committee of the PKP. Another Huk leader was the American communist, William J. Pomeroy, who was also in charge of information and often wrote Huk or PKP position papers under various pseudonyms. In 1949, Luis Taruc 'decided' to write his autobiography (which was published by New York's International Publishers in 1953). In fact, it was written by Pomeroy on the run and finished in a 'temporary shelter, newly built, and it may have to be abandoned quickly, perhaps today, perhaps this afternoon' as battles raged around him in Central Luzon.

Continuously pursued by US forces and the US-trained Philippine Constabulary, constantly betrayed by starving peasants who were offered fat bribes by the government, the guerrillas began to suffer heavy losses in the late forties and early fifties. By then, most of the PKP's leadership was already in jail. Early in 1952 Pomeroy was captured (jailed until 1961, he was finally released and came to England where he still lives). Then Luis Taruc, the self-educated tenant peasant's son, turned national hero, defected—and talked. Finally, in 1956, the PKP, whose armed struggle policy seemed closely akin to China's, switched tactics, officially adopted Moscow's coexistence line, and ordered the Huks disbanded. The guerrilla menace was over—or so it was thought. The PKP got set to enter the legal (i.e. parliamentary) 'road to power'.

But under US direction, the Philippine government remained unrelenting. In 1957, its 'Anti-Subversion Act' not only outlawed the party but also made membership a felony. The constabulary continued to hound its leaders, and many are still in jail, including Dr Jesus Lava, the PKP secretary general who was caught in 1964. Nevertheless, presumably under Russian 'guidance', the PKP stuck to its peaceful policy. It called for a 'broad anti-imperialist united front'.[74] Lava himself insisted that 'we want to be independent and nationalistic, and then socialistic, these steps taking form under democratic process'.[75] In England today, Pomeroy supports this view completely, insisting that the 'political struggle' is primordial. In the Philippines, that struggle is limited mostly to organizational activity within the ranks of the National Youth Movement (Kabataan Makabayan—KM) and the Labour Party (Lapiang Manggagawa—LM). Though neither KM nor LM are PKP 'fronts', the 'nationalistic' tendencies of all three seem to coincide and they have waged joint campaigns against Philippine involvement in the Vietnam war.

But such political manoeuvres remain quite irrelevant outside Manila union and intellectual circles, where peasants still live in miserable pre-war conditions.

In Central Luzon, seven out of every ten farmers are still tenants. The total of unemployed is estimated at over a million (out of 8,000,000). Corruption in government is rife. All over the country there is rampant crime and a pervading sense of helplessness among the poor. And while the good life eludes the masses, they see profligate ostentation among the irresponsible elite . . . and American aid has only maintained the status quo.[76]

To these poor, what—or who—can be relevant? The 'Robin Hoods': who execute rustlers, crooked officials and bandits;[77] who pay for services rendered, expropriate land and carry out agrarian reforms;[78] and who operate an invisible government in the countryside, 'seemingly immune from counterattack'.[79] And who are these Robin Hoods? The Huks.

No longer led by communists of the PKP (who sometimes refer to them as bandits) but by such populist-nationalist-communists as Faustino del Mundo (Commander Sumulong) and Pedro Taruc (Luis' cousin), today's Huks are made up of old die-hard partisans who refused to give up their arms, and of 'radical reformers' who abandoned all hope of substantive structural changes without revolution. Although the picture is occasionally confused by Mafia-type gangsters who call themselves Huks to obtain local help, the guerrillas 'have wide mass support ... and reportedly have been moving around in company strength where a year ago they moved in groups of 20 or 30'. According to US News and World Report,[81] *'the Huks control 176 villages, roughly 1 out of 12, in the poorest areas of Central Luzon'. And* Time[82] *reluctantly admits that the Huks 'are supported by thousands of sympathetic or frightened peasants'.*

The tactical reason why the Huks have not only survived but grown so spectacularly in the late 1960s is that they have combined self-defence terrorism to frighten would-be informers with genuine concern and aid for the impoverished countryside population. Also, all Huk leaders today are actual fighters in close, constant, personal contact with peasants. The analytic reasons why Huks fight, however, have not changed since the forties and fifties. Pomeroy himself explained those reasons quite clearly many times then. In Ang Komunista, *which he edited clandestinely, he wrote (under the pseudonym Ernesto Diaz):*

Unlike other countries, where the growth of capitalism fostered its own national bourgeois class, in the Philippines capitalism failed to develop to a significant degree to end the feudal methods of production. The imperialists did not force our country 'to embrace bourgeois methods of production'. On the contrary, it set about to preserve the precapitalist social structure in order to realize excessive profits at little risk and with cheap labor, at the same time restricting the growth of the proletariat. In this way, feudalism formed the backbone of imperialism in this country. Feudal landowners and the comprador-bourgeoisie soon became the cohorts of the imperialists. . . . In solving the national question, we must therefore face the fact that we cannot gain national liberation in our struggle against American imperialism by embracing bourgeois democracy. Another course is required. This course is the one blazed by the Chinese revolution.[83]

In Born of the People, *his 'autobiography' of Luis Taruc, Pomeroy eloquently detailed the more profoundly human reasons why the Huks fight. Those reasons are just as true today.*

Luis Taruc (William J. Pomeroy): *From Patriots to Liberators*[84]

In a barrio betwen Mexico and San Fernando, our GHQ sat in January 1945 waiting for the American army to come. The Hukbala-hap and the people were the masters of Central Luzon. The enemy was everywhere in flight; Japanese stragglers were being killed in the barrios by women; puppets had been chased from their positions and the people were ruling themselves through their own elected provisional representatives. The Huks hoisted the Philippines and American flags and waited in the town of Tarlac for two days before the American armoured spearheads entered. It was a great occasion for the Huks, who received the GIs as our allies. Our squadrons paced the American army all the way to Manila. Huks, following up an American plane and artillery bombardment, captured Calumpit, the gateway to Bulacan. When the Americans asked for coordination in fighting at Meycauayan and Obando we were able to inform them that Huks were already there.

The capture of Manila is often described as a race between two American units. Obscured entirely is the shock absorber role played by the Bulacan Regiment of the Huks and the squadrons of Regional Command 7. As a matter of fact, if there had been even a small amount of coordination between the Huks and the USAFFE at least half of the city could have been captured long before the arrival of the Americans, and the massacre of thousands of inno-cent Filipinos might have been avoided.

Huk squadrons entering Manila established their command post in the building on Lepanto Street which was later occupied by the House of Representatives. That was as close as most of our heroes ever got to representation in the government. On 5 February, our squadrons in Manila, where the battle was still at its height, were suddenly ordered to be disarmed by the American army. Astonished, our comrades refused. Instead they packed up and started back to Central Luzon. Just beyond the city our squadrons were halted and disarmed at the point of guns by American MPs under the personal authority of Colonel Eaton, whom I had met and spoken to only a few days before in Calasiao. Two squadrons were disarmed in Obando and another at Meycauayan. Our comrades were stunned. Some of the GIs with whom they had fought side by side into Manila were present and cried when they witnessed what was happening; others gripped our comrades' hands and said it was all a mistake, the arms were sure to be returned in a couple of days. The reason Colonel Eaton gave was that armed civilians would not be tolerated behind the American lines. The USAFFE units behind the American lines were considered not civilians but soldiers attached to the US Army! Our soldiers were not even given truck transportation; they were set afoot and forced to walk back to Central Luzon.

On 7 February, with the full knowledge of the American CIC, the men of Maclang dragged the 109 Huks of Squadron 77 into the courtyard, forced them to dig their graves, and there shot and clubbed them all to death. It was one of our best squadrons, containing many of the most promising leaders of the people produced by our struggle against the Japanese. Most of them came from Santa Rita, and from my home town of San Luis; many were Manila students; many were my relatives. The anger of the people forced the Americans to place Maclang under arrest. Almost immediately, however, he was set free. Two days after his release, at the behest of the CIC, he was appointed mayor of Malolos. . . .

Another situation arose when the Philippine Civil Affairs Unit (PCAU) came in the wake of the American army. Trained in American army schools and reflecting the MacArthur policy of reaction, the PCAU refused to recognize the authority of our provisional governments. The CIC demanded to know who had placed mayors in office. When told that the people had elected them, they ordered the removal of provisional officials. The elected officials in Concepcion, Tarlac, under Mayor Marciso, were the last to be ejected; the people did not recognize the authority of the PCAU.

In many cases, the mayors appointed in place of the elected officials were former USAFFE, and many were rabid anti-Huk elements.

Squadron 50, bringing into Concepcion two Japanese prisoners whom they had captured in the barrios, was surrounded by American MPs and disarmed. Commander Remy was accused of being a collaborator because he had two Japanese with him! The squadron was imprisoned in Concepcion. In Magalang, Squadron 3 was disarmed and imprisoned.

The attitude of MacArthur during the entire war was to play down and repress popular democratic movements organized to fight the enemy. His awaitist and lie-low orders had enabled the puppet government to exert a wide influence on the Filipino people and had helped the enemy consolidate his occupation, at a time when the people themselves were everywhere ready for mass resistance. As the 'liberation' progressed it became increasingly obvious that what MacArthur wanted was a return to the *status quo,* that he was carrying out a colonial policy of an imperialist group. Osmena,* well-meaning as he was, came back into relationships that were strange to him and tried to conduct himself in the spirit of the *status quo,* enabling MacArthur to manoeuvre at will. Even men like Tomas Confesor, who came into office as Secretary of the Interior shouting anti-collaborationist slogans, had little understanding of the issues in Central Luzon, having himself disturbed none of the feudal relationships in his type of guerrilla movement on Panay.

On top of preconceived prejudices, the American army, the officers in particular, were greeted with open arms by collaborators, landlords and USAFFE alike. American officers, wined and dined in the wealthy homes of landlords, came to feel much closer to their hosts and their opinions than to the ragged peasants in nipa huts. Every liquidation of a dangerous traitor was distorted into murder; our Harvest Struggle was termed robbery because it kept the profits from the landlords which they might have acquired from selling to the Japanese; our local governments were falsely called Soviets.

On 22 February the members of the GHQ of the Hukbalahap were suddenly arrested by the American CIC. We were brought to San Fernando for a 'conference' at gun point. When the 'conference' ended we were thrown into the San Fernando jail. I was particu-

* Pre-Second World War President of the Philippines, who was reinstated in 1945–ed.

larly impressed by the date on which it happened. It was Washington's birthday.

Throughout Central Luzon the Huk leaders had been placed on the wanted list by the CIC. Planes dropped leaflets in the barrios with names listed. Luna, on 5 March, picked one up in a barrio with his name on it, asking him to come for a conference; when he did so he too was arrested and imprisoned with us. In San Luis they raided the schoolhouse in which our intelligence and communications department was located at the time; our men there were boxed around by the American MPs. We were peasant leaders, therefore we were dangerous Reds in their eyes. We had organized the people to fight against the enemy, therefore we were plotting an insurrection. They implied that we were subversive because we fought against the puppet government.

'Is this the attitude of the State Department towards the Huks?' asked G.Y.*

'The army, not the State Department, has the authority in the Philippines,' answered the brass hat, Captain Fredericks.

They wanted to know the location of all our commanders. They kept asking questions about how many communists there were in the Huks, and who they were. It seemed as if they had forgotten the Japanese and considered the communists their main enemy. They never asked us to name the traitors and collaborators in Central Luzon. They demanded that we give up our arms, and presented us with prepared statements for us to sign, calling upon the Huks to surrender arms. We were promised high rank if we did so. We refused everything with counter-offers to place all our strength and abilities at the disposal of the American army to drive the enemy out of the Philippines.

In the San Fernando jail we were held incommunicado, kept in solitary cells. There were no beds; we slept on the cement floor. We could not bathe. Each of us had two tin cans, one to urinate into and one to drink from. We had no eating utensils. Outside there were machine-guns mounted around the prison. Luna used a nail to cut a bitter phrase into the wall of his cell: 'Democracy in the hands of the US Army.'

The Americans had come back not to liberate us but to reclaim us.

---

* G.Y. stood for Guan Yek, the war name of the Huk commander and communist leader Casto Alejandrino (whose features looked some what Chinese). He is in jail–ed.

We had been a colonial people, but the Hukbalahap, founded on national liberation, was destroying the colonial mentality. Because we believed in a free Philippines, with its people educated not only in words about democracy but in democratic actions, we were called anti-American. The American officers in the CIC called us subversive. If the American way of life was imperialism, then we meant to be subversive of it.

In Iwahig [prison] GY and I examined our work and our mistakes over the past three years. One mistake, we felt, had been the failure to emphasize sufficiently our expansion work, which, properly pressed, might have mobilized far wider sections of the people. More important, however, in our estimation, had been our failure to emphasize and to clarify the true meaning of imperialism to the people. We had neglected to point out that imperialism was the same, whether Japanese, American, British or Dutch. In so doing we had narrowed down and weakened the basic issue of the Second World War, which, in its positive aspect, was a war for national liberation, a struggle which unharnessed not only the anti-fascist forces but also the anti-imperialist forces. We had left our people unprepared for what to expect from the return of the Americans. That is why our soldiers, gladly greeting the GIs and fighting beside them, were stunned when the same GIs turned around and disarmed them, arrested them, and permitted them to be massacred.

MacArthur and the other American imperialists were not the only group that considered the Hukbalahap dangerous. This opinion was shared by the comprador feudal landlord group that had always been the backbone of American rule in the Philippines, that had, in the main, automatically switched to the Japanese masters when they arrived, and now were ready to accept American rule once again. Always they followed their narrow class interests, and were ready to sell out people and country for their property and profits. If we had so many it is because we have been oppressed by foreign powers for so long that the compradors have become well-entrenched. At the end of the war, however, they were in a weakened and discredited position. The anti-Japanese and anti-collaborator feeling was so high that it threatened to sweep away the whole framework of imperialist control. The threat was felt to be greater because of the existence of the militant and well-organized Hukbalahap. The persecution and attempted suppression of the Huk, therefore, were the results of the joint efforts of the American imperialists and the comprador-feudal landlord group of Filipinos to maintain their rule.

When the Americans came in 1898 they crushed the people's movement that had come into being in the struggle against Spain, and found and installed elements whom they could depend upon to guard their interests against the people. When the Americans came in 1945 they tried to crush another people's movement that had come into being in the struggle against Japan, and they again found and installed elements who could guard their interests against the people. History, we determined, was not going to repeat itself. This time the Filipino people were not going to be crushed; they were going to win.

Where, in this developing switch of alliances, did Osmena stand, and a number of leading elements who were with him? Why was Osmena, who had grown up under the wing of the imperialist eagle, being discarded in favour of Roxas? We studied our answers. Osmena was old, Roxas was young. Osmena showed tendencies of going along with the will of the people; Roxas, with the shadow of punishment for collaboration hanging over him, could be depended upon to go all the way with the imperialists. Most important, however, was the tendency for Osmena to ally himself with a group that we termed the nationalist bourgeoisie, those elements among our capitalists that wanted independence with the least possible imperialist control, and wanted to profit from an industrialized Philippines. Roxas, on the other hand, would accept puppet-hood and complete imperialist control. We saw the promotion of Roxas into leadership as the greatest danger to the interests of the Filipino people.

We fretted impatiently in the cells of Iwahig.

Upon our imprisonment, Mariano Balgos had become the acting commander-in-chief of the Hukbalahap. He had offered to the American army a full division of the Hukbalahap soldiers to be used in the then planned invasion of Japan proper. He had urged the induction of Huks into the regular Philippine Army to help complete the liberation of the country as swiftly as possible. Both offers were ignored.

It was in July that the news came to us of the formation of the Democratic Alliance [DA]. The Hukbalahap supported it as did the peasant unions and other active fighters for our freedom. The Democratic Alliance (significantly under the chairmanship of Judge

Jesus Barrera) recognized the revolutionary nature of the people's fight against Japanese fascism and called for our independence and for our development as a free nation on the basis of the widest extension of democracy and the greatest attention to the welfare of the common people. The Democratic Alliance came into being because of the fact that the Nacionalista Party had been exposed as the party of treachery and betrayal which had abandoned the people, and the majority of whose leaders had participated in the orgy of plunder of the people during the occupation. We saw in the Democratic Alliance a medium of expression for the masses of people who wanted a better life in the postwar years.

Previously in May, the merger of the pre-war peasant movements took place, and the PKM—Pambansang Kaisahan ng Magbubukid (Confederation of Peasants)—came into being under the leadership of Mateo del Castillo and Juan Feleo. That gave us tremendous encouragement. It was a unity cemented in the Hukbalahap, in the struggle against fascism.

In July, too, the most significant sections of the trade union movement reconstituted themselves in the Congress of Labour Organizations, in Manila. Among the founders of the CLO was Mariano Balgos. Many of the other active CLO leaders had fought with the Hukbalahap also, and the new trade union movement in general was crowded with workers who had participated in guerrilla movements.

The pre-war organizations of the people had not only been kept alive; they had burst forth now in even greater number and at a higher stage of advancement. Such was the contribution of the Huk and its allies.

The DA programme was not revolutionary. It believed in the ballot and the peaceful petition as the instruments through which the people's will should be expressed and achieved. It did not propose even the mildest socialization or change in the system of society as we know it. The path it proposed would have led no further than the development of a healthy industrialized capitalist country out of the feudal agricultural colonial condition that we had. Nevertheless, it was a tremendous change, which the people wanted.

The Roxas group was also sensitive to the general desire throughout the Philippines for a change. It, too, was aware of the stigma attached to the very name 'Nacionalista'. When, in January, the Roxas group split away from the old party to form their own political organization, it adopted the name 'Liberal Party' and conducted a campaign during which they promised everything to everybody. Reaction, without a mask, could never have succeeded in the postwar Philippines. After the war a new qualitative change had entered the people's struggle. During the war it had been a struggle for national liberation, with the military phase uppermost. Now it had become a struggle for independence and democracy, with the political phase uppermost. During the war, so to speak, our methods had been underground and illegal; now they were open and legal. In the postwar Philippines, however, we had to face one fact; whoever used legal methods to resist the ruthless drive to power by the Roxas faction was operating strictly at a disadvantage.

To recite the facts of Manuel Roxas' life is to draw a portrait of a puppet of a man who serves and shields the masters against the masses. As such he was not alone, nor was he even the most outstanding example. History is full of men like Manuel Roxas. The capitalists use them to fill their governments, and call it democracy; the imperialists place them in power in their colonies, and call it independence. They are the apologists, the spokesmen, and the tools.

Before the war Manuel Roxas was one of the lawyers who handled the interests of Andres Soriano, the monopolist and fascist. By marriage he was related to the De Leon interests, big feudal landlords and sugar magnates in Central Luzon. During the Japanese occupation he urged the surrender of guerrillas, he was a member of the Preparatory Commission on Philippine Independence which organized the puppet republic, he was chairman of the BIBA which robbed the people of rice to feed the enemy, he was Minister-without-Portfolio in the puppet cabinet, he supported the declaration of war against the United States.

Following the war he was whitewashed and protected by MacArthur and US High Commissioner Paul V. McNutt, he was financed by Soriano and the Elizaldes and the feudal landlords, he gave our economy to the American imperialists with the Bell Act and parity, he gave our sovereignty to the American army with the military bases treaty, he sought to drown the people's movement in blood.

After my release I had returned to San Fernando, the central point of people's organization in Pampanga. There my wife resumed the operation of her beauty parlour, which had been interrupted so violently in 1941. The war was over, but the Philippines was still like a huge armed camp. The American army in many places out-numbered the Filipino civilians. San Fernando was teeming with American vehicles and GIs. They were a constant reminder that the liberation was like a new occupation. The CIC kept us under continual surveillance.

From the time the election campaign got under way it became obvious that the Roxas forces were taking no chances on losing. As early as October 1945 the Democratic Alliance had become the target of intimidation and terror in Central Luzon. Pro-Roxas mayors had refused to permit rallies to be held in municipalities, and when meetings did take place they were broken up by American MPs and by civilian guards on the pretext they were a threat to peace and order. The DA was organized in the shadow of imperia-list and landlord guns.

Unrest was widespread across Central Luzon at this time. The 60–40 crop-sharing programme urged by the PKM and agreed upon by Osmena to supplant the old 50–50 arrangement had been dis-carded by the administration due to the pressure and the sabotage of the big landlords. The PKM organized protest rallies. They were answered by Montelibano, the new Secretary of the Interior, who announced that he was declaring war on 'lawless' elements.

Montelibano's declaration of war, which fitted in perfectly with the strategy of Roxas, was backed up with great strength. In January control of Central Luzon was transferred from American MPs to the Philippine MP command, which had a force of over 22,000 men and was still under the direct supervision of the American army. The great majority of the MPs, both officers and enlisted men, had been members of the Philippine Constabulary in the service of the Japanese. The US army gave them a gift of 10,000 sub-machine-guns. Among the elements utilized as civilian guards by the landlords was the religious sect known as the Iglesia ni Cristo. During the Japanese regime, the sign 'I am Iglesia' written on a house guaranteed its protection from the enemy's touch.

Montelibano's little demonstration of statesmanship was imple-mented at once in Nueva Ecija, where martial law was declared, although this province was completely peaceful. Curfews, raids and provocations became the order of the day across the province. Peaceful, unarmed citizens were fired upon for gathering in private houses for celebrations. Many were killed and wounded. Cocky

MPs raced about the roads in tanks and armoured cars, firing in the air to frighten the people in regions where the PKM was strong.

At the same time, the 86th Division of the American army, stationed in Central Luzon, was suddenly ordered to reorganize itself along battle lines, to deal with 'possible unrest which may grow out of the political crisis in the Philippines'. The people, however, found they had an ally in the American soldiers, who called a huge demonstration in Manila, protesting against the intended use of American troops against Filipinos by groups that wanted to keep a stranglehold on our economy, and demanding that American GIs be sent home to the states. It showed that Americans themselves could not swallow the intentions of their imperialist-minded leaders, and they forced the US army to change its mind about using GIs to shoot down Filipino peasants.

Our election campaign emphasized independence and democracy. Wherever I spoke I stressed the fact that our people had fought for national liberation, and for the rights of free men that went with it. Unlike the Osmena group, which conducted a half-hearted campaign, I centred my attacks on the collaborators, who had sold our country once and were about to sell it again. I denounced the new assaults against the peasants in Central Luzon as the opening guns of an attempt to impose fascism on the Philippines.

In the weeks immediately before the election, the Roxas forces used everything from terror to trickery in Central Luzon. Peaceful meetings were dispersed and fired upon, homes were illegally entered and searched, and countless citizens were unlawfully detained by MP and Special Police forces. The MPs made it openly known that they were for Roxas, and threatened that everyone who voted for Osmena would be regarded as a Huk and a communist and would suffer for it. Armoured cars rumbled daily in Central Luzon.

We made every effort to guarantee a peaceful election, going out of our way to avoid clashes with the aggressive armed men of the opposition. Later an attempt was made by the Roxas administration to prove that the people's organizations intimidated voters. The only violence that occurred during the campaign, however, was committed by Roxas thugs and by landlord terrorist gangs. On the eve of the election Edilberto Joven, chairman of the Pampanga DA, and his son, a senior medical student at the University of the Philippines, were kidnapped in Bacalor and their bullet-riddled bodies were flung upon their own doorstep, as a warning to DA voters. Delegations demanding an investigation were ignored by the MP command, which covered up for the murderers, hired by Pablo Angeles David, Joven's own uncle-in-law.

Intimidations were intensified especially just prior to election day. Roxas began to shout hysterically about the 'Red menace' and dangers of a 'Huk uprising'. On election eve he actually went into hiding, claiming that the Huks were out to kidnap him! In Pampanga the Liberal Party went to the extent of circulating leaflets in the 2nd District purportedly supporting my candidacy, and calling for the election of a 'Roxas–Taruc' ticket!

Roxas was repudiated in Central Luzon, which elected six Democratic Alliance Congressmen and one Nacionalista, and gave Osmena a majority. Roxas had won nationally, but was his victory the expression of the people's will? A little over six months after I was released from the imperialist prisons I was elected to the Congress of the Philippines by the people of Pampanga. For the son of a peasant to become a Congressman is not a small honour in our country.

In all our history as a people there is nothing to equal the campaign of suppression and persecution launched against the peasant movement by Manuel Roxas in August 1946, and later continued by President Elpidio Quirino. The Spanish execution squads, the butcheries carried out by the American army when it crushed the first Philippine Republic, even the terrors of the Japanese, were all exceeded by the orgy of killing, torture, burning, and looting that was let loose upon Central Luzon.

In every town the jails overflowed with arrested peasants. Zoning was carried out in many barrios, and everyone suspected of being an active Huk or PKM was dragged off to the MP prisons, beaten and tortured. In Manila, too, scores of men who were now pursuing civilian life, were arrested in their homes and in the street, indicating that no one was safe from the surveillance of government agents. Well-known Huks were charged with an astonishing list of crimes, for every act that we had ever committed against the collaborators during the war. Huks who had fought desperately for the defence of their country were railroaded to long terms in prison for 'kidnapping', 'murder', and 'banditry'. The traitorous landlords took their revenge.

In the zoned barrios all male inhabitants were rounded up by the

MPs and grouped in an open space. Masked informers then went among them, pointing out active comrades to the MPs. In the jails the arrested men were beaten and tortured sadistically, in an effort to make them reveal the whereabouts of Huk leaders or bivouacs. Repeatedly they were given the water-cure, that torture of fiends in which water is poured into a man until his stomach is swollen and the water runs from his nose and ears, and then he is beaten. Bullets were placed between their fingers and they were given electric shocks. Our most active comrades were killed, and then reported 'shot while trying to escape'. It was a terror campaign, aimed not merely at annihilating us but at smashing our mass base. MPs and civilian guards swarmed into the barrios. From that moment until today, the life of the barrio people has not been free from fear, death, looting, and persecution.

The armies of Roxas and the landlords were far worse than the armies of the Japanese had been. They were Filipinos like ourselves, for one thing, who knew our language, our customs, our countryside, in a way that the Japanese could not know. Many had received their training from the Japanese; the majority of the MPs, with their officers, at that time came from the ranks of the puppet constabulary, and in the civilian guards were large numbers of USAFFE troops who had fought Huks even during the occupation. The MP recruited, wherever it could, the scum of the Manila streets. The 'cream'—the most ruthless and venomous—were organized into a battalion, appropriately called the 'Skull Unit'. They were sent against the people with the freedom to perpetrate whatever crime they wished.

These measures far exceeded the cordoning and zoning by the Japanese. At a moment's notice barrios were evacuated into the towns, where the people lived huddled in churches, in the overcrowded homes of friends, or in makeshift huts. In the barrios their homes were systematically looted, the pigs, chickens, goats, and carabaos stolen, and the homes finally put to the torch. The smoke of burning barrios dotted the plain of Central Luzon. Women were raped in the barrios, men were shot down in the fields on the mere suspicion of being Huks. MPs, afraid of Huk fighting ability, shelled many barrios before entering them, killing helpless people. Tanks and armoured cars ran through cultivated fields, destroying crops. It was total warfare against the people.

The masses of the people were at first demoralized, in varying degrees, depending on the depth of their political consciousness. The members of the mass organizations, who had a better understanding of what was happening, were least affected and recovered from the shock of the blow the quickest. The people outside the mass organizations, however, were confused and shaken.

The most important feature of the people's reaction was the fact that, despite the terror, goodwill towards the Huk was maintained practically everywhere. Their experience with the Huk during the war had convinced them that beyond all doubt our organization was fighting for their interests and was a part of them. Even when they were demoralized and were afraid to participate in activity themselves, they still gave supplies to the Huk when our squadrons visited them. At no time, in spite of the brutal advantage gained by the enemy, were we severed and isolated from the masses.

The demoralization that prevailed among large sections of the people was caused by the natural desire for peace and security after the difficult years of the Japanese occupation. Although they did not trust the demagogy of Roxas, many of them wanted to believe it. Many were even willing to accept the peace of slaves, just as long as it was peace. It was the path of least resistance, whereas the path of the Huks was the path of long and bitter struggle. The test of the revolutionary spirit, of an individual as well as of a group, is the willingness and readiness to endure severe hardships over an indefinite period to achieve a goal. In 1946 only a part of the people of Central Luzon were willing to take this path. It was the mailed fist policy that convinced the people as a whole to give their complete support to the Huk, and compelled them to acquire the revolutionary spirit.

During the raids the MPs always arrest 'suspects'. The suspects are never formally charged. They are merely taken to the garrisons and 'questioned'. Sometimes the 'questioning' lasts for months before the suspect is released. Sometimes the victim never comes home. Relatives go to the garrison or to government officials and inquire anxiously about those who have disappeared. They are told, he was released long ago. But why hasn't he come home? Where did he go? The answer is always a shrug and the reply, I don't know.

In the new speech of Central Luzon the people refer to a missing member of the family by saying: 'He has gone to the barrio of I Don't Know.'

In April 1948 Manuel Roxas died unexpectedly. The man who

stepped into his place, his Vice-President, Elpidio Quirino, began at once to adopt different tactics towards the Huk. He let it be known privately that he was ready to negotiate terms acceptable to us. In our analysis of Quirino we saw him first as a leader of the Liberal Party, the chosen party of the American imperialists, who could be expected to carry on the relations established by Roxas, and we saw him second as a politician anxious to build enough following, by hook or by crook, to fulfil his ambition of being elected president in 1949. Under the Roxas administration he had been pushed into the background by the Liberal Party chieftains led by Jose Avelino, and his ambitions had suffered. We did not expect to win a democratic peace from Quirino, but we concluded that we could at least establish a wider acceptance of the legitimacy of our cause, and prove the sincerity of our demands. We accepted the Quirino overtures, and the negotiations commenced.

It became obvious at once that Quirino's intention was to dupe us into surrender of our arms and thus place us at his mercy. Our arms were at all times the key question. They were the means by which we had twice defended the cause of the people, and had kept alive. Without them we were helpless before fascist terror. To trick us into giving them up, Quirino promised everything. He agreed to our demand that we keep our firearms. He publicly promised land reforms and democracy, and he privately agreed to work toward the abrogation of the Bell Trade Act,* military bases, and in general to fight against American imperialism. Judge Antonio Quirino, the president's brother and emissary with full powers, was a smooth bargainer who agreed with us on all points that we advanced.

We went along with him as far as we dared, waiting for evidence that he would keep his promises. To prove our good faith, I relinquished the field, under a truce, and came to Manila on 29 June 1948 (my birthday) to confer directly with Quirino. I was overwhelmed by the enthusiasm and the sympathy with which the people greeted me. All the attempts of Roxas to brand us as bandits had failed. My reception was the best proof of that.

To enter the city after two years of underground struggle in the

* The Bell Trade Act opened the Philippines to US exports while limiting Filipino exports to the US to quota-regulated raw materials. It also restricted the Filipino peso to the US dollar and, worst of all, established 'parity' whereby US firms owned half of all Filipino utilities. The military treaty gave Philippine bases to the USA for ninety-nine years—ed.

H

forests and mountains was a strange, throat-catching sensation. The contrast between the relative security of the city-dweller's existence and that of the hounded peasant was sharp and painful. My mind was constantly on my hungry and sick comrades in the field, who were so anxiously awaiting the outcome of the venture. Many had warned me against trusting unduly those whom I had come to see.

While the negotiations were proceeding, I was granted my right to sit in Congress. Almost everyone in Congress vied to pose in pictures with me, claiming that they, too, were 'Huks at heart'. Government spokesmen loudly asserted that the Huks had surrendered. On the floor of Congress I denounced the attempt of the government to distort the negotiations, pointing out that I was in Congress by the will of the people and not by the will of the administration. In my maiden speech I said bluntly that I was grateful to no one but the people for that honour, and pledged to continue to fight for their cause. I pointed an accusing finger at those who had betrayed the national honour in the previous two years.

We made two serious mistakes in our negotiations with Quirino. We allowed ourselves to be put in the position of accepting an amnesty proclamation from him without challenging its implication that we were the guilty party. Second, we kept too much in the background the basic consideration of struggle against American imperialism. Peace depended entirely upon Quirino's implementation of his promises, which failed to develop. During the period of truce the PCs,* and civilian guards continued to raid and to terrorize, and ambushed our soldiers on several occasions. Huks and PKMs who dared to register under the amnesty proclamation were told directly by civilian guards and by PCs: 'Now we know who you are. We will take care of you later.' Quirino finally got around to announcing his 'agrarian reforms', which turned out to be a charity offering that he called 'social amelioration'. It involved an appropriated sum of four million pesos, enough to give a few cans of milk and some old clothes to landless peasants.

Eagerly the administration put forward its much-publicized plans for the registration and surrender of our firearms. The promises of Quirino grew emptier as the days passed, and the ominous outlines of a double-cross took shape. On 14 August, a day before the deadline, I went to see President Quirino to give him my final appraisal

* Philippine Constabulary–ed.

of the situation, and to remind him of our agreements, both written and verbal. My visit failed.

The same day I gave the press my first statement accusing Quirino of bad faith and treachery. That same evening our intelligence unearthed a scheme to kidnap me. My brother-in-law was mauled by thugs gunning for me. I left the city and went back to the field early the next dawn. The following day the PCs and civilian guards made simultaneous raids throughout Central Luzon. Amnesty was over.

The terror immediately launched by Quirino exceeded by far the worst of the Roxas brutalities. Murder, torture, raping, looting and wholesale evacuations ensued across Central and Southern Luzon. The bulk of the victims at the beginning were those who had trustingly registered under the amnesty proclamation of Quirino. The hopes of the people for peace, raised during the negotiations, were smashed again.

The most important conclusion forced upon us by our experiences was that we could no longer hope to achieve a democratic peace through normal, legal, constitutional processes alone as long as we were under imperialist-feudal rule. We had been driven gradually toward this conclusion by an accumulation of events: the unseating of the Democratic Alliance Congressmen in 1946; the rigged parity plebiscite of 1947; the senatorial, provincial, and municipal elections of 1947, in which tremendous frauds were perpetrated to keep the Liberal Party in power; and now the fraudulent amnesty of Quirino in 1948. All of this was compounded by the incredible graft and corruption of Liberal Party rule, which mercilessly and without check robbed the public treasury.

In consequence of this assessment of our situation, we decided henceforth to place our main emphasis on the necessity for an armed struggle to overthrow the corrupt puppet regime of the American imperialists. Although we had previously understood the need for such an extension of the struggle, it had been necessary for the masses as a whole to accept its importance. The Bell Trade Act and the military bases agreement provided the foundation for such a mass understanding. American disinterest in the industrialization of the Philippines while rebuilding Japan, United States support of other colonial powers which sought to stem the rising liberation movements, laid bare the nature of the imperialist enemy.

How, then, does American imperialism affect our people?

For over half a century the Philippines has become largely the private landed estate of a handful of big businessmen who live ten thousand miles away in the United States. They acquired possession by taking us away from a previous owner, Spain, as the spoils of war in 1898 and they made sure of their possession by using the iron fist in 1899 to crush with blood our revolutionary movement for real independence. Since then, posing as our friends and benefactors, they have robbed and plundered our wealth, and they held back the achievement of our democracy and freedom. When they pretended to give us independence, in 1946, it was only as a smokescreen to hide an even greater domination.

The American imperialists used many excuses to justify their taking of the Philippines. President McKinley said that he had been advised to do so by God. Some said that it was the duty of the United States to civilize the Filipino. Others said that it was their duty to teach us how to govern ourselves. None mentioned publicly that they could make huge profits in our country.

To guarantee those profits, American imperialism has kept us a backward, colonial people, with the majority living in the misery of poverty and ignorance. It has prevented our growth as an independent nation, forcing us to act according to its own wishes, both in our internal and in our external affairs. It has stood in the path of our free economic development, compelling us to endure the narrow, outworn system of feudalism and keeping us from using our own means and our own energies to advance the welfare of the people.

It has boasted that it 'educated the Filipinos', but today nearly fifty per cent of our people are still illiterate and a large proportion of the rest can barely read or write. It has said that it raised our standard of living to the highest in the Orient, yet today tens of thousands of Filipinos die each year of tuberculosis and beri-beri, the diseases of poverty. It has claimed that it trained us in the ways of democratic government, but today the most corrupt regime in our history, with American approval, massacres the people and conducts itself like the worst emperors of pagan Rome.

The Philippines is a backward agricultural country, and has been for centuries. There was a general impression, fostered by both Spaniards and Americans, that Filipinos were incapable of achieving anything better, at least not until they were taught to do so over a long, long period of time. In the meantime, the Americans would protect us and guide us along the right path. I believed that. I even believed that America was noble because it was doing so much for us.

What they neglected to teach us, and what we had to find out for ourselves, bitterly, was that American imperialism had deliberately perpetuated the backward, feudal agrarian system which had been used by Spain. The American rulers had not broken up the big landed estates because they wanted us to remain an agricultural country, and the feudal tenant system was the best way to maintain the *status quo*, since it kept the largest mass of the people impoverished and disciplined and easy to control.

The American imperialists did not want our country to become industrialized because they wanted our people to buy only the products made in American factories. Our country was to be a market for their goods. It was also supposed to remain a source of raw materials needed by the American factories: unrefined sugar, copra, abaca, metallic ore, lumber, tobacco. Under our backward system of economy such raw materials could be obtained cheaply because our workers were paid very low wages. The raw materials were converted into finished products by the American factories and then sold back to us, by American import companies. All the Filipino ever received from this process, which involved the exploitation of the resources of his country, were very low wages.

The Filipino moves about in an American-made world. The clothes he wears, the cigarettes he smokes, the canned food he eats, the music he hears, the news of the world he reads (and the books and the magazines) are all American, although his own country has the ability to produce all these. He eats pineapple canned in California, but he grows it in the Philippines. His country grows millions of coconuts, but he has to buy toilet soap made in New Jersey out of coconut oil. He buys sugar refined in American mills, but grown on his own island of Negros; if he wants to buy Filipino-made sugar, he must be content with *muscovado* or *panotsa*. He rides on American-made buses or an American-made train. On the radio, made in New York (if he is one of the very few who have a radio), he listens to recorded American programmes. American movies dominate his theatres. His schools use American textbooks that explain science, economics, history, and politics from the American standpoint. The value of his peso depends entirely on the value of the American dollar. The very home he lives in (if he lives in the city) is virtually American-made: the corrugated iron roof, the nails in the walls, the electric wiring and switches, the kitchen utensils, the plates and spoons, his toothbrush, the bed clothes, the ring with which he weds his wife. And, finally, of American make, are the guns, the tanks, the planes, the artillery, the vehicles, and even the uniforms of the troops that have been used to shoot down the Filipino people who would like to see a Filipino-made future for their children.

Some small American industries have been established in the Philippines; cosmetics, soft drinks, electric fixtures. They are subsidiaries of large corporations in the United States which have set up Philippine branches because they can hire cheaper labour and thus sell their products for a greater profit. The American worker who does the same work is paid a wage three times as great.

There is another reason why the imperialists do not want to industrialize the Philippines. They would create an industrial working class that would undoubtedly organize and form powerful unions to fight for higher wages and living standards, as the large industrial trade unions do in the imperialist countries. The imperialists are afraid of creating a large, militant industrial working class; it would threaten their super-profits and eventually their control.

Before the war, when I worked as a labourer for the Metropolitan Water District in Manila, I received a wage of one peso, seventy centavos per day. I was told by the good American friend I met in those days that an American labourer received more for a single hour's work. Yet we were told that Filipinos were being taught the American way of life. The clever American imperialist! He came into our country with his talk about democracy and about the superiority of the American way of life, painting a picture in colours about his big cities and his luxuries and his opportunities, dazzling the humble Filipino who lived on rice and fish, telling him that he too could be fortunate if he would just trust in the American way. He would pat Juan de la Cruz on the back and say: 'You should feel proud. You are the only Christian nation in the Orient. Look at all the sugar and copra you produce and all the gold you dig and all the abaca you grow. One of these days, too, you'll be independent and then you too can be like your Uncle Sam.'

The Filipino peasant, who slept on the floor and whose chair was an empty box, plastered the walls of his nipa hut with American magazine illustrations of mansions in the country and hotels and advertisements of luxurious beds and furniture. In the city the

labourer who lived in a *barong-barong* that became flooded when
it rained, went to the American movies and saw the well-dressed
glamorous characters moving around in the handsome drawing-
rooms and the modern kitchens that had refrigerators and washing
machines and electric toasters.

After the war the imperialist said: 'Here is your independence.
You see? Just as we promised.' The Filipino could look around and
see the American army, stronger than ever, still on his soil, and see
the Bell Trade Act operating so that he still produced nothing but
sugar, and copra, and abaca, and metallic ores. He could still cut
pictures out of the magazines and still go to the movies. The worker
was now paid three pesos instead of a peso-and-a-half, but he now
paid one peso and thirty centavos for a *ganta* of rice instead of the
pre-war twenty-five centavos.

The Americans soon realized they could not rule forever with an
iron hand; it was too expensive. They solved their problem by getting Filipinos to rule for them. A group of Filipinos stood ready and
willing to play such a role, the landlord-*ilustrado* class, the landed
gentry. A large number of this group had not even joined the
struggle against Spain. Their own fortunes were derived from the
exploitation of the masses and they were content to have a strong
external power upon which to rely, to help them maintain their
exploiter's position. They were afraid the revolution would go too
far and would get rid of them as well as of the Spaniards. The
Americans were stronger than the Spaniards; they were even more
reliable. The American Civil Government, operating through the
Philippine Commission, at first based itself upon this class of Filipinos. They formed the first political party in the Philippines, the
Partido Federalista. It existed during the period when no Filipino
political party advocating independence was allowed to exist.

American rule brought into prominence a new economic group,
the compradors, the middle-men through whom raw materials left
our country and finished products entered. The compradors had
been a weak group under Spain but they grew and flourished under
the United States, particularly after the passage in 1909 of the
Payne-Aldrich Act,* establishing free trade as a basis for imperia-

* Under this tariff act, unlimited quantities of US goods were permitted into
the Philippines duty-free, but the amount of Philippine sugar, the chief export,
which might be imported into the United States free of duty was limited to 300,000
tons per annum–ed.

list relations. Owing their fortunes to the operations of imperialism, they became the right-hand men of foreign rule.

The whole process of 'training to govern', about which American imperialism has boasted so much in the Philippines, has been built around the training of these groups to govern in the interests of American imperialism. One reason for perpetuating the feudal system of landowning that had functioned under the Spanish regime was to keep the big landlords in power because they were an integral part of the new American pattern of rule.

In the old Spanish universities, as well as in the new University of the Philippines and in the other higher schools of learning established by the Americans, the theory of 'intellectual aristocracy' was driven home to the students. The school systems grew less and less adequate the closer down it got to the masses until, in the barrios, it was mere perfunctory instruction. The gap between the educated and the uneducated or poorly educated was a sharply accentuated class difference. In addition, American textbooks were moved from the United States into Philippine schools without a line of revision, regardless of how great a difference existed between the two countries. The sociology of the American big city and of the American rural community was clamped grotesquely upon the mind of the Filipino student, to whom the cacique and the governor-general were the symbols of authority.

Politics is a special sort of occupation under imperialism. It is made attractive by the opportunities for politicians to enrich themselves through corruption. After the war, when American imperialism needed ruthless and unscrupulous men to carry out its policies in the face of a strong people's movement, this corruption was magnified a hundred times. It went so deep that it is impossible to uproot until the whole of imperialist control is uprooted. Japanese collaborators, anxious to get back into the good graces of American imperialism, jumped at the bribes dangled in the form of surplus army equipment and war damage payments. Once they had sold themselves thoroughly, imperialism then had a weapon to hold over them to enforce even greater acts of puppetry. This phenomenon was not new, nor was it a product of the break-down of morals during a war. It was the culmination of the type of political rule that was fostered from the beginning by American imperialism in the Philippines.

What happened in 1945 was almost a duplication of what had

happened in 1898. The American army, on both occasions, landed to find a revolutionary movement fighting against the common enemy. On both occasions they took steps to crush it and on both occasions they found allies in the exploiting classes of Filipinos. In 1945, however, there was a difference; the revolutionary movement was not led by vacillating elements who would sell it out; it was led by the working-class leadership of communists. Within three years after the end of the war, the operation of American imperialism had resulted in converting the Hukbalahap guerrilla struggle into a national liberation movement. The Hukbalahap, the people's army, had thus become the rallying centre of all Filipinos in the struggle for national liberation.

PALESTINE

Because each side includes contradictory and opposing forces, the Israeli–Arab confrontations have long generated a series of myths which have tended to obscure the real revolutionary picture in the Middle East. In the West, for example, a great many radicals, who normally sympathize with the liberation movements of Asia, Latin America and Black Africa but who also retain their sense of guilt for the liquidation of six million Jews by Nazi Germany, look upon the reactionary Arab regimes as proof that anti-Zionists are really anti-Semites. On the other hand, confirmed Jew-haters can oppose Israel on the safe issue that Zionists stole the Arabs' land. And, of course, both are right—as far as they go. For the majority of the Arab countries are indeed ruled by regimes much more anti-democratic than the Israeli government, and the Zionists did steal Arab lands. The only way, then, to look clearly at the situation, is to separate the analysis. Since Israel is a Zionist state, its ideology and activity should be laid bare without recourse to what Hitler did in Europe or what Arab rulers do at home. And, likewise, the class-conflict inside the Arab countries should be investigated on its own, without taking the statements of one or more of the rulers as representative of the masses.

The first point to remember is that Zionism was and is a colonialism. That is, settlers came to Palestine, seized or bought land, and decided to live there. Whether or not their ancestors had preceded them two thousand years ago is immaterial to the form of society they established, the structure of the economy, how they treated the natives, etc. These settlers were a minority which imposed their ways on the majority. What were those ways? Usually, when foreign settlers colonize an area, they use the native population as a labouring class—for their benefit. But in Israel this did not take place. The Jews or newcomers simply drove the Arabs or natives out. And that is exactly what the Zionist leaders wanted. In The Complete Diaries of Theodor Herzl, *for example, that founder and leader of*

Zionism stated, long before the Jewish immigration began (in fact, Herzl was still thinking of Uganda, not Palestine, as the site for a Jewish state):

When we occupy the land . . . we shall expropriate gently the private property on the estates assigned to us. We shall try to spirit out the penniless population across the border by procuring employment for it in the transit countries, and by denying it any employment in our country. . . . Both the process of expropriation and the removal of the poor must be carried out discreetly and circumspectly.

Zionism, then, was clearly meant to be territorial colonialism. And it still is. The following exchange is from the TV programme Face the Nation:

Sidney Grusen (of the New York Times*): Is there any possible way that Israel could absorb the huge number of Arabs whose territory it has gained control of now?*

Moshe Dayan (Israeli Defence Minister): Economically we can, but I think it is not in accord with our aims for the future. It would turn Israel into either a bi-national or a poly-Jewish-Arab state and we want to have a Jewish state. We can absorb them but it wouldn't be the same country.

Grusen: *Now is it necessary, in your opinion, to maintain this as a Jewish state and a purely Jewish state?*

Dayan: *Absolutely, absolutely, we want a Jewish state like the French want a French state.*[85]

So Zionism is also territorial expansionism. From this policy alone, the Palestinian Arabs, who have been deprived of their land, their livelihood and their country, are entitled to wage a patriotic war against the Israeli regime—and, by any analysis, revolutionaries and radicals should support them, at least until they have gained their right to self-determination.

Governments are not peoples. Even the Vietnamese, after massive bombings and invasion by half a million US troops, still make a difference between the US government, or literally, Giac My ('US imperialists') and the US people. That distinction must be maintained by all revolutionaries, even if the Zionist state itself, by its essence, has deliberately confused—and fused—Zionism with the Jewish people. Thus, it is non-revolutionary, in fact counter-revolutionary to talk of 'driving the Jews (or any people) into the sea'.

The governments of Jordan, Saudi Arabia, Kuwait and the Arab

Gulf are feudal-fascist governments who are just as close to imperialism as is Israel. The Lebanese regime is run by a commercial and banking bourgeoisie in partnership with and dependent upon imperialism. The governments of Egypt, Syria and Iraq are petty-bourgeois—a class that, because it came to power without revolutionary struggle (via coups d'état) has no revolutionary consciousness (but lots of revolutionary sounding rhetoric). In all these countries the masses are agitated. They want or need a socialist revolution. To curtail their internal activities, these Arab regimes talk of 'liberating' Palestine. Most don't really want to. And if Egyptian or some of the Ba'athi leaders in Syria and Iraq do, it is not in order to establish a new social structure for all of the Middle East, but as a way of generating a nationalist unity of the Arab countries. All these regimes, then, are either reactionary or opportunist, or both. All must be overthrown by people's revolution.

The above analysis, in brief, is detailed in the following articles. The first, by the Israeli Socialist Organization, a Marxist–Leninist group founded in 1962, explains best what Zionism is, why and how it has always been tied to imperialism (first British, then USA), why the Arab states' leaders play the revolutionary role and what their links to imperialism are, and finally makes the class-analysis needed by all genuine revolutionaries who are bent on launching people's war. The next article is the Seven Point Platform of Al-Fatah, the Palestine Revolutionary Liberation Movement, which was one of the first Palestine organizations to engage in terrorist activity inside Israel (through its armed wing, Al Assifa). Though led by petty-bourgeois intellectuals, Al-Fatah did begin to make the kind of analyses described above and did condemn any other so-called movement which 'did not spring from the masses themselves but was artificially imposed from above'. It also stressed the fact that Al Assifa operations 'are in no way aimed at the Jewish people as such with whom [Palestinians] have lived in harmony in the past for so many centuries'.[86]

The next two articles come from the same source, but technically have different authors—the Popular Front for the Liberation of Palestine (PFLP) and the Democratic Popular Front for the Liberation of Palestine or sometimes just the Democratic Front (DPFLP or just DPF). In August 1968 these two groups were still one, the PFLP. It had been formed shortly after the Six Day June 1967 defeat out of a merger between the Palestine branch of the Arab

Nationalist Movement (ANM), which collapsed altogether as a consequence of the June fiasco, and a bunch of Palestine commandos known as the Jibril-Shruru group. Because strong Marxist–Leninist elements were included among the former, the PFLP as a whole came into conflict with the anti-communist Ba'ath Party of Syria (which arrested three PFLP leaders). The Jibril-Shruru group then swore allegiance to the Ba'athi regime and seceded from the PFLP. Thus, when PFLP met for its second annual conference in August 1968, it appeared solidly Marxist–Leninist. It is then that 'The August Platform' (article III) was presented by the left. The right wing, viewing itself out-numbered, voted for the platform—but only to gain time to regroup. When it did, the left wing quit the PFLP and set up the DPF (by October 1969 all three liberation fronts represented here were coordinating their activities through the Palestine Struggle Command).

The DPF is by far the most revolutionary of the lot. It knows that a socialist Palestine can never be established until not only the Zionist but also the Arab reactionary and petty-bourgeois regimes are overthrown. It also knows that another set of coups will accomplish nothing: genuine liberation, it says, must come from the people who must win, through long protracted people's war, their right to self-determination—be they Arabs, Kurds, Armenians, or Jews.

I Israeli Socialist Organization: *The Other Israel*[87]

(1) Of all the problems bequeathed to the world by European imperialism, Palestine is among the most intractable. It is a peculiarly emotional issue, not only for those immediately involved. In the West the burden of guilt left by Hitler's crimes against the Jews has created a barrier which the injustices suffered by the Palestinian Arabs cannot penetrate. In many Arab countries hatred of the Jews is whipped up to divert the internal struggle against reactionary regimes into external channels. Western economic interests in the area, and the tendency of both East and West to exploit the situation for ideological or strategic advantage, further complicates the problem. To make matters worse, in both Israel and the Arab countries there is almost total ignorance of the other's history, people and aspirations.

Emotions, however, whether rightly or wrongly based, cannot solve complex political problems. They are much more likely to lead to disaster. At the centre of the emotional miasma surrounding Palestine lie two hard facts—the displaced Arab population who still live in refugee camps round Israel's border; and a new nation of Israel, with a complete class structure of its own, who by incessant propaganda and, to a certain extent, real achievement, are beginning to carve a place in the world. Neither can be forgotten, ignored, or annihilated. A political solution must sooner or later be found, that is both realistic and just. The alternative is—eventually—war, which will at best only defer, not solve, the political problems.

In the first half of the twentieth century the population of Palestine was about 700,000, the overwhelming majority being Arabs. There were various minority communities, including some 70,000 Jews. Economically and politically these Jews were an integral part of the indigenous population, differing only by religion. They had nothing to do with colonization or Zionism.

The first step in the modern Jewish colonization of Palestine was taken in 1870 when Baron Edmund de Rothschild of France acquired some land near Jaffa and established an agricultural school (Mikveh Israel—'Gatherer of Israel'). This was followed by the building of some twenty villages, inhabited by some 5,000 Jews, mostly from Russia. Up to 1900 the Baron invested about £2 million in Palestine. The Rothschilds were (and still are) among the world's leading financiers, with the French and British branches of the family holding influential positions in the economy of these two countries. Baron Edmund combined his Jewish sentiments with his support from French interests in colonizing Palestine following the Algerian model. He wished to amalgamate the emigration of East European Jews with the colonial interests of French imperialism. He did not entertain the idea of an independent Jewish state in Palestine (he was no Zionist) but used his financial power in the Ottoman treasury in order to prepare a new sphere of influence for French interests, employing Jewish immigrants as settlers. His Palestine activities were thirty years old when Zionism was born.

Political Zionism was founded in 1897 at a congress held in Basle, Switzerland. It differed significantly from the Rothschild colonization in that it declared its intention of solving the Jewish problem by creating a national Jewish state. However, the Viennese journalist T. Herzl, the founder and first leader of the Zionist movement, did not consider Palestine as the indispensable location for such a state. On the contrary, he advocated Uganda as the most suitable place for Jewish colonization. But the majority of the Zionists rejected the Uganda scheme and insisted on fulfilling the Jewish religious sentiment towards Palestine.

From the very beginning, Zionism sought to achieve its aim by means of a deal with one imperialist power or another. The guiding principle of Zionist diplomacy was always to affiliate itself with that world power within whose sphere of influence Palestine happened to be. Herzl courted mainly the Turkish Sultan and the German Kaiser. After the First World War Zionism was oriented towards British imperialism. Again after the Second World War Zionism switched its orientation to the US and occasionally flirted with France.

When at the beginning of this century organized Zionist immigration started to pour into Palestine, the surprising fact that the country was already populated could no longer be ignored. Like every colonizing society, the Zionist settlers had to shape a definite policy towards the indigenous population. Here we come to the specific feature of Zionism which distinguishes it from all other colonizations of modern times. The European settlers in other colonies sought to exploit the riches of the country (including the labour potential of the 'natives') and invariably turned the former population into a proletarian class in a new capitalist society. But Zionism wanted not simply the resources of Palestine (which were not very great in any case) but the country itself to serve for the creation of a new national state. The new nation was to have its own classes, including a working class. The Arabs were, therefore, not to be exploited, but totally replaced.

The Rothschild colonization clashed with the Palestine Arabs only over one issue—land ownership. The Baron bought land from feudal Effendis, sometimes by bribing the Ottoman administration, and drove the fellahin off the land. The expropriated fellahin were then employed as labourers in the Baron's settlements, following the usual colonial pattern. The Zionist colonization, however, raised the slogan 'Jewish labour'. Aspiring to create a Jewish working class as part of a new nation, it advocated a transition of people from middle-class occupations to manual labour, and it insisted that Jewish employers use Jewish labour only. The Zionists, therefore, clashed not only with the expropriated Arab peasants but also with the interests of the Baron's settlers who preferred to use the cheaper Arab labour. This issue was the main conflict within the settlers' community during the first three decades of the century. The main protagonists of the 'Jewish Labour' policy were the left-wing elements within Zionism. The bourgeois elements were always tempted to employ the cheaper Arab labour. Had the bourgeois attitude prevailed, Palestine might have developed along much the same lines as Algeria, South Africa or Rhodesia. It was, however, the left wing of Zionism which prevailed. The funds of the Zionist movement were often used to cover the difference between the cost of Arab labour and the more expensive Jewish labour.

The nascent Zionist society clashed with all the various classes of Palestine Arab society. It brought from Europe capital, modern technological know-how and skills. Jewish capital (often backed by Zionist funds) gradually displaced the feudal elements simply by buying up their lands, and Zionist regulations forbade re-sale of land to Arabs. Possessing technological and financial advantages, the Zionist capital economy blocked the emergence of an Arab capitalist class. Having clashed with the Arab peasants by driving them off their land, Zionism also prevented them from becoming a proletariat in the Jewish sector of the economy. Since the Arab sector's capitalist development was retarded and hindered, the peasants (as well as the Arab intelligentsia) found it hard to get any employment at all—except in the British Mandate administration and public services.

This socio-economic deformation was reflected in the political sphere. Since the bourgeoisie, the proletariat and the peasantry were denied a normal path of development, they did not produce parties and leaders of sufficient calibre. Political leadership of the Palestine Arabs inevitably remained in the hands of the landowning class, who, although they liquidated themselves as a class by selling their land to the Zionists, made enormous financial gains by these transactions. They retained the political leadership of the Arabs by covert cooperation with the Zionists and the British. In order not to be branded as traitors they assumed in public the most extreme anti-Zionist stands, even declaring the sale of the land to the Zionists to be treason.

But understanding existed between the Zionists and the Hashemite kings, who were the main ally of British imperialism in the

Middle East. In 1922 in London King Faisal (the son of Sherif Hussein of Mecca) signed a joint political agreement with Weizmann, Chairman of the Zionist movement. Article 3 of this Agreement *endorsed* the Balfour Declaration. Article 4 states: 'All necessary measures shall be taken to encourage and stimulate immigration into Palestine on a large scale.' This agreement was the ancestor of the secret agreement between Ben Gurion and Abdullah in 1948, when they divided Palestine between them and virtually arranged the result of the war.

Meanwhile, the anti-imperialist struggle throughout the Arab countries reached an unprecedented scale. In Syria, a general strike was declared in 1936 against French imperialism. This strike proved to be effective and on the whole successful. It brought Syria substantially nearer political independence. This made a great impression in Palestine, and there, too, a long general strike was declared. Conditions in Palestine were, however, very different because of the presence of Zionist economic infrastructure, which did not, of course, take part in the strike. Moreover, the Zionists exploited the fact that Arab workers in government administration and services (e.g. railroads, ports, etc.) were on strike, and that Arab commerce was paralyzed, to secure a grip of these large and important sectors of the economy. The strike coincided with a great influx of Jewish capital from Europe. Thus, while the Arab sector of the economy suffered a blow from which it never recovered, the Zionists secured a new and decisive hold on the whole economy.

British imperialism, which ruled Palestine from 1918 to 1948, used the familiar tactics of 'divide and rule', exploiting to the utmost the possibilities which rivalling nationalistic movements offered. For the masses it employed nationalist and religious incitement and provocation, which proved to be effective. It employed Jewish policemen against Arab population and vice versa. For the leaders it employed diplomacy, 'white papers', round-table conferences, giving contradictory promises to both sides and acting as 'mediators'. It succeeded in diverting what threatened to become an anti-imperialist struggle into the channels of nationalist strife.

The calculated ambiguities and 'contradictions' in the British foreign policy increased the unrest and hostilities between Jews and Arabs, and involved considerable bloodshed. In the late thirties this factor turned from an asset into a liability. The religious, feudal and bourgeois elements in Arab Nationalism welcomed the rise of fascism in Germany and Italy, as fellow enemies of British imperialism. Contacts between these camps worried the British. The oil-fields, pipelines and Suez canal seemed in danger. Zionist demands for more independence and increased immigration quotas for European Jews fleeing from persecution were other issues which had to be handled, too. But the Foreign Office, confident that the Nazis would never consider the Zionists as potential allies, produced another white paper in 1939, aimed at currying favour with the Arabs. It stated : 'His Majesty's Government now declare unequivocally that it is not part of their policy that Palestine should become a Jewish state. . . . It should be a state in which the two peoples in Palestine, Arabs and Jews, share authority in government in such a way that the essential interests of each are secured. . . .'

Before the war, the Palestine economy (especially the industrial and manufacturing sector) was dominated by the British metropolitan economy. The development of local light industry particularly was hampered by imports of consumer goods from Britain. Partly as a result of this, even in the Jewish community (numbering on the eve of war about 500,000 out of a total of 1,750,000), noticeable anti-British tendencies were beginning to form.

The war brought about an unprecedented boom in the Palestine economy. Palestine became a major base for the British garrison in the Middle East, which had to be housed, clothed, equipped and fed. Supply lines from Britain were disrupted by the war, and the British economy was overstrained by the war effort. The British had to rely to a large extent on the local economy, and they encouraged its rapid development. In the Arab sector unemployment disappeared as thousands of workers were employed to build camps, roads and airfields. But whereas Arab industry was not ready to benefit fully from the enormously increased demand, the Jewish sector was already organized along modern lines and had considerable reserves of manpower.

It therefore drew the maximum benefit from the increased demand and entered a period of great expansion, known as 'The Prosperity'. Whole industries grew from modest beginnings to formidable size within a period of four to five years. By 1942 there were 6,600 Jewish industrial enterprises, employing about 56,000 workers and producing at the rate of £20 million per year. The level of production in 1942 was more than double that of 1939 in the food, textile, metal, machinery and chemical industries—treble in the electrical appliance industry. The Palestine diamond industry (exclusively in Jewish hands) grew at an even more spectacular rate as the European centres were cut off from their raw materials (in South Africa) from 1,000 carats (valued at £25,000) in 1940 to 58,000 carats (valued £2.6 million) in 1943 and to 138,000 carats (£6 million) in 1945.

When the war ended, industrial growth slowed abruptly, and imports from Britain again menaced local industry—but by now the wartime growth had made the Jewish sector of the economy a force to be reckoned with. It did not want to return to the pre-war dominance by Britain and by now a much larger section of the Jewish population had a stake in maintaining industrial expansion. This new situation provided the economic impetus for the postwar demands of the Jewish community for political independence. Unlike the Arabs, the Jewish community had made no such demands before the Second World War because it was clear that an independent Palestine would be a state with an Arab majority. The new Jewish dominance of the economy was one of the main factors that brought about a change of policy.

Even more significant were new political factors, which derived chiefly from the rise and defeat of fascism in Europe. During the thirties many right-wing Arab nationalists had regarded German and Italian fascism as allies in the struggle against British imperialism. Like other nationalists throughout the British empire, they maintained this attitude throughout the war. In 1945 this policy was shown to have been wrong in principle, and also to be a grave tactical and moral disadvantage. Few Arabs served in the British army and, as a result, the Arabs, unlike the Jews, failed to gain experience in modern organized warfare. Moreover, the right-wing nationalists, having supported the losing side, were demoralized by the allied victory and found it difficult to resume the momentum of the pre-war struggle for political independence.

For the Jews the question of which side to support in the war hardly arose at all. A fascist Zionist party had existed during the thirties and had collaborated closely with Italian and Polish fascism. But the majority of Zionists maintained their pro-British orientation. By 1939 Nazi policy towards the Jews had forced even the fascist faction into the British camp. Of the 500,000 Palestine Jews, 50,000 volunteered for the British forces, encouraged and organized by the Zionist leadership. By the time the war ended ten per cent of the Jewish population had considerable military experience.

The Nazi crimes against the Jews also gave Zionists an entirely new status in the international arena. Previously, it had been a minority trend amongst the world's 18,000,000 Jews, with the majority either indifferent or hostile. After the extermination of 6,000,000 European Jews by Nazism, many more were attracted by the idea of an independent Jewish state. Zionism, which had always accepted anti-Semitism, became a major political tendency even among Jews who had no intention of personally emigrating to Palestine. The world powers began to regard Zionism as the representative of the whole Jewish people.

The war left large numbers of Jewish refugees in Europe, many of whom, encouraged by the Zionists, wanted to emigrate to Palestine. The Palestine Arabs had no wish to become a minority in their own country, and pressed the British government to stop Jewish emigration. The Zionists thereupon began to organize clandestine emigration on a large scale. The British tried to prevent this not only because of Arab pressure but also because they were worried by the rising tendencies towards independence among the Palestine Jews. World opinion, especially in Europe and the US, was still reeling with the shock of discovering the enormity of the Nazi war-crimes and inevitably sympathized with the refugees. The resulting political atmosphere was hostile both to the British government and to Arab nationalism. This atmosphere persists today and is one of the major assets of Zionism.

The emergence of the US as a major world power after the Second World War and the decline of British imperialism brought about a gradual shift of Zionist orientation from Britain towards the US. A strong Zionist lobby was built up in Washington and at the same time the pro-American elements in world Zionism gained supremacy over the pro-British faction.

The combined effect of these economic and political factors precipitated the clash between the Zionists and the British government. The war had transformed the Jewish community in Palestine into a nation with its own economy, army, political organizations, language and ideology. Its economic interests had become incompatible with direct colonial rule. It clashed with British policy on immigration, in a world atmosphere favourable to Zionism and hostile to Britain. Zionist re-orientation towards the US and the growing American interests in the Middle East hastened the colli-sion.

In this new situation the Zionists demanded political independ-ence in Palestine. The right wing demanded immediate inde-pendence for the whole of Palestine under Jewish minority rule; the centrists favoured the partition of Palestine between Arabs and Jews; the left-wing Zionists (among them parts of the present-day 'Mapam' party) wanted to postpone independence until the Jews became a majority through increased immigration.

In essence there were three parties involved in the Palestine problem. British imperialism; the Jewish minority (about 0.6 mil-lion); and the Arab majority (about 1 million). Each of these had its own demands, in conflict with the other two. But—mainly owing to the deformation of Arab society by the process of Jewish colonization—the Palestine Arabs did not in fact constitute a major independent political force in the period 1945-7. The struggle was waged mainly between the Zionists and the British.

During these years a series of conflicts, accompanied by armed violence, occurred between the Jewish community and the British administration. The Palestine Arabs, although they still outnum-bered the Jews by about two to one, remained relatively passive—a complete reversal of the situation during the twenties and thirties, when Arab struggle for independence had a mass character and often used violent means. The British government, preoccupied with a fuel crisis and Indian independence, neared desperation.

In 1947 Britain referred the Palestine problem to the UN expect-ing disagreement in the UN to lead to a renewal of the mandate. This would lend a new lease of life to the precarious British autho-rity in the area. In November 1947 the General Assembly adopted a resolution recommending the partition of Palestine into two inde-pendent, but economically linked, states. This solution was a victory for Zionism and was strongly opposed by the Arabs (who, of course, demanded an undivided independent Arab Palestine), and by British imperialism which struggled to retain its influence and power.

Both the US and the USSR supported the resolution; the US because they considered it a convenient way of gaining a foothold in the Middle East and replacing British imperialism; the USSR because it considered it the most practical way to drive British im-perialism out of one of its strongholds. The USSR probably underestimated the strong links between Zionism and American imperialism. As for the Foreign Office, it was worried not only because the creation of a Zionist state meant loss of influence to the US but also because the establishing of an independent Arab state in Palestine could have repercussions in the Arab world.

After the UN partition resolution, the British tried to provoke the Palestine Arabs against the Jewish population, to prove that a British presence was necessary to keep law and order. This attempt failed. Next, the British organized in Syria an irregular volunteer army (headed by Fawzi el Kaukji) which entered Palestine and attacked Jewish settlements. When this attempt failed too, the British finally decided to employ the regular armies of Trans-Jordan, Syria, Egypt and Iraq in order to wage open war against the Zionist state, which (according to the UN resolution), was to come into existence on 15 May 1948. The political and military plans for this invasion were drawn up by General I. C. Clayton (one of the main British colonial agents in the Middel East) in a meeting of the Arab chiefs of staff held early in 1948 at Bludan, Syria.

The 1948 war became a military conflict between the Zionists and the Arab armies. These armies were not, however, playing an independent role for achieving Arab independence in Palestine, but rather serving British interests, through the puppet regimes of Farouk, Abdullah and Nuri Sa'id. The war was used by these regimes to divert the internal anti-imperialist struggle (especially in Egypt and Iraq) into an imperialist-sponsored Holy War. The conduct of the war exposed the utter corruption of these regimes and hastened their downfall.

The fate of Palestine was decided not on the battlefield but also in secret talks between the Zionist leaders and Abdullah. These talks started immediately after the adoption of the partition resolution by the UN and went on until 1950. In these talks the two 'friendly enemies', although ostensibly at war with each other, agreed to divide between them the territory which the UN resolution had allotted to the Palestinian Arabs, as well as Jerusalem which, according to the resolution, was to become a separate unit under the UN administration. The armistice agreement coincided, more or less, with the results of the political negotiations between the Zionist leaders and Abdullah.

A new set-up was thus established in Palestine: 20,000 sq. km (instead of the 14,000 sq. km allotted to it in the UN resolution) became Israel; and the remaining territory (except the Gaza strip) was annexed by Abdullah, who renamed his kingdom 'Jordan' (instead of Trans-Jordan). This new set-up expressed the new balance of influence among the Western Powers. The area of the Zionist state was lost to British imperialism and came under US influence; while the area annexed by Abdullah represented the remnants of British influence. This new division of spheres of influence received formal confirmation in the Tripartite (US, Britain and France) Declaration of May 1950.

This state of affairs, established as a consequence of the 1948 war, persists today and is referred to as the '*status quo*' in the Middle East. It is an inherently unstable situation because the war was not terminated by a political solution of the Palestine problem but only by a temporary Armistice Agreement. Since Israel is interested in preserving the *status quo,* it has become more and more dependent on the Western Powers who guarantee its continuance. The same applies, of course, to the Jordanian regime, which because of its military weakness also depends indirectly on Israel. In spite of their seemingly hostile relations, these two regimes share a common interest—to preserve the *status quo.* Thus, the sum total of the relations between imperialism, the Zionists, and the various Arab parties which was known up to 1948 as 'the Palestine Problem' was transformed in 1948 into the 'Israeli–Arab conflict', the latter being a direct continuation (albeit in a new form) of the former.

The losers and victims of the 1948 war were the Palestine Arabs, who hardly participated in the war. Their right to self-determination, which previously nobody—not even the Zionist leaders—had denied, was violated. Most of them became homeless refugees. The fate of those who remained in the area held by Israel was hardly better. They have lived ever since under military rule and are subject to constant and severe repression. The land remaining in Arab hands was gradually but systematically expropriated, often by administrative subterfuge, to make way for Zionist development. The Arabs are second-class citizens in their own country.

In the early fifties the anti-imperialist struggle intensified throughout the Arab world. In the Arab East this intensification was, in part, a result of the Palestine war. Britain, already too weak to defend its old positions, had to accept the fact that the US was becoming dominant in this part of the world as in others. The global policy of the US to surround the USSR by a chain of bases and military pacts was welded in the Middle East with the traditional British colonial policy into a single anti-Soviet and imperialist policy. Throughout the fifties these two powers tried to create a military alliance of Middle-Eastern countries, to serve as a link in the chain of anti-Soviet alliances stretching from Scandinavia to Korea and to strengthen Western domination in the Middle East.

This policy encountered great difficulties, because the Arab masses were aware of its imperialist character and opposed it violently. On the government level, the consistent refusal of Egypt and Syria to participate in such pacts undermined the whole of Western policy in the region. The Israeli government, on the other hand, was always willing to participate actively in any such scheme, not only because of the traditional links between Zionism and Imperialism, but also (and more specifically) because Israel's adherence to the *status quo* made it a natural ally of imperialism—an ally who identified his own natonal interests—indeed his very existence—with the imperialist presence in the Middle East.

The Israeli position was fully understood and utilized by the West. Whenever the governments of Egypt, Syria or Jordan attacked the Anglo-American schemes, Israel was used as a threat against them. These threats often materialized in the form of armed raids by Israeli forces. Jordan, particularly, was raided during the period when the el Nabulsi government there conducted anti-Western policies. Usually, after such a raid, the Arab government concerned would turn to the West and ask for arms. The reply was always: 'Join the Baghdad Pact, and you will get arms.'

This Western policy was finally defeated when, after the big Israeli raid on Gaza on 28 April 1955, Nasser refused to submit to Western pressure and turned to Czechoslovakia for arms. This broke the arms monopoly of imperialism in the area, and considerably weakened its political influence. From this time onwards, the Soviet Union emerged as a protagonist in the Middle East scene. This development, followed by the nationalization of the Suez Canal, drove Britain and France to desperation. Employing an Israeli invasion of Egypt as a pre-arranged pretext, they launched a direct military attack on Egypt in order to regain possession of the Canal and to overthrow the neutralist and anti-imperialist governments in the Middle East. For Israel the failure of the Suez invasion meant that she was unable to force the Arab world to accept the *status quo*.

From that time the Palestine problem entered a period of stalemate.*

Israel is the most stable and reliable ally of imperialism in the area. In return, imperialism—which has an interest in preserving such an ally—grants Zionists its protection. Their hope is that the West will always be able to grant them this protection and will never let them down. Zionism has a powerful ally in Western public opinion. The five million American Jews constitute a strong pressure group exerting considerable influence not only on US official policy but also on American public opinion. Even that section of Western public opinion which opposes imperialism is reluctant to criticize Israel. This is a result of the deep feeling of guilt in the West after the massacre of six million Jews by the Nazis. Even socialists in the West often mistakenly identify anti-Zionism with anti-Semitism. Zionist propaganda has another great advantage: it aims at consolidating an existing situation and therefore preaches peace. Arab policy wishes to change the situation, and cannot simply preach peace, but has the difficult task of explaining the injustices of the *status quo*. Thus the Zionists appear as peace-seekers, the Arabs as aggressors.

The Zionists rely on military forces. Knowing that eventually the balance of conventional forces will be against them, they have recently started to develop nuclear weapons. They hope that possession of such weapons will make it impossible for the Arabs to upset the *status quo*. Alternatively, should the Great Powers force them to give up possession of nuclear weapons, the Zionists hope to get in exchange for this an East–West guarantee to maintain the *status quo*.

In the long run, the Zionist policies cannot succeed. Even if they do manage to maintain the *status quo* for a relatively long period, Israel will remain a small besieged fortress, economically unviable and dependent on outside economic aid for its very existence (about $400 million per year have been flowing into the country since 1950, to balance a constant deficit in the balance of payments). Its own natural resources are meagre, and its markets extremely limited. It cannot compete with the advanced economies of the European countries, and Arab markets are closed to it. It is only the world-wide fund-raising activities of Zionist organizations such as the Jewish Agency, and the reparations paid by the Germans, which

* Until the Six Day War (see below). This was written before the Israeli attack–ed.

keep the standard of living in Israel at an artificially high level. If Israel's carefully cultivated image in the West—of a democratic, refugee-sheltering, peace-loving country—were seriously dented, the economic consequences could be very serious. The inevitable decline of imperialist influence coupled with the progressive unification of the Arab world will make Israel's position even more precarious.

Arab attitudes can be broadly divided into two: those of the feudal regimes; and those of the bourgeois nationalist parties. Superficially similar, the attitudes of the two groups are backed by very different deeds and motivations. Neither propose a political solution to the Palestine problem.

The Arab feudal regimes, like Zionism, had always been natural allies of Western imperialism. Today, as in the past, they share common political interests with Zionism as both depend for their existence on imperialist influence in the area. The feudal regimes cannot uphold such a policy publicly in the Arab world where the masses are anti-imperialist and clamour for political independence. To cover up their cooperation with imperialism they put out virulent anti-Zionist and anti-Jewish propaganda. A classic example occurred during King Faisal's visit to Washington in June 1966. While conferring with President Johnson on containing Nasser and his policies, and thereby running the risk of revealing his pro-imperialist policies to the Arab world, a press question gave him the opportunity to declare that 'all the Jews in the world support Israel, and therefore are enemies of the Arabs'. The mayor of New York City, which has more Jews than Israel itself, promptly cancelled an official dinner with him. Faisal could only congratulate himself on this chance to consolidate his tarnished image in the Arab world.

Publicly, the feudal regimes advocate the annihilation of Israel: privately, they cooperate with it. In some cases (Jordan particularly), they depend on it for their existence. Whenever the Palestinian Arabs in Jordan threaten the regime of King Hussein (grandson of Abdullah), the Israeli army moves to the armistice lines, ready to intervene if Hussein is overthrown. The rebellious masses are immediately 'pacified' on the grounds that only Hussein's army can defend them from the aggressive Israelis. Although Hussein's throne has rocked violently more than once, it has withstood all attacks up to now, thanks to the intervention of Israel, which would

regard the overthrow of Hussein as a violation of the *status quo* —
a new regime in Jordan might refuse to recognize the Abdullah–Ben
Gurion pact of 1948, and the Tripartite Declaration of 1950.

Thus, whereas on the surface the feudal regimes appear to be the
most extreme enemies of Zionism, they are as concerned as Israel
to consolidate and perpetuate imperialist influence and presence in
the area. Zionism, and Arab feudalism are, as always, 'friendly
enemies'.

The bourgeois and petty-bourgeois parties throughout the Arab
world approach the Palestine problem through the United Nations
resolutions. This policy was first formulated by Nasser at the
Bandung Conference (1955) and it was unanimously adopted. This
policy meant essentially that Israel should repatriate the Arab refugees (according to a 1949 UN resolution); and that Israel should
give up the territory annexed by it as a result of the secret pact
with Abdullah. This policy would reduce the area of Israel but
would not affect its Zionist character.

In fact, this conciliatory programme (which represents a considerable concession to Zionism) would not provide a stable solution of the Palestine problem. It would probably be as dangerous as
the *status quo*. A smaller Zionist state would still be dependent on
Western imperialism, and as such would continue to threaten Arab
progress towards unity and socialism. This programme was raised
again by Bourguiba in order to embarrass Nasser, who dropped this
formula after Suez, realizing that although the slogan of adhering
to the UN resolutions had an attractive propaganda value, it did
not provide for a stable solution. Moreover, since Nasser's approach
to the problem of Arab unity is a basically bourgeois one, relegating
class contradictions within Arab society to second place, he was
led to seek an understanding with the reactionary regime in Jordan.
But this regime is as much opposed to the UN partition resolution
as the Zionists are, because Jordan too annexed part of Palestine
territory. Nasser is now not so keen to raise the UN formula.

Today, the Nasserites and Ba'athists do not have any political
solution. Instead, they talk in military terms and argue endlessly
with each other whether to go to war with Israel ('liberate Palestine')
in the near future (Syrian Ba'ath) or to postpone the war until a
considerable progress is made towards Arab unity (Nasser). This
military approach evades the main question. War can, at the very
most, serve as a means to political solution; it can never replace one.

Even if a war against Israel were to be won, the question of the political future of Palestine would remain unsolved. A military Arab victory would, at most, destroy the Zionist regime, but two million Jews would remain, and probably constitute a problem similar to the Kurdish problem, unless a political solution is implemented. As is well known, the Nasserites and the Ba'athists do not have a political solution even to the Kurdish problem.

The slogan of 'liberating Palestine', although emotionally satisfying, has even more serious political disadvantages. In the first place, it forces moderate Israelis and even anti-Zionist Israelis (there are some) to side with the Zionist government in sheer self-defence. The result is a rare degree of solidarity between public opinion and government. Internal dissension, which would inevitably arise in a normal situation, is muffled. In this atmosphere few Israelis dare question their country's reliance on imperialism, which at least protects their lives.

Moreover, this simple slogan damages the Arab case in the world arena. Apart from the unpopularity of military solutions, it also has the fault of identifying an entire population with the policies of the state, and requiring them to pay the price for those policies. Such over-simplifications are no longer acceptable to progressive world opinion, especially anti-imperialist elements who demand political solutions to political problems. Even the North Vietnamese are careful to draw a distinction between the policies of Washington and the American people. As a result of these factors the Arab nationalists, in spite of the moral rightness of their case, have been consistently losing the propaganda war ever since 1948.

Any serious political solution to the Palestinian problem must take into consideration that, unlike the European settler communities in South Africa, Rhodesia or Algeria, the Jews in Palestine constitute not an upper class but a whole nation, with a complete class structure of its own. The fact that this new nation was created artificially through Zionist immigration does not alter the fact that it exists. Whereas the political set-up of this community can be changed or destroyed, the nation itself cannot be eliminated. A stable solution must therefore fulfil two basic requirements: it must abolish the Zionist character of Israel; and it must establish the self-determination of this nation in a form which is in accordance with the interests of the Arab masses, with socialism and unification.

It is clear that the existence of an Israeli state (whatever the size of its territory) isolated from the Arab world is contrary to the interests of the Arab masses. It is also contrary to the interests of the Israeli masses. Such a state cannot exist without outside support and will always necessarily be dependent on imperialism. The inherent instability of such a situation will always be a threat over the heads of the Israelis. A stable solution must therefore provide for a non-Zionist form of self-determination for Israel within the framework of an Arab Socialist Union. The Palestine problem is, in fact, closely linked with the class struggle in the Arab world and with the problem of unification. This is the reason why those forces in the Arab world which are unable to solve the problem of Arab unity are also unable to solve the Palestine problem.

Another aspect of the Palestine problem is the self-determination of the Palestinian Arabs. Should they exercise this right and establish a state of their own? Naturally, both the Zionists and Hussein are hysterically opposed to any such suggestion. But progressive elements are also undecided on this issue, believing that the creation of a new small Arab state would have a harmful effect on the process of unification.

Here, too, any solution must be compatible with the interests of unification and socialism throughout the Middle East. If a political form of self-determination of the Palestine Arabs be established (because it is theirs by right) it must come about in a way that will conform with the interests of the masses throughout the Middle East. A unification based on the denial of the right to self-determination is morally, and politically, wrong, and whenever practised in the past has introduced suspicion, mistrust and instability into the union. If these are to be eliminated from the Union of the Middle-Eastern states, the fundamental national rights of the constituent members must be fulfilled. They should be given up by consent, not coercion.

The Palestine problem demonstrated the fact that nationalistic policies are unable to overcome the problem of unification of national states and unable to solve the problem of national oppression. They can only turn oppressed into oppressor. The underlying problems remain. Only those socialists who have gone beyond nationalistic ideology and policies hold the key to a stable solution to the joint problems of abolishing national oppression and unifying the national states.

(2) The 1967 June War exposed and succinctly expressed fundamental contradictions and processes in the countries of the Middle East. In Israel, the Zionist character of this state and of its leadership was made more prominent; the propensity for annexation and expansion, half-dormant since the Suez War, has now re-awakened. The bonds between Israel's Zionist regime and imperialism have also been manifested and strengthened sevenfold.

On the eve of the June War, Israel's rulers still disclaimed any desire for territorial expansion. But on the morrow all these declarations were forgotten. Appetite was whetted by eating. The truth is that the propensity for annexation and expansion had always been inherent in all the trends of political Zionism—not only in the Heruth party, which openly declared it, but also in the more moderate trends that did not openly admit it, for political and propagandist reasons, when times did not seem opportune.

After the June War, Israel controls the whole of the Palestine Mandate territory as well as vast tracts of Egyptian territory and a region in the south of Syria. In the beginning, the leaders of Israel claimed that in this situation, where 'Israel holds all the cards', they would be able to force a settlement to their liking upon the Arabs, who would have to accept Israel's terms. But these hopes proved to be false. Victory in the war, far from solving the Israeli–Arab problem, has actually intensified it.

The historical conflict between Zionism and Israel in its present form, on the one hand, and the Arab world on the other, springs from the fact that the 'Zionist Endeavour' was from its very beginning a planned and deliberate process of colonization by outsiders who settled in this country, displacing its indigenous people; in this, Zionism was backed by imperialism and sided with imperialism against revolutionary developments in the Arab world.

The short-sighted attempt of Zionism to exploit this 'opportune moment' for territorial gains and for forcing its own terms upon the Arabs will no doubt boomerang back in the long run on Israel itself. The belief that Israel's control over vast territories would improve her current security has also proven mistaken. Victory in the war has not put an end to guerrilla and sabotage actions. On the contrary, in this new situation they have assumed larger dimensions. But whereas world public opinion before the war largely took exception to such actions, they are now increasingly regarded as natural and legitimate means of resistance of a conquered and subjugated people.

The Palestinian Arab people, the chief and direct victim of Zionist colonization, a people whose greater part was reduced during and after 1948 to the state of pauperized refugees, and another part of which has lived for twenty years in Israel under severe conditions of discrimination and persecution — that people has now entirely become a conquered people. It has been robbed not only of the most elementary political rights, but also of the very prospect for national and human existence. Regarding the fate of that people, the various schemes suggested by Israeli government circles range from outright annexation to Israel (accompanied by pressures to emigrate from the annexed territory and even by measures intended to reduce Arab birthrate, 'to deal wisely with them lest they multiply' — as Pharaoh had once put it . . .) to the setting up of a Bantustan, a political 'strategic hamlet' in the form of a protectorate camouflaged as a 'federation' between Israeli overlord and Arab subject.

It is both the right and duty of every conquered and subjugated people to resist and to struggle for its freedom. The ways, means and methods necessary and appropriate for such struggle must be determined by that people itself and it would be hypocritical for strangers — especially if they belong to the oppressing nation — to preach to it, saying 'Thus shalt thou do, and thus shalt thou not do.'

While recognizing the unconditional right of the conquered to resist against occupation, we can support only such organizations which in addition to resisting against occupation also recognize the right of the Israeli people for self-determination. On such a basis the struggle of the Palestinian people can become combined in a joint struggle of Arabs and Jews in the region for a common future.

One thing is obvious — tightening the yoke of repression, mass collective punishments, blowing up houses, large-scale massacre assaults (like that against Kerameh on 21 March) — all these are quite incapable of putting an end to resistance.

To those who express their abhorrence and indignation in view of the innocent Israeli victims of sabotage actions we say: your abhorrence and indignation are perfectly justified. This situation of horrible tragedy must be terminated at once; and the way to terminate it is immediate withdrawal from all the occupied territories. Only from that point will it be possible to advance towards a complete solution of the Israeli–Arab dispute and the Palestine problem.

The collapse of the Egyptian army in the June war exhibited before the world's eyes the grave social contradictions rending Egyptian society. These contradictions were only mirrored, and enlarged, in the army. The 'Free Officers' group, led by Gamal Abd-el Nasser, established in Egypt a petty-bourgeois regime. It was a 'halfway revolution'. By its very nature, this regime is ever trying to balance between anti-imperialism and the tendency to compromise with imperialism; between left and right; between the pressure of the masses and the interests of the over-privileged bourgeoisie, bureaucracy and officer caste.

That regime has carried through a series of important reforms, some of them quite far-reaching, it also severed Egypt's exceeding dependence upon imperialism. But it has not fulfilled the hopes of the masses or realized their interests; it did not go over to a socialist revolution turning the toilers from subjects to masters of the state. The exploiting classes of the ancient regime were battered, not shattered. They have largely continued to exist side by side with a new bureaucratic-military stratum which is related to them by origin and outlook.

We hold that the solution of the main problems of the Middle East, including the Israeli–Arab problem, requires a radical transformation of the regimes throughout the region; a socialist revolution which will bring the working class to power, liberate the immense energies latent in the masses and channel them to actuate social and economic progress. Such a transformation is needed not only in countries now under feudal monarchy, but also in the relatively progressive Arab countries which are now under a petty-bourgeois, self-styled 'socialist' regime.

As for Israel, here a socialist revolution is needed radically to change the character of this state, transforming it from a Zionist state, an instrument for furthering Zionist colonization, a natural ally of imperialism, into a socialist state representing the true interests of the Israeli masses, a state oriented towards the surrounding region and both willing and capable to integrate itself in it.

We hold that the revolutionary socialist solution to the Israeli–Arab conflict remains valid—is, in fact, more valid than ever—in the new situation created after the war. De-Zionization of Israel and its integration in a socialist union with the Arab countries — this is the road for solution.

II Al-Fatah: *Seven Point Platform*[88]

1. The National Liberation Movement of Palestine (Al-Fatah) is the expression of the Palestinian people and of its determination to liberate its territory from Zionist colonization and to re-establish its national identity.

2. Al-Fatah is not fighting against the Jews as an ethnic and religious community. It is fighting against the Zionist and colonialist state of Israel with its racist, theocratic and expansionist structure.

3. Al-Fatah rejects any solution to the Palestine problem which does not recognize the existence of the Palestinian people and its right to self-determination.

4. Al-Fatah categorically rejects the Security Council resolution of 27 November 1967 and the Jarring mission resulting from it. This resolution disregards the existence of the Palestinian people and its national rights. Any so-called peaceful solution which disregards this basic fact is bound to fail. In any case, the acceptance by this or that party of the 22 November resolution is not binding, in any manner whatsoever, on the people of Palestine which is determined to pursue its resolute struggle against foreign occupation and Zionist colonization.

5. Al-Fatah solemnly declares that the final aim of its struggle is the restoration of the independent democratic Palestinian state where all citizens, whatever their creed, can enjoy equal rights.

6. Palestine forms part of the Arab Homeland. Al-Fatah will work for the active participation of the Palestinian state in building a united and progressive Arab society.

7. The struggle of the Palestinian people, like that of the Vietnamese people and all other peoples of Asia, Africa and Latin America, forms part of the historical process of liberating the oppressed people from colonialism and imperialism.

I

III Popular Front for the Liberation of Palestine: *The August Platform*[89]

Immediately after the First World War the imperialist countries took over the Arab east, and Britain issued the Balfour Declaration of 1917 which granted Zionists the right to a 'national home' in Palestine. This pledge was not incidental but a logical outcome of the imperialist policies in the Middle East: to establish an armed, imperialist base to confront the rising tide of the Arab liberation movement whose victory would endanger the imperialist interests in this vital area of the world. This was why the Zionist colonizing ambitions found such a favourable response from Britain.

The Arab feudal-bourgeois regimes had, from their inception, thrown in their lot with the imperialists, in a broad counter-revolutionary front against the Arab movements for national liberation. Their feudal-bourgeois composition made them unable to face the imperialist-Zionist designs with armed force and patriotic popular revolution: reactionaries everywhere fear the people more than they do the imperialists. To oppose these designs effectively required the mobilization and arming of the people—and it is this that the reactionary regimes, the enemies of national liberation, absolutely refuse to do since it would endanger their very existence which is linked to imperialism (in its old and new aspect) in the Arab lands.

For Palestine, from the beginning of the modern era, it was apparent that its fate would depend on the outcome of the national struggle—i.e., the class struggle between the forces of national liberation on one hand, and the imperialist-Zionist camp and its allies, the Arab reactionary regimes, on the other. The control, by the feudalists and compradors, of the state machine and its numerous instruments of repression and even of the leadership of parts of the nationalist movement up to 1948, made the fate of Palestine a foregone conclusion. The defeat of 1948, brought about by the feudalist-theocratic leadership of Haj Amin Husseini, the major bourgeois parties (Istiqlal, Difa') and the Arab feudalist regimes, provides the concrete example for the dialectical relation between the Palestinian and the Arab situation, and between this situation and the international one.

The Palestinian resistance movement must pass judgement on the Arab regimes where the stand of these regimes on the problem of

Palestine is concerned. Otherwise, the resistance movement would lose its identity, becoming a quantitative addition to the Arab regimes and institutions responsible for the abortion of the rebellion of 1936, the catastrophe of 1948 and the defeat of June 1967. The problem of Palestine could never be understood in isolation from a study of the Arab regimes responsible for the 'historical impasse' facing the Palestine problem after the June defeat. The present Arab regimes, together with the Palestine resistance movement, now face a basic choice: either 'liquidation' or the adoption of a programme for a people's war. The choice that they will make is not divorced from the programme of action actually implemented by the Arab regimes and the Palestinian and Arab national liberation movements.

And just as the defeat of June was not merely military, so the catastrophe of 1948 was a defeat for all that the feudal-bourgeois regimes stood for. The formation of the state of Israel was the logical outcome for the backwardness of Palestine and the other Arab countries ruled by the feudal-bourgeois regimes, the allies of imperialism. The need arose clearly to view the catastrophe [of 1948] not by itself, but [as a function of] class rule, the economic and military [backwardness]; and to see that the liquidation of the state of Israel and the liberation of Palestine depend on the destruction of the feudal-bourgeois regimes—the liquidation of the real causes of the catastrophe. Nasser was correct when he told his comrades during the siege of Fallouja, 'The defeat was not decided on the battlefield, but there, in Cairo.' And, 'The liberation of Cairo from the feudalist-bourgeois regime of Farouk, the ally of imperialism and Arab reaction, is the central concern in any programme of action for the liberation of Palestine.'

Thus, for Arab and Palestinian liberation movements, the central concern became the liquidation of the feudalist-bourgeois regimes responsible for the catastrophe of 1948, in order to open the way for the solution of the problems presented by the phase of national liberation which demand the construction of a modern national economy (industrialization and land reform), independent in its development of the world market. For without the construction of a solid economic base, it is impossible to build regular and popular armies capable of waging a protracted battle against the camp of counter-revolution on Palestine and the Arab lands (Israel and imperialism and Arab reaction).

After 1948, the bourgeoisie, leader of the Arab national liberation movement, produced a programme of action, petty-bourgeois
in character, for the destruction of the feudalist-capitalist-imperia-
list alliance responsible for the defeat. Proclaiming the alliance of
workers, poor peasants, soldiers and the petty bourgeoisie—the last
providing the alliance with its ideology and leadership—it came to
power then or shortly thereafter in the UAR, Syria and Algeria (and
in Iraq to some extent). Its petty-bourgeois programme called for
the construction of an economy based on light industry in the first
instance, then for solving of the land question in the interests of
poor peasants, and finally for the electrification of the country. The
forces of counter-revolution, faced with the violence of the national-
class struggle, did not stay passive for long. In 1956, the tripartite
aggression (British–French–Zionist) was organized with the objective of liquidating the patriotic anti-imperialist regime which was
threatening the interests and positions of the counter-revolution in
Palestine and elsewhere in the Arab world. After the aggression of
1956, neo-colonialism, represented by the USA, attempted to contain the Arab liberation movements and the patriotic regimes 'from
the inside'. But these regimes turned the approaches down, continuing, desultorily, in their indecisive petty-bourgeois fashion, to wage
their patriotic fight against imperialism and neo-colonialism. The
American neo-colonialists then recognized the failure of their
'peaceful containment' policy for the subjection of the Arab
national liberation movements. Hence, the objectives of the June
war were not the reactionary regimes, but the patriotic regimes and
all the sections of the Arab and Palestinian national liberation
movements. Why, then, the defeat? And with what programmes
did the patriotic regimes and liberation movements face the June
defeat?

Petty-bourgeois theoreticians have offered explanations for the
defeat. In essence they all centre around the question of technical,
scientific and cultural superiority of Israel, and American imperialism supporting it. And as small, backward countries, they say, we
could not confront American imperialism which has a war-
machine vastly superior to any in the underdeveloped world of Asia,
Africa and Latin America. These analysts then conclude that our
victory over Israel requires overtaking it in science and technology.

Other petty-bourgeois theorizers explain the defeat by a series of
military errors committed by this or that army—e.g., the unpre-

paredness of the UAR air force at the time of the sudden Israeli attack. These theorizers blithely disregard the facts of contemporary history when they discuss the Arab defeat in June. They purposely avert their eyes from the real causes of the defeat in six days despite such noisy sloganeering immediately before 5 June as '[Liberation] inch by inch!', 'Scorched earth!' and 'People's war of Liberation!' And if the technical superiority of Israel and imperialism was the decisive factor in the defeat, how then could one account for the Vietnamese people's confronting half a million American soldiers in addition to half a million puppet regime troops? And if the defeat was merely the result of certain military errors, why then were they accepted?

In Vietnam and Cuba there are patriotic, revolutionary regimes which are proletarian and poor-peasant in composition. They place all the countries' resources, material and cultural, at the service of the struggle to overcome the problems of national liberation; the liquidation of all class privileges—material and cultural—and the construction of a solid base for economic and political independence by heavy industrialization, mechanization of agriculture and electrification. The revolutionary classes in society stand at the head of the alliance of all class and political forces opposed to the capitalist-imperialist camp. Such a patriotic economic and political programme is able to mobilize and arm all the classes struggling for the solutions of the problems of national independence against imperialism and colonialism. The slogan of 'people's war!' takes a concrete expression: the vast toiling masses are mobilized in people's militia, partisan groups and the ranks of the regular army for the defeat of imperialism and all its allies.

In our countries the situation is different. It is the petty bourgeoisie which assumes the leadership of the Palestinian and Arab movements for national liberation. This class had effected the social, economic and military transformation of these countries—a transformation that remained within the ideological orientation of this class, and it was this ideology and the whole programme that evolved from it that were defeated in June 1967. The economy could not withstand the Zionist-imperialist attack because it was mainly a 'consumer economy' geared to light industry. In agriculture, division of land was at the expense of productivity. After the closure of the Suez Canal, an economy like this had to turn to the reactionary 'oil regimes' for help.

In the field of ideology and politics the petty bourgeoisie remained at the top of the pyramid of power; the broad masses of the people remained at the base. The petty bourgeoisie, by nature, fear the masses as much as they fear the feudal-bourgeois alliance. They failed to build a national economy developing independently from the capitalist world market, and therefore could not sever all relations with the imperialist camp—especially the USA.

After the defeat, the petty-bourgeois regimes were faced with a choice. They could choose the Vietnamese and Cuban way, which would mean a complete transformation of their programmes of action: mobilizing all the material and human resources of society, arming the people for a revolutionary war against all imperialist, Zionist and reactionary interests and positions, translating the slogan 'Fighting Israel and those behind it' into a daily armed action on the widest possible front against all forces of counter-revolution. Only then would the balance of forces favour the Arab and Palestinian movements for national liberation. Or they could remain within the limits of the pre-June 1967 policies, which means that the Palestinian and Arab liberation movements would be doomed to continuous withdrawal in the face of Israel, imperialism and Arab reaction. We note with bitterness that this choice was made by the Arab regimes. Their class composition and ideology could not allow them to implement a policy of 'people's war', for this would have demanded of them the renouncing of their privileges, politically and materially.

A look at the UN resolution of November 1967 suffices to show that its acceptance and implementation herald the liquidation of the Palestine problem. The resolution itself is precisely such an imperialist attempt to liquidate the problem. It stipulates:
—The right of all states in the Middle East to live within 'secure boundaries.
—Recognition of each state by all other states.
—The right of 'innocent' passage in the waterways of all states.
—A 'just' solution for the refugee problem.

The problem now for the Arab regimes and the Arab and Palestinian movements of liberation is not to weigh the pros and cons of the UN resolution. It is also not to argue whether the official stand regarding it is or is not merely a matter of tactical convenience. It is to see whether the economic, political, military and ideological programmes being adopted by the regimes and the liberation movements could lead to the liquidation of the effects of the June aggression, i.e., the liberation of Sinai, the Western bank and the Golan heights as a first step in the protracted war for the liberation of Palestine and the liquidation of the aggressive, racist Zionist structure.

The experience of the national liberation movement in our countries (Palestine and the Arab world) and in the underdeveloped countries proves that the road to national salvation and liberation starts with the necessity of arming oneself with 'revolutionary tools' capable of defeating the militarily and technically superior imperialist countries: revolutionary anti-imperialist, anti-Zionist ideology — a scientific ideology (the ideology of the proletariat). . . .

We must raise the patriotic, radical consciousness. Our people face a modern enemy supported by the largest imperialist power, the USA. The relation between the people and the resistance movement should be based on a scientific outlook which implements 'the concrete analysis of the concrete situation'. The raising of the political level of consciousness starts by exposing the causes of the failures of the Palestinian and Arab liberation movements, whose glaring examples are the defeat of the rebellion of 1936 in Palestine at the hand of Palestinian and Arab reaction, the catastrophe of 1948, and the defeat of 1967. In those defeats are the lessons for our future victory.

We must reject all defeatist policies and the UN resolution and the insistence on a programme for a popular war of liberation by arming and mobilizing the people in popular militias, so that the war can be fought on the widest possible front against Israel and those who are behind it (including the pro-imperialist Arab forces).

Protracted war waged by a mobilized, self-reliant people, armed with proletarian ideology, is the sole road for national salvation and for the defeat of the technically superior Israeli-imperialist enemy.

IV Democratic Popular Front: *We are Marxist–Leninists*[90]

Q: *What is the strength of the Democratic Front at the moment, compared with the PFLP?*

A: The basis and resources of the Democratic Front are mainly and even exclusively the workers, peasants and poor refugees of Palestine. On the other hand, the Popular Front represents in its leadership and in its ideology sizeable sectors of the Jordanian and Palestinian bourgeoisie. Consequently the measure for the weight of each of the two should be not the numerical strength of each but rather the militancy of each. It is very unlikely that an organization representing the ideology and the class structure of the bourgeois class in Jordan could have the militancy and efficacy of an organization representing both the ideology and the class basis of the workers, peasants and the poor masses in general. Even numerically the Democratic Front is stronger than the Popular Front at the present.

Q: *What is the position of the DPF [LP] in relation to the regimes of Syria, Egypt, Iraq, and Algeria, and how does this compare with the attitudes of the Popular Front and the Al-Fatah as you see them?*

A : That those regimes are the regimes of the petty-bourgeois ruling class and have amply illustrated and proved during the June war 1967 their incapacity of waging a long protracted popular war which would achieve victory. No victory is possible without an adoption of the revolutionary ideology of the working class and without a popular protracted war based on the Arab and Palestinian workers and peasants. The ruling petty-bourgeois class in Syria, Egypt, Iraq and Algeria is incapable of organizing those classes because it is afraid of the revolutionary potential contained in the Arab workers and peasants which would obviously be directed against their regimes as such. The basic difference between the Democratic Front and the Popular Front is the refusal of the right-wing leadership of the Popular Front to analyze critically the reasons and causes that led to the military defeat of June 1967, under the pretext of refusing to interfere in the internal affairs of the Arab states and the Arab regimes. In this sense the Popular Front has a position not dissimilar to the position of Fatah. The Democratic Front believes that the struggle for national liberation of the Palestinian people is intimately related to the struggle of the Arab masses against imperialism, reaction and the petty-bourgeois regimes and as such it does not conceive of its own struggle except as part of this overall struggle in the whole of the Middle East.

Q: *What is the ideological and organizational make-up of the Democratic Popular Front?*

A : The Democratic Popular Front believes that all its members should actively participate in military activity, thus forging a well built and strong military and militant detachment that will be capable of defeating imperialism, Arab reaction and Zionism. This necessarily means that the Democratic Front is not divided into a political and military wing. All militants are equally political militants [and their politico-military activity is] based on the revolutionary ideology of the working-class Marxism–Leninism. This distinguishes the DPF from the other organizations of the Palestinian Liberation movement. The DPF looks at the Palestinian people as one people without distinction of religion or creed. While refusing the concept of a bi-national state the DPF looks at the inhabitants of Palestine as one people. As the DPF puts the struggle in Palestine in its proper context, it aims at establishing in Palestine a Palestinian state under the leadership and hegemony of the working class. This Palestinian state would obviously grant *all* its inhabitants equal rights.

Q : *Does this imply that the DPF would be happy to achieve a socialist Palestine in which, for a while, the Jews might be a majority, provided of course that the Zionist structure and the Zionist organizations abroad were dismantled?*

A: Jewish numerical majority would be unlikely at present because the last census of population in Israel puts forward the figure of $2\frac{1}{4}$ million among whom 350,000 are Arabs. On the other hand, the Palestinian people now number about 2,000,000 which would mean that the situation would approach numerical equality between Arabs and Jews. Nevertheless the DPF accepts that Palestine is for all inhabitants, Arabs and Jews, which has to have as a pre-condition the ending of *institutionalized* Jewish immigration to Palestine. Further immigration into Palestine would have to be decided by the new social order that is going to be instituted in Palestine. This means that any possible immigration would be discussed and decided upon its merits, and obviously that would not exclude anybody and needless to say it wouldn't exclude Jews from immigrating to Palestine.

Q : *As I am sure you know, there is a small but growing left-wing revolutionary movement inside Israel. Do you foresee that at some*

I*

*time in the future the struggles of the Palestinian revolutionaries
and the Israeli revolutionaries may be united?*
A: The revolutionary left you mention still emphasizes the need to
preserve the national entity of the Jews in Palestine which negates
what we have been emphasizing on the Palestinians as one people,
one undivided people. As far as the second part of the question goes,
in as much as this revolutionary left proves itself in practice and
proves by its activity the extent and militancy of its opposition to
the Zionist regime presently controlling Palestine, cooperation and
coordination with the revolutionary national liberation movement
of the Palestinian people is possible. Only then could there be one
broad class struggle in Palestine.

Q : *What is the general military strategy and objectives of the
Democratic Popular Front and how does this tie up with the
political struggle inside the occupied territories?*
A : The DPF seeks to move its bases from the eastern bank to the
western bank so that the east-bank bases would only be relay bases
for the basic centres of its activities inside the occupied territories.
At the same time the Democratic Popular Front prepares for mass
action and mass participation of the workers of the east bank to
offset any attempts at counter-revolution. This dual strategy in the
view of the DPF is a specific implementation of the principles of
popular protracted warfare in the context of Palestine, namely the
activity and operations against Zionist occupation from within the
occupied territories proper, and at the same time mass action and
preparation inside the east bank against Hashemite and Arab reaction. The Democratic Front aims at building a wide popular front
of all the forces that are opposed to Arab reaction, imperialism and
Zionism.

Q :*Do you see a useful part being played by the civilian struggle
in the occupied territories and are you trying to develop this aspect
as well as the military aspect?*
A : The Democratic Popular Front considers that civilian resistance in the occupied territories is complementary to the military
activity waged by the Palestinian liberation struggle. We would also
like to emphasize that as far as the Democratic Front is concerned
we do not distinguish between military and civilian activity. We believe that what popular warfare essentially means is that all the
people carry out the most varied active participation in the struggle
against occupation. What is a daily activity of the Democratic

Front in the east bank is propaganda and action among Palestinian and Jordanian masses. This entails, for example, weekly visits of Democratic Front doctors to villages that are not regularly visited by the doctors of the Jordanian monarchy, political education, propaganda, etc. As for similar activities within the occupied territories it should be borne in mind that the recent emergence of the Democratic Front, and the extreme difficulties that face its attempts to establish itself as an independent armed movement, has not yet given it ample chance to develop its political organization inside the occupied territory. It should also be remembered in this context that in spite of those enormous difficulties the volume of activities of military operations carried on by the Democratic Front inside the occupied territories is quite considerable.

The Democratic Front has carried on a series of military activities inside the occupied territories which include the regular activities carried on by any liberation movement, namely, attacks on military Israeli occupation units, military targets, etc. Two or three operations of the Democratic Front are worthwhile commenting upon. These three operations have a clear propaganda value aimed especially at the Jewish community in Palestine and in this sense the Democratic Front is carrying on armed propaganda or propaganda by deeds. The first of these operations is the bomb in the cafeteria of the Hebrew University of Jerusalem. This operation carried out in March 1969 has been interpreted as follows in an official statement of the DPF : 'The Hebrew University is responsible for producing the main cadres for the Israeli state, namely the administration, the police and the army. It is also responsible for the inculcation of reactionary Zionist culture in the ranks of Jewish intellectuals. This is why the Democratic Front feels responsible to discourage Jewish intellectuals from criminally following the imperialist and Zionist policy.' The meaning of this text is quite clear. The bomb in the cafeteria of the Hebrew Univerisity is a warning and at the same time an active propaganda act aimed at the Jewish intellectuals to open their eyes to Zionism and to turn them from it. The second operation of the Democratic Front was the demolition of the Labour Exchange at Nablus, carried on in the second half of April 1969. The DPF explained this activity in the following terms: 'The Democratic Front aims at hitting the prominent Zionist military and political institutions in the occupied territories. This is why the demolition of the Israeli Labour Exchange in

Nablus expresses the rejection by the Democratic Front and the masses of Nablus of the Zionist, political and military policy of employing Arab labour in order that Israeli workers can be drafted into the occupation army. Moreover, the establishment by the enemy of Labour Exchanges in occupied territories is designed to employ cheap labour thus furthering the exploitation practised by Zionist capitalism and increasing its wealth.' The third operation was the demolition of a factory in the Golan Heights. The aim of this operation was the propaganda value directed at the Jewish workers in a similar manner as the Hebrew Univerisity operation was directed towards Jewish intellectuals.

Q: *It is often said that the Zionist state thrives on the existence of war. Can it not be said that the carrying out of military operations against purely civilian targets as opposed to military or economic targets will make the task of the revolutionary left inside Israel more difficult and tend to solidify the Israelis more and more behind Zionism?*

A: Three points could be made in answering this question. First point: military operations against civilians form part and parcel of any struggle for national liberation. In this sense the national liberation struggle of Palestinian people is no different from any struggle, no different from the national liberation struggle waged by the Vietnamese people. Second point: the military operation carried on by the armed struggle of the Palestinian people is designed to create as much disturbance and as much dislocation in the Zionist state occupying Palestine, to prove by deeds that the Zionist design is no longer comfortable, no longer profitable for anybody and no longer viable even for the one people who initially believed in it. Third point is that those same military operations are designed to warn the Jewish community in occupied Palestine of the crimes committed in its name by Zionism against the whole people, i.e., against the Palestinian people.

The Palestine problem has uneven effects. Zionism is equally dangerous to both Arabs and Jews. One basic fact should be borne in mind: the principal victim of Zionism is the Palestinian people. The condition of the establishment of the Zionist state in Palestine has been the displacement of the Palestinian people. Consequently, the principal contradiction at present is between the Palestine people in its majority—either under Israeli rule and the victim of racial persecution and oppression or displaced and in exile in the surrounding Arab countries on one side and the Zionist structure that binds the Jewish community together in Palestine on the other. The second point pertains to that concept of the Hebrew nation. This concept implies an inherent contradiction. If by asserting the existence of a Hebrew nation one implies from this the legitimate right of the Hebrew nation to possess and establish its own state then we sink back obviously into Zionism. Clearly this implication of the concept goes against the whole interpretation and the whole rejection of Zionism. But if by the term Hebrew nation is meant that the Jewish community in Palestine possesses its peculiar cultural features and implies a code for respecting these cultural peculiarities, then clearly any revolutionary socialist platform in the Arab world respects and helps further the cultural development of all minorities in the Arab world. Not only Jews but Kurds, Armenians, etc. To clarify further, when we talk of minorities in this context, we refer to minorities in the context of a united socialist Arab republic in the Middle East.

IRAQ

Except for traditional communists, politicians tend to be a violent lot in Iraq. For years, the youthful King Faisal and his perennial prime minister Nuri el-Said thought nothing of torturing and killing their critics. Then, on 14 July 1958, a batch of army officers, including Major General Abdul Karim Qassem ('Kassim' in the Western press), Colonel Abdel Salam Aref and Major General Ahmed Hassan al-Bakr, overthrew the monarchy and established a republic; the king and his prime minister were promptly killed by a vengeful mob.

Qassem consolidated his power, 'retired' Hassan al-Bakr, jailed Aref and condemned him to death, but forgot to kill him. So, on 8 February 1963, when a Ba'ath Party coup overthrew Qassem and installed Aref as a figure-head president, Aref remembered the past but did not forget to dispose of Qassem. He had him executed in front of television cameras. The Ba'athis then went on a rampage, slaughtering thousands of communists who had been Qassem's allies. Once that was taken care of, Aref tossed the Ba'athis out of power and ruled until April 1966, when he died in a helicopter crash. His brother, General Abdul Rahman Aref, took over next—until General Hassan al-Bakr made his comeback, and, with the Ba'ath right wing, seized power in July 1968.

With each coup, of course, hundreds of opponents were quietly liquidated and thousands tossed into jail. But one group, though constantly harassed, remained faithfully peaceful—members of the Communist Party of Iraq (ICP). This was not because they abhorred violence but because throughout Qassem's regime they were convinced that they 'had the President's ear'. In fact, the Central Committee of the ICP condemned as 'leftist violationist extremist' every communist cadreman who advocated peasant land seizures, defence committees, arming the people, even just criticizing Qassem. As a result, when Qassem was overthrown, the ICP was totally unprepared for the ensuing repression—in which, among thousands,

Salam Adel (Hassan Al-Radawi) and Jamal Haidat, respectively first and second secretaries of the ICP, were tortured to death.

Instead of challenging the whole ideological base and analysis of the Central Committee, the 1963 coups of February and October (Aref's ousting of the Ba'ath) brought about a hardening of the so-called 'rightist tendency' within the ICP. The Central Committee's policies coincided totally with Soviet strategy: peaceful coexist-ence, non-anti-capitalist road to socialism, full cooperation with the petty-bourgeois nationalist movements of the Arab world (Nasser-ism), then Ba'athism, which is a so-called Moslem-Arab form of socialism).

To support Aref or the Ba'ath just because they called themselves Arab nationalists and declaimed against Zionism was unacceptable to many communists, however, especially after so many of their comrades had been massacred by both. Thus many left the party and, eventually, created two new groups: the Armed Detachment of the ICP, which began urban guerrilla activities, and the Group of Revolutionary Cadres which undertook preparations for rural armed struggle. These two groups then forced a split in the ICP, with the revolutionary elements calling themselves the Central Com-mand of the Iraqi Communist Party (ICP-CC). Headed by Aziz Al-Hajj, a member of the old Central Committee, it issued the self-critical analysis (below) in September 1967 and called for a Party Congress early in 1968.

By the time it convened in January, the urban guerrilla Armed Detachment had been uncovered by the police and liquidated. The Group of Revolutionary Cadres insisted that armed struggle be con-sidered as 'the decisive means' of attaining revolutionary power. The ICP-CC wanted the Plenum to consider it 'one means of revolu-tionary struggle'. A compromise was reached: the Front for Popular Armed Struggle (FPAS) would begin guerrilla operations in the south as an independent movement open to all revolutionaries, and Aziz Al-Hajj's ICP-CC would officially and publicly support it. Meanwhile, it reported (pamphlet, dated 5 January 1968) that 'the Plenum saw the need to subordinate diplomatic considerations to the principle of class struggle and to the requirements of interna-tionalist solidarity, and the need to consolidate the fighting front against world imperialism led by the US'. And it concluded that 'the Plenum stressed that subjective conditions for achieving victory do

*not all ripen simultaneously, but crystallize through direct and reso-
lute revolutionary struggle.'*

The FPAS began operations—*successful attacks on a series of
police observation posts near the marshlands of Al-Ahwar, where
the guerrillas had their base. They were led by Khaled Ahmad
Zaki, the ex-President of the Iraqi Students' Association in Britain
and a former member of the secretariat of the Bertrand Russell Peace
Foundation. Three days later, Zaki and twelve men were caught in
an army encirclement. For thirty-six hours they fought, trying to
retreat deep into the marsh, shooting down an army helicopter in
the process. When the shooting stopped, five had made it, five were
caught and three guerrillas were dead—Zaki among them.*

On 11 June the ICP-CC issued the following communiqué:

*The sustenance and development of armed struggle in the Arab
countryside; the passing over of the Kurdish revolution to the stage of
revolutionary offensive; the role our Party can play in strengthening it
and increasing its participation in it; the revolutionary operations in the
cities and the crucial role that the popular revolution expect the revolutionary forces inside the army to play in order to tip the balance of power
decisively to the side of the people – all these varied forces of revolutionary
armed struggle are interlocked and interacting on one another; and they
must all merge into one revolutionary drive in order to achieve final
victory. Moreover, the mass struggles – both economic and political –
play a concrete and necessary role in preparing for the armed struggles,
for they help raise the general revolutionary mood, weaken the enemy
forces and spread confusion in its ranks.*

It was a mild statement of support—*presumably because the
FPAS had been wiped out. But it was a beginning.*

Central Command of the Iraqi Communist Party: *Self-Criticism*[91]

In both its socio-political content and participating forces, the July
Revolution was a national-democratic revolution. It is impossible
to understand the causes of its sudden eruption without a compre-
hensive knowledge of the preceding popular struggles of which our
Party was the prime organizer. The national and social mass strug-

gles in both city and countryside, the leading role played by our Party in those struggles, the deep national democratic consciousness developed by the masses over decades and the total isolation of the reactionary puppet regime — all are factors which account for the transformation of the military *coup d'état* of 14 July (in which military units occupied strategic positions in Baghdad) into the bridgehead of a genuine popular revolution in which millions of people participated. But the low level of class consciousness and the control of bourgeois and petty-bourgeois officers over the military operation which unleashed the revolution led to the transfer of state power to the representatives of the national bourgeoisie and of certain sectors of the petty bourgeoisie, to the exclusion of representatives of the working class and its Party. Despite the fact that our Party had taken the initiative in forming the 'National Unity Front'* and in uniting the various groups of 'free officers', it was the only party of this front which had no representatives in the 'Revolutionary Government'.

The nature of any political regime can be defined on the basis of the ideology that guides it, its policies and the interests it represents. The revolution achieved political independence, dealt a mortal blow to the Baghdad Pact, initiated a progressive — though not radical — agrarian reform, established some basic democratic freedoms and recognized certain national rights of the Kurdish people. Those national democratic steps were implemented under constant pressure from the masses led by our Party. The ICP developed at a rapid rate after the revolution and came to play a decisive role in organizing the masses of workers, peasants, students, youth and women; led the mass campaign for arming the people and was primarily instrumental in uncovering and defeating the successive reactionary plots.

Since the first days of the revolution, a number of contradictions arose between the interests of the national bourgeoisie and some sectors of the petty bourgeoisie on one hand, and those of the working class and its natural allies on the other. So long as the national bourgeoisie was not in possession of state power, those contradictions were relegated to the background. But, once the revolution put state power into the hands of the military representatives of the

* Formed during the struggle against the monarchy and including the ICP, the Ba'ath, the National Democratic Party and the Istiqual Party with the indirect participation of the Democratic Party of Kurdistan – Translator's note.

national bourgeoisie, the latter sought to contain the revolution within prescribed limits, afraid lest its radicalization and progress led to working-class control over the state. Those attempts soon clashed with the mounting revolutionary wave among the masses and their constant pressures—matters which the government had to take into account, especially since it was permanently subjected to reactionary plots.

It is true that Qassem was neither a 'classic' representative of the national bourgeoisie, nor the leader of a bourgeois party in power. It is also true that he came from a petty-bourgeois background. Nevertheless, the spirit with which he conducted the country's policy shows that he was, from the beginning, a *conscious* representative of the national bourgeoisie. Or else, how can we explain his initial fears from the increasing influence of the ICP and the upsurge of working-class and peasant militancy, his reluctance to grant genuine popular freedoms, his leniency towards reaction or his preservation of the reactionary state machine? All this occurred at a time when our Party was pursuing a policy of alliance with Qassem, lulled by the belief that the man is a revolutionary democrat who is bound to join the camp of the working class! At a time when we were foremost in propagating his cause and mystifying people about him.

Our first mistake did not lie in the lack of 'diplomatic charm', but in our idealist, non-Marxist characterization of Qassem which put him over and above all classes and parties and considered him a member of the camp of the toiling masses and their revolutionary movement. This rightist view ultimately led to exaggerated support for Qassem and reluctance to criticize his wavering or provide the masses with a correct appreciation of the man and of the regime he leads. Consequently, our calculations for the development of the revolution were based on Qassem's own person, and his 'goodwill'. We lacked any revolutionary plan to radicalize the revolution, free it of the strait-jacket imposed by Qassem and the national bourgeoisie and drive it forward towards fulfilling its essential tasks, namely a radical land reform and preparatory steps for its transformation into a socialist revolution.

Among the rightist, opportunist concepts deeply entrenched in our Party is the one which considers erroneous any attempt made, after 14 July 1958, to realize revolutionary democratic demands by relying on the masses, by starting 'from below', 'from the streets', etc. Such attempts, labelled 'leftist', are considered liable to alienate our ally—the bourgeoisie—and even superfluous, since the same demand, more or less, can be realized by secret negotiations with the government or through diplomatic channels. In fact, this concept does not seek at educating the masses through practical revolutionary struggle, nor at deepening the revolution or pushing it forward. It is a concept based on immediate, narrow interests which is alien to the Party's basic goals.

The Party opened offices for 'Popular Resistance', started accepting recruits and called upon the government to train and arm them. However, the immediate reaction of Qassem's government was to issue a military order to close down these offices. The question of acquiring arms by revolutionary means was then put on the agenda of an extraordinary meeting of the Central Committee, held in the last days of July 1958. The discussion ended by the victory of the rightist tendency which put forward a rare piece of wisdom : 'Why this alarm about the new order? It has come to stay, and will know how to defend itself when the need arises!' 'Reason' defeated 'burning revolutionary passion' and the defence of the revolution was entrusted to the bourgeoisie. Qassem's government, facing counter-revolution, was forced to establish and train popular resistance units, but kept the arms under lock and key in the police stations; the arms for the defence of the revolution were put under the watchful eye of counter-revolution!! (For the security forces never changed during Nuri Said, Qassem's dictatorship or the Ba'athi dictatorship of 8 February 1963.)

Thus, the 'Revolutionary Government' paralyzed the popular resistance even before it was born. Qassem did not even call it to arms when he was in danger just before 8 February 1963. What is even more surprising is that the rightist tendency, which opposed arming the people in July 1958, blamed the Party for calling the masses to armed resistance on 8 February 1963, without providing them with arms!

It is a well-known fact that our Party took the initiative in forming the National Unity Front composed of all Arab patriotic forces in Iraq and established a bi-lateral alliance with the Kurdish Democratic Party because the front did not recognize the national rights of the Kurdish people. Our Party also took the initiative in uniting all the organizations of patriotic officers in the Army and connected them with the front. Despite all that, ours was the party in this front which was not represented in the 'Revolutionary Government'. At the enlarged plenum of the Central Committee (on 6 September 1958), the slogan of 'abolishing competition' was adopted to bridge the gap between the fact that our Party was not represented in the government composed of representatives of bourgeois and petty-bourgeois groups and its active participation in the National Unity Front, whose emergence was the prime condition for the victory of the 14 July revolution.

We never went beyond propaganda and agitation for the democratic demand that our Party be represented in the government in order to transform it into a genuine National Coalition Government. After the Shawwaf armed conspiracy in Mossul,* Qassem found himself in an embarrassing situation *vis-à-vis* his clique of officers because of his policy of conciliation between the nationalists and the democrats. This embarrassment ultimately led Qassem to seek to coopt some communists into his Cabinet, but without formally recognizing this as a representation of our Party in Government and refusing to relinquish his personal dictatorial powers to the Cabinet and by so doing transform it into a genuine National Coalition Government composed of representatives of all the patriotic forces, including our Party. This embarrassment and Qassem's reaction led the rightist tendency in our Party to seek to abolish the difference between a genuine Coalition Government, which can only come through mass struggle, 'from the streets', and a fake coalition government whose members are chosen according to the leader's personal whim.

Our Party lost about two months—from 8 March to the end of April 1959—in secret negotiations with Qassem on the participation of some comrades in the government. This phase was termed by reactionaries the period of the 'Red Menace'. At the end of these fifty days, the American commander of NATO forces in Turkey sounded the alarm and solemnly declared that the situation in Iraq had become hopeless. At a time when the enemies of the revolution were extremely vigilant, our Party passed through a unique revolutionary situation without even realizing it. The only means of those enemies of the revolution was then to clamour and to slander, reflecting their deeply engrained fear of victory of the revolutionary

* An abortive Nasserite coup led by Colonel Shawwaf in Mossue during the summer of 1959, which led to violent reprisals by Qassem and the ICP against the nationalists – Translator's note.

wave in Iraq. This fear soon found its way into our ranks through the infiltration of rightist conceptions and the existence of a strongly entrenched rightist tendency, and because of our constant fear of 'leftist deviation'. Our bourgeois enemy-allies scared us off by evoking the threat of a civil war, which is an ever-present possibility. Yet, had one occurred then, it would have turned out in our favour. Whereas, when it did start effectively in February 1963, it took the form of an atrocious butchery against communists and revolutionary democrats. Reaction emerged victorious because it chose the appropriate time and place. As for our fear of civil war in 1959, it did not serve to avoid the catastrophe, but, on the contrary, helped render it inevitable.

During the revolutionary situation of the spring of 1959, there was no way out of the revolutionary crisis except by seizing power from Qassem, whose bargaining with the right wing had been evident before the [Shawwaf] conspiracy and who found himself in an embarrassing situation after it. Qassem knew how to retreat after the conspiracy and until the end of April 1959. As for us, we missed a historic opportunity and lost for the people a unique revolutionary situation.

The rightists claim that the main battle until mid-1959 was against imperialism and counter-revolution. Therefore, it was incorrect to press—even to press!—for developing the revolution and the seizure of power by the revolutionary classes. The fact is that the national and the democratic contents of the revolution are interlocked and therefore inseparable. We all know, for example, that the conflict with the nationalists and Cairo revolved essentially around the question of political democracy (in its popular, not bourgeois, sense); and that the fear of Iraq's development along the road to democracy and the scare of our Party's influence and that of the peasant movement are the only explanation why those parties were so keen on imposing their unionist policy (i.e., Arab unity devoid of any political democracy in which the communist parties would be banned) on Iraq at any cost. Furthermore, the complete victory against imperialism (and its oil companies in particular) and the efficient resistance to the mounting wave of reactionary plots were only possible by relying on the broadest masses in an atmosphere of ample freedom, by winning over the great mass of peasants to the revolutionary camp and by organizing them on the basis of a radical agrarian reform in the implementation of which the peasant would have direct, structural participation. Therefore, the establishment of a revolutionary, national-democratic regime was required in order to sustain a resolute struggle against imperialism and to successfully defeat counter-revolution.

In the conditions of Iraq, this regime can only come about through an active and efficient, if not leading, role played by the working class and its Party in state power. As for us, we have idealized bourgeois nationalism and consolidated the bourgeois regime which was not even capable of preserving itself or its leader on 8 February 1963 — all this in the name of fighting against imperialism and counter-revolution. The slogan of 'defending the revolution' exemplified this idealization of bourgeois nationalism. Whereas we should have raised, from the beginning, the slogan of a 'revolutionary, national-democratic regime', educated the masses about the need for the participation of the ICP in state power, constantly exposing the ambivalence of the national bourgeoise and its political organs, and organized the broadest masses to impose the implementation of a revolutionary democracy through the escalation of mass pressure, then moved to the overthrow of Qassem himself when he persisted in refusing to heed the will of the masses. Had we followed this strategy and adopted the appropriate revolutionary tactics, we would most probably have succeeded in seizing state power during the period of revolutionary upsurge in 1959, or at least initiated civil war in such a way as to make sure that we would have emerged from it victorious.

The principal factor which led to the defeat of armed resistance against the 8 February coup* is a strategic and not a tactical factor: our adoption of an erroneous strategy based on negative defence. We resolved not to initiate armed struggle in defence of this regime when faced with a military coup. In other words, we decided not to initiate civil war, but avoid it at all costs — at a time when the other forces were preparing for it, sharpening their knives to butcher us. Indeed, we resigned initiative to the counter-revolution to choose the most appropriate moment to realize its dream of liquidating our Party and crushing the revolutionary movement.

The rightist ideas which dominated our Party since 1959 are the cause of the defeat of armed resistance in 1963. But those ideas say

* 8 February 1963 is the date of the Ba'athi *coup d'état* and the anti-communist witchhunt–ed.

the Party committed the mistake of calling the masses to arms on 8 February without providing them with a sufficient number of arms and ammunition. In fact, our Party had a following of thousands of officers and soldiers, and the great mass of soldiers at large was opposed to the coup. But four years of negative defence and leaving the initiative in the hands of the enemy paralysed those effective 'reserves' from launching armed resistance against the putschists (and the same applies to thousands of armed peasants).

In our plans for armed resistance, before 8 February, we relied heavily on our peasant comrades-in-arms only to discover after the coup serious flaws in this vital sector. We lacked small armed bands composed of trained comrades devoted to armed struggle who can constitute the nucleus and the pole that attracts the mass of armed peasants. Those are serious tactical and technical flaws, but our basic mistake was a tactical one: we left the peasant masses in a vicious circle during the years 1958–9, did not encourage them to settle accounts with their class enemies—the big landowners and the feudalists—and refrained from training them to defend their acquisitions after Qassem's retreat which started in mid-1959. We left them 'in reserve' to defend the Republic when the 'decisive day' comes, but without relating this to any of their vital interests. And when this 'decisive day' finally came, only the vanguard of the peasantry moved.

Setting up revolutionary organizations inside the armed forces is a relatively easy task, but it is quite difficult to preserve such organizations for long in a country dominated by political reaction which deprives the people of its most elementary rights. The official, military command of the army, as distinct from its revolutionary command, controls military discipline which banks on a huge force—the force of habit. The military commander can move his troops by one order, whereas the revolutionary commander (i.e. the Party) requires the existence of a high revolutionary mood among his revolutionary forces, and needs strong levers in the form of special organizations (special armed detachments, shock troops, a vanguard, etc.).

One of the big flaws in our previous defence plan resided in that everything depended on winning or losing the battle in Baghdad. Our military and civilian organizations did not possess a plan to pursue armed struggle outside Baghdad. This was bound to lead to confusion or even sheer desperation. After the defeat of our first resistance, we should have operated a provisional, organized retreat, or at least withdrawn our cadres to a relatively safe area. Nothing of the sort happened. As usual, our organizations and cadres were put under strict emergency regulations; furthermore, they remained in the cities and did not take refuge as a whole in the countryside— a fact which facilitated their capture. Had there been a plan ready before the coup for withdrawal of some of our military and civilian comrades to the countryside, then we could have started the civil war in a relatively forceful manner, or, at least, our forces would not have been annihilated without fighting as was the case when some of our cadres defected.

Our military strategy was one of quick decision which resolves the conflict in one decisive blow ('all or nothing') and thus we lacked a long-term defensive plan. But this military flaw is a consequence of our political line which refrained from furthering the workers' and peasants' revolution but limited itself to 'defending the revolution' or ameliorating the situation in alliance with the bourgeois forces inside or outside government. It never occurred to us to organize the agrarian revolution or push it forward by encouraging the peasants to enforce the land-reform law as a *fait accompli* by confiscating the lands of the feudalists or refusing to pay rent.

From the beginning of 1964, 'the spirit of the age'—i.e., the age of transition to socialism on the world scale, the age of increasing might of the socialist camp and of its influence on the course of world events, the age of the disintegration of the colonialist system, etc.—was used to give priority to peaceful struggle (at a time when the country was plagued with a reactionary military dictatorship). Thus giving priority to other means of struggle over the armed struggle was not conceived on the basis of the specific internal situation in Iraq (the enemy's strength, the strength of the democratic movement, the level of revolutionary consciousness among the masses, the Kurdish revolution, Iraq's strategic location, the oil economy, historical conditions, etc., etc.) but on a multitude of factors which contain not one single reference to internal conditions.

The rightist tendency further used the 'spirit of the age' to prove that our Party and the democratic movement at large now play a secondary role not only in all the Arab countries but also in all the newly independent states. Time and time again our party stressed the positive impact of the 'spirit of the age' on Nasser, Ben Bella and even Aref, to point out the possibilities of the development of the Arab Socialist Union in Iraq into an organization for all revolutionaries—only to discard the leading role of the working class in the revolution, political democracy and even the dictatorship of the proletariat.

How can communists exercise their political, intellectual and educational influence and carry out their vanguard role without possessing their independent party, with its developed ideology and organization? Is the dissolution of communist organizations in some independent Arab countries and the integration of communists into a formless organization which includes six million members*—full of reactionaries, characterized by ideological disunity and political apathy and constituting an integral part of the existing regime—a solution in the interest of the revolutionary movement in this country? Were communists really able to exercise real and effective 'political, intellectual and educational influence'? Or have they been totally submerged in the dominant petty-bourgeois *milieu*? Was it not in the interest of the national-democratic—not to say socialist—revolution in [newly independent countries] that strong communist parties should have existed *at least* in order to face the threat of counter-revolutionary coups (e.g., the experiences of Ghana and Algeria)? Isn't the existence of such parties necessary *at least* to organize the masses for resisting those coups?

As for Cairo's Arab policy, it is a wavering opportunistic and shortsighted policy which is by no means governed by general revolutionary principles, despite its dominant anti-imperialist character. Although Nasser recognized, in 1962, the error of establishing a truce with Egyptian and Arab reaction, he nevertheless initiated the Arab Summit conference [in 1964] in which he once more concluded peace with the ruling Arab oligarchies and bestowed upon them a false nationalist white-wash, only to launch a recent attack against summit conferences and so on, alternating between glorifying Bourguiba and Hussein and denouncing and attacking them.

As regards Iraq, Cairo's policy is to collaborate with any Iraqi government which is not openly hostile to it, whichever its nature may be and irrespective of the feeling of the Iraqi people towards it. Indeed Cairo wishes, and tries to get its Iraqi friends in power. Yet it is well aware of their weakness and isolation. Therefore, it prefers to collaborate (with its friends) with any Iraqi government which is willing to be friendly with Egypt, however reactionary its

* Reference to the Arab Socialist Union (ASU), the ruling party in Egypt—ed.

internal policy might be. But, Cairo would never accept a revolutionary, democratic solution to the government crisis in Iraq, i.e., a solution in which our Party would play a major role.

In view of Cairo's empiricist, opportunist policy, it is hardly surprising that it supported the February [1963] coup and concluded the April [1963] agreements with the putschists.* When Cairo failed to convince the Ba'athis to subordinate their rule to hers, she broke relations with them. In fact, Cairo did not break those relations because of the Ba'athis' bloody, fascist policy against the communists and democrats, nor for their aggressive chauvinism against Kurdish nationalism or their soft policy towards the feudalists and the oil companies; the conflict revolved around the refusal of the Ba'athis to bow down to Cairo orders. It is precisely for this same reason that Cairo then supported the October [1963] coup, collaborated with Aref and Taher Yahia and concluded the 'coordination agreement' with their regime. In practice, this agreement ran counter to all of Cairo's statements and platforms on 'the unity of the Arab toilers' and to its 'new' concept of Arab unity. For what has the 'unity of the toilers' to do with concluding a 'coordination agreement' with a reactionary military clique isolated from the vast majority of the Iraqi people? What 'progressive union' is the one that does not care to collaborate with the revolutionary progressive forces in Iraq, but collaborates instead with a terrorist, chauvinist gang which is suppressing those forces? What is important is not the new unionist platforms, but their execution—i.e., the practical policy which Cairo is still following.

In Iraq, meanwhile, the Communist leadership hailed the 'coordinating agreement' as the first step towards the unity of all Arab toilers and a guiding-light to all the future battles against imperialism in the area at large. The rightist tendency raised the slogan of the 'identity of conditions in Egypt and Iraq', calling for the simulation of Egypt in all fields, 'especially in internal policy and agrarian reform'. Our position on the 'coordination agreement' should have been, instead, one of opposition because it was concluded with a reactionary dictatorship in Iraq and without any popular participation or control.

Repeating slogans of neutralism, peaceful coexistence and of the need for closer relations with the socialist countries is not enough,

---

* Which called for the establishment of a tripartite union between Egypt, Syria and Iraq–ed.

presently, as a criterion to judge the anti-imperialism of a regime. One should be aware of the methods of neo-imperialism which is willing to concede to the raising of such slogans, provided the regime in question implements an anti-communist policy and preserves the economic interests of imperialism, especially oil. The real criterion for assessing the anti-imperialism of any regime is its position on the economic positions of imperialism, its acceptance of, or opposition to, the main imperialist policies concerning the major world issues.

The rightist line of our Party has simply forgotten that the question of political power is the central question in any revolution and that progressive economic measures which are taken under various pressures cannot be implemented or consolidated if state power remains in the hands of reactionary groups which are hostile to the people. Even the 'progressive' regimes in Syria, Egypt and some African countries cannot last and push the revolution forward without liberating the initiative of the masses and granting them freedom of organization and action, without effective and active participation of the masses in the running of the state. The struggle for political democracy (in its popular, revolutionary—and not bourgeois—sense) is a struggle for the right of the working class and the toiling peasants to organize themselves, have their independent class activity and defend their vital interests.

AFRICA

No black man has more influenced African revolutionary thought and activity than Frantz Fanon. Born 20 July 1925, in Fort-de-France, in the impoverished French colony of Martinique, Fanon wrote his first outcry against colonialism when he was barely thirteen. Later, he journeyed to France and studied medicine at Lyons University, then enlisted in the French army and fought the Germans under General de Lattre de Tassigny. Reaching Algeria in 1952 in the midst of the Maghreb Rebellion, Fanon went to work in the psychiatric hospital of Blida, where, commented a friend, every day 'he discovers in his patients the scars of colonialism— delirium, mental disturbances, fury, paranoia— all the evasions invented by the colonized in order to escape oppression. He finds a sort of refuge in madness: this— for lack of anything better— is his means of liberating himself.' Fanon himself wrote then: 'I want only one thing; for the exploitation of man by man to cease forever on this earth.'

To help bring that end about, Fanon began to write furiously against French exploitation in Algeria. His voice gained listeners— and the wrath of the French occupiers. So, in 1956, he fled to Tunisia, where he joined the Algerian National Liberation Front, which appointed him editor of El Moujahid, *the official organ of the Algerian revolutionaries. As the Algerian War progressed, Fanon changed— and showed it in his articles. 'The challenging of the very principle of foreign domination,' he wrote, 'brings about essential mutations in the consciousness of the colonized, in the manner in which he perceives the colonizer, in his human status in the world.'*

Fanon went on to endorse Pan-Africanism and, as he travelled throughout Africa representing the Provisional Government of the Algerian Republic (GPRA), to proselytize it. In fact, he became an African revolutionary, above and beyond his loyalty to Algeria. Finally, by 1961, as he hurriedly wrote his last and greatest book, The Wretched of the Earth *(for he knew he was dying of leukaemia),* he broadened Pan-Africanism to Pan-Third Worldism — and advocated revolution by all peoples exploited by 'the Americans [who] take their role of patron of internal capitalism very seriously'. Colonialism (by which he also meant imperialism) 'is not a thinking machine, nor a body endowed with reasoning faculties. It is violence in its natural state, and it will only yield when confronted with greater violence. At the decisive moment, the colonialist bourgeoisie, which up till then has remained inactive, comes into the field. It introduces that new idea which is in proper parlance a creation of the colonial situation: non-violence.'

The cry against violence is heard only when the victims are white, Fanon said. Who among America's liberal bourgeoisie talked about non-violence when blacks were being beaten, lynched, slaughtered by whites in the South? Then, everyone insisted on non-violence. 'In 1945,' Fanon wrote, 'the 45,000 dead at Setif could pass unnoticed; in 1947, the 90,000 dead at Madagascar could be the subject of a simple paragraph in the papers, in 1952, the 200,000 victims of the repression in Kenya could meet with relative indifference.' Had he lived until 1965, he would have pointed out that the murder of one million Congolese elicited almost no outcry while the whole Western world wailed and shouted when the Congolese revolutionaries retaliated on a few hundred whites. Colonialism, concluded Fanon, must be racist to justify its violence to itself. And then, once a man is racist, his violence eggs him on to be more of a colonialist.

Fanon was also one of the first Africans to understand that the USA and Russia basically see eye to eye; their entente, he said in 1961 (just before he died), eliminates progress, thus 'peaceful coexistence between the two blocs provokes and feeds violence in the colonial countries'. Against that violence — the violence of hunger, poverty, disease and ignorance, as well as modern warfare, and especially the violence caused by the privation of dignity — Fanon posited counter-violence, the violence of the revolutionary. 'At the level of individuals,' he said, 'violence is a cleansing force. It frees the native from his inferiority complex and from his despair and inaction; it makes him fearless and restores his self-respect. Even if the armed struggle has been symbolic and the nation is demobilized through a rapid movement of decolonization, the people have the time to see that the liberation has been the business of each and all and that the leader has no special merit.'

In the passages below, Fanon also concludes that in the struggle against imperialism, only the friendship 'wrought in combat' is reliable. The passages are notes written after the summer of 1960, while the author travelled through Africa on diplomatic missions for the GPRA. In the first series, he is moved by the murder (by poison) of Felix Moumié, leader of the Union of Cameroon Population party (UPC). Organized by Moumié, Reuben Um Nyobe (who was also murdered, presumably also by French agents) and Osendé Afana, three of black Africa's greatest intellectuals, the UPC had tried to oppose the colonialism of France and Britain from the end of the Second World War to 1955, by legal means. That year, UPC launched an armed struggle which brought about official independence in 1960 and a partition of the Cameroons into a Federation in 1961. That Federation, totally submissive and directed by French-English neo-colonialists, provoked a new uprising, the UPC again launching guerrilla warfare operations. The first battles, in which Afana was killed, almost destroyed the National Liberation Army (ALN) of the UPC. But it regrouped, reorganized and retrained. By mid-1969, the ALN had secured two fronts—despite the intervention of a French expeditionary force.

The second set of notes by Fanon was triggered by the murder of Patrice Lumumba (see Congo–Kinshasa). What galled Fanon was the number of African leaders who were willing to betray their people for the pay of the imperialists—which, as he said, are led by the USA. He was convinced that part of the trouble was the absence of ideology. Had Africans been firmly imbued with a sense of unity, they would have had a better perspective on the Congo and the role there of Belgians, South Africans and Americans, he said. Lumumba himself would have realized that the UN is nothing more than a 'legal card of imperialists'. His mistake, said Fanon, was 'to believe in the friendly impartiality of the UN'. Grounded in a sound ideological base, other African leaders of independent countries would not have sent troops to serve under the UN command but directly to help Lumumba. Fanon concluded that Africans must learn to be self-reliant and build mutual cooperation through mutual commitment—'friendship wrought in combat'—to a united Africa.

Fanon himself cannot be pigeon-holed into any of the world's prevalent revolutionary ideologies. He was a militant nationalist, Third World-ist (or Tri-continentalist), and anti-imperialist. He often did fall back on Marxist class analysis but was no communist —except in the most profound sense that he believed that all men should live and act and make decisions and rule themselves collectively. More than anything else, he was anti-exploitation and he understood that man's exploitation of man will never end until the wretched of the earth have shaken off their inferiority complexes by grabbing arms and forcing their exploiters and all of their institutions, propaganda, aid-programmes and cultural paternalisms out of their hands.

Frantz Fanon: *Missions, Martyrs, Movements*[92]

To get Africa on the move, to work for its organizations, for its restructuring behind revolutionary principles; to participate in the ordered movement of a continent—that's what I really wanted to do. The take-off point, the first base, was represented by Guinea. Then Mali, ready for anything, fervent and brutal, coherent and singularly sharp, extended the bridgehead and opened precious perspectives. To the East, Lumumba was marking time. The Congo, which constituted the second beach-head for revolutionary ideas, found itself in a painful morass of sterile contradictions. It was not time yet to assault the colonialist citadels of Angola, Mozambique, Kenya, Rhodesia, the Union of South Africa. Yet everything was ready. And the the colonialist defence system was reviving old particularisms and undercutting the liberating lava. For the time being, then, it was necessary to hang on to the Congo and advance in the West.

For us, Algerians, the situation was clear. But the terrain remained difficult, very difficult. From the West, we had to prove that the continent was one concrete demonstration. Behind the general options available to leaders it was possible to determine the precise points where the peoples, the men and the women, could help, help each other, build in common. The spectre of the West, the European tinges, was everywhere present and active. The French, English, Spanish, Portuguese areas remained in existence. Oxford opposed the Sorbonne, Lisbon was against Brussels, the British bosses against the Portuguese bosses, the pound against the franc, the Catholic Church against Protestantism or Islam. And on top of all this, the United States penetrated everywhere, dollars in the vanguard, also the black American diplomats, scholarships, broadcasts of the Voice of America. Difficult work. Fortunately, in every corner, arms signal us, voices answer us, hands grasp ours. Things move.

The rapid and reassuring noise of the liberated cities that smash their moorings and advance grandiloquent but not at all grandiose, these veteran militants today having definitely passed their exams, who sit down and — remember. But the sun is still very high in the sky, and if one listens to it, with an ear glued to the red earth, one distinctly hears the sound of rusty chains, the groans of distress, and the shoulders droop from the bruised flesh in this stifling noonday. The Africa of everyday, oh not that of the poets, not the one that puts to sleep but the one that stops you from sleeping, for the people are impatient to do, to play, to say. The people who say: I want to build myself as a people, I want to build, to love, to respect, to create. That people who cry when you tell them: I come from a country where women are without children and children without mothers and who chant: Algeria, brother country, country that calls, country that hopes.

That is the real Africa, the Africa we had to let loose in the continental furrow, in the continental direction; that Africa that we had to orient, mobilize, throw to the offensive. That Africa to come. The West. Conakry, Bamako. Two cities dead on the surface but below the temperature is unendurable for those who calculate, who manoeuvre, who profit. In Conakry and in Bamako men strike Africa, forge it with love and enthusiasm.

Colonialism and its derivatives do not, as a matter of fact, constitute the present enemies of Africa. In a short time the continent will be liberated. For my part, the deeper I penetrate into the cultural and political circles, the more I am convinced that the greatest danger menacing Africa is the absence of ideology. For nearly three years I have been trying to bring the misty idea of African unity out of the subjectivist wells, to expose clearly the phantoms posited by the majority of its supporters. African unity is at the same time a dream, a myth, a nightmare, a willpower and what not. African unity is a principle from which we propose to establish the United States of Africa without going through the bourgeois chauvinist phase, with its procession of wars and mournings. To initiate this unity all combinations are possible. Some, like Guinea, Ghana, Mali and tomorrow maybe Algeria put political action to the forefront. The UAR, on its side, puts a greater emphasis on cultural aspects. Everything is possible, and one and the other should avoid trying to discredit or denounce those who see that unity, that rapprochement among African states, differently from them.

Moumié. On 30 September, we met at the Accra airport. He was going to Geneva for some very important meetings. In three months, he told me, we would see a massive decline of colonialism in the Cameroons. In Tripoli, the fog stopped all landings for three hours and the plane had to circle above. The pilot wanted to land anyway. The tower refused to give him permission but the courageous and heedless pilot decided to land his tens of thousands of tons. 'These guys are gambling with people's lives,' Felix said to me.

It was true. But were we not also gambling with ours? What was this intrepidity in comparison to our lives perpetually in suspense? Today, Felix is dead. In Rome, two weeks later, we were to meet again. He was not there. When I returned to Accra his father saw me arrive alone at the airport and his face betrayed deep anguish. Two days later, I was informed that Felix had been hospitalized. It was suspected that he had been poisoned. Kigué, the Vice-President of the UPC, and Marthe Moumié decided to go to Geneva. A few days later, we heard: Felix Moumié was dead.

We hardly felt his death. An assassination, but a bloodless one. Neither machine-gun volleys nor bombs; thallium poisoning. It made no sense. Thallium! How to understand such a cause? An abstract death striking the most concrete, the most alive, the most impetuous man. Felix's tone was constantly high, aggressive, violent, choleric, in love with his country, hating cowards and manipulators. Austere, hard, incorruptible. Of revolutionary essence packed into sixty kilos of muscle and bone.

In the evening we went to comfort the Cameroon comrades. The father, his face seamed, impassive, inexpressive, listens to me talk of his son. And gradually the father made way for the militant. Yes, said he, the programme is clear. We must stick to the programme. Moumié's father, at that moment, reminded me of those Algerian parents who listen, stupefied, to the story of how their children died; who, from time to time, question, demand a detail, then relapse into that inertia of communion that seems to draw them to where they think their sons have gone.

Yet, that's where the action is. Tomorrow, in a moment, we'll have to take the war to the enemy, allow him no rest, no respite, no chance to breathe. Let's go.

We're now in Bamako, capital of Mali. Modibo Keita, always militant, understands rapidly. No need to make long speeches. Our work sessions are short. We're eight. One commando, the Army, transmission, political commissars, the sanitary corps. Each of the pairs is to prospect according to his own discipline the possibilities of work. Our mission: to open the southern front. To transport arms and munitions from Bamako. Stir up the Saharan population. To infiltrate to the Algerian high plateaux. After having brought Algeria to the four corners of Africa, to come back with all of Africa towards Algerian Africa, towards the north, towards Algiers, the continental city.

What I want: great lines, great navigation canals through the Sahara. Subdue the desert, deny it, reassemble Africa, create the continent. That from Mali may descend on our territory Malians, Senegalese, Guineans, Ghanaians. And those from Nigeria, Togoland, the Ivory Coast. That all climb the slopes of the desert and flow over the bastion of colonialism. To turn the absurd and the impossible inside out and throw a continent into an assault against the last ramparts of colonial power.

We must hurry. Time presses. The enemy is still tenacious. In reality he does not believe in military defeat. But me, I have never felt it so possible, so within reach. We need only to march, to charge. It's not even a matter of strategy. We have mobilized and furious cohorts, loving our combat, eager to work. We have Africa with us.

But who's preoccupied? A continent is set to explode and Europe is languishingly asleep. Fifteen years ago, it was Asia that stirred. Then, Westerners were having fun. Today, Europe and the United States hunch their backs. The 650 million Chinese, calm possessors of an immense secret, are building a world by themselves. Are giving birth to a world.

Observers who happened to be in the capitals of Africa during the month of June 1960 could be aware of a certain number of things. All sorts of strange people from the Congo, which had just made its appearance on the international scene, kept showing up. What did these Congolese have to say? It didn't matter.

But if one took aside one of these Congolese and interrogated him seriously, then one could become aware that something very grave was being plotted against the independence of the Congo and against Africa.

Shortly after the independence celebration, Congolese senators and deputies left the Congo and went to the United States. Others installed themselves for a few weeks in Brazzaville. Trade unionists were invited to New York. Still in Africa, were one to buttonhole one of these deputies or senators, one would have learned that a whole very precise course of action was about to be put into motion.

From before 1 July 1960 had been launched the Katanga operation. To be sure, to safeguard the Union Minière. But it was Belgian interests that were being defended behind this operation. A unified Congo, with a central government, went counter to Belgian interests. To support the decentralization of the various provinces, to provoke such demands, to pour fuel over them, such was Belgian policy before independence. In their task, the Belgians were helped by the authorities of the Rhodesia-Nyasaland Federation. Today it is known—and Mr Hammarskjöld knows it better than anyone—that, before 30 June 1960 a Salisbury-Elizabeth airlift supplied arms to Katanga. Lumumba had once proclaimed that the liberation of the Congo was the first phase in the complete liberation of Central and Southern Africa and had set his next objectives very precisely: support for the nationalist movements of Rhodesia, Angola and South Africa.

A unified Congo with an anti-colonialist at its head constituted a very real danger for that southern Africa, that very southern Africa before which the rest of the world veils its face. Or rather: before which the rest of the world is content to weep, and during Sharpeville, or to perform stylistic exercises on anti-colonial day celebrations. Lumumba, as leader of the first country in that region to obtain independence and in concrete awareness of what colonialism was all about, had taken the responsibility, in the name of his people, to help physically bring about the death of that Africa. That the authorities in Katanga and Portugal had put everything at their disposal to sabotage the Congo's independence does not surprise us. That they reinforced the action of the Belgians and augmented the thrust of the centrifugal forces of the Congo is a fact. But this fact does not explain the coldly planned, coldly executed assassination of Lumumba. This colonialist collaboration is insufficient to explain why, in February 1961, Africa is about to experience its first great crisis over the Congo.

Its first great crisis because it will have to decide whether it wants to go forward or backward. It will have to understand that it is no longer possible to advance by regions; that, like a great body that fights off all mutilations, it will have to advance on all fronts; that there will not be one Africa which fights colonialism and another Africa that comes to terms with it. It will be necessary for Africa, that is to say Africans, to understand that there can never be greatness in procrastination and that there can never be dishonour in saying what one is and what one wants, and that in reality the advantage of the colonized, in the last analysis, can only be his courage, the lucid awareness of his objectives and of his alliances, and the tenacity that he brings to his liberation.

Lumumba believed in his mission. He had an exaggerated faith in his people. For him, the people not only could not deceive themselves but also could not be deceived. And in fact he seemed to be right. Each time, for example, that in some region or other the enemies of the Congo managed to undermine his policy, it was sufficient for him to appear, explain, denounce, for the situation to return to normal. But he would forget that he could not be everywhere at the same time and that the truth of his explanation was less than the truth of his person.

Lumumba had lost the battle for the presidency of the Republic. But, because he embodied from the beginning the confidence that the Congolese people had placed in him, because the African peoples confusedly understood that he alone was concerned with the dignity of his country, Lumumba continued to express the Congolese patriotism and the African nationalism which is most rigorous and noble.

As a result, other countries that are more important than Belgium or Portugal decided to take a direct interest in the matter. Lumumba was contacted, interrogated. After his trip to the United States, the decision was made: Lumumba must go.

Why? Because the enemies of Africa were not fooled. They realized perfectly that Lumumba had sold himself. Sold himself to Africa, of course. That meant that he was no longer up for sale.

The enemies of Africa realized with some horror that should Lumumba succeed in the very heart of the colonialist empire—with a French Africa being transformed into a renovated community, and Angola into a Portuguese 'province' and finally Eastern Africa—it was finished with 'their' Africa, for which they had very precise plans.

The great success of the enemies of Africa is to have compromised the Africans themselves. It is true that these Africans were directly interested in the death of Lumumba. Chiefs of puppet governments, in the centre of a puppet independence, confronted day after day by the massive opposition of their peoples, did not take long to convince themselves that the real independence of the Congo would put them personally in danger.

There were other Africans, a little less puppet, who became frightened of the idea of separating Africa from the West. One could say that these African chiefs of state always feared facing Africa. They too, although less actively but consciously, contributed to the deterioration of the situation in the Congo.

Little by little the West agreed that it was necessary to intervene in the Congo, that one just couldn't let things evolve at such a rate. Little by little the idea of intervention by the UN took shape. Then, as we can see now, two errors were committed by Africans. The first was by Lumumba, when he asked the UN to intervene. It was not necessary to appeal to the UN. Never has the UN been capable of solving a single problem raised before the conscience of man by colonialism, and each time it has intervened it has done so to give concrete help to the colonialist power of the oppressing country.

Look at the Cameroons. What peace do Ahidjo's subjects enjoy when they are held down by a French expeditionary force which, in large part, got its experience fighting in Algeria? Meanwhile, the UN has controlled the self-determination of the Cameroons and the French government has installed a 'provisional executive'.

Look at Vietnam. Look at Laos.

It is not true to say that the UN has failed because the cases are difficult. In reality, the UN is the legal card used by the imperialists when the card of brute force has failed.

The partitions, the joint control commissions, the trusteeship are all international legal means of torture, meant to crush the will to independence of the peoples, to cultivate anarchy, banditry and misery.

For after all there were no massacres in the Congo before the UN arrived. Despite the hallucinating rumours propagated to coincide with the departure of the Belgians, one could count only some ten dead. But since the UN arrived we have become accustomed to learn every morning that the Congolese massacre each other by the hundreds.

Today, we are informed that repeated provocations were made by Belgian soldiers acting as soldiers of the United Nations. Today we learn that civilian functionaries of the UN had set up a new government already on the third day of Lumumba's investiture. So now we can understand much better what has been called Lumumba's violence, rigidity and susceptibility.

In fact, everything shows that Lumumba was abnormally calm.

The chiefs of the UN mission made contact with Lumumba's enemies and with them decided to destroy the State of the Congo. In such a case, how should the head of government react? The aim sought and hoped for is the following: to manifest the absence of authority, prove the failing of the state.

And with that, then, motivate the sequestering of the Congo.

Lumumba's mistake, then, was, in the first place, to believe in the friendly impartiality of the UN. He forgot that in the present state the UN is nothing more than a reserve assembly, under the boot of the Great Ones, to carry on, between armed conflicts, the 'peaceful struggle' for the partitioning of the world. If Ileo, in August 1960, was telling anyone who would listen to him that Lumumba had to be hanged, if the members of Lumumba's cabinet did not know what to do with all the dollars which at that time invaded Leopoldville, if, finally, Mobutu went to Brazzaville every evening to do and hear what we can now guess, why then turn with such sincerity, with such absence of reserve towards the UN?

Africans must remember this lesson. If outside help is needed, let us call upon our friends. Only they can really and totally help us to realize our objectives because the friendship which binds us has been wrought in combat.

But for their part the African countries committed a grave error in sending their troops under the control of the UN. By that fact they let themselves be neutralized and, without suspecting it, allowed the others to do their work.

Surely, they should have sent troops to Lumumba—but not within the framework of the UN. Directly. From friendly country to friendly country. The African troops in the Congo have suffered an historical moral defeat. With crossed feet, they watched without reacting (because they were UN troops) the disintegration of a state and nation which all of Africa had saluted and praised. A shame.

Our mistake, we Africans, comes from the fact that we forgot that the enemy never really means his withdrawals. He never understands. He may capitulate, but he is never converted.

Our mistake was to have believed that the enemy had lost his combativeness and his nefariousness. If Lumumba gets in the way, Lumumba gets put out of the way. Imperialism has never hesitated to murder.

Look at Ben M'Hidi, look at Moumié, look at Lumumba. Our mistake was to have been slightly confused in our action. Naturally, in the Africa of today, traitors exist. It is imperative to denounce them and combat them. That this is hard after the magnificent dream of an Africa bound together and subject to the same exigencies of true independence does not change the facts.

Africans have swallowed the imperialist policy in the Congo, have served as intermediaries, have swallowed the activities and the weird silences of the UN in the Congo.

Today they are afraid. They compete with one another in shedding hypocritical tears over the murdered Lumumba. Let us not be fooled any more: they fear their bosses. And the imperialists themselves are also afraid. And with reason, because many Africans, many Afro-Asians have understood. The imperialists are trying to mark time. They want to wait for the 'legitimate emotion' to die down. We must take advantage of this short respite to abandon our fearful acts and to decide to save the Congo and Africa.

The imperialists decided to strike down Lumumba. They have done so. They decided to raise voluntary legions. Those are now in place.

The Katanga air force, under command of South African and Belgian pilots, began a few days ago to strafe the ground with machine-guns. From Brazzaville, foreign planes come full of volunteers and paratroop officers destined to rescue a certain Congo.

No one knows the name of the next Lumumba. There is in Africa a certain tendency represented by certain men. It is this tendency, dangerous for imperialism, which is at stake. Let us be on guard never to forget it: that is our fate, the fate of all of us, that is at stake in the Congo.

MOROCCO

Though Che Guevara popularized the slogan, he was not the only early exponent of the 'Many Vietnams' theory. If he gets most of the credit for it today, if he is hailed as one of the all-time great revolutionaries by the thousands of liberation fighters engaged in actual combat in over sixty countries of the world, it is because Che himself lived and died as one of them. But the Moroccan Nationalist, El Mehdi Ben Barka, ultimately played just as crucial a role in establishing solidarity among the liberation fighters of the Third World, and in developing what is known today as the tri-continental spirit (of which the Many Vietnams theory is its military characteristic). That is why he, too, had to be killed.

The son of a Moroccan cop, Ben Barka grew up in Rabat as one of a hundred small-time rabble-rousers against the French. At twenty-two, with a handful of Moroccan intellectuals, he organized the Istliqal Party, which was strictly an independence movement, and hoped for a constitutional monarchy. (In fact, to earn his living, he gave maths lessons to the royal prince who, later, as King Mohammed v, once appealed to him to stop his international intrigues by pleading, 'I need my mathematics teacher here with me.')

Repeatedly jailed by the French, Ben Barka repeatedly escaped — and kept organizing. Small, mysterious and self-effacing but with a disarming smile and a warm handshake, he remained in the background as much as possible, even after Morocco became an independent monarchy and he was elected president of its first National Council. Realizing, as he said, that true independence comes only when the wealth is owned by all the people, not just a small upper class in partnership with foreign capitalists, Ben Barka moved to the left, and organized another party, this time called the National Union of Popular Forces (UNFP). Its single motto was then 'Land for the Peasants'.

Early in 1963 Ben Barka and twenty-eight of his comrades were elected to the National Assembly. But a few weeks later the UNFP

K*

was accused of plotting to overthrow the monarchy, and Ben Barka was condemned to death. Escaping once again, he first tried to organize internal resistance, then went into exile to stir things up outside.

Hounded by the Moroccan secret police, which acted under the direct supervision of Morocco's Minister of Interior, General Mohammed Oufkir, a Foreign Legion veteran of Vietnam and longtime CIA operant, Ben Barka dodged assassins' bullets as he hopscotched from Cairo to Geneva, Algiers to Hanoi, Paris to Havana. As he did so, his vision expanded: no longer did he work for the liberation of Morocco alone; he now sought the liberation of all of Africa, and eventually of the whole Third World. Indefatigable, persuasive, coldly thorough, it was he who did most to convince the Afro-Asian representatives attending the 1965 Conference at Winneba, Tanzania, that their common enemy was capitalism. That Afro-Asian Solidarity meeting proclaimed that 'all the wars, aggressions and interventions of imperialism, its maintenance of military bases in foreign lands and its support for cruel and corrupt dictatorship, spring from and are dictated by economic exploitation'. Ben Barka then drew the logical consequence: 'We must achieve greater coordination in the struggle of all the peoples, as the problems in Vietnam, the Congo and the Dominican Republic stem from the same source: US imperialism.'

That coordination was to be the Organization of Solidarity of the Peoples of Africa, Asia and Latin America (OSPAAAL), known today as the Tri-Con. And as Ben Barka had done more than anyone to weld it together, he was elected chairman of its preparatory committee (see the Conclusion of Volume II). But he never actually attended the Tri-Con. For, one autumn day in 1965, he was 'arrested' by French policemen as he chatted with friends in a Paris café, taken to the villa of a French mafioso and murdered apparently in the presence of Minister Oufkir (who was indicted for the crime but released when Ben Barka's body was not found). Dumped in the Essonne River near Corbeil, the body was presumably recovered and discreetly disposed of by France's Gaullist 'Police Parallel', a para-political organization of Marseilles underworld figures who carry out 'delicate missions in the interest of the State'—anything Gaullism dislikes, from the kidnapping of rightwing rebellious generals after the Franco-Algerian entente to the liquidation of potential revolutionaries (e.g. Felix Moumié and Reuben Um Nyobe of the Cameroons).

Ben Barka's greatest contribution to Third World revolutionary theory was his perceptive analyses of neo-colonialism. In the first article below, a report written in January 1960, he clearly foretells how imperialism will adapt itself to ruling the underdeveloped world from afar—through neo-colonial institutions. Pushing their so-called concept of so-called liberal democracy, he says, the imperialists will try to convince the newly independent nations of Africa that pluralism, religious freedom, open unions, market oriented economics, and the use of the old intellectual bureaucracies are all fundamental ingredients for the creation of a new viable country. In fact, and the imperialists know it full well, each of these ingredients confuse and debilitate the new state. Pluralism leads to the creation of new parties, the richest of which will represent the interests of the old profiteers (the imperialists themselves and the reactionary classes); religious freedom is merely a way to justify the existence and political activity of extreme right-wing sects; open unions lead to the influx of CIO-AFL agents who are more committed to capitalist structures than proletarian welfare; market-oriented economics is nothing less than the laissez-faire system by which the trading bourgeoisie links up with international capitalists (imperialism); and reliance on the old intellectual bureaucracy is the way by which imperialists propagate their value system, socially and psychologically. A newly independent country which seeks an independent economy—without which, Ben Barka said, there can be no real independence—cannot afford any of these 'ingredients'. It must stick firmly to its objective: the nationalization of the whole country. The basic task of national liberation, he said in 1963 (second passage below) is 'the effective and total transfer of power to the genuine representatives of national revolution, even if this causes a resumption of armed struggle'.

El Mehdi Ben Barka: *National Liberation and African Solidarity*[93]

When the representatives of the various countries of Western Europe gathered around the Berlin Conference table to divide

Africa into Zones of influence, that action in itself demonstrated that behind their quarrels and disagreements lay unity, a solidarity of colonizers. For through them, through their national diversity, the rising capitalism of the nineteenth century was continuing its march towards unification and its irrepressible tendency to create a world market and secure the sources of raw materials and energy for itself.

The impact of western capitalism was everywhere the same for African societies, too, which differed in their traditions and the pattern of their civilizations but whose productive forces were at similar stages of development. The way in which these societies were disorganized, in which a new structure has, gradually, taken the place of the traditional one, was essentially the same. The liberation movements too, which are a necessary and inevitable reaction against the colonial presence, have consequently also had a common origin, a common make-up and a common aim.

Because of its geographical position, Morocco was the first and last to receive the blows of Western imperialism. It was on the soil of the Maghreb that Portugal, the first modern colonizing people, first tried its strength, closely followed by Spain.

In 1912, after the first negotiations between the European powers on the subject of the division of Africa (*Entente Cordiale* of 1904 and Franco–German Agreement of 1911), Morocco fell under French rule. But resistance did not falter and, after half a century of various types of struggle, military (in particular the 1925 Rifi revolt under the leadership of Abdel Krim al Khettabi) then political ('Pacification'), and finally in the form of popular armed resistance from 1952–6, Morocco gained its independence.

Here a whole people was involved. It was not just the action of a bourgeois or intellectual minority. In Morocco the liberation movement is the conjunction of three basic forces: the peasantry, the middle-class townspeople, and the proletariat.

The rural masses constituted one of its basic elements. They were the first to suffer from the military operations and then from eviction from the land that was their livelihood. The French colonists settled, in less than twenty-five years, over more than one million hectares of agricultural land, one-third by means of direct seizure made possible by the complicity of a Moroccan feudal system.

The townspeople were very soon to benefit from the means of communication, information and education which settlement inevitably brought with it, thus engendering the agents of its own destruction. It was then that nationalist political organizations emerged.

Finally, the industrial revolution achieved by French capitalism created a working class that was significant numerically and aware of its rights. The struggle which brought it into conflict with the foreign ruling class, safeguarded by the administration of the protectorate, was as much political as economic.

This is why the whole of Moroccan society remained united in the face of imperialism. The only elements excluded from this nationwide union were those cliques who, vestiges of a dead past, saw only the colonial presence as a guarantee of their outdated privileges. These were the administrative overlords or the religious auxiliaries of the protectorate and part of the big trading bourgeoisie which grew up as an intermediary during the establishment of the colonial structures and which could not continue except through the continuance of these structures.

This is the explanation for the profoundly popular, progressive and broadly national character of the Moroccan liberation movement. The same is true of the liberation movements of all African countries where the organized labouring masses are increasingly in the fore.

The work of this movement, which has been growing particularly during the last few years, is already producing results. The year 1960 will welcome the independence of several African states. But other peoples must continue the struggle against entrenched colonialism. Their cause is ours as well. Here we must examine their situation and the conditions in which they are carrying on their just fight, with the greatest attention.

The path of progress towards political independence is imposed upon each people by the machinery the relevant colonial powers put into action. It is they who force liberation movements to have recourse to violence and armed struggle. Negotiation is never rejected the moment it appears possible in conditions that could conceivably hasten the achievement of national aspiration.

Those African countries which are approaching independence possess considerable reserves of energy and enthusiasm, thanks to their national forces of liberation. The problem is therefore to safeguard this potential. What measures should be taken to avoid the disillusion which has followed independence almost everywhere in

Asia and which is already appearing in a number of independent African countries? In other words, our problem is to know how to prevent the persistence of neo-colonialism, which is a new form of foreign presence in our country.

It is quite clear that the declaration of independence which is a purely political achievement, indeed even a legal one, cannot change the fundamental structures of a country that was originally colonized. Independence is the condition, the promise of a liberation, not liberation in itself.

During the first three years of its independence Morocco has seen the features of its economic dependence and backwardness on the administrative and technical level perpetuated and even intensified. Its foreign trade has remained centred on the French market. Its currency has remained a camouflaged French currency. Most of its dynamic industrial sectors are still controlled by French capitalism which had free transfer between Morocco and the franc zone in its power. The growing of export produce, which is modern agriculture *par excellence*, is dominated by the powerful French settlers.

No policy of independence can be truly followed if the country's economy is not first of all freed from a crushing dependence. By the creation of a national currency, breaking away from the French franc; by the setting up of an Economic Development Bank to encourage and direct investments in the vital sectors; by a Foreign Trade Bank to supervise the diversification of Morocco's trading patterns with other countries of the world; and lastly, by a general control of the transfer of capital. Any independence which is satisfied with representing the features of colonial domination under new names can only be a snare and a delusion.

The former colonial powers use their economic superiority to keep important military forces in our countries. Capital investment, the presence of a settler colony, constitute both a reason and an excuse for their military presence which also fits into the world strategy of the cold war.

The foreign military forces of occupation, far from being a stabilizing factor, constitute a constant threat to the very existence of the young sovereign states. Furthermore, they utilize the liberated territories as bases for aggression to carry on the colonial war with neighbouring peoples. Suffice it to cite here the example of the dissidence of the Moroccan governor (Addi ou Bihi) whose revolt, organized in the first year of our independence by reactionary and anti-nationalist elements, was armed by the French forces stationed on our territory and was to make possible the reinforcement of the Algerian war via the south of Morocco.

But it is not only a question of the liquidation of the after-effects of colonial occupation. Our chief concern is to get our country working to build itself up economically, politically and socially. Such a long-term task demands that we establish a lasting peace and keep our country out of all military alliances and block quarrels alien to us.

Our efforts in this context have just culminated in our declaration that the American bases are to be evacuated.* We shall continue to work for the evacuation of other foreign forces, the French and Spanish, so as to guarantee complete success to our foreign policy of non-dependence.

This policy of non-dependence is all the more vital since new ideas in neo-colonialist *milieux* in Europe regard Africa as a stake and trump in the politics of world equilibrium.

In this context, Africa is still considered in these *milieux* as an endless source of the minerals and energy necessary to the economy of the industrialized countries of the West. All the projects aiming to associate Africa with the European Common Market to build a Eurafrica or to found bodies of shared investments may well move in a direction which gives primacy to foreign capitalist interest and can only slow down the smooth and rapid development of the African economy.

We must not forget that for a quarter of a century, as the prices of manufactured products imported from Europe increased, the price of raw materials sent out of our continent has been falling continuously. The economic ability and expansion of the industrial countries of Europe have therefore taken place at the expense of the underdeveloped sources of raw materials.

Faced with the growing liberation movement in Africa, these same imperialist interests try to perpetuate the relations of economic exploitation in the deceptive guise of cooperation. Our countries are finding themselves faced ever more clearly by positive blocs whose aim is to dictate a new colonial pact.

The duties of our African countries, like other developing countries in Asia and Latin America, is to organize themselves so as to produce and proclaim a common attitude, to seek out effective

* By May 1970 those bases were still in US hands–ed.

formulae of cooperation and to arm themselves against every dangerous form of exploitation.

Our analysis of the evidence for neo-colonialist manifestations in Africa would be incomplete if we did not stress the dangers constituted by the national forces of reaction. Imperialism would stand no chance of survival in Africa if it could not camouflage itself behind the interests of certain retrograde elements. With the conquest of political power, certain positions have changed their meaning and certain sectors of the population which, during the period of struggle, remained neutral or supported the liberation movement, have taken quite another attitude after independence. The rural or pseudo-religious feudal system, or what remains of it, is intensified by independence and striving to take the place of the weakened colonial power. Escaping the purge, it makes use of the new power given it by the democratic and parliamentary organization to sink its privileges into new legal bases.

The forms of political organizations of a European type, whose pluralism no longer expresses the same economic or ideological realities for us, act as havens for those anti-nationalist elements aiming to corrupt political *mores*. The pointless polemics, the demagogic campaigns sow doubt and scepticism which prepare the people to undergo any disguised form of colonial exploitation.

These reactionary elements, instruments of neo-colonialism, are now tackling even the working classes whose unity was forged during the period of national struggle. The vain attempts to create an artificial union movement are simply another form of neo-colonialism.

Side by side with these anti-national and reactionary elements, imperialism finds a second ally. The big trading bourgeoisie, which derives all its power from liberal economic policy, suddenly finds itself allied with the colonial presence the moment it is no longer experiencing the misdeeds of the political preponderance of imperialism. Then it sets itself up ferociously against all attempts to guide economic and commercial policy towards a real independence, which forces it either to enter the production cycle or else to disappear.

Lastly, habitual servitude has left a large part of the intellectual and administrative cadres, inherited from the colonial period and which took scarcely any part in the liberation movement, with a lack of imagination, enthusiasm and honesty that makes them unfit to work effectively for popular aspirations, and they soon find themselves enslaved by the holders of power.

The danger dogging the newly independent countries is that the conjunction of these forces of evil may perpetuate an economic dependence, underdevelopment, which makes political independence pointless. The alliance of a powerful and reactionary feudality, a servile and craven bourgeoisie and ineffective and rotten administrative mandarinate, threatens to constitute a regression even in comparison with certain forms of imperialism.

A popular and progressive political force is absolutely vital to ward off this danger, to fight this alliance. In Morocco this was done by the creation of the Union Nationale des Forces Populaires. In our manifesto of 6 September 1959 we noted the bankruptcy of the parties with bourgeois structures which frequently resort to manipulating the popular masses for specific ends, the failure likewise of three years of hesitation and indecision which have blunted popular enthusiasm. We have succeeded in drawing all the basically popular forces into the Union in our desire to build up a true independence and real democracy, so as to be able to tackle the real problems.

Faced with local reactionary forces, which inevitably come together sooner or later and rally to imperialism to defend their interests, which sow division in the ranks of the people and try to interest them in secondary problems like those of formal democracy and thus leave the field free to the real dangers of an economy based on neo-colonialism, which try to involve us in quarrels which have nothing to do with us, it is vital that in each African country the popular patriotic forces should unite and form the structured and united political organization which will be the instrument of genuine African Liberation.

If we consider the lessons to be learned from the experiences of India and China, the countries of central Europe, the Middle East and Latin America, we come to the conception of a model of economic growth which is of scientific inevitability. In this realm, we have gone beyond the stage of sectarian discussion.

We know now that in no case can the way of liberal capitalism be followed in our countries. This is why liberalism with us is nothing more than the excuse of reactionary forces.

We know now that the conditions necessary for us to emerge from underdevelopment are, internally, a rapid reform of the agrarian structure, rapid and genuine industrialization, an effective and logical investments policy and, externally, the furtherance of foreign and technical cooperation.

In the economic and social building up of the new Africa, we must stress the predominant role of the working class and organized peasantry. These forces are the only guarantees and permanent up-holders of this policy—because it is bound to be attacked both by external imperialism and by its agents within the country itself. We know now that progress towards independence is a difficult and obstacle-strewn path. Imperialism knows it too. That is why in Africa it no longer puts up as savage a resistance as hitherto to political independence, hoping to safeguard its economic domination with time.

We must take care that political independence, when it has been granted and not fought for, does not become an arm in the hands of imperialists to get others to defend its main economic privileges. To fight this alliance of imperialism and the national forces of reaction we must work for alliance with the liberal and progressive forces of other former colonies and the union of the national patriotic forces of all African countries.

It is in this context that the various unification movements in Africa will have their full meaning. These Unions will be founded on economic and political necessity: they will be a defensive reaction against the union of imperialist interests in Africa.

Based on an independent economic policy founded on cooperation and mutual aid; on a peace policy tending to give a new direction to the competition between east and west, and on a reaction against the alliance of the imperialist forces and those of national reaction, tendencies towards unification in Africa constitute the main element of the successful development of our continent.

If political independence is not an end in itself, if it is not sufficient in itself, it is nonetheless the necessary condition for all the changes which can undermine a colonial structure. The union of Africa, the building up of Africa's future, demand the liberation of all Africa.

We are thinking in particular of the atrocious struggle which for five years has been bloodying a territory bordering our own, which is dear to us and which is faced with a blind and stubborn coloni-alism.

We must not forget that it was Algeria, though it is still struggling for its independence, that gave the signal for the liberation of French Africa. When French imperialism was bleeding itself white in an inconclusive war in Indochina there was no shortage of pundits to launch the slogan: 'Quit Asia and hang on to Africa.' They thought that they had fat years of peace and exploitation ahead of them. It was the revolt of All Saints Day of 1954 that tolled the knell of these hopes for Africa. Everything happened as though these same pundits were applying the following policy: 'Abandon everything in Africa and hang on to Algeria.' Whatever the obstinacy of the French government, whatever the skill of French diplomacy (which consists of recognizing the right to self-determination for the Algerian people without agreeing to guarantees elementary for free choice, after five years of struggle and suffering), we ourselves know that French colonialism will ultimately loosen its grip on Algeria as it has loosened its grip on its Asian and other African possessions. But we must do all we can to hasten the end of this conflict whose horror we are constantly presented with through every possible variety of evidence, and indeed even by Red Cross reports.

This same blind colonialist obstinacy emerges from the decision of the French government to explode its atomic bomb in the middle of the African continent, defying world opinion and taking no account of the repeated protests of the African peoples and the condemnation of the UN General Assembly.

And to hasten the liberation of these territories, still under colonial domination, as well as to consolidate already acquired independence, the deeply-felt desire for unity that has emerged all over Africa must be made concrete.

First, within each country, all the forces of progress, unionist, political and intellectual must unite to formulate and apply a policy worthy of our aims. The long and difficult struggle now beginning, to make up for a time lag of a century and give our countries a modern and prosperous economy, requires the union of all relevant forces and the abandoning of every form of selfish and sterile partisan sectarianism.

This movement for the concentration of forces must be extended to all Africa.

To counter colonial solidarity, we must promote a solidarity of the African peoples to intensify our struggle, both internally against the reactionary forces and externally against imperialist manoeuvres.

To counter the economic bloc of the imperialist powers, we must consider every form of aid and economic and commercial cooperation capable of withdrawing our economic relations from the domination of imperialist monopoly.

To study our problems and experiences, our successes and sometimes our failures deeply and seriously, we must encourage all forms of cultural cooperation, the only way to educate consciences in the mystique of African union.

Lastly, this solidarity must extend even further to all the liberation movements throughout the world, particularly to genuinely progressive movements in the West which have the same basic aims as ourselves : the material well-being and the dignity of man.

It is certain that the colonizer's desire is that the political power that he holds should be transferred to an heir (individual or group of interests) able to ensure him the running, by remote control, of the affairs of the new state and above all the continuity of economic power to the benefit of the original mother country.

But matters do not always work as the colonizer would like, particularly where the popular will in the interested country is expressed through a movement of national liberation. Which leads to the variety of solutions offered us by current experience.

We know the extreme cases of People's China, Vietnam and Cuba, for instance, where the struggle which began as national liberation moved gradually towards economic and social revolution with the seizure of power by the People's Army after total victory over the colonial or reactionary forces.

At the other end of the scale we have the purely neo-colonial solutions.

Between these two extremes the problem of power finds intermediate solutions after negotiations, compromises which are dependent on the relation between the forces of the two factors involved. But experience shows that a single path leading to independence may arrive at different solutions to the problem of power.

In the case of Algeria, for example, the compromise reached at Evian is a revolutionary compromise, i.e., it makes possible a definite achievement, the recognition of Algeria's independence and does not shut off any of the vistas of revolution, in so far as the latter's instrument is safeguarded, i.e., the armed forces of the FLN, the vanguard of the fighting people of Algeria. But for months we have been watching the unmistakable neo-colonialist manoeuvres working towards an unwavering goal: to destroy the solution of the problem of power from the start, and to act in such a way that the Evian solution shall be harmful to the basic interests of the Algerian people's revolution.

In Guinea, even if the operation has taken place without any bloodshed, it is nonetheless true that power has been gained for the people thanks to the activity and vigilance of the Guinea Democratic Party.

In the case of Morocco, the power held by the French, Spanish and international protectorates was transferred—under the pressure of the liberation movement—not to the king alone, though he is theoretically the sovereign, but to a coalition including the popular forces. It took more than six years for the heirs recognized by colonialist interest to succeed in seizing power and getting themselves set up in 1962 with a prefabricated Constitution, and going from corruption and falsification to violence and repression.

The pseudo-constitutional method was also used at the same time by neo-colonialism to consolidate the fascist regime in South Korea.

Similarly in Kenya we find stubborn attempts to impose a prefabricated coalition to prepare for the subsequent transfer of exclusive power to the heir presumptive of British authority.

What must we conclude after this brief survey?

That the basic problem in our national liberation movement is that of political power: every care must be taken for independence to be immediately expressed by the effective and total transfer of power to the genuine representatives of national revolution in the country concerned, even if this causes a resumption of armed struggle.

The prime role of a national revolution is to gain hold of the machinery of the colonial state to put it at the service of the people.

The condition for independence not resulting in the creation of a neo-colonialist state is naturally the existence of a popular organization whose leadership must be fiercely convinced that everything except political and economic power is mere idle dreaming. It must be armed against the risks of gradual degeneration after the seizure of power, be constantly alert to the manoeuvres of imperialism and its internal allies and ready at all times to counter the aggressor, whoever he may be.

Our duty is to talk openly and frankly to our masses so as to protect them from the disappointment a false security can give. It is important to promote and develop a sense of vigilance which will make them permanently aware of the manoeuvres of imperialism without closing our eyes to our own weaknesses and mistakes.

On the national level of each country, as an Afro-Asian Peoples' Solidarity movement, we must draw particular attention to the daily struggle, help with the improvement, however partial, of the lot of the labouring masses, educate and organize the people, sharpen their awareness and build up their revolutionary potential so that they can come to power when the time is ripe. We must not relax our bonds of solidarity, but help it to confront all foreign or counter-revolutionary intervention.

On the inter-African, inter-Asian, Afro-Asian level, too, we must welcome any attempt at rapprochement, regrouping or unity as positive, provided it is the genuine expression of national will, even if there are temporary divergencies or contradictions of interests. The principles on which these meetings will be based will remain those of each country's complete equality of rights, mutual co-operation and independence.

The success of this double action, on a national scale and internationally, lies in the feeling of innate fraternity and solidarity among all these people, and in their ever deepening awareness of our common destiny.

It is in the common struggle of our popular organizations against all forms of colonial, capitalist and feudal exploitation, and through the success of this struggle, that we shall develop this awareness of our common destiny, and that new international relations, whose aim is to serve mankind, will develop.

ALGERIA

If the Algerian revolution has indeed failed—as its left-wing op-
ponents claim—the cause is not to be found in its leaders. For they,
like the whole country, were products, and, yes, deformations, of
one of the most brutal colonialisms the modern world has known.
For 132 years the French ruled Algeria with the kind of vicious
racism that does not establish Apartheid separation but permeates
so deeply into the minds and hearts of men that the victims end up
colonizing themselves. It was such destruction of spirit that con-
vinced Frantz Fanon that the colonized man would never be free
until he drowned the last colonizer-exploiter in his own blood—in
self-expressive violence of liberating epuration.

The war of national liberation was violent all right, but not
cleansing. During the more than seven years of struggle, the French
devastated the country, razed 8,000 Algerian hamlets and killed more
than 1,000,000 people—one-tenth of Algeria's population. Thou-
sands of acres of forest land, which served to stop soil erosion, were
burned. Four out of the seven million head of cattle, the Algerian
fellah's main food, were slaughtered. Three million Algerians were
rendered homeless; 400,000 were interned in concentration camps;
400,000 went into exile; and 300,000 fought with the National
Liberation Army (ALN) of the National Liberation Front (FLN).

The Algerian war divided the population into three basic ele-
ments—the veterans; the collaborators; and the émigrés. Many of
these latter were in French jails (like Ben Bella), but many more
joined the Algerian Army which was formed in Morocco and
Tunisia. Among these was Colonel Houari Boumedienne. This army
was well-trained, well-equipped and well-fed, and by war's end,
with the guerrilla movement basically collapsing, it moved into
Algeria, quashed those elements of the guerrilla ALN trying to
seize power, and established order.

Ben Bella and Boumedienne were friends (the former had enlisted
the latter into the FLN in 1954 when Boumedienne was an Arabic

teacher in Cairo). Released from jail only a few months before the Evian agreement, Ben Bella was alone. He had no aides, no strong ALN allies, not even any bodyguards, and certainly no legal party with which to contest the power of the Provisional Government of the Algerian Republic (GPRA), then headed by elements of the national bourgeoisie. Ben Bella despised these professional old-style politicians who, he correctly thought, would end up establishing a neo-colonial regime in Algiers. Nor could Ben Bella turn to the ALN guerrillas who were either in disarray or else wanted to seize power themselves. So, Ben Bella called on his old friend with his efficient army—Boumedienne.

Boumedienne was equally opposed to the old politicians. In fact, he disliked all civilians, especially in government; they were all corrupt or corruptible demagogues, he thought. To the colonel (highest rank in the FLN Army), Ben Bella was a veteran fighter, a longtime militant with army-like discipline. Thus he gave him full support, installed him in power and put the army at his disposal— within limits. And Ben Bella, who defended Boumedienne before the party, felt those limits. He made Colonel Tahar Zbiri, a veteran ALN commander, the People's Army Chief of Staff, and kept a wary eye on Boumedienne. He once even introduced him to an Egyptian journalist as 'that man who is preparing a plot against me' and asked the colonel, 'How is the intrigue progressing?'

Boumedienne, who answered, 'Very well, thank you,' kept an even firmer watch on Ben Bella. But for three years the duo seemed to get along. They appeared almost everywhere together—Ben Bella in front, quick, sharp, at ease in all situations; Boumedienne behind, shadowy and silent. Ben Bella was no petty-bourgeois reformer; he tried to move Algeria towards a socialist revolution. He pushed the agrarian reform, stimulated the youth movement, generated a strong labour movement, which advocated workers' control (called 'self-management' by Algerians), wiped out the landowner class and fought his traditional-minded colleagues' view of women ('Now the men will again shut us up in our homes,' women complained when Ben Bella was overthrown). But totally lacking a non-colonialist bureaucracy, Ben Bella was too hamstrung to move faster. Besides, as a residue of the war and his own colonized spirit, he trusted no one, jailed too many critics, justified himself with too many speeches. He was too much of a politican and too little of an army man to satisfy Boumedienne, too much of a dictator to please

Colonel Zbiri, too secretive to elicit mass support. On 12 June 1965 he told the Political Bureau (half filled with Boumedienne's men) that he would present a plan for changing the Army Command and crushing its opposition at the next week's session. At 2 a.m. on 19 June, a few hours before that session was to begin, Colonel Zbiri arrested Ben Bella. A few moments later Colonel Boumedienne was in full control.

Boumedienne did not drastically change Algeria's foreign or rhetorical policies. But he stopped the socialist revolution. The land reform was no longer carried out. Workers' control stopped, then was reversed as government-appointed functionaries displaced the workers' council. French economic interests grew and labour militancy was forcibly curtailed. Even the New York Times *concluded (26 April 1968) that industrial planning in Algeria should be described not as socialism but as state capitalism.*

Meanwhile, a left-wing opposition sprang up through the Organization of Popular Resistance (ORP), headed by militant FLN veterans Hocine Zahouane and Mohamed Harbi and one of the secretaries of the Algerian Communist Party, Bachir Hadj Ali. These three were quickly arrested, however, and the ORP enlarged itself into a militant popular revolutionary front called the Socialist Avantguard Party (PAGS, though generally still known as the FLN-ORP). Then, in November 1967, Chief-of-Staff Colonel Zbiri demanded a meeting of the Revolutionary Council (the FLN's supreme body, which neither Ben Bella nor Boumedienne listened to very much); Zbiri wanted an end to Boumedienne's arbitrary rule and the establishment of collective leadership. Instead, Boumedienne rigidified the FLN Party machinery under Kaid Ahmed, his former Minister of Finance and a close personal friend. On 14 December, Colonel Zbiri rebelled. But he was defeated and condemned to death (in absentia, *as he escaped*).

Where the Algerian Revolution will go from here is hard to say. The FLN-ORP is still active, though in 1969 it began to give limited support to some of Boumedienne's policies (and ORP leaders were tranferred from jail to house detention). The labour unions are still agitating for workers' control and Boumedienne has not succeeded in smashing their militancy. Many FLN guerrilla veterans have regrouped and are demanding a return to the revolutionary march. The Kabylie mountain berbers are in open defiance (their leader, Ait Ahmed, who rebelled against France, Ben Bella and Boume-

dienne, escaped from jail in 1966). And Boumedienne himself is reverting to more socialistic measures. What is still missing is the commitment in practice, to the Algerian Charter, that magnificently idealistic programme adopted by the FLN after the French were driven out of Algeria.

The Algerian Charter was actually based on the programme written and adopted by the National Revolutionary Council of the FLN in exile, at Tripoli, Libya, in June 1962. Known as the Tripoli Programme, it is an eloquent testament to a people's struggle, what it means, how it can be perverted and what Algerian revolutionaries' hopes were then. Since those who wrote it and survived are now within the ORP, the following programme is still alive in Algeria today.

The National Liberation Front: *The Tripoli Programme*[94]

The Evian agreement of 19 March 1962, ending the long war of extermination conducted by French colonial imperialism against the Algerian people, constitutes an irreversible political victory ending the colonial regime and longstanding foreign domination. However, this victory of principles should not let us forget that victory was obtained above all by the continuous revolutionary processes and political and social factors of historical significance created by the armed struggle of the Algerian people.

It was these factors, brought into play in the course of the war of liberation, that secured the only durable victory. It has been through direct action against colonialism that the Algerian people have achieved and consolidated their national unity. In the course of this action, they have ejected from their ranks the sectarianism of the old parties and cliques, and have overcome the many divisions that the French occupation instituted as a political system.

It is in the unity of its action against colonial oppression that the nation has regenerated itself and has achieved the full measure of its dynamism. Through this action, in which the Algerian nation has revived the tradition of struggle, the task of achieving independence and national sovereignty has been brought to a successful conclusion.

It was the participation of the masses that has shaken the foundations of colonialism and has exposed definitively the old reactionary institutions, accelerating the destruction of the many taboos and social structures of feudal origin which acted as obstacles to the further development of Algerian society.

The participation of the Algerian masses has created a new collective awareness of the tasks required for the reconstruction of our society on new bases. The Algerian people, by taking the situation into their hands, and by persistently affirming their will to struggle, consciously or unconsciously have tied this will to struggle to the historical necessity to conquer and untiringly promote every aspect of progress in its most efficient revolutionary form.

The colonial war conducted by France against the Algerian people took the form of a campaign of extermination. It necessitated sending to Algeria the strongest army of all times. Equipped with the most modern weapons, backed by a strong colonial administration, and helped in this campaign of repression, terror and collective massacre by the French population in Algeria, this army concentrated its attacks on the defenceless civilian population, and harassed the ALN (Algerian Liberation Army) in vain. In this way, more than a million Algerians were annihilated and a million more either deported, imprisoned or forced into exile. This war of colonial domination could not have lasted as long as it did without the support of NATO, or the military and diplomatic support of the USA. The extreme degree of cruelty with which this war was waged can only be explained by the very nature of the French policy of colonialization, and the acquiescence of the French people, who long have been deceived by the myth of a 'French Algeria'. The nationalistic and chauvinistic character of this colonial war was well illustrated by the constant participation of the different classes of the French society, including the working class. The French political left, which has always played a role in the anti-colonial struggle on a theoretical level, revealed itself powerless in face of the unforeseen implacable development of the war. Their political action remained timid and ineffective because of their old assimilationist conceptions, and their erroneous idea of the evolutionary nature of the colonial regime, and its ability to reform itself peacefully. The obstinate struggle of the Algerian people forced French colonialism to show its true nature as a totalitarian system, producing in turn militarism and fascism. This truth, demonstrated by events, escaped the attention of the French democrats for a long time.

Despite the colossal tactical and material reinforcement of the French forces in Algeria, of which the Challe Plan has been one of the most significant contributions, their failure became obvious. The Gaullist government was pressed to change the classical colonial regime into a neo-colonialist regime, aiming to maintain under a different form the essential financial and strategic interests of France in Algeria. The Constantine Plan, conceived during the worst period of the war in order to create the economic basis of a 'third force in Algeria', was the first outline of this pseudo-liberal policy.

Under the many pressures of the liberation struggle and the international situation, France finally admitted to the necessity of a peaceful solution to the Algerian situation by agreeing to negotiate with the GPRA. The conferences of Melun in June 1960, Evian in 1961 and Lugrin in July of the same year, successively failed due to the obstinacy of the French government, which asked for a camouflaged surrender, and insisted on the division of the Algerian territory, claiming that section in the Sahara. However, the resurgence of the people's struggle, progressing during the historic days of December 1960, and the insistence of the GPRA on the basic positions of the revolution, forced the French government to begin serious negotiations.

The Evian agreement of 18 March 1962 guarantees the recognition of national sovereignty to Algeria and the integrity of its territory. However, this agreement includes a policy of cooperation between Algeria and France as a counterpart to independence. This cooperation as outlined in the agreement implies a maintenance of ties of dependence in the economic and cultural fields. It also gives, among other things, precious guarantees to the Algerian French of an advantageous place in our country. It is evident that such a concept of cooperation constitutes a typical feature of the neo-colonial policies of France. This is the phenomenon of neo-colonialism substituting itself for classical colonialism.

The immediate task of the FLN is to liquidate, by all means, colonialism as it still manifests itself after the cease-fire in the virulent form of the criminal actions of the OAS.* But it must also elabo-

* Organization de l'Armee Secrète, the ultra-right-wing Organization of the Secret Army, which tried to stop Algerian independence by terrorizing the liberal and reformist community, both in France and in Algeria–ed.

rate at this time an effective strategy to deal with neo-colonialist manoeuvres, which constitute a grave danger for the revolution as they appear under the seductive features of liberalism and apparently disinterested economic and financial cooperation.

The present antagonism between the old and the new colonialism must not deceive us. At any rate, there is no question of preference between one or the other : both must be opposed. The hesitations of the Gaullist power in its fight against the OAS is due to the natural affinity that exists between the French colonialists of both sides of the Mediterranean, and this hesitation expresses a tactical collusion aiming to force the Algerians into a choice in favour of neo-colonialism. This attitude of the French government leads in fact to an opposite reaction. The refusal to effectively repress the activities of the OAS proves without a doubt the complicity of the French government with the ultra-colonialists of Algeria, dealing a hard blow against cooperation.

In this regard, French propaganda aims to perpetuate the myth that the French are indispensable to the economic and administrative life of this country. But for over a century more than three-quarters of Algeria, the agricultural regions in particular, have been abandoned to their fate without any serious planning or proper equipment. Except for their technical skills, the great majority of the French of Algeria, because of their colonialist mentality and their racism, cannot be useful to the Algerian state.

Even if the traditional colonialists are forced to realize that Algeria is lost to them, they do not look upon themselves as being definitively defeated. The OAS aims to institute fascism in France and to begin the colonial war in Algeria again. In practising terror, the colonialists hope to arouse brutal reaction from the Algerian people, and by so doing to annul the cease-fire agreement. It is evident that this plan consists in making Algeria a springboard for a coming fascist *coup d'état* supported by the French army and directed against the governmental power in France. It is important, however, not to underestimate the colonialist threat directed towards Algeria. One of their methods, in fact, is the systematic sabotage of the Algerian economy. This tactic is not new. It was used previously in Vietnam, more particularly during the colonialist débâcle.

By the Evian agreement, the French of Algeria will not be considered entirely as foreigners. They will enjoy for a three-year period all rights as Algerian citizens, after which time they will have to make a definite choice as to their nationality. This presence of the French in Algeria gives rise to a complex problem, in fact one of the most serious the Algerian state has to solve. The predominant influence of the French of Algeria remains in the economic, administrative and cultural spheres, and contradicts the fundamental perspectives of the revolution. It must be noted that the abolition of privileges, the 'acquired rights' of colonization, is an inseparable part of the struggle against neo-colonialism in general. A correct solution of the French minority problem will be found in a consistent policy of anti-imperialism.

According to the terms of the Evian agreement, the French government has the right to maintain its troops in Algeria for a certain period and use the naval airport of Mers El-Kebir, and military airports and atomic installations in the south of the country. This military occupation, which is the result of a neo-colonialist strategy directed towards North Africa in general and Algeria in particular, will be lessened at the end of the first year of self-determination. The contingent of the French army will then be reduced to 80,000 men, the evacuation being scheduled for the end of a second two-year period. As long as Algerian territory is occupied by foreign forces, the freedom of the state is limited and its national sovereignty endangered. The first months of independence will be particularly difficult.

The Provisional Executive has not succeeded two months after taking power in imposing its authority or in controlling the colonial administration, most of the members of which actively support the OAS. It is a vital necessity to regenerate and completely reorganize the administration. This task will prove to be a very delicate one considering the vast territory, the acute daily problems and the lack of qualified Algerians, many of whom were killed in the war.

The national and moral consequences of the practice of genocide carried on for so many years against the Algerian people will be felt more and more. Hundreds of thousands of orphans, tens of thousands of invalids, and thousands of families of only women and children abandoned to their fate, are waiting for adequate measures to be taken by the national power. The wounds of the nation are deep and will not disappear before many decades. Some of them are extremely serious, and could paralyze our society in its forward march. Two million Algerians, most of them women and children, are leaving the camps to which they had been driven. The hundreds of thousands of refugees from Morocco and Tunisia must be repatriated soon.

The problems resulting from this situation are economic and social, but their solution is a matter of politics and organization. To launch national and international campaigns to obtain aid for housing, nutritional and hygienic problems will not be sufficient. These problems, the most serious, brought to us by the war, show tragically the immense chaos our country finds itself in. Not partial and immediate measures, but a basic solution and decisions of a strong social bearing and in accord with an overall plan, are required. The economic and social revolution will deal first with these problems or it will fail to even make a beginning. The revolution will be judged by this test which will determine its future development.

The future government of Algeria inherits an anaemic and exhausted country. Large rural zones, once throbbing with life, are now only desolate areas. In the large and middle-sized cities crushing misery consumes the population, who are crowded in the old sections and in the 'bidonvilles' (villages built of used oil drums). We have to see immediately about removing this intolerable condition by procuring work for the adults, providing schools for the children, fighting against famine and sickness, bringing back a zest for life by means of the collective reconstruction of the country.

Sovereignty has been won, but now we must face the task of giving substance to the national liberation. After having opposed our independence, the French government is trying to interfere according to its imperialist interests. The Evian agreement constitutes a neo-colonialist platform which France is ready to use to propagate its new form of domination.

The French government will not only use its armed forces and its French minority to divert the evolution of Algeria. It will exploit above all the political and social contradictions of the FLN and will attempt to find in this movement of allied currents some which might be detached from the revolution and turned against it. This imperialist tactic can be summarized as follows: to develop a 'third force' in the ranks of the FLN composed of moderate nationalists dedicated to independence but hostile to any consequent revolutionary action, and to oppose the elements of this 'third force' to the militants and cadres who remain faithful to popular aspirations by continuing the anti-imperialist struggle. The obvious intention of the French government is to see a 'moderate' tendency gain control over the revolutionary forces of the FLN, making possible a French–FLN agreement in the framework of neo-colonialism.

The FLN, which at the beginning of the insurrectional action of 1 November 1954 had decided upon an armed struggle for the sole purpose of national liberation, could not have foreseen all the implications and different developments resulting from the war in the popular consciousness and in Algerian society in general. The FLN was not aware of the profound revolutionary potential of the rural people. The little they knew about the situation was confined to a superficial evaluation which was the traditional outlook of the old nationalist parties.

We can say in fact that the FLN, a vanguard tendency at its very beginning, broke with the practices, methods and conceptions of the old parties as it became a movement. But this break could not have been beneficial and definitive without being accompanied at the start by a vigorous effort of ideological demarcation, and a far-reaching programme to cope with the coming events that the struggle was to provoke in Algerian society.

The FLN did not intend to surpass the one objective inscribed on the traditional programme of nationalism, that is, independence. On the other hand, the FLN neglected to foresee the eventuality of two major facts that classical nationalism had never been able to conceive : (a) the very character of the colonial war in a country where the foreign population plays the role of agent and auxiliary of French imperialism; and (b) that the armed struggle involving massive participation by the colonial population, rejecting domination, never develops according to a simple scheme, a guidebook, resulting in national liberation without difficulty.

The inevitable consequences of the totalitarian colonialist oppression on a nation newly freed is a thorough criticism and revision of the structures of the oppressed country. This revision in question completes itself spontaneously, simultaneously and in an infallible manner by the search and the discovery of new structures, of new modes of thought and action, in a word by a process of continual transformation which constitutes the direction of the revolution.

Paradoxical as it may appear, the national revolutionary struggle is perceived and felt in its newness and its originality by the popular masses more than by the leadership and the directorates. The latter are inclined to underestimate or overestimate certain new facts, to artificially compare their own revolutionary movement to other revolutionary movements and to copy other ideologies, which often gives their conceptions an irrelevant and unrealistic character. The view of the world is confused and unformulated in a country at war. The people will express themselves in a very incomplete and empirical way as long as the struggle lasts and facts cannot be analysed with the help of precedence, example and analogy.

This original thinking, the result of a real evaluation by the people of their revolution and of their collective experiences, has not been taken sufficiently into consideration by the revolution as one of its treasures.

Instead of the revolution taking this thinking into consideration, we have witnessed and are still witnessing a very serious lack of contact between, on the one hand, the collective consciousness tested in reality, and on the other hand, the practice and authority of the FLN at all levels. Very often, in a paternalistic manner, this authority has purely and simply substituted itself for political responsibility which is inseparable from the search for an ideology. This authority, which was most of the time on the level of technicalities and removed from an ideological research, produced concepts which could be termed as anti-revolutionary.

The FLN, sworn enemy of feudalism, even though it has fought feudalism throughout our old social institutions, has done nothing in return to preserve itself from feudalistic concepts at certain levels of its own organization. It has forgotten in this regard that naïve conceptions of authority, the absence of rigorous criteria, and political ignorance, favour the development of a feudal mentality.

This feudal mentality does not only develop within the traditionally preponderant class, that class which possesses the land and exploits the people. It continues to survive under various forms as a relic of a past epoch, in African and Asian countries, even under popular revolutions when the latter lack ideological vigilance.

Just as there is feudalism in land—material feudalism—there can also exist political feudalism of the bosses and their cliques, whose coming to power was made possible by the absence of all democratic education on the part of the militants and the citizens.

In addition to the feudal mentality which has impregnated all the life of Maghreb since the end of the middle ages in the economic, social, cultural and religious spheres, and which the FLN

L

has been unable to completely eradicate, we must note also one of its most surreptitious effects—*paternalism*.

Paternalism constitutes a real hindrance to political development and to the conscious and creative initiative of the militant and of the citizen. It conveys a deceptively mild, anti-popular and secret type of archaic authority and, inevitably, an infantile conception of responsibility.

This distortion of revolutionary values has also resulted in substituting deficient political maturity with superficial attitudes, resulting in *formalism*. It is in this way that patriotism and revolutionary spirit are interpreted in terms of being only frantic gestures. This artificial romanticism and shameless taste for heroic bombast is contrary to the reserved temperament of our people. Formalism serves as an alibi for those who seek to escape from their day-to-day revolutionary duties.

Next we must denounce another state of mind, one never denounced enough because it has caused numerous catastrophes and has done as much harm to the revolution as the feudalistic inheritance—the *petty-bourgeois* attitude. The lack of ideological firmness within the FLN has allowed this attitude to infiltrate the ranks of a great part of the rank and file and the youth.

The easy ways inherited from the old parties with an urban base, the escape from reality due to a lack of revolutionary education, the individualistic longing for stability, for the seeking of profits and ostentation, the prejudice that many have towards the peasants and obscure militants, all this constitutes the salient characteristics of the petty-bourgeois attitude. This attitude becomes easily impregnated and pseudo-intellectualized—empty of any knowledge—with the most outmoded and harmful concepts of Western mentality. In addition, this attitude tends towards a new bureaucratic class, demarked from the majority of the people.

The ideological poverty of the FLN, and the feudal mentality and petty-bourgeois attitudes which are the indirect result of this poverty, could reduce the future Algerian state to a mediocre and anti-popular bureaucracy in fact, if not in principle.

One of the essential causes that slowed the development of the FLN on the ideological plane, aggravating its weaknesses and worsening the general situation of the war in Algeria, arises out of this chasm between the leadership and the popular masses. The installation of the headquarters of the FLN outside Algeria at the end of the third year of war, even if it was necessary at the moment, nevertheless isolated the FLN from the national situation.

This isolation could have been fatal to the liberation movement as a whole. One of the most obvious consequences of this state of affairs has been the progressive de-politicization of those organs which remained in Algeria as well as those groups created or taken outside of Algeria by the Directorate. It must be understood here that by the de-politicization is meant the absence of all general ideological direction constituting a firm tie between the Algerian people and their leaders on both sides of the frontiers. By de-politicization is also meant the toleration during the armed struggle of disparate and contradictory political currents, and individualistic actions escaping all control, and allowing some people to become dignitaries without precise functions.

Besides, the GPRA, which merged at its beginning with the leadership of the FLN, has contributed to the weakening of the two concepts of State and Party.

The amalgamation of the state institutions and the organs of the FLN has reduced the latter to a merely administrative apparatus. In the interior, this amalgamation resulted in depriving the FLN of its responsibilities to the advantage of the ALN, and, with the help of the war, practically annihilated it.

The experience of the seven and a half years of war proves that, without an elaborate ideology developed in contact with the national reality and the popular masses, there cannot be a revolutionary party. The *raison d'être* for a party is its ideology. It ceases to exist should its ideology fail.

The war of liberation victoriously conducted by the Algerian people has re-established national sovereignty and independence. However, the struggle has not ended with this victory. On the contrary, it must continue with the construction of a revolutionary state in order that the conquests of the armed struggle may be extended and consolidated.

If we look into the general situation, we see that Algeria is only starting to emerge from colonial domination and a semi-feudal status. These two characteristic features of Algeria will not automatically disappear with the coming of independence. They will persist as long as a radical transformation of society has not been achieved.

Algeria, as with most of the countries of Africa and Asia, has known feudalism as an economic and social system. This system has continued to exist until today after having undergone a series of retreats and transformations since 1830.

At the time of colonial conquest, the Algerian feudal proprietors, who were already unpopular, immediately joined with the enemy, not hesitating to participate in their war of looting and continued repression. Emir Abdelkader, chief of the Algerian state and artisan of the resistance, undertook an implacable fight against them. He succeeded in destroying their coalition at the battles of Maharez and Mina in 1834. In its traditional politics, colonialism has constantly leaned on the support of these Algerian feudal proprietors in order to defeat nationalist aspirations. To save them from destruction and popular vengeance, colonialism organized them officially in 1838 as a permanent corps.

From the military and land-holding caste that it was, the Algerian feudal gentry gradually became an administrative caste. This role permitted them to pursue their exploitation of the people and to enlarge their landholding wealth. Thus, this corps of *caïds* has been perpetuated until today and is the most typical expression of this feudalism.

Parallel to this agrarian and administrative feudalism, we must note the existence of another type of feudalism—that of the great congregations of the Marabouts. The Marabouts, who played a positive role in the national struggle before 1830 and at various times up until 1871, have been converted partially into this administrative feudalism. In the obscurantist context of colonialism they have exploited the religious sentiment of the people by superstition and other ignorant practices.

In the course of the liberation struggle the Algerian people shook the colonial structure and dealt a death blow to feudalism as an administrative and patriarchal power. However, even if the institutions of feudalism have disappeared, its ideological relics and social vestiges remain. These relics and vestiges have contributed to the alteration of the Islamic spirit and have carried along with them the immobility of Moslem society.

Feudalism, product of the decadence of Maghreb at a certain moment of its history, could only be perpetuated in the context of declining social, cultural and religious values. Based upon the principle of patriarchal and paternalistic authority, a source of arbitrariness, it represents as well an acute form of parasitism.

It is from these two aspects that it encourages the persistence of structures and concepts of another age: tribal attitudes, regionalism, discrimination against and segregation of women, obscurantism and taboos of all kinds. All these conceptions and reactionary practices which still exist in the rural life of Algeria constitute an obstacle to progress and the liberation of man. The Algerian peasantry, which has always fought against oppression and the immobility inherent in the feudal system, could not alone triumph. It is the role of the revolution to liquidate definitively the anti-national, anti-social and anti-popular relics of feudalism.

Since 1 November 1954 a new dimension has appeared in Algerian society which had remained static until then. This new dimension was the collective participation of the people in the national struggle. This movement of the masses, by its depth and continuity, has put into question all the values of the old society and posed the problems of the new society.

An analysis of the social content of the liberation struggle makes it clear that it is the peasants and the working people generally who have been the active base of the movement and have given it its essentially popular character. The massive participation of the workers swept the other social layers of the nation into the struggle along with them. More particularly, it has created the important phenomenon of the total participation of Algerian youth regardless of their social background. We must note in this respect that it is largely the youth who come from the bourgeoisie who have determined the support of the bourgeoisie themselves to the cause of independence.

This popular movement resulted in the armed struggle being impelled beyond the objective of national liberation towards a further perspective—that of the revolution itself. But with its continuity, its untiring effort, and its immense sacrifices, it has given the fragmentary national consciousness a more homogeneous form. Furthermore, it has resulted in a collective consciousness oriented towards the revolutionary transformation of society. This fact, which we cannot over-emphasize, has given to the liberation movement its essential character in contrast to the other nationalist movements in the Maghreb.

This implies necessarily an effort of analyses, of adequate arrangement, a firm and correct orientation and clear decisions. Two main criteria should inspire our action: (1) we should proceed from

Algerian reality in the direction of the objective conditions and the aspirations of the people; (2) we should express this reality taking into account the requirements of modern progress, the achievements of science, the experiences of other revolutionary movements, and the anti-imperialist struggle across the globe.

The word 'revolution' has long been thrown about carelessly without any precise content. However, it has never failed to galvanize the popular masses, who instinctively give to the word a meaning beyond the objectives of the war of liberation. What was lacking in the meaning of 'revolution', and what is still lacking to reveal its full significance, is an essential ideological basis. During the war of liberation the momentum of the struggle was sufficient to propel and carry forward the revolutionary aspirations of the masses. To-day, when the struggles have stopped with the end of the war and the re-establishment of national independence, it is important that this momentum now be carried over onto the ideological plane without delay. After the armed struggle must come the ideological struggle, after the struggle for national independence must come the Popular Democratic Revolution.

The Popular Democratic Revolution is the conscious construction of a country according to socialist principles with the power in the hands of the people. In order that the development of Algeria be rapid and harmonious, and in order that the primary economic needs of the people be satisfied, it must be conceived within a socialist perspective, within the framework of the collectivization of the basic means of production and within the framework of a rational plan.

An important task of the revolution is to consolidate the newly independent nation, and restore all the values stifled and destroyed by colonialism, by restoring a sovereign state, a national economy, and a national culture. These values must be conceived and organized within a modern perspective. This means the abolition of the social and economic structures of feudalism and its hangovers, and the establishment of new structures and institutions favouring and guaranteeing the emancipation of man and the full and entire enjoyment of his liberties.

The sense of responsibility, the greatest emanation of the democratic spirit, must everywhere replace the principle of authority which is the essence of the feudal paternalistic character. The democratic spirit must not be a matter of purely theoretical speculation.

It must be concretized in clearly defined state institutions in all sectors of social life of the country. The economic conditions of the country determine in a large measure its social, cultural and political character.

Since the fate of the individual is tied to the fate of society as a whole, democracy for us should not only mean the expansion of individual liberties, but above all the collective expression of popular responsibilities.

The building of a modern state on a democratic anti-feudal basis will be possible only through the initiative, the vigilance, and the direct control of the people. Only such a state will be able to find an effective solution to the problem of health, housing, and the improvement of the living conditions of the families.

In this framework, the Algerian woman, emancipated by the revolutionary struggle, will be able to assume the full responsibility to which she is entitled.

The tasks of the democratic revolution in Algeria are immense. They cannot be realized by one class alone in society, as enlightened as it might be; only the people can carry these tasks to their completion—the peasants, the workers, the youth, and the revolutionary intellectuals.

The experience of certain countries which have recently gained their independence teaches us that a privileged social layer can take power to its exclusive benefit. In so doing it robs the people of the fruits of their struggle and isolates itself from them in order to ally itself with imperialism. In the name of national unity, which it exploits for opportunistic purposes, the bourgeoisie pretends to act in the interests of the people, asking for their support.

The seizure of power in Algeria must be clearly understood. National unity is not unity based upon the bourgeoisie. It affirms the unity of the people on the basis of the principles of the Popular Democratic Revolution to which the bourgeoisie must subordinate its interests. The logic of history and the basic interests of the nation make this an imperative. The patriotism of the bourgeoisie will be demonstrated to us by their acceptance of this imperative, by their support of the revolutionary cause and by their renunciation of the aim of directing the destiny of the country.

The bourgeoisie is the purveyor of an opportunist ideology of which the main characteristics are defeatism, demagogy, an alarmist spirit, a contempt of principles, and a lack of revolutionary conviction—all the characteristics favouring the establishment of neo-colonialism.

The revolution is not a series of formulae to be applied in a routine and bureaucratic fashion. There is no finished ideology; there is only constant and creative ideological striving.

The construction of a modern state cannot take place without the complete rejection of all forms of subjectivism: improvisation, approximation, intellectual laziness, a tendency to idealize reality and to emphasize only those aspects which are spectacular and romantic. Furthermore, we must be on guard against moralizing, an idealistic and infantile tendency which consists in wishing to transform society and to resolve its problems on the basis of moral values alone. That is a concept which leads to errors and confuses revolutionary action in its constructive phase. Moralizing, often professed by a few, is an easy excuse for an inability to act on social reality and to organize constructively. Revolutionary endeavour cannot be narrowed down to good intentions alone, as sincere as they might be; it requires, above all, actions based on objective conditions. Individual moral values, even if they are respectable and necessary, cannot be the determinant factors in the construction of society. In a sound society the conditions will be created for their collective flourishing.

Algerian culture will be national, revolutionary and scientific. Its role as a national culture will consist, first of all, in restoring to the Arab language, the living expression of the cultural values of our country, its dignity and its effectiveness as a language of civilization. To this end, it will work to reconstitute, revitalize, and promote our national inheritance and its dual classic and modern humanism in order to reintroduce it into the intellectual life and the education of the people. In so doing, it will combat cultural cosmopolitanism and the overwhelming Western influence which have contributed to the contempt which many Algerians have held towards their language and national values.

As a new revolutionary culture it will contribute to the emancipation of the people. It will neither be a caste culture, closed to progress, nor a luxury of the mind. Popular and militant, it will enlighten the masses and assist them in their political and social struggle in all its forms. Being a dynamic culture dedicated to the service of the people, it will enhance the development of the revolutionary consciousness, always reflecting the aspirations of the people, their real situation, their new conquests and thus all forms of their artistic traditions.

This necessity is imposed upon us because the Arab language has not been used as an instrument of modern scientific culture and therefore has to be developed for its future role by rigorously concrete and perfected methods. Algerian culture developed in this way must constitute the indispensable living link between the ideological effort of the Popular Democratic Revolution and the concrete everyday tasks of building the country. In this light, the indispensable raising of the cultural standards of the militants, the cadres, those holding administrative responsibilities, and of the masses becomes of the utmost importance.

The revolutionary vanguard of the people must provide an example by adopting the objective of raising its own cultural level, and making this objective its motto. We must vigorously denounce the tendency to underestimate intellectual effort and to profess, as sometimes happens, uncalled for anti-intellectualism. To this attitude another extreme—close to petty-bourgeois moralism—often responds. This flows from a tendency to exploit Islamic values for demagogic purposes in order to evade the real problems. No doubt, we belong to Moslem civilization, which has a lasting and profound impact on the history of humanity, but it would be doing an injustice to this civilization to believe that its revival could take place by repeating simple subjective formulas relating to general behaviour and religious practice.

We cannot ignore the fact that Moslem civilization, in order to become a concrete reality, had to begin and develop through positive effort on the level both of work and thought, of economy and culture. Moreover, the spirit of discovery which animated it, its orientation towards science, foreign cultures and the universal character of the epoch, brought a creative exchange between Moslem civilization and other civilizations. These criteria—of creativity, of efficient systematization of values and contributions of Moslem culture—contributed greatly to human progress in the past. In a genuine cultural renascence this heritage must be taken into account. A nostalgic attitude toward the past, however, will certainly result in impotence and confusion; we must use the past as a source of inspiration for building on the basis of concrete realities according to rigorous methods. Once Islam is freed from all its excrescences and superstitions, which have strangled and distorted

L*

it, it will be certain to contribute more than as a religion, but as a vehicle of two essential factors—culture and national identity.

The Algerian economy has been a colonial economy, dominated by France and entirely in the hands of foreigners. Algeria has been primarily a source of raw materials and a market for manufactured products. Its dependent status is demonstrated by the high proportion of foreign trade in relation to national production, and by the preponderance of France in this foreign trade—Algeria has always been the major customer and supplier of France—by the extent of foreign investment and of foreign control of Algeria's balance of accounts, and by the lack of important industrialization.

Two economic sectors united by a fragile commercial link coexist in Algeria : (a) the modern and dynamic sector is the capitalist sector. It constitutes a real outpost of the French economy and involves European agriculture geared to urban markets and export trade, diverse industrial branches, transportation, big commerce and goods and services. Algerian contribution to this sector is mainly in manpower. And (b) the traditional sector, in which the essential part of the Algerian population (5,225,000 persons) makes a living, still retains the structures inherited from the past. A subsistence economy and pre-capitalist production relationships are dominant. Financial and technical means are almost nil.

The social consequences of this dependent, disjointed and dominated economy are severely felt by the majority of the Algerian population as is shown by the great disparity in income. The average income of the French Algerian is more than 340,000 francs annually, whereas the average income of Algerians is less than 50,000 francs annually, which means less than 20,000 francs annually for the masses living in the old sector.

The social consequences can be seen equally in the failure to integrate into the economy 2,500,000 Algerians (990,000 of whom are partially or totally unemployed in the cities, and 1,500,000 of whom are unemployed in the countryside)—the rural exodus, the emigration of 400,000 to France, the illiteracy of more than four-fifths of all those over six years of age, in housing shortages, in the lack of sanitation, which has resulted in many slums and 'bidon-villes', and the very poor sanitation in the countryside.

In countries newly freed from foreign domination, the methods of classical liberal economics do not permit a real transformation of society. This method of economic development creates anarchy of the market, reinforces dependence upon imperialist countries, establishes the state as an apparatus for transferring the wealth of the country into the hands of the possessing classes, and contributes to the maintenance of parasitic social layers tied to the imperialist world.

The native bourgeoisie gradually replaces the foreign bourgeoisie in the deteriorating sectors of production, and enriches itself while the people remain in misery and ignorance.

The limited national revenue and private capital in our country, the export of most of the profits, the use of local capital for speculation purposes, commercial profits and high-interest loans, the waste encountered from unemployment of our powerful working force, are all factors which exclude the capitalist method of developing our economy.

Our Party cannot leave the very important work of solving the fundamental problems of our country in the hands of an embryonic bourgeoisie tied by the nature of their activities to imperialism. In 1954, out of 4.5 billions of private investments in our country, eight per cent of this amount was local capital. We cannot allow foreign capital to dominate our economy and expect that they will modernize our industry.

Foreign capital is reluctant to invest in low-profit industries and will not therefore take an interest in certain fields which are the most urgent. The fields to which foreign investment are attracted relegate it to a secondary role in the development of our economy.

Planning and nationalization of the industries involving the participation of the workers are essential measures in order to achieve three main aims: to eliminate the power of the monopolies as basic changes are made in economic relations with foreign powers, mainly France; to eliminate internal obstacles to planning by a radical change in the structures of rural life; to industrialize our country in order that we might supply our people with the necessities of life.

Only planning allows the necessary accumulation of capital required for productive industrialization within a relatively short period; only planning allows the centralization of the most important investments and eliminates unnecessary spending caused by competition between industries.

Workers' participation in the management of the economy will permit the control and execution of the plan and its continual adaptation to the possibilities inherent in the situation.

The creation of an internal market and the laying of the basis of industrialization can only be achieved with a revolution in the rural mode of life. From an economic point of view, due to the present conditions in the farming areas—due to the nature of production on the farms of the big French *colons* and big Algerian proprietors and the degree of mechanization on these farms—our Party advocates collective farms, a policy of the land being distributed without fragmentation. This solution should be applied with the consent of the peasants themselves in order to avoid the disastrous consequences of forced collectivization.

The agrarian reform must be accomplished according to the slogan 'The Land to Those Who Work It' and according to the following rules: (1) immediate ban on transactions in land and in means of agricultural production; (2) restrictions on landholding according to the kind of crop and the size of the crop; (3) expropriation of properties larger than the maximum allowed; (4) distribution of the expropriated land to the poor peasants; (5) democratic organization of the peasants into cooperative forms of production; (6) creation of state farms on the expropriated land and participation of the agrarian workers in the administration and the sharing of benefits. These farms will facilitate contact with the market and will constitute a training-ground for the formation of better qualified agrarian cadres; (7) a ban on sales or rental of land in order to avoid the re-constitution of the big properties; (8) the annulling of the debts of peasants, 'khammes', and workers owed to land-holders, moneylenders or to public services; (9) material and financial aid from the state.

The overpopulation of rural areas will allow the rapid mobilization of the work-force to reconquer the land. This is of the utmost importance. The democratic organization of rural workyards will eliminate unemployment, will help recuperate large areas and will liberate all our productive forces.

This transformation of the agricultural structure must be the point of departure for the development of the foundation, the nationalization of credit and foreign trade, in a first stage, and the nationalization of natural resources and energy in a second stage. These measures will accelerate the tempo of the industrialization of our country.

The rail and road systems of our country were built according to the economic and strategic requirements of the period of colonization. During the war, numerous new rail lines and side roads were built to facilitate the mobility of French troops. These can now be used as a basis for the development of a suitable foundation to facilitate the progress of trade and to eliminate all obstacles to the broadening of the internal market and to the exchange of agricultural produce. The policy of the Party must be in the direction of the nationalization of the means of transportation and of the establishment of connecting communication lines between the main routes and the rural markets.

The nationalization of banks has to be completed within the next period. The banks are so numerous that they are not easily brought under national control. They have been recently converted into 'societies for development' but this change must not obscure the fact that their essential character is to be an instrument of financial blackmail.

Algerian commercial policies must be inspired by the following principles:

—to drastically eliminate at an appropriate rate the preferential status that France has long had with Algeria,

—to assure trade based on equality and reciprocal advantage with other countries. To increase trade with countries offering stable prices and long-term agreements where we may buy our supply of equipment at the lowest possible prices,

—to nationalize on a scale of priorities the essential branches of foreign trade and of wholesale commerce, and to create state societies for each different product or group of products—such an organization allows a real state control on imports and exports, facilitates efficient action towards the fulfilment and procuring of commercial benefits for investments in the productive branches,

—to control prices and create state stores in the rural centres in order to combat speculation and usury.

Unless there is an economic and technical base provided by industrial development, the development of the agrarian sector of our economy and the mobilization of the masses cannot meet the problems confronting our country. A sector of our industry is already nationalized. The state has to extend this sector to mines, quarries and cement factories.

The long-term development of the country is conditional upon the development of basic industries necessary to modern agriculture. In this respect Algeria presents tremendous possibilities for the petroleum and uranium industries. In this domain it is the responsibility of the state to provide the necessary conditions for the development of a heavy industry.

During the period when it will be necessary to allow a private sector to exist it will be necessary to have a correct orientation. On no account should the state contribute in any way to the creation as has happened in certain countries of an industrial basis for the benefit of the native bourgeoisie, whose development it must check by appropriate means. Foreign private capital is desirable within the confines of certain conditions—as a complementary factor within the framework of mixed enterprises. The rate of profit must be controlled and a certain percentage of profits must be re-invested within our country.

The enthusiasm of the masses and their social mobilization must become a constant factor in the life of the country. In order to make this possible, extravagant spending, waste of public funds, extreme luxury and very high incomes must be severely condemned. These abuses contribute to the conviction of the masses that they alone carry the burden of building the country. Moreover, the administration by the state of certain enterprises must under no circumstances justify a deterioration in the living conditions of the workers, who must keep the right to go on strike.

Previous to 1 November 1954 the Algerian people expressed their attachment to national values elaborated in the framework of the Arab–Moslem civilization by creating and maintaining the 'medersas libres' (free cultural organizations) in spite of the opposition of the colonial authorities. And, in the course of the struggle for independence, some of the leaders of the 'willayas' (military zones) strove to make Algerian culture accessible to the masses. In our country, the cultural revolution involves many tasks:

(a) The restoration of a national culture with a progressive introduction on a scientific basis of the Arab language and culture into the schools. Of all the tasks confronting the revolution this is the most delicate one requiring modern cultural media, and cannot be accomplished rapidly without great danger of disorientating and confusing whole generations.

(b) The preservation of the popular national culture.

(c) The broadening of the school system to ensure all levels of education for everyone.

(d) Adaptation of educational programmes to Algerian reality.

(e) Extension of the methods of mass education and the mobilization of all national organizations to fight against illiteracy and to teach all the citizens how to read and write in the shortest possible period.

The economic and social stagnation in rural society, the hasty resettlement of the population after the conquest, has resulted in a proliferation of slum areas in the country around the big cities and urban centres. The war aggravated this phenomenon by 'regrouping' two million peasants. The Party must take immediate measures to give decent housing to citizens harassed by the long war and initiate a plan of building projects to locate them close to points of production.

Medical care and clinical facilities must be rapidly nationalized so that everyone can get free medical attention with the least possible delay. This should be done by developing a National Health Service in charge of hospitals and medical installations. This National Health Service will employ full-time physicians who will enjoy the best working conditions and opportunities for research. Only these doctors will be admitted to university or hospital careers. This National Health Service will gradually replace the old classical liberal sector.

The contribution of the Algerian women to the struggle for freedom brought favourable conditions for their liberation from their traditional yoke. They should take part fully in the administration of public affairs and in the general development of our country. The Party must remove all obstacles to the liberation and development of women, and support and promote women's organizations. In the past we have had a negative attitude regarding the role of women in society. In many ways the idea of feminine inferiority still permeates our society, and women themselves are imbued with these traditional prejudices.

The Party cannot go forward without a persistent struggle against reactionary beliefs and social prejudices. In this field, the Party must not only denounce anti-feminine prejudices, but must make absolutely irreversible an aim that it has inscribed in its declaration, by allocating responsible posts in the Party to women.

A foreign policy with a correct orientation can be an important instrument in consolidating our independence and in constructing a national economy. Algeria has gained its independence at a time when the world relationship of forces continues to unfold in favour of the masses and against imperialism. The struggle of the liberation movements in Africa, Asia and Latin America, the consolidation of independence in countries which had long been colonies, the action of democratic forces in the imperialist countries, and the gains accomplished by socialist forces—this struggle has accelerated the disintegration of imperialism. In the last few years, this struggle has claimed many victories.

This new situation has brought numerous changes in imperialist policies. The imperialists have become more and more flexible, trying to associate with small groups of the native bourgeoisie or bureaucracy in the interest of exploiting the people. They are attempting to demobilize the forces of liberation in order to maintain their economic and strategic interests in the colonized countries.

The alliance of imperialist countries with the governments of some African, Asian and American nations has temporarily delayed the ebb-tide of imperialism. But the general trend of our epoch is the reduction of imperialism's capacity to manoeuvre, not the enlargement of it.

The foreign policy of Algeria, in view of the constant dangers threatening our country, must be directed towards fighting colonialism and imperialism, towards helping the movements of unification of the Maghreb, of the Arab world, and of Africa, and towards supporting liberation forces and the fight for peace.

The great lesson we draw from our own struggle for independence is that the imperialist countries, confronted by the rising tide of the masses, are seeking solidarity in spite of their minor differences. Our struggle has raised an echo from the masses in these countries, but it has also met with hostility from certain groups. In its drive to maintain its domination over Algeria, France received material and moral support from all the Western countries, especially from the USA. Our revolutionary struggle will still meet many more obstacles. This must not keep us from making the maximum effort to persist in our anti-imperialist fight.

The struggle against imperialism has produced political and social forces which have been oriented in the same direction towards attainment of the unity of the Maghreb, the Arab world, and Africa.

The achievement of unity among different countries is a gigantic task which' must be considered in the framework of the ideological, political and economic paths common to all their people. In the Maghreb, and in the Arab world as in Africa, the divide-and-rule policies of imperialism, the conflicting and particular interests of the ruling classes are the main obstacles to realizing unity which they often reduce to a mere demagogic slogan.

The main task of our Party is to help the Maghreb, the Arab world, and Africa to reach a correct evaluation of the formidable challenge of such an accomplishment as unification. Meeting this challenge must be done through the vanguard organizations and mass organizations so that we can see concretely what obstacles must be overcome.

At the level of the governments, the development of trade, the realization of common economic projects, a concerted foreign policy, and a total solidarity in the fight against imperialism are objectives which, being in the interest of the peoples, impel us towards unification.

The Algerian war of liberation, because of its power and intensity, increased the tempo of the struggle for freedom in all African countries. Independent Algeria must give complete support to the masses who are constantly struggling to liberate their countries. We must pay close attention to Angola, South Africa, and the nations of East Africa. Our solidarity against colonialism will broaden our line of defence against imperialism and reinforce the movement for unification.

International cooperation is needed to utilize all human and material resources for progress in a climate of peace, and can only be won by a permanent mobilization of the masses against imperialism.

CONGO–KINSHASA

In recent African history, few countries have suffered more than the old Belgian Congo. Second only to the Sudan in size, second only to South Africa in wealth (and potentially richer), it has been ravaged by slave-hunters and mercenaries, UN troops and US guns, Cuban exiles and CIA agents. And though the fate of its many revolutionaries has been bleak, it is the source and inspiration of people's armed struggle for all of black Africa.

Lying just south of the continental centre, the Congo was first conquered by the Portuguese, then by Arab merchants of Zanzibar and finally by the Belgians, whose King Leopold 'owned' it as his personal property until 1908 when it was annexed to Belgium. The first colonial administration was not established until 1930, and by 1959 the country was ruled by 9,600 Belgian colonists and 7,000 missionaries—besides civil servants and the army (reinforced repeatedly since 1895, date of the first of many Congolese rebellions). The Belgians never attempted to develop the country's infrastructure, and by 1959 there was not a single Congolese secondary school teacher and only thirty university graduates. More than seventy-five per cent of the colony's fourteen million people lived below subsistence level, engaged in primitive agriculture, hunting and fishing. Meanwhile, the Congo was turning out three-quarters of the world's industrial diamonds, sixty-nine per cent of its cobalt and a large share of its copper, zinc, gold, tin, silver, cadmium, manganese, tungsten, bismuth and germanium, plus of course high-grade uranium (from which the Hiroshima bomb was made).

But the Congolese got none of the profits. These went to the Belgians, British, French and, through stock ownership in Britain's Tanganyika Concessions (TANKS) and the Oppenheimer combine, to America's Rockefeller group. In 1960 alone, for example, net mining profits from Katanga reached $407 million. From 1950 to 1959, Union Minière (mostly Belgian but also some English and

American interests) derived 31 billion Belgian francs from its Congolese investments.[95]

At a mass rally in Leopoldville (now Kinshasa) on 3 January 1959 the head of the Congolese National Movement (MNC), Patrice Lumumba, said that such conditions could not go on. He demanded immediate and total independence. The next day 30,000 Congolese demonstrated in the streets—and were savagely put down by the Belgian army. But as the movement grew, Belgium agreed finally to pull out in 1960. General elections were held before independence and Lumumba's MNC won most of the elective posts, with Joseph Kasavubu's ABAKO party second. Independence came on 29 June 1960. Two weeks later, egged on by the Belgians, the Congo's richest province announced its secession and on 12 July 1960 Lumumba, who was then Prime Minister, appealed for help from the United Nations.

That act would be his undoing. Guided by members of the UN's 'Congo Club' (one Englishman, two Indians and three Americans), the UN Forces immediately stepped in to prevent Lumumba from consolidating his power. Under the direction of the Congo Clubman, Andrew W. Cordier, later President of Columbia University but then Executive Assistant to UN Secretary-General Dag Hammarskjöld (and, through his membership in the Century Association and the Council on Foreign Relations,* a close associate of Dean Rusk, Allen Dulles, McGeorge Bundy, David and Nelson Rockefeller, et al.), the UN occupied the Leopoldville airport, stopping aid to Lumumba, and seized the radio station, prohibiting Lumumba from speaking to his people. The UN force, however, did not stop the rebellious and pro-American troops of Sergeant (later 'General' and now 'President') Joseph Mobutu from kidnapping Lumumba and taking him to Camp Hardy near Thysville, beating him all the way. Once there, Katanga secessionist (and later Congo 'Prime Minister') Moïse Tshombe had him killed in his presence. Shortly before his death, Lumumba, then thirty-six, wrote to his home:

My dear wife,

I am writing these words not knowing whether they will reach you, and whether I shall still be alive when you read them. All through my struggle

* In 1960, the Council received $112,200 from American Metal Climax, Inc., IBM World Trade Corp., Mobil International Oil Co., (whose director, Grayson Kirk, was Cordier's predecessor at Columbia University), the *New York Times*, the Rand Corporation, Standard Oil Co. in exchange for 'free consultation with members of the Council's staff on problems of foreign policy'—ed.

for the independence of my country, I have never doubted for a single instant the final triumph of the sacred cause to which my companions and I have devoted all our lives. But what we wished for our country, its right to an honourable life, to unstained dignity, to independence without restrictions, was never desired by the Belgian imperialists and the Western Allies, who found direct and indirect support, *both deliberate and unintentional,* amongst certain high officials of the United Nations, *that organization in which we placed all our trust when we called on its assistance.*

They have corrupted some of our compatriots and bribed others. They have helped to distort the truth and bring our independence into dishonour. How could I speak otherwise? Dead or alive, free or in prison, by order of the imperialists, it is not myself who counts. It is the Congo, it is our poor people for whom independence has been transformed into a cage from whose confines the outside world looks on us, sometimes with kindly sympathy, but at other times with joy and pleasure.

But my faith will remain unshakeable. I know and I feel in my heart that sooner or later my people will rid themselves of all their enemies, both internal and external, and that they will rise as one man to say No to the degradation and shame of colonialism, and regain their dignity in the clear light of the sun.

We are not alone. Africa, Asia, and the free liberated people from all corners of the world will always be found at the side of the millions of Congolese who will not abandon the struggle until the day when there are no longer any colonialists and their mercenaries in our country. As to my children, whom I leave and whom I may never see again, I should like them to be told that it is for them, as it is for every Congolese, to accomplish the sacred task of reconstructing our independence and our sovereignty: for without justice there is no dignity, and without independence there are no free men.

Neither brutality, nor cruelty nor torture will ever bring me to ask for mercy, for I prefer to die with my head unbowed, my faith unshakeable, and with profound trust in the destiny of my country, rather than live under subjection and disregarding sacred principles. History will one day have its say, but it will not be the history that is taught in Brussels, but the history which will be taught in the countries freed from Imperialism and its puppets. Africa will write her own history, and to the north and south of the Sahara it will be a glorious and delightful history.

Do not weep for me, my dear wife. I know that my country, which is suffering so much, will know how to defend its independence and its liberty.

Long live the Congo! Long live Africa!

Patrice.

Following Lumumba's murder, on 14 February 1961, and the violent repressions unleashed by Mobutu, Lumumba's forces rallied. First Antoine Gizenga set up a rebel regime in Stanleyville (now Kisangani) and held out until 1962 when he was crushed by Mobutu's forces assisted by the UN. Then, Bocheley Davidson and Pierre Mulele, who had been Lumumba's Minister of Education, created the National Council of Liberation (CNL). Mulele journeyed to China for training and, in November 1963, opened the first guerrilla centre in the south-western province of Kwilu. Next Gaston Soumaliot and Christophe Gbenye led a rebellion in Kivu which swept down into Stanleyville and again established a rebel regime, this time called the Revolutionary Congolese Government, with Gbenye as president.

But towards the end of 1964 a few hundred Belgian paratroopers and mercenaries from Rhodesia, South Africa and West Germany, and some 200 Cuban exiles commanded by CIA 'operatives', were dropped from US-piloted, US C-130 planes, and a massacre began that would cost 30,000 Congolese lives before Gbenye was beaten. Soumaliot fled into the jungles and, like Mulele, adopted guerrilla warfare tactics. The war spread. More mercenaries came. US bombers, US military aid, and US 'advisers' were dispatched to the area in increasingly heavier quantities—on the justification, as US Under-Secretary of State Harriman said, of 'the dangers of Chinese communist influence in the Congo' although London's Guardian *reported that there was 'no proof of Chinese intervention while the presence of US bombers and military personnel was public knowledge'.*

The Kivu rebellion failed. Only Mulele's CNL kept fighting, joined now by the forces of Soumaliot and Gaston M'Galo. Meanwhile, General Mobutu deposed Tshombe, who had manoeuvred himself into the Congo's premiership. In 1967, Mobutu ordered the assassination of Lumumba's wife and four children. That same year, in June, the Patrice Lumumba Battalion, headed by Thomas Mukwidi, went into battle, opening up still a new rebel front. Che Guevara and other Cuban guerrilla fighters had helped organize it, and had even fought with it for a while. It was Che's theory (as it had been that of Frantz Fanon) that the Congo was the key to all of black Africa. But Mulele was no longer interested; he had stopped fighting. In September 1968 he was publicly offered a pardon and a cabinet post by Mobutu's Foreign Minister Justin-

Marie Bomboko (who had worked first for Lumumba, then Kasa-vubu, then Tshombe and now Mobutu). Mulele accepted. Bomboko went to escort him home from Brazzaville. The next day, Mulele was arrested, tried for war crimes—and executed two days later.

The articles which follow are from Mulele's forces. They are ex-tracts from two of six notebooks found near Lake Leopold II after an assault in June 1965 on Nioki by his CNL forces. The notebooks were all of the same type: school size of 100 pages each. Other documents found with them indicated that the rebels had been trained in Boanga and Gambona, just across the Congo River into Congo-Brazzaville, and that it was at these camp sites that the lectures recorded in these notebooks were given. All six notebooks, written in longhand by various people, give accounts of lectures which were obviously delivered by professional revolutionaries of Maoist conviction (though the only non-Congolese name to appear is that of the Cameroon scholar-revolutionary, Osendé Afana, who died in the first 1961 guerrilla assault on the neo-colonial Came-roon regime). The lectures were in French and were transcribed with photostatic longhand samples by Belgium's Centre de Recherche et d'Information Socio-Politique (CRISP). In his introduction, Benoit Verhaegen, CRISP's scientific consultant, explained that the lec-tures' changing tone was caused by the fact that there were various instructors giving the lectures.

Basically these lectures explain Mao's United Front theory for revolution, complete with class analyses and a definition of 'demo-cratic centralism' which is the apparatus of leadership crucial to all Marxist–Leninists. The lectures are interesting, however, be-cause they are aimed at political unsophisticates. They also show how Maoists are perfectly willing to adapt themselves to local conditions—in the case of the Congo, even to the point of defining a three-stage revolution: the national (armed struggle), which is anti-imperialist; the democratic (nationalization), which is anti-reactionary; and the socialist, to be put into effect much later when a consciousness for socialism exists. But once again, like all Maoists, one point remains a firm dogma: that the national bourgeoisie is a revolutionary force during the national revolution phase. In the Congo, General Mobutu, who had killed most of the rebels and who was president in 1969, is the perfect representative of that pro-imperialist so-called national bourgeoisie.

Notebooks of War[96]

First Notebook: Politics—Lecture One: The Enemies of the Congolese Revolution and What it has to Do (28–12–64)

Wherever there is revolution you will find its friends on one side and its enemies on the other. Like every other revolution the Congolese one has its friends and its enemies; and every revolution has its duties which it must undertake so that it can achieve its ends.

In this lecture we are going to study the enemies of the Congolese revolution at the present moment and consider what it has to do.

What is the Congolese revolution against? It is against the enemies of the Congolese. And who are these enemies? They are: (1) Neo-colonialists and imperialists (Belgians, Americans, the British, the Italians and the French). (2) The Congolese bureaucratic or comprador bourgeoisie. (3) Reactionary feudal elements in the Congo (traditional or *de facto* tribal chiefs), the agents of imperialism and neo-colonialism.

The main enemies of the Congolese revolution are the neo-colonialists and the imperialists. These are the foreigners whose military presence tramples the people of the Congo day in and day out. They have military bases in the Congo and military specialists etc. here as well. They use them to oppress the Congolese.

Of the enemies of the Congolese, the American and Belgian imperialists are the most important, followed by British and Italian imperialists and then by the French and Japanese. Remember that the number one enemies of the Congolese are the American and Belgian imperialists. Collaborating in their dirty work—exploiting and enslaving the people of the Congo, murdering hundreds of them —there are:

(a) The Congolese bureaucratic or comprador bourgeoisie; tools of imperialism such as these hold managerial positions in government offices, in the gendarmerie, in the police, throughout the administration, as magistrates, as teachers, in short in every branch of the public services including deputies of the puppet Assembly and members of the foreign House in the Congo. This class of Congolese have united their interests to those of imperialism.

(b) Then there are the natural allies of imperialism. When we attack them we attack imperialism and vice versa. The class interests of these elements are also unshakeably bound to those of imperialism: thus, for example, this is so of traditional and *de facto* chiefs such Kiamvou in Kwango province and Mpaneline in Kwilu province. If imperialism is to be eradicated in the Congo these class enemies must be fought and crushed:

1. Imperialists.
2. Congolese bourgeois bureaucrats and compradors.
3. Feudal reactionaries.

The struggles against the bureaucratic or comprador bourgeoisie and against the reactionary feudal minority which oppresses the people is part of the democratic revolution. But if these two struggles are carried out together, that is, if they are combined, then this is *National* Democratic Revolution. These struggles must be waged together, because imperialism in the Congo will never be eradicated if its local agents are not fought, nor can the agents of imperialism in the Congo be eradicated alone.

These two struggles, then, are intimately bound together, although they are, to some extent, separate.

Remember that the struggle against imperialism is the basic duty, the core of the revolution, but remember too that the democratic revolution should not be neglected although it is of secondary importance. They must be taken together while the priority of the national revolution is understood. Our task is a National Democratic Revolution.

The duties of the democratic revolution

1. To overthrow the regime of the reactionary classes, that is the minority which governs the interior; the agents of imperialism, the bureaucratic or comprador bourgeoisie and the Congolese feudal reactionaries.
2. To achieve agrarian reform.
3. To establish and to honour the democratic and trade union rights of all the national anti-imperialist forces.
4. To give the country political institutions popularly elected and under democratic control: a National Assembly and a government which is answerable to it, etc.

The duties of the national revolution

1. To overthrow the neo-colonialist regime.

2. To get rid of all foreign military bases, to abrogate all the unjust treaties which were forced on the country by the imperialists.

3. To reorganize the army, the gendarmerie, the police, the administration, justice and teaching, etc. so that their primary object is the service of the whole people.

4. To put patriots in all positions of authority, to set up an independent currency.

5. To nationalize the national resources (mines, forests, etc.), agriculture, ranching, commerce, banking and industry which have been grabbed or controlled by foreign capitalists, to establish an independent national economy.

6. To give a national scientific and popular content to the courses of instruction at all levels, primary, secondary and higher. To ensure that the teaching programme from the primary grades through the secondary stages to the higher levels is organized inside the country and that the same applies to technology as well. To nationalize all teaching and welfare institutions (hospitals, dispensaries), all the organs of the press, information and propaganda which are instruments of neo-colonialism, and to prevent the establishment or opening of further channels for them.

If the National Democratic Revolution carries out its duties, it will achieve its ends, otherwise it will have to continue its struggle.

Lecture Two: The Driving Forces of the Congolese National Revolution (13–1–1965)

If we compare the National Democratic Revolution to a train and its passengers, then we can call the driving forces those who can board the train. The station from which they leave is the beginning of the revolution and their destination is its end. These forces are made up of these classes and subdivisions of classes which are listed below, but before going into this question in depth I should like to draw the attention of the comrades to two points: *class origin and the class to which one belongs*. One's *class origin* is the class into which one is born, the class to which one *belongs* is the class whose interests one defends and in which one finds oneself :

Feudal anti-imperialist elements and landlords: those who basically make their living from the unpaid labour of peasants on their land can be called landlords. If Mr Smith is to be considered as a landlord three conditions must be satisfied:

1. Mr Smith must own land.
2. Mr Smith must either not work his own land himself or at least his own work on his land must be a subsidiary source of income to him.
3. His major source of income must come from the exploitation of peasants. Such exploitation may take numerous forms, but the most important is *ground rent,* that is, the landlord takes some of the peasants' time and what he has produced (harvest, cattle or fish) for free. He pracitises usury and exploits the labour of the workers.

Politically speaking most of these elements are the natural agents and allies of imperialism. They are bound to imperialism by flesh and blood. They are not the driving forces of the revolution, they are its enemies. On the other hand some of them can, under certain conditions, join in the revolution.

The bourgeoisie: A bourgeois owns the means of production and exchange as a feudal person does or as a landlord of feudal character. Basically the bourgeois makes his living by the exploitation of wage labour, i.e., a worker produces goods of the value of 1,000 francs, the bourgeois gives him a salary of 200 francs and keeps the rest to himself. Economically and politically the bourgeoisie can be divided up into major classes :

1. The upper middle class, the bureaucratic or comprador bourgeoisie.
2. The middle or national bourgeoisie.
3. The petty bourgeoisie.

The so-called *bureaucratic or comprador middle class* gets its wealth by using the state apparatus (senior civil servants and politicians) or by trading with foreign capitalists or by filling positions in the management of imperialist business undertakings, etc. In a colonial country or in a neo-colonial one this class serves imperialism and is supported by it. It is an enemy of the revolution. For example, Kasavubu, Tshombe, Mobutu, Nendaka, Bomboko, etc.

However, under certain conditions and at the right moment various strata of the upper middle class may join in the National Democratic Revolution, for example when it is engaged against feudalism or when it is in conflict with those monopolies under whose influence it does not find itself, or even against another imperialist power. Thus, in 1961 the agent of American imperialism,

Adoula, claimed to be a nationalist when he opposed Tshombe of Katanga who was an agent of Belgian, French and British imperialism.

The middle or national bourgeoisie owns fairly substantial means of production and exchange, but it does not serve the imperialists and it is not supported by them. From a political and an economic point of view this group of the bourgeoisie stand for an independent Congo, but one which is under its leadership. It wants to develop a national capitalist economy which is under its own and not imperialism's control. For this reason imperialists call this group of the national bourgeoisie revolutionary when they are concerned with the overthrow of foreign control, during the national revolution that is. The moment it seems that the tide of revolutionary consciousness is sweeping through the masses of the people, it goes over to the side of counter-revolution. The middle or national bourgeoisie plays two parts: with its left hand it fights imperialism and with its right it fights the workers and peasants.

The petty bourgeoisie, like the middle bourgeoisie, is independent of the imperialists but it owns much less important means of production and exchange. In Black Africa capitalists of this class do not employ more than ten employees. This class comprises small traders and carriers, artisans and members of the liberal professions (doctors and lawyers), lesser civil servants and state employees, the lower levels of the intelligentsia, students and primary and secondary teachers, etc.

In Tropical Africa, the petty bourgeoisie is both more numerous and more revolutionary than feudal elements, the bureaucratic or comprador bourgeoisie and even the middle bourgeoisie. It has the following political weakness : individualism and unsteadiness, and one of its faults is going from one extreme to another, sectarianism. The petty bourgeoisie, is, however, one of the important forces of the African revolution in general and of the Congolese revolution in particular.

The peasants are the most numerous section of the population of the Congo, comprising more than eighty per cent of the total, but it does not consist of a homogeneous class. The peasants of the Congo can be divided into three classes :

Rich peasants or capitalists; middle peasants; and finally the third group which is relatively poor, very close to the proletariat.

The rich or capitalist peasants exploit a paid labourer. In general they take the same political line as the town middle bourgeoisie. At the present state of the revolution they are consequently anti-imperialist and nationalist.

As their name suggests *the middle peasants* are those who own some land themselves but do not exploit the labour of another. This is the case for the vast majority of Congolese peasants. Politically they are close to the upper strata of the petty bourgeoisie which they want to join. A number of middle peasants who exploit the labour of a paid hand to a limited extent already belong to that class. Their exploitation is not continuous, however. For example, they only do so at important moments such as the harvest. They have only just got enough to live on, and often their condition worsens from one year to another. These peasants are anti-imperialist.

Small peasants and poor peasants have no land nor do they have alternate means of production sufficient to enable them to live by their labour alone. In order to get the minimum they need to live they are forced to some extent to work either for feudal landlords or for other landlords, or rich or middle peasants. They are more revolutionary than the rich or middle peasants and every year that passes their standard of living deteriorates.

Passing on from the poor peasants, we arrive at the *proletariat* with almost no evident disjunction by way of the semi-proletariat.

The semi-proletariat are workers who have a few means of production, e.g. a plot of land, a workshop, but do not have enough to guarantee a subsistence wage. To make a living they are forced to work for capitalists or on the land.

The proletariat are those who own no means of production or exchange. Their only means of gaining a living is by the sale of their labour force to capitalists. In Black Africa this class has not yet developed much. History shows, however, that the semi-proletariat is the most revolutionary class. They are those who are most ready to make any sacrifice to fight imperialism and to construct a Congo which is entirely free, democratic and prosperous.

Thus the forces of the National Democratic Revolution are:
Exploiters:
1. The middle bourgeoisie.
2. The petty bourgeoisie.
3. Anti-imperialist elements of the feudal classes and of the bureaucratic or comprador bourgeoisie.

4. The middle peasantry.
5. Poor peasants.
6. The semi-proletariat.
7. The proletariat.

To this list should be added the lumpen proletariat, a class which can become a revolutionary force so long as it is guided and given attention. The members of this class are the unemployed, groups of bandits, card players and so forth. If we contrast the side of the revolution with that of the counter-revolution:

1. The revolutionary camp has a just cause, the other side's cause is a lost one and is unjust.

2. There are more in the camp of the revolution than there are in the camp of the counter-revolution. Ninety per cent of the population of the Congo belongs to the side of the revolution and outside the Congo an overwhelming majority of mankind are its allies.

3. It is easier to unite the revolutionary side on a firm foundation than it is for the counter-revolutionary forces to unite. Despite alliances between one another, imperialists and all reactionaries are driven by insuperable problems which arise from their very nature which is always to oppress and exploit. This can be seen very clearly in the sharp struggles which occur today between the main imperialist powers who want to dominate the whole of the West for their own gain. As long as there is imperialism it will be the deadly enemy of all mankind. If it is not crushed no group of humanity, especially not those of the countries of Africa, Asia and Latin America, will be able to achieve its aspirations of liberty and happiness. Because it is so important, the struggle against imperialism can unite men of all classes, all countries, whatever the contradictions between them, to fight against their common enemy, imperialism led by America.

4. The ultimate victory of the revolution is inevitable. Sometimes oppressed peoples and classes are not sufficiently aware of this truth, so that they do not unite with each other closely enough or soon enough. Then again they do not enjoy the powerful technological means which imperialism can exploit in its struggle today. These are weak points of the revolutionary side. But these are only temporary. The imperialist oppression and exploitation of the people must unite them against imperialism so that they can find the means to defeat their mighty enemy. This is what we learn from all revolutions, from the great socialist revolution of October 1917 to the Algerian revolution, from the Chinese revolution, from Cuba, and

from Congo-Brazzaville, to mention only a few. This is why we can say that imperialism is only a scarecrow, and the reactionaries only bogeymen. They may appear strong, but they are puny in the long run. Strategically, we can scorn them, but in our tactical plans we must take them very seriously, we must carefully study how to deal them their death blow and how to mobilize everybody to do so.

Lecture Three: Leadership and Guidance of the Revolution (no date, 1965)

Our text is taken from the book by Comrade Osendé Afana,* Doctor in Science in economics, politics and philosophy, and a barrister. The book is called *Economic Growth and Monoculture in West Africa*.

What is the leadership? It has the role of guiding a social class during the revolution. According to the teaching of the greatest revolutionaries and from daily experience, leadership has nothing to do with shouting commands all day long nor with making others agree to one's point of view by brutality or arrogance.

Guidance consists of persuading and showing others by setting a just example, by giving them the example of work well done and getting them to do likewise and to accept our precepts willingly. To be a successful leader, three essential conditions have to be satisfied:

1. A policy, a programme has to be designed which is just and adequate and which corresponds to the interests and needs of everybody.
2. A good example must be set by working well, so that the programme can be realized.
3. All the revolutionary forces inside the country have to be thoroughly organized and mobilized so that the programme can be realized.

Who satisfies these conditions best: members of the peasantry, the petty bourgeoisie or the proletariat?

Leadership by the peasantry has no consistent or unequivocal quality since there is no single class of peasants. There are numerous social classes, all more or less different, from the richest to the poorest. Overall, the peasantry is full of contradictions which are

---

* Cameroon sociologist, political scientist, nationalist and revolutionary killed in combat as a guerrilla against the neo-colonial regime in 1961–ed.

more or less sharp and even opposed. Consequently the only scientific approach to the problem is to study whether a group of the peasantry can exercise leadership.

The most progressive groups of the peasantry, poor peasants and the intermediate strata of the middle peasants, are necessarily called upon to play a very important part in the national democratic revolution of the African people. As has been the case in China and Cuba, to quote only two examples, the main body of revolutionary soldiers can only come from the peasants in underdeveloped countries which are basically agrarian. But can the peasants be thought of as the avant-garde at the head of the revolution, can they exercise the kind of leadership we have just described, especially in view of the fact that they are not homogeneous? This question can only be answered by studying the leadership potential of each rural group. All the evidence shows that feudal elements, landowners whose character is essentially feudal, the bureaucratic or comprador bourgeoisie, cannot lead the revolution on to victory.

The middle bourgeoisie is weak in Black Africa, but it is revolutionary to some extent, in so far as it struggles against the domination of foreign capital and for the establishment of a society whose politics are under its control, and for the development of a national capitalism which is independent. Once that is achieved though, the political programme of the middle bourgeoisie becomes illusory and leads to a neo-colonial or neo-feudal regime under the bureaucratic or comprador bourgeoisie. Furthermore, to achieve even that, the middle bourgeoisie has to struggle not only against imperialism, bureaucratic capitalism and reactionary feudalism, but also against the workers who cannot allow themselves to be exploited. This is why the actions of the middle bourgeoisie are as much directed against progressive forces led by the proletariat as they are against reactionary forces led by imperialism. The middle bourgeoisie's economic ambiguity makes it incapable of mobilizing the revolutionary forces.

The petty bourgeoisie also has two aspects, particularly in Black Africa. It too, consequently, suffers the same problems regarding leadership as does the middle bourgeoisie. Despite this, the revolutionary qualities of the African petty bourgeoisie are worth a special study. Its characteristics are very pronounced and will endure, because the petty bourgeoisie of Africa is of very limited power, and because it has had to struggle long and hard against imperialism to reach the stage it has. On the other hand, the African proletariat which has come into being in foreign businesses is relatively more mature and more combative than the African petty bourgeoisie. The former has been under greater threat from members of its own class in the West and even in Asia and Latin America.

When his enemy is strong and ruthless, when it crushes him as it did during the classical colonial regime, the bourgeoisie makes an alliance with the popular masses to fight him. Once, however, a revolutionary consciousness develops amongst the working masses, the bourgeoisie allies itself with the enemy to defeat them.

Because of its strong tendency to subjectivism and individualism, by reason of its sectarianism and its economic shakiness, Africa's new petty bourgeoisie falls an easy victim to neo-colonialism in the Kennedy style. History will show that despite its indubitable worthiness at the present stage of our struggle, this class cannot lead the African revolution to its ultimate and final victory.

Only *the proletariat* is capable of this historic task. Why? In the first place because all the other social classes are unable to do so. But furthermore, and more importantly, because the proletariat is far and away the most revolutionary class. The proletariat knows better than any other class how to bring this just programme to fruition. In fact this class knows better than any other that it is exploited.

There are those who claim that in Africa the peasants are more exploited. In monetary terms this may be so, but in terms of real value, and especially if a comparison is made between the pay of each in contrast to the amount they add to the national wealth, then there can be no doubt that the proletariat is subject to greater exploitation. Obviously they produce more than the peasants but their real wealth and purchasing power is usually the same if not lower. In fact, despite all his means of production, the African proletariat resembles the grossly underpaid peasant with this further disadvantage that he has to buy goods at prices which are often too high, whereas the peasant consumes a proportion of what he produces and thereby avoids the exploitation of imperialism and its allies to some extent. This is especially so where peasants are neither serfs nor slaves, which is true of the majority of peasants in Black Africa.

Anyway, the proletariat are more aware that they are being exploited. This higher level of consciousness arises in the great difference between their own permanent wretchedness and the effrontery with which the class enemy, personified in the employer, gets rich quick.

But the enemy of the landowning peasants of Black Africa is almost disembodied. His enemy helps himself to public money, he is the moneylender and the merchant. As far as the peasant is concerned it is immaterial whether they are imperialists or not. Consequently the peasants' resentment is vague. So far as organization is concerned the proletariat is far more significant than the peasantry and can easily organize itself into an independent political force. This, together with its association with the more advanced forms of the economy, means that it is more accustomed to discipline.

All these advantages contribute to the superiority of the proletariat which everyone can see in the social life of the African people. Workers' unions are invariably set up before peasant organizations and they generally exhibit a higher degree of aggressiveness. The proletariat also shows its superiority when it comes to organizing and mobilizing the shattered remnants of other classes, especially those of peasant origin. This is particularly true of Africa where there are such large numbers of semi-proletarians. Furthermore, there is a natural affinity between the proletariat and their most trustworthy ally, the peasant.

In international relations the proletariat can also count on the total solidarity of the international working-class movement. Foreign capitalists, however, only support the African bourgeoisie in so far as the latter offer them no competition. It is true that the proletariat is a smaller class than the peasantry and that it has a lower cultural level than the bourgeoisie, but all the evidence shows that no other class in society unites in itself so many leadership qualities as it does. The only reason why it has not exercised its role of leadership in Africa yet is because the objective and subjective conditions have not yet occurred in sufficient degree. The countries of Africa are still far from achieving the objective and subjective conditions necessary for the setting up of a socialist government.

When we state that the people of Africa have obviously got an interest in choosing socialism we are taking the long-term view and not speaking of an immediate transition to socialism.

Lecture Four (no date)

But in the stage in which the Congolese revolution is at present,

M

if it is to provide a satisfactory answer for the interests and aspirations of the whole people, it cannot—must not—be a bourgeois revolution. Yet it cannot be a socialist revolution either.

At present the Congolese revolution must be a new democratic revolution. (a) Politically the new democracy is typified by an alliance between all the national revolutionary classes under the leadership of the proletariat. All these classes take an effective share of political power but it is accepted that the proletariat is at the helm. (b) The economy of the new democracy is characterized by the nationalization of business enterprises which belong to foreign capital, and to the bureaucratic or comprador bourgeoisie. Priority is given to the development of the public sector, to agricultural reform, and to the formation of cooperatives of independent agricultural workers, artisans, traders, etc.

Priority will be given to existing establishments and to the development of socialized public property. The speedy development of the country will be kept up. In passing we should stress the main similarities and differences between the national democracy and the new democracy. Both regimes are based on the alliance of all revolutionary classes; as such they are against the imperialists, their aggressive military blocs and against feudalism. Both regimes insist that all revolutionary forces and the government should respect democratic liberties. By contrast with the reactionaries they are anxious to protect all aspects of political independence and to strengthen them by achieving ever increasing economic independence. The people must choose between these two transitional regimes, between the capitalist and the socialist paths of development.

The main differences between the regimes are as follows: a national democracy can only be found in a country where the social classes are not yet sharply distinguishable from one another and where, in consequence, the proletariat can hardly exercise its leadership uncontested (e.g., Guinea, Mali, Indonesia). Once the social classes are sufficiently differentiated, and once the leadership of the proletariat is more markedly imposed, the regime becomes a new democracy. It is the more progressive of the two. The new democracy turns into a popular democracy, essentially, when the political and economic power of the bourgeoisie shifts over to the proletariat allied to the poor peasantry.

Could a new democratic regime win through in the Congo? Yes.

Why? Because every day the requisite conditions come together in a way which is almost ideal. What are these basic conditions which favour the new democratic revolution?

(a) The determination of the vast majority of the people to overthrow the neo-colonialist regime by any means and to set up a new democratic regime. This determination expresses itself by the development of mass movements despite the conditions of virtual fascism. The Congolese proletariat has an increasingly important avant-garde role. It is the most numerous, the most conscious and the most combative of all Black Africa.

(b) The discrediting of intermediary forces and semi-revolutionary solutions (e.g. the petty bourgeoisie and the middle bourgeoisie) which have suppressed all democratic liberties and even attacked moderate nationalists. They are allied to the neo-colonialists whose regime has shown the people that the only way of satisfying the just aspirations of the population was that of total revolution as advocated by the CNL [National Council of Liberation].

(c) The developing contradictions within the counter-revolutionary camp, first between the various imperialists. The English, Italian and American imperialists are attempting to supplant their Belgian colleagues. One may expect contradictions, though only infrequently, between the imperialists and their puppets, and finally between the puppets themselves. Thus Tshombe and his group refused to join Kasavubu's ABAKO* and there is already open competition between these two for the next presidential elections. There will be contradictions between the new bureaucratic bourgeoisie which is somewhat favourable to agrarian reform and the feudal elements who are opposed to it, etc. It is true that there are also contradictions amongst the revolutionaries, but our differences can and will soon find peaceful solutions, while the contradictions between our enemies should, by and large, exacerbate as time goes on.

Lecture Five: *The Weapons of the Congolese New Democratic Revolution* (no date)

As usual we should ask ourselves today what are the long-term objectives of the Congolese revolution. Will it be a capitalist regime, guaranteeing political power and cultural and material comforts to

---

* Neo-colonialist but verbally anti-imperialist movement which held power in 1964–5–ed.

a small minority of the bourgeoisie and the feudal elements; or will it be a socialist regime, which will enable the country to achieve complete independence and the speedy development of all its potentialities, so that all social classes which are anti-imperialist and anti-colonialist, can benefit?

First of all, however, we must tackle the major problem which confronts us today. Once the Congo has its natural independence the burning question for the Congolese revolution will be whether it can continue to go forward or whether it will be blocked in a prolonged or complete checkmate. The victory of the revolution depends on critical weapons, which are:

1. An avant-garde revolutionary party.
2. A fine liberation army.
3. A powerful peasant movement.
4. A united front of all these.

The party is the most important of these. This is why we will go over the basic question of the party again and again and why we will do no more than simply outline the basic needs of the other principal weapons of the revolution.

A political party is the means by which a class or a part of a class wields its dictatorship. Parties are political organizations by means of which classes or parts of classes take power, hold it, reinforce it, broaden its base and thus look after their interests and aspirations.

Political parties, therefore, have a well defined class content, even if some parts of their programmes serve the interests of many classes. Their primary objective is the promotion and consolidation of the interests of a given class.

This is the essential difference between a political party and a political movement; a movement chooses generalized objectives which satisfy the needs of numerous classes at any given time, rather than the particular interests of one class or part of a class. In practice, however, the dominant class always leads the movement according to its class interests, e.g., the peace movement, the movement for national integrity and independence, for African unity, etc. These movements meet everybody's objectives, but every class interprets their meanings differently and attempts to achieve them according to their own interests.

If a party is to enable a class to gain and reinforce its hold on power it must fulfil four functions:

1. Mobilize the masses, give them a sense of direction and educate

the class and all the people according to the class interests which it wishes to protect.

2. Mobilization of the masses means pushing them into this kind of action.

3. Organize actual struggles against whatever stands in its way so as to achieve the party's objectives.

4. Keep a tight grip on the way the party's orders are carried out.

The CNL must have theory—if it is to lead the Congolese revolution to final victory. It must satisfy certain criteria, of which the following are the most important:

1. It must comprise a unified body of the Congolese revolutionary class. In the interests of unity all CNL militants must be one in the intention and unshakeable determination to serve the interests of the Congolese revolutionaries, i.e., they must be willing to translate their unity of intention into unity of action. Their every act must be directed to the same class interests and directives. Unity has no place for intra-party rivalries. Our experiences in recent years stress that the CNL cannot defend or consolidate its unity if it does not fulfil the following conditions satisfactorily.

2(a). It must be an avant-garde body of the most revolutionary classes in the Congo, which entails three consequences: the CNL must be guided by revolutionary theory. Without that no party can distinguish the enemies of the revolution from the forces which are driving it forward, no party can pick out what has to be done and how that relates with other needs, and, therefore, no party can succeed in closely uniting revolutionary forces so as to isolate the reactionaries and pick them off one by one. For example, we have had many illusions about the United Nations: they prevented us from making serious preparations for armed struggle. In the Congo we have often overestimated the revolutionary capacity of the Congolese bourgeoisie. We must avoid the sin of sectarianism, we must not write off all except a tiny minority of Congolese as revolutionary. We must not exclude militants and those from certain clans and tribes. If we do so we will be failing to mobilize important revolutionary elements and may even provoke violent attacks against them. All this shows that there can be no revolutionary movement without a revolutionary theory, that without it we cannot lead the revolution to final victory.

2(b). If the CNL is to be an avant-garde body, it must recruit its militants and especially its leading cadres from the best elements of the national middle and petty bourgeoisie, from amongst the intellectual revolutionaries and especially from the peasants and working class. There are certain class characteristics of organizations which do not primarily depend on the class origin of the constituent members but on the class interests which it serves, on its ideology, and on the actual political struggles in which it engages. Thus working-class parties are not proletarian parties even if the majority of their members are workers. Man's consciousness is determined by his social conditions. That is why the militants and leading cadres of an avant-garde revolutionary party should primarily be recruited from the avant-garde revolutionary classes.

2(c). To be an avant-garde body means that the CNL must set up, and then maintain and extend, close links with the masses. If the CNL is not well bedded in the masses everybody will not be able to support it, and it will not be able to lead the revolution to victory.

3. All the evidence shows that the CNL cannot be united, and cannot be an avant-garde body of the revolutionary classes, if it is not also a well organized body. What does that mean? The experiences of other revolutions in recent years show us that, in the main, good, revolutionary organizations mean three factors:

1. All CNL members must be active members of the grass root CNL organizations.

2. All CNL institutions, especially those of the leadership, must follow normal CNL procedure, i.e., our revolution must not suffer because the executive committee or less important institutions such as the financial control commission are not carrying out their duties properly so that the executive committee is consequently paralysed. Again it is most important that the upper echelons of the CNL carry out their duties in continuity.

3. All CNL organizations must work according to the principles laid down in the statutes of the Congolese National Revolution. These are the most important rules:

(a) Democratic centralism.

(b) There must be criticism and self-criticism at all levels of the CNL.

(c) The leadership must follow the mass line closely and avoid becoming separated from the people.

(d) The CNL must have better structure and a better organization than the other revolutionary parties. This will ensure that its leadership of the most revolutionary class organizations is effective. It must be the cutting edge of these organizations, the pattern which all other revolutionary classes will imitate.

The CNL is not the only means by which the members of the revolutionary classes defend their interests and aspirations. There are numerous other organizations which serve this purpose—unions, cooperatives, bodies of women, young people, students and peasants. There are cultural, sporting, religious associations, etc. Why should all these organizations have a single leadership? Because they are all defending the same class interests, they share a common purpose.

The CNL can lead all these organizations by becoming an even more closely united body, an avant-garde, a highly organized, revolutionary and class organization. The CNL must continuously develop its fundamental leadership qualities. Because it employs a theory of revolution it will be able to tailor its programmes to everybody's class interests. By constituting itself from the finest elements of the most revolutionary classes, its cadres will receive the best schooling. As the most experienced organization it will enjoy the greatest prestige amongst the masses. In short, by becoming a new kind of revolutionary party the CNL will be best able to lead all the other revolutionary organizations. The CNL should lead through its militants within these organizations. This means: CNL militants should play an active part in all existing organizations and in any which may be formed; CNL militants should lead by example. Those who do not agree with their party's line should be persuaded by the example of the militants' conscientiousness and selflessness within their respective organizations. To act otherwise is a violation of the letter and spirit of the revolution.

Why does the CNL need its own army? The army is the main instrument of class dictatorship. Reactionaries are always the first to resort to violence, e.g., South Vietnam, Cuba, Algeria, Angola, South Africa and our own country, the Congo. If oppressed nations and classes do not learn how to handle weapons, if they only try to liberate themselves by using peaceful means, they will never be free. In the Congo, especially, armed struggle is essential because:
1. The armed forces of the counter-revolution oppresses our people and butchers them daily.
2. The people have no democratic liberties or political rights.
3. The imperialists and their stooges invariably rebuff all peaceful

attempts of liberating the Congo whether we attempt to negotiate for it or win it electorally.

The imperialist and people's armies recruit from different strata of society. But there are other extremely important differences. The army of the CNL is the blade of an avant-garde revolutionary party, a new kind of people's army, because there are only Congolese patriots in it and no foreign mercenaries. It takes orders only from Congolese, not from foreigners. It is closely tied to the people and the party by the same revolutionary theory and the same just cause as that of the CNL; by the CNL leadership, the party actually having set up organizations within the army; by democratic methods of organization and control, notably the practice of political, economic and military democracy within the ranks; and by its productive labour, as it works to mobilize and organize the masses.

Third Notebook: The Revolution (no date, 1965)

The revolution is the expression of the revolt of the masses. Once they have tried every peaceful means of implementing their demands and have been thwarted by the brutality and the violence of their enemies, they resort to violence themselves as the only and necessary means of getting what they want.

Wherever there is a revolution you will find the objective causes of it. Take the struggle against neo-colonialism in the Congo or in the Cameroons. Rightfully the Congo should be held to belong to the people of the Congo, first, last and always. Its political, economic and military administration should be in Congolese hands alone. All inhabitants of the Congo, natives and foreigners alike, should be subject to Congolese law.

Such would be the case if men treated one another honestly, with justice and equality. But in fact this is not the case. Hence the Congolese, who never stopped hearing how rich the Congo was, saw only how wretched they were, and they looked for the cause of their misfortunes. The work of whose fruits they were cheated cleared their eyes and led them to ask, and peacefully, for the complete independence of their country. But their enemies answered their peaceful demands with violence and denied them their legitimate requests (e.g., the arrest of Patrice Lumumba before the Brussels round table meeting).

As we all know the Congo was declared independent by the Belgian imperialists in 1960, but we also know that the Belgians interpreted the meaning of independence differently from the Congolese patriots. The proof of this is the death of Patrice Lumumba and his friends and what is happening in the Congo today.

The people of the Congo repeated their demand that their country should have genuine independence and peacefully asked the Belgian neo-colonialists to discontinue all meddling in Congolese affairs. Instead the Americans, the Belgians, the French and the English have sent bombers, weapons of all kinds, mercenaries and paratroops to slaughter the peaceful and unfortunate people of the Congo. But the Congolese had determined to win full independence and they made up their minds to answer the violence of the imperialists and their stooges with popular violence.

The people can rely, essentially, only on themselves. They must wage their own war and win it by relying on their own forces. But they are not alone in their struggle. They can depend on the stalwart support of all revolutionary men and women the world over, led by the mighty socialist camp. As for the supply of weapons, the people of the Congo have already learnt that they must be taken from the enemy. The cause is just, we are determined to defeat our enemies at any cost.

But if we want to win, if we want to build a united, democratic, vigorous party, a party with room in it for everyone, tribalism must be eradicated. We must denounce this scourge, and expose it in whatever form it takes. We must fight it, drive it out of politics. This is the only way we will be able to pursue policies which will promise us victory against the enemies of liberty and progress in our country.

Tribalism is an undesirable form of thought and action in which priority is given to the selfish interests of one's own tribe or clan. More or less overtly a tribalist believes that the men and women of his own tribe or clan are better than other people who should wait on them and obey them. The tribalist tries to impose the sovereignty and pre-eminence of his clan or tribe on others. Usually tribalist ideas and sentiments are exploited so as to form a following which will serve their interests and selfish ambitions.

Tribalism takes different forms. These are the main ones:

1. The tribalist is always exaggerating and boasting of the fine

M＊

qualities and deeds of the people of his clan or tribe. He ignores or tries to minimize their faults, but he behaves in quite the opposite way when it comes to people of another clan or tribe.

2. The tribalist practises favouritism towards the members of his own tribe or clan. They are usually allowed to do what they like, even if it is against the law, or the rules and regulations of the party. He trusts them and will tell them his secrets, even those which are critical to the party and the state. But in his dealings with members of other clans or tribes, the tribalist is sectarian. He has no confidence in their efforts or their honesty and sometimes he will not even pass their orders on to them.

3. A tribalist will try to offer privileges and responsible jobs to members of his own tribe or clan, e.g., study grants, and responsible posts which are not appointed by open election are usually picked out by tribalists for the members of their own tribe or clan.

4. Again he will try to let these same people out of their duties and obligations, especially if hard work or danger is involved, or if the assignments are tough or humiliating.

5. The tribalist also hands out drugs, clothing, food and party, army and governmental funds to his cronies. He hurriedly compiles reports for them and keeps the best beds in hospital for them. All his zeal and devotion vanishes the moment he has to work for members of another clan or tribe.

6. Occasionally a tribalist will even decide that a member of another clan or tribe is too wealthy or fortunate to deserve any help from him. He may even refuse them help when they are really in difficulties. Sometimes he will go so far as to say they should not have the little they have and that they should hand it over to the members of his tribe or clan. The next step is an easy one, which has, alas, been taken by many tribalists who see nothing wrong in stealing from or exploiting the members of other tribes and clans.

7. There are even those who take tribalism so far that instead of contemplating marriage with a member of another tribe they would rather see marriage between blacks and whites. The Kasavubu government, for example, could have given competent personnel, who had come from the south, posts in the north but it preferred simply to hand over that part of our country to colonialists who were well known to have committed atrocities in the south or in Indochina or Algeria.

8. Politically, tribalism finds its highest expression in attempts to

set up so-called independent republics which are actually tribal enclaves. If this device does not succeed they campaign for 'a federation with regional autonomy' by which, of course, they mean the parcelling up of political and administrative power in little tribal lots. We have all met cases of such 'federalism' and of such tribal 'autonomy'. The most glaring examples are Congo-Leopoldville and the federalist fancies of the Kenya African Democratic Union (KADU).

History has shown that imperialists and all reactionaries are constantly trying to stimulate tribalist feelings amongst the people so as to divide them amongst themselves, so that their exploitation can be more effective and grinding. Even when tribalism is not met in its worst forms, it is a factor which causes splitting and weakness so that the masses are less able to struggle against foreign domination and underdevelopment. History also shows that every tribalist is primarily interested in satisfying the selfish interests of his own tribe at the expense of other tribes, that within the tribe itself he is promoting the interests of his own clan and that within the clan itself he is looking after his own family. In the last analysis tribalism is a feudally engendered kind of selfishness. This is the reason why tribalist associations always end by splitting and going under, usually in very sharp internecine struggles.

All the evidence indicates that the primary cause for the survival and development of tribalism is backwardness in the formation of the nation. The concrete evidence of this backwardness is the host of tribes found in the body of the state. Thus there are 140 in the Cameroons and 300 in Nigeria, etc. But this is not such a serious problem, for these tribe-families all belong to the same racial stock, either because of natural parenthood, or because of the way they have been geographically mingled together, or because they have shared a common history for a fairly long time. What's more, prolonged colonialist and imperialist domination has done much to unite the different tribes. It is true that no country in tropical Africa has made itself a nation yet, that is, established a stable community, set up historical institutions, and integrated its tongue, land, economic life and physical characteristics into the culture of the community. But small racial groups and the fact that the nation has not yet constituted itself in an ideal way is not a major bar to the campaign against tribalism. Already a national consciousness has developed in the course of the struggle against foreign domination.

The main obstacles to the campaign against tribalism are underdevelopment and imperialism. Imperialism, neo-colonialism and colonialism intend to govern; that is why they are continually stirring up hatred and rivalry between tribes. They say to the members of this tribe or that, there are more of you and you are the wealthiest. You should govern the Congo. Then they say to some others: you are the clever ones, you should lead the country. And even while they are saying this other imperialists agents or neo-colonialist stooges are saying the very same words to other tribes or clans.

The most important fact to grasp is that the Congolese revolution will never win if the majority of the Congolese cannot take part without discrimination. History shows this clearly. Consider the Iraqis who are obviously in a majority position in their own country and who receive substantial support from abroad. Despite this they cannot overcome and defeat the Kurds, nor can they build a genuinely independent, democratic and prosperous country. In the Congo itself there have been extraordinary developments in the revolution which have been, unfortunately, confined to one or two regions, not to say tribes. Sananga-Maritime is a well-known recent example. Despite exceptional feats of heroism and self-sacrifice in these districts, despite even the anti-tribalist policy of the CNL, we have not been able to overthrow the colonialist or neo-colonialist government. The liberation of the Congo will naturally begin in one or a few regions, but the revolution will not win if it is not actively supported by the great popular masses throughout the length and the breadth of the land.

Every man must be equal before the law which imposes duties upon us but also accords us rights. The campaign for democracy and equality of rights should encompass the struggle against tribalism and here the best weapon is education, which must have a national, popular and scientific character at one and the same time. Educationalists should never cease putting the evils of tribalism under the limelight and emphasizing the necessity of uniting the people of the Congo against the enemies which they all have—imperialism, neo-colonialism and underdevelopment. People must be taught that every individual and all men have good and bad qualities and that everybody should be judged according to what he says and does, not according to whether he is a member of this family or that tribe. Education should also be scientific insomuch as it should encompass technical knowledge and practical skills and progressively eradicate subjectivist and irrational concepts. Schooling and education should be available to all, so that everyone can exploit his abilities, develop his personality, and win the regard and respect of others no matter what tribe he belongs to.

The struggle against tribalism is an integral part of the struggle within the party. It is consequently absolutely essential. This is particularly so because every party militant or leader in the CNL has come from one tribe or another and has been and still is under the influence of tribalism. Others will have to campaign continually, tenaciously, for many years. The struggle is at once the condition and the reward of our victory over imperialism, neo-colonialism, misery, ignorance and disease.

Tribalism and nepotism are the essence of factionalism. Nepotism is family spirit translated into the field of politics. A man who has this fault, consciously or unconsciously, regards the party, the army, the state and the revolution as family businesses. With all his heart, the nepotist wants to give all the advantages he or she can to his or her parents, children, spouse, brothers and sisters. Like the puppet Ngo Dinh Diem he reckons that power and all the advantages which can be derived from it should be given to the members of his own family in the first place.

Should it happen in our ranks, it will be used by the imperialists and all other reactionaries to attack and denigrate the whole party and its revolutionary policies. The inevitable consequence is the paralysis or even the death of the organizations which are afflicted by tribalism and nepotism and their resulting power struggle. The pity of it is that good elements allow themselves to be drawn into these fratricidal struggles unleashed by a handful of individualists pursuing their personal ambitions. A house divided against itself cannot stand. If we want to survive and win, we must remove this cancer from our midst.

Everything shows that the main source of the power struggle lies in individualism, pride and selfishness. One thinks oneself superior to everyone else, and as such worthy of power and all that normally goes with it, honours, glory and material benefits. In addition, the absence of strong traditions about the birth and development of political power and the way personal relations are more important than indispensable programmes or theories, together with many other social factors, can make the leaders dizzy, tempting them to build up their personal power to the point of making themselves into chieftains each with their own clients and vassals.

Naturally imperialists, neo-colonialists, right-wing nationalists and all the other enemies of our party's revolutionary line try to exploit to the full all the factors mentioned above in order to split our leadership, weaken and smash our revolution, and finally force puppets in their pay upon us as our leaders.

Even in truly independent countries that are economically and technically advanced and well organized, political consciousness is invariably unevenly spread. Society renews itself continually, and, after it has done so, the militants of the party, the army and the state must do so. Now, militants and young cadres need to struggle for a fairly long period in order to familiarize themselves with the party's principles and just methods of leadership. During this period many rapid and often profound social upheavals occur. The leaders do not always quickly succeed in finding the just principles and methods that should govern the new relationships among the leaders, between the leadership and the rest of the party, between the party and the masses, between fraternal parties and so on. Even in the most advanced societies it can be said that, to various extents of course, the power struggle had its origin in ignorance and violation of just principles, or even pure and simple betrayal of the revolution.

The campaign against the power struggle is hence an integral part of struggle within the party. To fight the power struggle we must therefore show through education and personal example that the exercise of power is a heavy burden and an inexhaustible source of sacrifices, not of personal satisfaction. To take on a responsible post means above all to accept serving others, not one's self or one's own. It means putting myself at the disposal of the body that gives me responsibility at all times. And the higher the responsibility the more heavy and dangerous the burden. First, because peaks attract lightning. It is against the leaders and those in responsible positions that our enemies are dead set. They murder them without pity at the very first opportunity.

Those who see in positions of responsibility a way of helping themselves and those close to them should realize that their selfishness and their pride are bound to bring them many personal enemies, in addition to imperialists and all other reactionaries, the sworn enemies of the revolution.

How is one to avoid the blows of so many enemies? There is only one solution: giving up one's ambitions and selfish interests and putting oneself wholeheartedly at the service of others. But how is one to serve somebody else without knowing his specific needs and difficulties? How is one to know them without their help? The inevitable conclusion is that to fulfil his task a leader must put himself disinterestedly at the service of others and learn from them. He also needs everyone's support and must surround himself with many capable, dynamic and disinterested elements like himself.

In a country like the Congo, engaged in a struggle as difficult as the one against imperialism, neo-colonialism and underdevelopment, a country in which everything has to be done, it is not responsible positions which are in short supply but dignified cadres able to fill them usefully. One of the safest criteria for telling whether somebody is a true revolutionary, capable of giving good leadership, consists in seeing if he wants to unite without discrimination all elements capable of taking part in the revolution and if he establishes effective links with the masses, that is, follows the mass line.

If the revolution is to triumph there must be fidelity to a correct political line, one in the interests of the whole people. A general truth should be stated clearly: it is necessary to satisfy everyone's legitimate needs, including spiritual ones such as the need for prestige, if we are to struggle effectively against the power struggle. The vital and fundamental principle is that everyone's needs should be satisfied according to their work and merit alone. Once this principle is accepted we should apply ourselves to the correct definition of the relations between leaders and led. All societies need leadership. Effective and correct leadership must exist in its organization as a fish lives in water, in close unity with the led. The leader has the right to more private goods and funds than those under him but only so far as they are absolutely necessary to permit him to carry out his duties. For example, a leader needs a car for his work but there is no need for it to be a luxurious one. Generally speaking one must ensure that the honours and material benefits of leadership do not separate him from the masses and don't encourage him to think of himself as a god or demigod.

All these measures and others analogous to them have the same end in view : to combat the causes of and pretexts for the power struggle, to check the tendency towards personal power and the establishment of privileged castes, but, at the same time, to promote the development of a democratic and socialist society in which all will thrive free from any exploitation. Thus you can see that the problems of everyday life are closely linked to the problems of organization.

The Conference of Cadres, convened in Accra in December 1960, stipulated that the greatest care must be taken to see that responsible comrades are:

1. The most faithful to the mass line.
2. The most capable of taking decisions rapidly.
3. The most devoted to the party and the most disciplined.
4. The most dynamic.

The CNL must add another criterion which is not mentioned here: class background. Revolutionary theory and history show that the classes are not equally revolutionary. The proletariat lead, followed by the semi-proletariat, the poor peasants and the small peasants. In those of our countries which are economically little developed, the petty bourgeoisie has, so to speak, a higher revolutionary potential that it has in the economically developed countries. In short, experience shows that the best cadres are those who follow the most revolutionary class line.

It is unusual for a single person to fulfil all these conditions to a very high degree. We should at least make sure that the organization and leadership teams are well balanced and that they form a perfect blend of all these qualities. Leadership organizations at all levels must above all be relatively stable. Every time replacement occurs an important fraction of members of the outgoing organization should be included. This allows continuity of action and experience to be maintained by the leadership.

It is neither enough to elect good leaders nor to make up the organization of the leadership sensibly. Cadres must also be correctly formed, chosen and treated. The great importance of these questions is due to the fact that once a political line has been adopted, everything depends on the cadres. Under every unexpected condition and situation, their application may be good or bad, their adaptation correct and revolutionary or incorrect and even counter-revolutionary. The only way of handling cadres correctly is to give them proper working conditions while placing obstacles to the foolish ambitions which lurk in all of us, and of arousing in them unlimited devotion and enthusiastic dynamism for the service of the whole people. Such a policy cannot be achieved without respect for democratic centralism.

Democratic centralism simultaneously unites discipline and democracy while ensuring that democracy is subordinate to discipline. Discipline means that every individual party member obeys his committee and the organization in which he is active. It also means that the minority obeys the majority, that junior organizations obey senior organizations and that the whole party obeys the congress of the executive committee in between congresses. Discipline should be the same for everyone. Everyone should obey the law, the statutes and other key party texts. Thus the principle of respecting the hierarchy applies not only to the led but also to the leaders. If discipline is to be really tight it must be freely agreed to. This means that democracy and free discussion should occur at all levels.

Comradeliness must be found throughout the leadership organization, that is, the collective leadership must be combined with individual responsibility. All important decisions concerning policy and organization must be talked over, collectively adopted and then applied to everyone. Similarly, the administration of their execution is a joint responsibility but the execution itself is entrusted to one or a few members of the leadership. All decisions concerning the jurisdiction of general assemblies which meet regularly should be taken by vote following discussion at which every party member has the same opportunity to express his opinions freely without having any pressure brought to bear on him or needing to fear any reprisals. Once decisions have been adopted in these circumstances the kind of discipline discussed above applies to all.

Democratic centralism also means that organizations and junior leaders are forbidden to give opinions on questions not yet treated by their superiors. They must learn to submit suggestions, and their superiors must not shirk their responsibility to solve difficult problems. These demands lead directly to the keystone of democratic centralism: the mass line.

The *mass line* is attained only when those who hold responsible positions at all levels of the army and the party gather opinions and criticisms from militants and people in general; consider these opinions together in the light of the party's policy and objectives, as well as in the experience of revolutions of other lands; consequently, take a just decision and convince militants and the people that the position is a just one; make sure that orders are carried out and then go on to repeat the process. This definition of the mass line literally allows leaders and those with responsibility to live with the people as the fish lives in water. In this way they can quickly spot where their policy is lacking and how they can put matters right. However little they are able to make scientific analyses and undertake self-criticism, as long as they are naturally honest, revolutionary leaders can find in the mass line the best conditions in which to know and to serve the people and their wishes and especially the effective way to wage the struggle for power.

SOUTH AFRICA

Towards the end of the 1960s, every nationalist, would-be nationalist, revolutionary and pseudo-revolutionary party or movement throughout Southern Africa tried to define itself as the most militant. What's more, each group spent a great deal of time and effort denouncing the others. In South Africa (Azania), for example, the two main liberation 'fronts'—the African National Congress (ANC) and the Pan-Africanist Congress (PAC)—were engaged in such savage verbal warfare that their true achievements often passed unnoticed. And those achievements were considerable, especially since both groups were declared illegal after years of open political activity, which made their leaders perfectly known to the repressive forces.

The South African government is surely one of the most vicious and totalitarian existing in the world today. With widespread collusion from all imperialist countries (whatever their 'official' policy towards apartheid), the white regime has brought the 3,000,000 whites the highest standard of living in the world, but only at the expense of the total subjugation and enslavement of the country's 15,000,000 blacks, who furnish the South African whites and foreign interests an unlimited supply of cheap labour.

The investment totals more than $4 billion just from the USA, West Germany, France and Japan alone. The country accounts for 43 per cent of the mineral output of the entire African continent and more than two-thirds of the world's gold production. It also exports capital: $600 million by 1963, of which almost $400 million was invested in the Rhodesias. Inside the country, the whites owned 87 per cent of the land. Their per capita yearly income in 1959 was $1,200, compared to $109 for Africans (blacks) and $151 for other non-whites, (Asians, West Indians, etc.). Today infant mortality for whites (27 per thousand) is among the lowest in the world, while for the blacks (400 per thousand) it is the highest. In addition, of course, the blacks have no rights whatsoever: they cannot vote, *join unions, organize parties, stage protests, refuse to obey whites, go for a walk after 11 p.m., and so on. Many are compelled to live in 'Reserves'—concentration camps. Families are split for the convenience of whites and, most symbolically degrading of all, every non-white is forced to carry a 'Pass Book', which can be demanded by any policeman or white person (of any profession) at any time.*

What is even more incredible, however, is that most of these conditions have existed for centuries—with few rebellions. Partly, this is due to Mahatma Gandhi, the same dogmatic pacifist who led India's millions of wretched to accept their exploited fates (see the chapter on India). For it was Gandhi who set the tone for the peaceful form of protest that permeated South Africa when, in 1894, he founded the Natal Indian Congress (which later became part of the South African Indian Congress). When the ANC was formed a few years later, it took its inspiration from Gandhi, and for the next half century, it consistently advocated non-violent, legal opposition to white rule. So firm was ANC's reformist line that in 1960 its President-General, Chief Albert John Luthuli, was awarded the Nobel Peace Prize. Though he was arrested for High Treason in 1956 and banished to his village under the Suppression of Communist Activities Act, in 1959, and though he recognized in 1966 that the 'fruits of moderation' have resulted only in 'new laws ... issued during the past thirty years which restrict our rights and our progress to the extent that today we practically have no rights at all', he and ANC remained basically reformist until past his death in July 1967. As late as January 1966, with the whole third world aflame with revolutionary fervour, ANC was still hoping to find a peaceful way to crush South African fascism, and at the Tricon meeting in Havana, ANC's delegate expected international pressure and UN sanctions to be the way.

But by then, as ANC leader Nelson Mandela explained at his trial for sedition, ANC had indeed created an armed wing—the Umkonto We Sizwe (MK) or 'Spear of the Nation'. How that decision came about in 1961 (partly as a result of the 1960 Sharpeville massacre and the banning of ANC), is well detailed in Mandela's statement before the court during the 'Rivonia Trial'—which convicted him to life imprisonment (he is now incarcerated at Robben Island). But in that statement (see article I below), Mandela clearly shows that ANC was still working for a non-violent solution, using the MK's sabotage tactics as a bargaining force to gain political points.

Mandela was clearly no communist. But so many of ANC's cadremen were that the policy and strategy of ANC were indistinguishable from those of the South African Communist Party (SACP). Indeed, by 1961, the SACP had also come out in favour of armed struggle. In the programme adopted by its Fifth National Conference in 1962 (article II), it stated categorically that 'the slogan of "non-violence" is harmful to the cause of the democratic national revolution in the new phase of the struggle.' But its reformism remained undaunted. Once people are armed, the SACP concluded, 'the crisis in the country, and the contradictions in the ranks of the ruling class, will deepen. The possibility would be opened of a peaceful and negotiated transfer of power to the representatives of the oppressed majority of the people.'

Such statements are not communist naïvety but communist policy. During his trial for sabotage at Pretoria in March 1966, Abram ('Bram') Fischer (who was also convicted to life imprisonment) said:

I believed when I joined the illegal Communist Party that South Africa had set out on a course which could lead only to civil war of the most vicious kind whether in ten or fifteen or twenty years. Algeria provided the perfect historical example of that. I believed moreover, and still believe, that such a civil war can never be won by the whites of this country. They might win some initial rounds. In the long run the balance of forces is against them, both inside and outside the country. In Algeria, a close historical parallel, a French army of half a million soldiers backed by one of the world's great industrial powers, could not succeed. But win or lose, the consequences of civil war would be horrifying and permanent. Clearly it is imperative that an alternative 'solution' be found, for in truth civil war is no 'solution' at all.

Bram Fischer was a daring, courageous man who lived by his conviction. But what kind of revolutionary 'ideology' could lead such a man to consider the Algerian revolution, which did win, as no solution at all? *It was inevitable, then, that either ANC and SACP dropped their reformism or else that new revolutionary groups seized the vanguard. And it is the Pan-African Congress (PAC) which has tried hardest to do just that. Strongly influenced by Maoism, at least in rhetoric, it has blasted both the ANC and the CP. Shortly after Fischer was convicted, for example, PAC leader*

K.A. Jordaan wrote of his statement to the court: 'He who wants to change the old society, but recoils from the only effective method of doing so [armed struggle], ends up by accommodating himself to that society.' Writing in the September 1966 issue of Azania News *(a PAC publication), Jordaan defined the CP as counter-revolutionary and concluded: 'It is only by changing their environment in the furnace of a revolution that Azanians can also change themselves and be fit to master their own affairs'—a view already made famous by Fanon (see above). And in a pamphlet published about the same time, Cardiff Marney, who had been an ANC ally but now joined the PAC, wrote that*

> *ANC's warning the world that unless a peaceful solution was imposed from the outside, preferably by UN intervention, South Africa would be engulfed in a bloodbath and reduced to 'chaos' and 'lawlessness' . . . means nothing less than saying that the independent armed struggle of the people is undesirable. The training of ANC saboteurs and guerrillas was therefore not seriously intended: it was merely to serve as a threat to extract sanctions from the imperialist powers [who rule the UN] and secure their intervention. Freedom, in other words, would be brought to the people on the point of imperialist bayonets! This peaceful approach of the ANC is in line with the policy and peaceful coexistence of the Soviet Union who is giving the ANC considerable financial backing.*

On its side, PAC got financial backing from China. It formed an alliance with the Zimbabwe (Rhodesia) African National Union (ZANU) and proclaimed it was unleashing guerrilla wars in both Rhodesia and South Africa. ANC, which made an alliance with the Zimbabwe African Peoples Union (ZAPU), then announced it would do the same. And each group has been claiming a better score ever since.

Both ANC-ZAPU and PAC-ZANU are indeed engaged in actual combat in Rhodesia and South Africa today. After some serious mistakes which almost wiped out its forces, the former is now slowly establishing a firm revolutionary base. The latter has been racked with informers, agents and militant speech-makers who spend their time hopscotching from one friendly country to another. By October 1969, PAC had not yet even elaborated a clear ideological-military position.

That, ANC did. At a conference in Morogoro, Tanzania, in April 1969, it worked out its strategy (see article III) which turned out

*to be the strongest condemnation yet of the Guevarist line. Justify-
ing its half-century of reformism as consciousness-building, ANC
clearly still saw armed struggle as only one weapon in the arsenal of
a political party's march towards power. Liberation was seen as the
overthrow of the regime. As for the future, that was to remain in
the hands of the party. Totally missing was the concept of armed
struggle as a way of liberating the men who fight from the decades
in which they have internalized their own oppression. That the
foundation of the future society is laid during the course of the
revolution itself seemed to remain an alien concept to the ANC
and its traditional communist ideologues.*

I Nelson Mandela: *I Am Prepared to Die*[97]

Some of the things so far told to the court are true and some are
untrue. I do not, however, deny that I planned sabotage. I did not
plan it in a spirit of recklessness, nor because I have any love of
violence. I planned it as a result of a calm and sober assessment of
the political situation that had arisen after many years of tyranny,
exploitation and oppression of my people by the whites.

I admit immediately that I was one of the persons who helped to
form Umkonto We Sizwe,* and that I played a prominent role in
its affairs until I was arrested in August 1962. I, and the others who
started the organization, did so for two reasons. First, we believed
that as a result of government policy, violence by the African people
had become inevitable, and that unless responsible leadership was
given to canalize and control the feelings of our people there would
be outbreaks of terrorism which would produce an intensity of bitterness and hostility between the various races of this country which
is not produced even by war. Second, we felt that without violence
there would be no way open to the African people to succeed in
their struggle against the principle of white supremacy. All lawful
modes of expressing opposition to this principle had been closed
by legislation, and we were placed in a position in which we had
either to accept a permanent state of inferiority, or to defy the

---

* 'Spear of the Nation', the military wing of the ANC. It is sometimes referred
to as MK as well–ed.

government. We chose to defy the law. We first broke the law in a way which avoided any recourse to violence; when this form was legislated against, and then the government resorted to a show of force to crush the opposition to its policies, only then did we decide to answer violence with violence.

But the violence which we chose to adopt was not terrorism. We who formed Umkonto were all members of the African National Congress, and had behind us the ANC tradition of non-violence and negotiation as a means of solving political disputes. We believed that South Africa belonged to all the people who lived in it, and not to one group, be it black or white. We did not want an inter-racial war, and tried to avoid it to the last minute.

The African National Congress was formed in 1912 to defend the rights of the African people which had been seriously curtailed by the South Africa Act, and which were then being threatened by the Native Land Act. For thirty-seven years—that is until 1949— it adhered strictly to a constitutional struggle. It put forward demands and resolutions; it sent delegations to the government in the belief that African grievances could be settled through peaceful discussion and that Africans could advance gradually to full political rights. But white governments remained unmoved, and the rights of Africans became less instead of becoming greater. In the words of my leader, Chief Luthuli, who became President of the ANC in 1952, and who was later awarded the Nobel Peace Prize:

. . . who will deny that thirty years of my life have been spent knocking in vain, patiently, moderately and modestly at a closed and barred door? What have been the fruits of moderation? The past thirty years have seen the greatest number of laws restricting our rights and progress, until today we have reached a stage where we have almost no rights at all.

Even after 1949, the ANC remained determined to avoid violence. At this time, however, there was a change from the strictly constitutional means of protest which had been employed in the past. The change was embodied in a decision which was taken to protest against apartheid legislation by peaceful, but unlawful, demonstrations against certain laws. Pursuant to this policy the ANC launched the Defiance Campaign, in which I was placed in charge of volunteers. This campaign was based on the principles of passive resistance. More than 8,500 people defied apartheid laws and went to gaol. Yet there was not a single instance of violence in the course of this campaign on the part of any defier. I, and nine-teen colleagues were convicted for the role which we played in organizing the campaign, but our sentences were suspended mainly because the Judge found that discipline and non-violence had been stressed throughout.

During the Defiance Campaign, the Public Safety Act and the Criminal Law Amendment Act were passed. These statutes pro-vided harsher penalties for offences committed by way of protests against laws. Despite this, the protests continued and the ANC ad-hered to its policy of non-violence. In 1956, 156 leading members of the Congress Alliance, including myself, were arrested on a charge of High Treason and charges under the Suppression of Communism Act. The non-violent policy of the ANC was put in issue by the state, but when the court gave judgment some five years later it found that the ANC did not have a policy of violence. We were acquitted on all counts, which included a count that the ANC sought to set up a Communist State in place of the existing regime. The government has always sought to label all its opponents as communists.

In 1960, there was the shooting at Sharpeville, which resulted in the proclamations of a State of Emergency and the declaration of the ANC as an unlawful organization. My colleagues and I, after careful consideration, decided that we would not obey this decree. The African people were not part of the government and did not make the laws by which they were governed. We believed in the words of the Universal Declaration of Human Rights, that 'the will of the people shall be the basis of authority of the government', and for us to accept the banning was equivalent to accepting the silenc-ing of the Africans for all time. The ANC refused to dissolve, but instead went underground. We believed it was our duty to preserve this organization which had been built up with almost fifty years of unremitting toil. I have no doubt that no self-respecting white political organization would disband itself if declared illegal by a government in which it had no say.

In 1960 the government held a referendum which led to the establishment of the Republic. Africans, who constituted approxi-mately seventy per cent of the population of South Africa, were not entitled to vote, and were not even consulted about the proposed constitutional change. All of us were apprehensive of our future under the proposed White Republic, and a resolution was taken to

hold an All-In African Conference to call for a National Convention, and to organize mass demonstrations on the eve of the un-
wanted Republic, if the government failed to call the convention.
The conference was attended by Africans of various political
persuasions. I was the secretary of the conference and undertook to
be responsible for organizing the national stay-at-home which was
subsequently called to coincide with the declaration of the Republic. As all strikes by Africans are illegal, the person organizing
such a strike must avoid arrest. I was chosen to be this person, and
consequently I had to leave my home and family and my practice
and go into hiding to avoid arrest.

The stay-at-home, in accordance with ANC policy, was to be a
peaceful demonstration. Careful instructions were given to organizers and members to avoid any recourse to violence. The government's
answer was to introduce new and harsher laws, to mobilize its
armed forces, and to send Saracens, armed vehicles and soldiers into
the townships in a massive show of force designed to intimidate the
people. This was an indication that the government had decided
to rule by force alone, and this decision was a milestone on the
road to Umkonto.

It was only when all else had failed, when all channels of peaceful
protest had been barred to us, that the decision was made to embark
on violent forms of political struggle, and to form Umkonto We
Sizwe. We did so not because we desired such a course, but solely
because the government had left us with no other choice. In the
Manifesto of Umkonto, published on 16 December 1961, which is
Exhibit AD, we said: 'The time comes in the life of any nation
when there remain only two choices—submit or fight. That time
has now come to South Africa. We shall not submit and we have no
choice but to hit back by all means in our power in defence of our
people, our future and our freedom.' This was our feeling in June
of 1961 when we decided to press for a change in the policy of the
National Liberation Movement. I can only say that I felt morally
obliged to do what I did.

As far as the ANC was concerned, it formed a clear view which
can be summarized as follows:—
1. It was a mass political organization with a political function to
fulfil. Its members had joined on the express policy of non-violence.
2. Because of all this, it could not and would not undertake violence.
This must be stressed. One cannot turn such a body into the small

closely-knit organization required for sabotage. Nor would this be politically correct, because it would result in members ceasing to carry out this essential activity: political propaganda and organization. Nor was it permissible to change the whole nature of the organization.

3. On the other hand, in view of this situation I have described, the ANC was prepared to depart from its fifty-year-old policy of non-violence to this extent that it would no longer disapprove of properly controlled violence. Hence members who undertook such activity would not be subject to disciplinary action by the ANC.

I say 'properly controlled violence' because I made it clear that if I formed the organization I would at all times subject it to the political guidance of the ANC and would not undertake any different form of activity from that contemplated without the consent of the ANC.

As a result of this decision, Umkonto was formed in November 1961. When we took this decision, and subsequently formulated our plans, the ANC heritage of non-violence and racial harmony was very much with us. We felt that the country was drifting towards a civil war in which blacks and whites would fight each other. We viewed the situation with alarm. Civil war could mean the destruction of what the ANC stood for; with civil war racial peace would be more difficult than ever to achieve. We already have examples in South African history of the results of war. It has taken more than fifty years for the scars of the South African War to disappear. How much longer would it take to eradicate the scars of interracial civil war, which could not be fought without a great loss of life on both sides?

The avoidance of civil war had dominated our thinking for many years, but when we decided to adopt violence as part of our policy we realized that we might one day have to face the prospect of such a war. This had to be taken into account in formulating our plans. We required a plan which was flexible and which permitted us to act in accordance with the needs of the times; above all, the plan had to be one which recognized civil war as the last resort, and left the decision on this question to the future. We did not want to be committed to civil war, but we wanted to be ready if it became inevitable.

Four forms of violence were possible. There is sabotage, there is guerrilla warfare, there is terrorism and there is open revolution.

We chose to adopt the first method and to exhaust it before taking any other decision.

In the light of our political background the choice was a logical one. Sabotage did not involve loss of life, and it offered the best hope for future race relations. Bitterness would be kept to a minimum and, if the policy bore fruit, democratic government could become a reality. This is what we felt at the time, and this is what we said in our Manifesto (Exhibit AD):

> We of Umkonto We Sizwe have always sought to achieve liberation without bloodshed and civil clash. We hope, even at this late hour, that our first actions will awaken everyone to a realization of the disastrous situation to which the Nationalist policy is leading. We hope that we will bring the government and its supporters to their senses before it is too late, so that both the government and its policies can be changed before matters reach the desperate stage of civil war.

The initial plan was based on a careful analysis of the political and economic situation of our country. We believed that South Africa depended to a large extent on foreign capital and foreign trade. We felt that planned destruction of power plants and interference with rail and telephone communications would tend to scare away capital from the country, make it more difficult for goods from the industrial areas to reach the seaports on schedule, and would in the long run be a heavy drain on the economic life of the country, thus compelling the voters of the country to reconsider their position.

Attacks on the economic life lines of the country were to be linked with sabotage on government buildings and other symbols of apartheid. These attacks would serve as a source of inspiration to our people. In addition, they would provide an outlet for those people who were urging the adoption of violent methods and would enable us to give concrete proof to our followers that we had adopted a stronger line and were fighting back against government violence.

In addition, if mass action were successfully organized, and mass reprisals taken, we felt that sympathy for our cause would be roused in other countries, and that greater pressure would be brought to bear on the South African government.

The affairs of the Umkonto were controlled and directed by a National High Command, which had powers of cooption and which could, and did, appoint Regional Commands. The High Command was the body which determined tactics and targets and was in charge of training and finance. Under the High Command there were Regional Commands which were responsible for the direction of the local sabotage groups. Within the framework of the policy laid down by the National High Command, the Regional Commands had authority to select the targets to be attacked. They had no authority to go beyond the prescribed framework, and thus had no authority to embark upon acts which endangered life, or which did not fit into the overall plan of sabotage. For instance, MK members were forbidden ever to go armed into operation.

Umkonto had its first operation on 16 December 1961, when government buildings in Johannesburg, Port Elizabeth and Durban were attacked. The selection of targets is proof of the policy to which I have referred. Had we intended to attack life we would have selected targets where people congregated and not empty buildings and power stations. The sabotage which was committed before 16 December 1961 was the work of isolated groups and had no connection whatever with Umkonto. In fact, some of these and a number of later acts were claimed by other organizations.

The Manifesto of Umkonto was issued on the day that operations commenced. The response to our actions and manifesto among the white population was characteristically violent. The government threatened to take strong action, and called upon its supporters to stand firm and to ignore the demands of the Africans. The whites failed to respond by suggesting change; they responded to our call by suggesting the laager.*

In contrast, the response of the Africans was one of encouragement. Suddenly there was hope again. Things were happening. People in the townships became eager for political news. A great deal of enthusiasm was generated by the initial successes, and people began to speculate on how soon freedom would be obtained.

But we in Umkonto weighed up the white response with anxiety. The lines were being drawn. The whites and blacks were moving into separate camps, and the prospects of avoiding a civil war were made less. The white newspapers carried reports that sabotage would be punished by death. If this was so how could we continue to keep Africans away from terrorism?

Already scores of Africans had died as a result of racial friction. In 1920 when the famous leader, Masabala, was held in Port Eliza-

* A concentration camp – ed.

beth gaol, twenty-four of a group of Africans who had gathered to demand his release were killed by the police and white civilians. In 1921, more than one hundred Africans died in the Bulhoek affair. In 1924 over two hundred Africans were killed when the Administrator of South West Africa led a force against a group which had rebelled against the imposition of a dog tax. On 1 May 1950 eighteen Africans died as a result of police shootings during the strike. On 21 March 1960 sixty-nine unarmed Africans died at Sharpeville.

How many more Sharpevilles would there be in the history of our country? And how many more Sharpevilles could the country stand without violence and terror becoming the order of the day? And what would happen to our people when that stage was reached? In the long run we felt certain we must succeed, but at what cost to ourselves and the rest of the country? And if this happened, how could black and white ever live together again in peace and harmony? These were the problems that faced us, and these were our decisions.

Experience convinced us that rebellion would offer the government limitless opportunities for the indiscriminate slaughter of our people. But it was precisely because the soil of South Africa is already drenched with the blood of innocent Africans that we felt it our duty to make preparations as a long-term undertaking to use force in order to defend ourselves against force. If war were inevitable, we wanted the fight to be conducted on terms most favourable to our people. The fight which held out prospects best for us and the least risk of life to both sides was guerrilla warfare. We decided, therefore, in our preparations for the future, to make provision for the possibility of guerrilla warfare.

All whites undergo compulsory military training, but no such training was given to Africans. It was in our view essential to build up a nucleus of trained men who would be able to provide the leadership which would be required if guerrilla warfare started. We had to prepare for such a situation before it became too late to make proper preparations. It was also necessary to build up a nucleus of men trained in civil administration and other professions, so that Africans would be equipped to participate in the government of this country as soon as they were allowed to do so.

At this stage it was decided that I should attend the Conference of the Pan-African Freedom Movement for Central, East and

Southern Africa, which was to be held early in 1962 in Addis Ababa and, because of our need for preparation, it was also decided that, after the conference, I would undertake a tour of the African States with a view to obtaining facilities for the training of soldiers, and that I would also solicit scholarships for the higher education of matriculated Africans. Training in both fields would be necessary, even if changes came about by peaceful means. Administrators would be necessary who would be willing and able to administer a non-racial state and so would men be necessary to control the army and police force of such a state.

I started to make a study of the art of war and revolution and, whilst abroad, underwent a course in military training. If there was to be guerrilla warfare, I wanted to be able to stand and fight with my people and to share the hazards of war with them. I also made arrangements for our recruits to undergo military training. But here it was impossible to organize any scheme without the cooperation of the ANC offices in Africa. I consequently obtained the permission of the ANC in South Africa to do this. To this extent then there was a departure from the original decision of the ANC, but it applied outside South Africa only. The first batch of recruits actually arrived in Tanganyika when I was passing through that country on my way back to South Africa.

I returned to South Africa and reported to my colleagues on the results of my trip. On my return I found that there had been little alteration in the political scene save that the threat of a death penalty for sabotage had now become a fact. The attitude of my colleagues in Umkonto was much the same as it had been before I left. They were feeling their way cautiously and felt that it would be a long time before the possibilities of sabotage were exhausted. In fact, the view was expressed by some that the training of recruits was premature. This is recorded by me in the document, which is Exhibit R 14. After a full discussion, however, it was decided to go ahead with the plans for military training because of the fact that it would take many years to build up a sufficient nucleus of trained soldiers to start a guerrilla campaign, and whatever happened the training would be of value.

The ideological creed of the ANC is, and always has been, the creed of African Nationalism. It is not the concept of African Nationalism expressed in the cry, 'Drive the white man into the sea.' The African Nationalism for which the ANC stands is the concept of freedom and fulfilment for the African people in their own land. The most important political document ever adopted by the ANC is the 'Freedom Charter'. It is by no means a blueprint for a socialist state. It calls for redistribution, but not nationalization, of land; it provides for nationalization of mines, banks and monopoly industry, because big monopolies are owned by one race only, and without such nationalization racial domination would be perpetuated despite the spread of political power. It would be a hollow gesture to repeal the Gold Law prohibitions against Africans when all gold mines are owned by European companies. In this respect the ANC's policy corresponds with the old policy of the present Nationalist Party which, for many years, had as part of its programme the nationalization of the gold mines which, at that time, were controlled by foreign capital. Under the Freedom Charter, nationalization would take place in an economy based on private enterprise. The realization of the Freedom Charter would open up fresh fields for a prosperous African population of all classes, including the middle class. The ANC has never at any period in its history advocated a revolutionary change in the economic structure of the country, nor has it, to the best of my recollection, ever condemned capitalist society.

As far as the Communist Party is concerned, and if I understand its policy correctly, it stands for the establishment of a state based on the principles of Marxism. Although it is prepared to work for the Freedom Charter, as a short-term solution to the problems created by white supremacy, it regards the Freedom Charter as the beginning, and not the end, of its programme.

The ANC, unlike the Communist Party, admitted Africans only as members. Its chief goal was, and is, for the African people to win unity and full political rights. The Communist Party's main aim, on the other hand, was to remove the capitalists and to replace them with a working-class government. The Communist Party sought to emphasize class distinctions whilst the ANC seeks to harmonize them. This is a vital distinction.

It is true that there has often been close cooperation between the ANC and the Communist Party. But cooperation is merely proof of a common goal — in this case the removal of white supremacy — and it is not proof of a complete community of interests.

The history of the world is full of similar examples. Perhaps the most striking illustration is to be found in the cooperation between Great Britain, the United States of America and the Soviet Union in the fight against Hitler. Nobody but Hitler would have dared to suggest that such cooperation turned Churchill or Roosevelt into communists or communist tools, or that Britain and America were working to bring about a communist world.

South Africa is the richest country in Africa, and could be one of the richest in the world. But it is a land of extremes and remarkable contrasts. The whites enjoy what may well be the highest standard of living in the world, whilst Africans live in poverty and misery. Forty per cent of the Africans live in hopelessly overcrowded and, in some cases, drought-stricken reserves, where soil erosion and the overworking of the soil makes it impossible for them to live properly off the land. Thirty per cent are labourers, labour tenants and squatters on white farms and work and live under conditions similar to those of the serfs in the Middle Ages. The other thirty per cent live in towns where they have developed economic and social habits which bring them closer in many respects to white standards. Yet most Africans, even in this group, are impoverished by low incomes and high cost of living.

The highest-paid and the most prosperous section of urban African life is in Johannesburg. Yet their actual position is desperate. The latest figures were given on 25 March 1964, by Mr Carr, Manager of the Johannesburg Non-European Affairs Department. The poverty datum line for the average African family in Johannesburg (according to Mr Carr's department) is R42.84 per month.* He showed that the average monthly wage is R32.24 and that forty-six per cent of all African families in Johannesburg do not earn enough to keep them going.

Poverty goes hand in hand with malnutrition and disease. The incidence of malnutrition and deficiency diseases is very high amongst Africans. Tuberculosis, pellagra, kwashiorkor, gastroenteritis and scurvy bring death and destruction of health. The incidence of infant mortality is one of the highest in the world. According to the Medical Officer of Health for Pretoria, tuberculosis kills forty people a day (almost all Africans), and in 1961 there were 58,491 new cases reported. These diseases not only destroy the vital organs of the body, but they result in retarded mental conditions

---

* One South African rand is worth ten shillings or $1.20–ed.

N

and lack of initiative, and reduce powers of concentration. The secondary results of such conditions affect the whole community and the standard of work performed by African labourers.

The complaint of Africans, however, is not only that they are poor and the whites are rich, but that the laws which are made by the whites are designed to preserve this situation. There are two ways to break out of poverty. The first is by formal education, and the second is by the worker acquiring a greater skill at his work and thus higher wages. As far as Africans are concerned, both these avenues of advancement are deliberately curtailed by legislation.

The present government has always sought to hamper Africans in their search for education. One of their early acts, after coming into power, was to stop subsidies for African school feeding. Many African children, who attended schools, depended on this supplement to their diet. This was a cruel act.

There is compulsory education for all white children at virtually no cost to their parents, be they rich or poor. Similar facilities are not provided for the African children though there are some who receive such assistance. African children, however, generally have to pay more for their schooling than whites. According to figures quoted by the South African Institute of Race Relations in its 1963 journal, approximately forty per cent of African children in the age group between 7 to 14 do not attend school. For those who do attend school, the standards are vastly different from those afforded to white children. In 1960/61 the *per capita* government spending on African students at state-aided schools was estimated at R12.46. In the same years, the *per capita* spending on white children in the Cape Province (which are the only figures available to me) was R144.57. Although there are no figures available to me, it can be stated, without doubt, that the white children on whom R144.57 per head was being spent all came from wealthier homes than African children on whom R12.46 per head was being spent.

The other main obstacle to the economic advancement of the African is the industrial colour bar under which all the better jobs of industry are reserved for whites only. Moreover, Africans who do obtain employment in the unskilled and semi-skilled occupations which are open to them are not allowed to form trade unions which have recognition under the Industrial Conciliation Act. This means that strikes of African workers are illegal, and that they are denied the right of collective bargaining which is permitted to the better-paid white workers. The discrimination in the policy of successive South African governments towards African workers is demonstrated by the so-called 'civilized labour policy' under which sheltered unskilled government jobs are found for those white workers who cannot make the grade in industry, at wages which far exceed the earnings of the average African employee in industry.

The government often answers its critics by saying that Africans in South Africa are economically better off than the inhabitants of the other countries in Africa. I do not know whether this statement is true and doubt whether any comparison can be made without having regard to the cost of living index in such countries. But even if it is true, as far as the African people are concerned it is irrelevant. Our complaint is not that we are poor by comparison with people in other countries, but that we are poor by comparison with the white people in our own country, and that we are prevented by legislation from altering this imbalance.

The lack of human dignity experienced by Africans is the direct result of the policy of white supremacy. White supremacy implies black inferiority. Legislation designed to preserve white supremacy entrenches this notion. Menial tasks in South Africa are invariably performed by Africans. When anything has to be carried or cleaned the white man will look around for an African to do it for him, whether the African is employed by him or not. Because of this sort of attitude, whites tend to regard Africans as a separate breed. They do not look upon them as people with families of their own; they do not realize that they have emotions—that they fall in love like white people do; that they want to be with their wives and children like white people want to be with theirs; that they want to earn enough money to support their families properly, to feed and clothe them and send them to school. And what 'house-boy' or 'garden-boy' or labourer can ever hope to do this?

Pass laws, which to Africans are among the most hated bits of legislation in South Africa, render any African liable to police surveillance at any time. I doubt whether there is a single African male in South Africa who has not at some stage had a brush with the police over his pass. Hundreds and thousands of Africans are thrown into gaol each year under pass laws. Even worse than this is the fact that pass laws keep husband and wife apart and lead to the breakdown of family life.

Poverty and the breakdown of family life have secondary effects.

Children wander about the streets of the townships because they have no schools to go to, or no money to enable them to go to school, or no parents at home to see that they go to school, because both parents (if there be two) have to work to keep the family alive. This leads to a breakdown in moral standards, to an alarming rise in illegitimacy and to growing violence which erupts, not only politically, but everywhere. Life in the townships is dangerous. There is not a day that goes by without somebody being stabbed or assaulted. And violence is carried out of the townships into the white living areas. People are afraid to walk alone in the streets after dark. Housebreakings and robberies are increasing, despite the fact that the death sentence can now be imposed for such offences. Death sentences cannot cure the festering sore.

Africans want to be paid a living wage. Africans want to perform work which they are capable of doing, and not work which the government declares them to be capable of. Africans want to be allowed to live where they obtain work, and not be endorsed out of an area because they were not born there. Africans want to be allowed to own land in places where they work, and not to be obliged to live in rented houses which they can never call their own. Africans want to be part of the general population, and not confined to living in their own ghettos. African men want to have their wives and children to live with them where they work, and not be forced into an unnatural existence in men's hostels. African women want to be with their menfolk and not be left permanently widowed in the reserves. Africans want to be allowed out after 11 o'clock at night and not be confined to their rooms like little children. Africans want to be allowed to travel in their own country and to seek work where they want to and not where the Labour Bureau tells them to. Africans want a just share in the whole of South Africa; they want security and a stake in society.

Above all, we want equal political rights, because without them our disabilities will be permanent. I know this sounds revolutionary to the whites in this country, because the majority of voters will be Africans. This makes the white man fear democracy.

But this fear cannot be allowed to stand in the way of the only solution which will guarantee racial harmony and freedom for all. It is not true that the enfranchisement of all will result in racial domination. Political division, based on colour, is entirely artificial and, when it disappears, so will the domination of one colour group by another. The ANC has spent half a century fighting against racialism. When it triumphs it will not change that policy.

This then is what the ANC is fighting. Their struggle is a truly national one. It is a struggle of the African people, inspired by their own suffering and their own experience. It is a struggle for the right to live.

During my lifetime I have dedicated myself to this struggle of the African people. I have fought against white domination, and I have fought against black domination. I have cherished the ideal of a democratic and free society in which all persons live together in harmony and with equal opportunities. It is an ideal which I hope to live for and to achieve. But if needs be, it is an ideal for which I am prepared to die.

II South African Communist Party:
National Democratic Revolution[98]

The conceding of independence to South Africa by Britain, in 1910, was not a victory over the forces of colonialism and imperialism. It was designed in the interests of imperialism. A new type of colonialism was developed, in which the oppressing white nation occupied the same territory as the oppressed people themselves and lived side by side with them.

A rapid process of industrialization was set in train, especially during the two world wars. South African heavy industry and secondary industry grew to occupy first place on the continent. This process had profound effects on the country's social structure. It concentrated great wealth and profits in the hands of the upper strata of the white population. It revolutionized the economy, transforming it from a predominantly agricultural into an industrial-agricultural economy, with an urban working class, mainly non-white, which is the largest in Africa.

On one level, that of 'white South Africa', there are all the features of an advanced capitalist state in its final stage of imperialism. There are highly developed industrial monopolies, and the merging of industrial and finance capital. The land is farmed along capitalist lines, employing wage labour, and producing cash crops for the local and export markets. The South African monopoly capitalists, who are closely linked with British, United States and other foreign imperialist interests, export capital abroad, especially in Africa. Greedy for expansion, South African imperialism reaches out to incorporate other territories—South-West Africa and the protectorates.

But on another level, that of 'non-white South Africa', there are all the features of a colony. The indigenous population is subjected to extreme national oppression, poverty and exploitation, lack of all democratic rights and political domination by a group which does everything it can to emphasize and perpetuate its alien 'European' character. The African Reserves show the complete lack of industry, communications, transport and power resources which are characteristic of African territories under colonial rule throughout the continent. Typical, too, of imperialist rule, is the reliance by the state upon brute force and terror, and upon the most backward tribal elements and institutions which are deliberately and artificially preserved. Non-white South Africa is the colony of white South Africa itself.

All whites enjoy privileges in South Africa. This gives the impression that the ruling class is composed of the entire white population. In fact, however, real power is in the hands of the monopolists who own and control the mines, the banks and finance houses, and most of the farms and major industries. The gold and diamond mines are owned by seven mining-financial corporations and controlled by a handful of powerful financiers. These seven corporations are closely linked with British and American imperialist interests. They control capital investment in mining alone of R490 million, and employ almost 500,000 workers. In addition, they dominate large sections of manufacturing industries. They are linked with the main banks, two of which control assets of over R2,000 million, mainly in the forms of loans to industry, commerce and the state. They own vast tracts of arable land and mining rights in almost every part of the country. In agriculture, too, monopoly dominates. Four per cent of the farms make up an area amounting to almost two-fifths of the total white-owned farmland. Thus, in mining, industry, commerce and farming, monopolists dominate the country's economy. They are also closely linked with *state monopoly capital* ventures, such as Iscor (Iron and Steel), Escon (Electricity) and Sasol (Petrol).

These monopolists are the real power in South Africa. The special type of colonialism in South Africa serves, in the first place, their interests. Low non-white wages; the reserves of poverty; the compound labour system and the importation of hundreds and thousands of contract labourers from beyond our borders; the pass laws and poll tax and rigid police control of labour and of movement— all are designed to keep their profits high. In 1961 these seven mining corporations and their subsidiaries made a working profit of nearly R212 million and paid out dividends of R101 million to shareholders.

One quarter of the capital of the seven mining-financial groups is owned abroad, mainly by British and American investors. In 1958, dividends of R3 million were paid out abroad. The two biggest banks are largely controlled from Britain, and in recent years United States capital investment in South Africa has grown rapidly, exceeding all other American investments in the rest of Africa put together.

Effective economic domination in South Africa is thus exercised by an alliance of local white monopoly interests in mining, industry and agriculture, together with foreign imperialists and representatives of state monopoly capitalism. These interests have conflicts among themselves, which are reflected in the main white political parties and groupings. But they find common ground in the perpetuation of the colonial-type subjugation of the non-white population.

On the whole, the white workers represent an 'aristocracy of labour'. The monopolists have extended numerous concessions to them. They receive relatively high wages. Non-white miners receive an average of R144 a year plus food and compound housing: white miners R2,470. African male farm workers average R68 a year; whites R1,050. Whites have a monopoly of the best paid jobs, and of entry into skilled trades. They are invariably given positions of authority over non-whites. The relatively high standards of life and wages enjoyed by white workers represent, in reality, a share in the super profits made by the capitalists out of the gross exploitation of the non-whites. Systematically indoctrinated with the creed of white superiority, the white worker imagines himself to be a part of the ruling class and willingly acts as a tool and an accomplice in the maintenance of colonialism and capitalism. However, in reality, the white worker, like the non-white worker at his side, is subjected to exploitation by the same capitalist owners of the means of production. White workers' wages in general are high in comparison with those of non-whites. But many categories of white workers are paid little more than non-whites, and also struggle to support their families. The white worker is subjected to the insecurity of the capitalist system, with its constant threats of depression, short-time and unemployment. The division of trade unions on racial lines weakens all sections of workers in their constant struggle with the bosses for better pay and conditions and shorter hours of work. The fundamental interests of all South African workers, like those of workers everywhere, lie in unity: unity in the struggle for the day-to-day interests of the working class, for the ending of race discrimination and division, for a free, democratic South Africa as the only possible basis for the winning of socialism, the overthrow of the capitalist class and the ending of human exploitation.

There are no acute or antagonistic class divisions at present among the African people. Most of them are wage-workers in industry or agriculture. There are no large-scale African employers of labour. The professional groups, mainly teachers, do not, as a rule, earn salaries or live differently from their fellow-Africans. Even the people of the reserves, especially the menfolk, spend much of their lives as migrant wage labourers in the mines, in agriculture or industry.

One third of the African people live on the reserves. The largest of these are the Transkei and Ciskei, in the Cape Province, but there are also other scattered areas widely separated in the other three provinces. The government speaks of the reserves as the 'home-lands' of the African people, but so far from being able to sustain additional population, they are grossly over-crowded already and far too small to maintain their present population of $3\frac{1}{2}$ million. Most Africans on the reserves are not independent peasants and have no land or insufficient to make a living. To support their families and avert starvation most of the men in the prime of life are usually away working for white employers and leaving the farming to old people and womenfolk. The smallness and the overcrowding of the reserves leads to soil exhaustion. There is no opportunity for intensive farming, crop rotation, or scientific cattle pasturing, because there is not enough land. The reserves are the most backward and underdeveloped areas in the country, typical of colonial Africa. They lack industries, communications and power resources. There is no capital for improvements or mechanization.

The government is attempting, through the 'Bantu Authorities' system, to enforce a return to tribalism, using chiefs who are prepared to collaborate, and deposing and deporting those who refuse. The effect is actually to hasten the breakdown of tribal institutions. Those chiefs who collaborate with the government have become the most hated group in the countryside, relying on dictatorship and terror, contrary to African traditions, to enforce the laws of the white authorities on the unwilling people. The people of the reserves are boldly calling the government's 'Bantustan' bluff. They are fighting bitter struggles, including armed struggles, against the Bantu authorities. The peasant in the countryside today is not the unsophisticated tribesman of the previous century. Millions have at some time or other come to work in the towns. They have come into contact with the challenging outlook and the advanced methods of organization of the trade unions, the Congress movement and the Communist Party. These 'new peasants' have awakened the countryside, transforming the African peasantry from a reserve of conservatism into a powerful ally of the urban working class in the struggle against white colonialism, and for freedom, land, equality and democracy.

Millions of agricultural labourers and labour tenants are employed on white-owned farms throughout the country. These are the most exploited workers in South Africa. They work without any protection from labour laws, from dawn to sunset, at hard and exhausting labour, for wretchedly low wages. The food they are given is too little, it is always the same, and it is an unhealthy diet. On most farms the housing for them is worse than what is provided for the farm animals. The use of convict labour, and compound labour, and other forms of forced labour, is common on farms in many parts of South Africa. Farmers and their foremen frequently employ physical violence against African farm labourers, beating them with sjamboks, often to death. Wages for farm labour are the lowest in the country. Agricultural labourers are not really free workers. They are tied, often for life, to a particular farmer because of the operation of the labour tenancy system, the pass laws and in particular the so-called 'trek-pass', the Native Service Contract and and Masters and Servants Acts. Organization of agricultural workers' unions and other bodies for farm workers is also made exceptionally difficult because of the close supervision maintained over them by the farmers.

*N**

The 400,000 African labourers working on the gold and coal mines have to do the most backbreaking, dangerous and unhealthy work, for wages which are a scandal and a disgrace in an industry which distributes millions of rands annually to its shareholders. They are separated, for long periods, from their wives and families. A large proportion of them are 'imported' from territories outside the Republic, the Protectorates, South-West Africa, the Portuguese Colonies, Nyasaland, Tanganyika and elsewhere, although conferences of African states have decided to work towards ending this practice. The migratory labour system leads to a continual turnover of personnel, making the organization of mine workers a difficult task, and the mine owners go to great lengths to stamp out the development of trade unionism among them. Especially since the great strike led by the African Mineworkers' Union in 1946, they are subject to constant surveillance by police, spies and informers.

The workers of the towns, the Africans employed in factories and in transport, in steelworks and power stations, in shops and offices, comprise the most dynamic and revolutionary force in South Africa. The wages of urban African workers, in relation to their high living costs, are scandalously low. They are forced to live far from their places of work, involving exhausting and expensive journeys by bus or train. In shops and factories they are relegated to the most arduous and least rewarding work. Pass laws and urban areas legislation make the tenure of their jobs and their residences precarious, and they are subjected to never-ending raids and surveillance by the police. It is illegal for African workers to strike and their trade unions are unrecognized and vigorously discouraged by the state. Even when employers are prepared to enter into collective bargaining with African workers, the state intervenes to stop it. Despite these and many other disabilities, and the daily struggle for existence, this class, the most numerous and experienced working class on the African continent, has time and again shown that it is the vanguard of the African people. It has built up a number of stable and effective trade unions, devoted to the cause of African liberation and of workers' unity on our continent and throughout the world. African workers constitute the core of the African National Congress and the Communist Party. They have repeatedly come out on nationwide political general strikes and have been the leading force in every major struggle of the liberation movement. Disciplined and taught the lessons of organization and unity in the harsh school of capitalist production, driven by their conditions of life into united struggle for survival, this class alone is capable, in alliance with the masses of rural people, of leading a victorious struggle to end white domination and exploitation.

The coloured and Malay people, a population of 1½ million living mainly in the Western Cape Province, are a national group comprising workers, farm labourers, professional people and small businessmen. Like all non-whites, the coloured people are subjected to many forms of racial discrimination, reflected in low standards of living, education, housing, nutrition and health. Coloured workers, despite a tradition of craftsmanship which is the oldest in the country, find access to senior posts is withheld from them and given to whites; coloured farm labourers work and live under wretched conditions. Their pay is scandalously low, and on the wine farms is partly made up by a liquor ration—the 'tot' system, which undermines their health. Coloured teachers and other state employees are paid much less than their white counterparts for doing the same work. Nevertheless, for many years, this community occupied a privileged position in relation to the Africans. The white ruling group extended various concessions—such as a qualified franchise, trade union rights, property rights—in order to prevent the emergence of a coloured national consciousness, and the formation of a united front of oppressed non-white peoples for equality and the ending of white colonialism. This policy was not without success. But, with the deliberate removal by the government, one after another, of all the privileges extended to the coloured people in the past—the abolition of the common roll franchise, the introduction of apartheid and job reservation, white baaskap in the trade unions and separate university education—working-class and democratic leaders have come to the fore. The coloured people are rejecting apartheid and moving towards the path of struggle, side by side with African and other freedom fighters.

The Indian community, of half a million, are mainly the descendants of indentured labourers who came to work in the Natal sugar fields a century ago. From the earliest times all sorts of degrading and discriminatory restrictions have been placed on South African Indians, restrictions which they have resisted in many historic struggles. Today there is a substantial class of Indian industrial and agricultural workers, especially in Natal, but also, increasingly in the Transvaal. There is also a considerable class of Indian merchants, factory owners and small shopkeepers. The Indian workers face appalling problems of unemployment and overcrowding in slum conditions. Indians do not have voting and other democratic rights. Indian businessmen, and all sections of the community, are subjected to innumerable disabilities, especially relating to land and property ownership and economic and educational opportunities. They are not allowed to move from one Province to another without special permits, and are completely debarred from the Orange Free State. The Nationalist government has applied the Group Areas Act with particular ferocity against the Indian communities in the cities and small towns, uprooting them from their homes and livelihood and threatening to 'resettle' them in isolated areas where they face complete ruination. The Indian people have turned their backs on the reformist bourgeois leadership which counselled paths of compromise with oppression and the seeking of sectional privileges regardless of democratic principle and the fate of the masses. They have unreservedly joined in the many united struggles of the African and other oppressed peoples over the past two decades.

The Nationalist Party, which has governed South Africa since 1948, has brought this country to the verge of revolution. The Afrikaaner nationalist movement, which was always corrupted by white chauvinism, has today lost all trace of the anti-imperialist element it once had, during the period of its struggle against British rule. Dominated by the Afrikaner capitalist class and large-scale farmers, the Nationalist Party is controlled by the fascist 'Broederbond' secret society. Deeply influenced by the Nazi movement in Germany, it adopted many of Hitler's ideas and worked for a fascist victory in the Second World War. The Nationalist Party has become the instrument of the most racialistic and imperialistic sections of the capitalist class. The declaration of a Republic in May 1961 in no way lessened the dependence of the South African economy on British and American finance-capital. The Republic left the British Commonwealth not by choice of the Nationalist government but because the unpopularity of its racial policy among African and Asian member countries faced it with expulsion. In all major questions of international policy the Nationalist government identifies itself with the most aggressive elements of international imperialism in the United States, Britain, France, West Germany and Japan. It is dependent on financial and armaments aid from these countries to maintain its rule in South Africa.

The other white parliamentary parties can offer no way out of this crisis. The United Party, traditionally the instrument of the goldmining interests and the English-speaking capitalists, laid the basis for all the excesses of the Nationalists during the many years in which it governed South Africa before 1948. As the main 'opposition' group in Parliament it has steadily retreated before Nationalist reaction. It is compromised by its own anti-democratic class character and afraid lest genuine opposition to the government might result in disturbances which would adversely affect business and the confidence of foreign investors. It vies with the Nationalists in appealing to the racial prejudices of the white voters. It has actively or passively assisted the Nationalist Party at every stage of its march to fascism.

Disgusted with the surrender of the United Party and alarmed at the dangers to the country's stability and future presented by Nationalist policy, a number of former United Party MPs and members broke away in 1959 to form the Progressive Party. Backed by influential business interests, such as the Oppenheimer mining group, and supported by a section of urban, middle-class whites, the Progressive Party seeks to avert the coming democratic revolution in South Africa by offering a 'qualified' franchise to middle-class non-whites and concessions to ease the intolerable burden of apartheid.

A more radical tendency among progressive middle-class and intellectual circles is represented by the Liberal Party. This party proposes a universal franchise, but since it expressly confines itself to 'parliamentary and constitutional methods' it suggests no realistic or convincing method to obtain this. Its insistence on anti-communist and anti-socialist policies and its failure to attack the roots of race-oppression in the economy of the country seriously lessen the Liberal Party's usefulness and effectiveness. Its adherence to the 'West' in the cold war continually conflicts with its opposition to the National government, and makes the liberation movement doubt its reliability as an ally in the struggle.

The deep-rooted crisis in South Africa can only be resolved by a revolutionary change in the social system which will overcome these conflicts by putting an end to the colonial oppression of the African and other non-white people. The immediate and imperative interests of all sections of the South African people demand the carrying out of such a change, a national democratic revolution which will overthrow the colonialist state of white supremacy and establish an independent state of National Democracy in South Africa.

The Communist Party considers that the slogan of 'non-violence' is harmful to the cause of the democratic national revolution in the new phase of the struggle, disarming the people in the face of the savage assaults of the oppressor, dampening their militancy, undermining their confidence in their leaders. At the same time, the Party opposes undisciplined acts of individual terror. It rejects theories that all non-violent methods of struggle are useless or impossible, and will continue to advocate and work for the use of all forms of struggle by the people, including non-collaboration strikes, boycotts and demonstrations.

The Party does not dismiss all prospects of non-violent transition to the democratic revolution. This prospect will be enhanced by the development of revolutionary and militant people's forces. The illusion that the white minority can rule for ever over a disarmed majority will crumble before the reality of an armed and determined people. The crisis in the country, and the contradictions in the ranks of the ruling class, will deepen. The possibility would be opened of a peaceful and negotiated transfer of power to the representatives of the oppressed majority of the people.

III African National Congress: *Strategy and Tactics*[99]

To ignore the real situation and to play about with imaginary forces, concepts and ideals is to invite failure. The art of revolutionary leadership consists in providing leadership for the masses and not just for its most advanced elements; it consists of setting a pace which accords with objective conditions and the real possibilities at hand. The revolutionary-sounding phrase does not always reflect revolutionary policy and revolutionary-sounding policy is not always the springboard for revolutionary advance. Indeed, what appears to be 'militant' and 'revolutionary' can often be counter-revolutionary. It is surely a question of whether, in the given concrete situation, the course of policy advocated will aid or impede the prospects of the conquest of power. In this, the only test, the advocacy of armed struggle can, in some situations, be as counter-revolutionary as the advocacy of its opposite in other situations. Untimely, ill-planned or premature manifestations of violence impede and do not advance the prospect for revolutionary change and are clearly counter-revolutionary. It is obvious therefore that policy and organizational structures must grow out of the real situation if they are not to become meaningless clichés.

Future historians may well be able to pause at some moments during the evolution of our struggle and examine critically both its pace and emphasis. But, in general, without the so-called reformist activities of the previous half century, the prospect of advancing into the new phase would have been extremely small. This is so because even in the typical colonial-type situation armed struggle becomes feasible only if:

— there is disillusionment with the prospect of achieving liberation by traditional peaceful processes because the objective conditions blatantly bar the way to change;

— there is readiness to respond to the strategy of armed struggle with all the enormous sacrifices which this involves;

— there is in existence a political leadership capable of gaining the organized allegiance of the people for armed struggle and which has both the experience and the ability to carry out the painstaking process of planning, preparation and overall conduct of the operations; and

— there exist favourable objective conditions in the international and local plans.

In one sense these conditions are connected and interdependent. They are not created by subjective and ideological activity only, and many are the mistakes committed by heroic revolutionaries who give a monopoly to the subjective factor and who confuse their own readiness with the readiness of others.

These conditions are brought about not only by developing political, economic and social conditions but also by the long hard grind of revolutionary work. They depend on such factors as the response of the enemy, the extent to which he unmasks himself and the experience gained by the people themselves not in academic seminars but in actual political struggle.

We reject the approach which sees as the catalyst for revolutionary transformation only the short-cut of isolated confrontations and the creation of armed resistance centres. Does this mean that before an actual beginning can be made to the armed challenge we have to wait for the evolvement of some sort of deep crisis in the enemy camp which is serious enough to hold out the possibility of an immediate all-round insurrection? Certainly not! We believe that given certain basic factors, both international and local, the actual beginning of armed struggle or guerrilla warfare can be made and having begun steadily develop conditions for the future all-out war which will eventually lead to the conquest of power. Under the modern highly sophisticated police state (which South Africa is) it is questionable whether a movement can succeed in a programme of mass political organization beyond a certain point without starting a new type of action. Also, it is not easy to determine the point at which sufficient concrete, political and organizational preparations have been carried out to give our armed detachments the maximum chances of survival and growth within any given area. There is no instrument for measuring this. But we must not overdo the importance of the subjective factor and before embarking upon a path which is in one sense tragic, although historically inevitable and necessary, certain of the basic minimum conditions already mentioned must be present and certain minimum preparations must have been made.

The opening step in 1961—organized sabotage mainly in the urban areas—served a special purpose and was never advanced as a technique which would, on its own, either lead to the destruction of the state or even do it great material damage (although guerrilla activity in the urban areas of a special type is always important as an auxiliary). At the same time there was a threefold need to be met in order to lay the foundations for more developed and meaningful armed activity of the guerrilla type.

The first was the need to create a military apparatus and, more particularly, to recruit large numbers of professional cadres who were to be trained and who would form the core of future guerrilla bands.

The second was the need to demonstrate effectively to all that we were making a sharp and open break with the processes of the previous period which had correctly given emphasis to militant struggle short of armed confrontation.

The third was the need to present an effective method for the overthrow of white supremacy through planned rather than spontaneous activity. The sabotage campaign was an earnest indication of our seriousness in the pursuit of this new strategy. All three needs were served by this convincing evidence that our liberation movement had correctly adjusted itself to the new situation and was creating an apparatus actually capable of clandestinely hitting the enemy and making preparation for a more advanced phase. The situation was such that without activity of this nature our whole political leadership may have been at stake both inside and outside the country and the steps which were simultaneously taken for the recruitment and preparation of military cadres would have met with less response.

When we talk of revolutionary armed struggle, we are talking of political struggle by means which include the use of military force even though once force as a tactic is introduced it has the most far-reaching consequences on every aspect of our activities. It is important to emphasize this because our movement must reject all manifestations of militarism which separates armed people's struggle from its political context.

Reference has already been made to the danger of the thesis which regards the creation of military areas as the generator of mass resistance. But even more is involved in this concept. One of the vital problems connected with this bears on the important question of the relationship between the political and military. From the very beginning our movement has brooked no ambiguity concerning this. The primacy of the political leadership is unchallenged and supreme and all revolutionary formations and levels (whether armed or not) are subordinate to this leadership. To say this is not just to invoke tradition. This approach is rooted in the very nature of this type of revolutionary struggle and is borne out by the experience of the overwhelming majority of revolutionary movements which have engaged in such struggles. Except in very rare instances, the people's armed challenge against a foe with formidable material strength does not achieve dramatic and swift success. The path is filled with obstacles and we harbour no illusions on this score in the case of South Africa. In the long run it can only succeed if it attracts the active support of the mass of the people. Without this life-blood it is doomed. Even in our country with the historical background and traditions of armed resistance, still within the memory of many people and the special developments of the immediate past, the involvement of the masses is unlikely to be the result of a sudden natural and automatic consequence of military clashes. It has to be won in all-round political mobilization which must accompany the military activities. This includes education and agitational work throughout the country to cope with the sophisticated torrent of misleading propaganda and 'information' of the enemy which will become more intense as the struggle sharpens. When armed clashes begin they seldom involve more than a comparative handful of combatants whose very conditions of fighting-existence make them incapable of exercising the functions of all-round political leadership. The masses of the peasants, workers and youth, beleaguered for a long time by the enemy's military occupation, have to be activated in a multitude of ways not only to ensure a growing stream of recruits for the fighting units but to harass the enemy politically so that his forces are dispersed and therefore weakened. This calls for the exercise of all-round political leadership.

Guerrilla warfare, the special, and in our case the only form in which the armed liberation struggle can be launched, is neither static nor does it take place in a vacuum. The tempo, the overall strategy to be employed, the opening of new fronts, the progression from lower to higher forms and thence to mobile warfare; these and other vital questions cannot be solved by the military leadership alone; they require overall political judgements intimately involved with the people both inside and outside the actual areas of armed combat. If more awareness of oppression combined with heroic examples by armed bands were enough, the struggle would indeed be simple. There would be no collaborators and it would be hard to find neutrals. But to believe this is to believe that the course of struggle is determined solely by what we do in the fighting units and further involves the fallacious assumption that the masses are rock-like and incorruptible. The enemy is as aware as we are that the side that wins the allegiance of the people wins the struggle. It is naïve to believe that oppressed and beleaguered people cannot temporarily, even in large numbers, be won over by fear, terror, lies, indoctrination and provocation to treat liberators as enemies. In fact history proves that without the most intensive all-round political activity this is the more likely result. It is therefore all the more vital that the revolutionary leadership is nationwide and has its roots both inside and outside the actual areas of combat. Above all, when victory comes, it must not be a hollow one. To ensure this we must also ensure that what is brought to power is not an army but the masses as a whole at the head of which stands its organized political leadership. This is the perspective which is rooted at all levels of our liberation movements whether within or outside the army. Our confidence in final victory rests not on the wish or the dream but on our understanding of our own conditions and the historical processes. This understanding must be deepened and must spread to every level of our movement. We must have a clear grasp not only of ourselves and of our own forces but also of the enemy— of his power and vulnerability.

On the face of it the enemy is in stable command of a rich and varied economy which, even at this stage when it is not required to extend itself, can afford an enormous military budget. He has a relatively well-trained and efficient army and police force. He can draw on fairly large manpower resources. In addition, the major imperialist powers, such as Britan, West Germany, France, the United States and Japan, who have an enormous stake in the economy of our country, constitute a formidable support for the apartheid regime. Already now before the crisis deepens the imperialist partners of South Africa have done much to develop the economy and armament programme of South Africa. In a situation of crisis they may pass over from support to active intervention to save the racist regime.

If there is one lesson that the history of guerrilla struggle has taught us it is that the material strength and resources of the enemy is by no means a decisive factor. Guerrilla warfare almost by definition presents a situation in which there is a vast imbalance of material and military resources between the opposing sides. It is designed to cope with the situation in which the enemy is infinitely superior in relation to every conventional factor of warfare. It is *par excellence* the weapon of the materially weak against the materially strong. Given its popular character and given a population which increasingly sides with and shields the guerrilla whilst at the same time opposing and exposing the enemy, the survival and growth of a people's army is assured by the skilful exercise of tactics. Surprise, mobility and tactical retreat should make it difficult for the enemy to bring into play its superior fire-power in any decisive battles. No individual battle is fought in circumstances favourable to the enemy. Superior forces can thus be harassed, weakened and, in the end, destroyed. The absence of an orthodox front, of fighting lines; the need of the enemy to attenuate his resources and lines of communication over vast areas; the need to protect the widely scattered installations on which his economy is dependent; these are among the factors which serve in the long run to compensate in favour of the guerrilla for the disparity in the starting strength of the adversaries. The words 'in the long run' must be stressed because it would be idle to dispute the considerable military advantages to the enemy of his high-level industrialization, his ready-to-hand reserves of white manpower and his excellent roads, railways and air transport which facilitate swift manoeuvres and speedy concentration of personnel. But we must not overlook the fact that over a period of time many of these unfavourable factors will begin to operate in favour of the liberation forces:

— The ready-to-hand resources including food production depend overwhelmingly on non-white labour which, with the growing intensity of the struggle, will not remain docile and cooperative.

— The white manpower resources may seem adequate initially but must become dangerously stretched as guerrilla warfare develops. Already extremely short of skilled labour — the monopoly of the whites — the mobilization of a large force for a protracted struggle will place a further burden on the workings of the economy.

— In contrast to many other major guerrilla struggles, the enemy's economic and manpower resources are all situated within the theatre of war and there is no secure external pool (other than direct intervention by a foreign state) safe from sabotage, mass action and guerrilla action on which the enemy can draw.

— The very sophistication of the economy with its well-developed system of communications makes it a much more vulnerable target. In an undeveloped country the interruption of supplies to any given region may be no more than a local setback. In a highly sensitive modern structure of the South African type, the successful harassment of transport to any major industrial complex inevitably inflicts immense damage to the economy as a whole and to the morale of the enemy.

In the vast expanse that is South Africa, a people's force will find a multitude of variations in topography, deserts, mountains, forests, veld and swamps. There might not appear to be a single impregnable mountain or impenetrable jungle but the country abounds in terrain which in general is certainly no less favourable for guerrilla operations than some of the terrain in which other guerrilla movements operate successfully. Also the issue must be looked at in the context of guerrillas, who are armed and operate in the terrain. The combination makes an area impregnable for the guerrilla. South Africa's tremendous size will make it extremely difficult, if not impossible, for the white regime to keep the whole of it under armed surveillance in strength and in depth. Hence, an early development of a relatively safe (though shifting) rear is not beyond the realm of practicality.

The main content of the present stage of the South African revolution is the national liberation of the largest and most oppressed group—the African people. This strategic aim must govern every aspect of the conduct of our struggle whether it be the formulation of policy or the creation of structures. Amongst other things, it demands in the first place the maximum mobilization of the African people as a dispossessed and racially oppressed nation. This is the mainspring and it must not be weakened. It involves a stimulation and a deepening of national confidence, national pride and national assertiveness. Properly channelled and properly led, these qualities do not stand in conflict with the principles of internationalism. Indeed, they become the basis for more lasting and more meaningful cooperation; a cooperation which is self-imposed, equal and one which is neither based on dependence nor gives the appearance of being so.

But none of this detracts from the basically national context of our liberation drive. In the last resort it is only the success of the national democratic revolution which—by destroying the existing social and economic relationships—will bring with it a correction of the historical injustices perpetrated against the indigenous majority and thus lay the basis for a new—and deeper internationalist—approach. Until then, the national sense of grievance is the most potent revolutionary force which must be harnessed. To blunt it in the interests of abstract concepts of internationalism is, in the long run, doing neither a service to revolution nor to internationalism.

PORTUGUESE AFRICA

In the so-called developed world, the poorest and most backward country is Portugal, where the nine million people have lived under an iron-fisted dictatorship since 1926. In all those years, the dicta-tors (Gomes da Costa for a few years, Oliveira Salazar for forty and now Marcello Caetano) have taken most pride in giving their people peace and stability. Actually, they achieved neither: rebellions oc-curred in 1931, 1936, 1946, 1947, 1952, 1959, 1961 and 1962, and some form of political agitation and unrest has continued ever since. But at home the dictators have so far managed to keep a tight hold on their people, whose rate of income, education, health, housing and mobility is the lowest in Europe.

Outside Portugal, however, the dictatorship has not been nearly as successful. To the Lisbon regime, Portugal's foreign colonies are 'overseas territories'—Goa, for example, which was seized by Nehru, is still referred to as 'our possession in India under temporary foreign occupation'. Though the government correctly interprets the policy of its NATO allies (especially the USA, England and France, who claim to oppose Portuguese colonialism) as nothing more than a manoeuvre to replace it with their own neo-colonial rule, Lisbon has learned very little from the wave of African libera-tion movements. It keeps its colonies, specifically in Africa, under very rigid control, giving local populations no political rights, no education (95 per cent illiteracy), no modern training of any kind. As Peter Ritner put it (in The Death of Africa*): 'Portuguese Africa is one of the worst governed areas of the world.' On the other hand, whatever the area produces of worth (iron, diamonds, copper, bauxite, uranium, oil, cotton, tea, coffee, sugar, nuts, rice) is owned and exported by foreign companies—Portuguese, Ameri-can, Belgian, Rhodesian, South African, Italian, British and*

German (Krupp). As a result of the Portugal–Rhodesia–South Africa alliance, more than 10,000 blacks from Portuguese Africa are sent to work in mines in the other two countries—as forced labour.

Portuguese Africa is composed mainly of three separate countries: Mozambique on the Indian Ocean, with Tanzania to the north, South Africa to the south and Zambia and Rhodesia to the west, has 7,000,000 blacks, 200,000 whites; Angola (and its Cabinda enclave just above the Congo River), framed by the Atlantic, the Congo—Kinshasa on top, Zambia on the east, and South Africa's colony, south-west Africa, on the bottom, is the sixth biggest country in the continent and is populated by 6,000,000 blacks, 300,000 whites; Guiné-Bissau, a tiny (36,000 sq. km) bush lowland squeezed on Africa's western hump, has only a few thousand whites and 600,000 blacks. Each of these countries is now in revolt, with armed liberation movements occupying considerable portions of the countryside. To fight them, the Portuguese have brought in 150,000 troops (the military eats up 42 per cent of Portugal's budget) and are constantly bombing the countryside—with napalm. They also use Vietnam-like strategic hamlet tactics to try to pacify the rural population.

Each country has various guerrilla operations. In Angola, where the rebellion was launched in 1961, and in Mozambique, where it began in 1967, the most successful liberation movements are those whose ideology approximates most to that of traditional communists: the Popular Movement for the Liberation of Angola (MPLA) and the Mozambique Liberation Front (FRELIMO). After initial successes both have had major difficulties, mainly because of internal squabbling and rivalries with other guerrilla fronts. In Angola, for example, MPLA fighters are often ambushed by the 'guerrillas' of Holden Roberto's GRAF (Republican Government of Angola in Exile) which is aided by the Congo (K)'s General Mobutu and the CIA. FRELIMO has also suffered from the infiltration of agents working for Portugal's secret police PIDE, and by the CIA. It is generally believed, for example, that the assassination of its president, Eduardo Mondlane, in Dar es Salaam in February 1969, was the operation of such agents.

Since then, however, both the MPLA and FRELIMO have increased their revolutionary activities. FRELIMO now fields some 12,000 guerrillas (against 60,000 Portuguese troops), controls twenty per cent of the countryside (where it is carrying out agrarian re-

forms), and is entering a new phase of trying to coordinate its actions with the forces of ANC-ZAPU. The MPLA, which is also linking up to this alliance, runs an even greater proportional area.

Ideologically, none of the liberation movements of Angola or Mozambique, neither the MPLA or FRELIMO, nor the Chinese-oriented movements which are also active, have offered new insights into guerrilla warfare. At FRELIMO's second Congress, which was held inside the liberated area from 20 to 25 July 1968, the resolution on Armed Struggle stated: 'Our war is essentially a political one, and its duration is defined by the party. The people's army is part and parcel of the party, and its strategic plans are made by the top leadership of the party.' On the other hand, it went on to state: 'In order to conduct correctly the struggle, all the leaders should be involved in the armed struggle. Only in this way, following the struggle step by step, may the leaders be able to solve all the complex problems arising daily. The people's army performs its task in accordance with the policy defined by FRELIMO.' As late as 1966, in a speech in London, Uriah Simango, the priest who became FRELIMO's vice-president and then one of three Council Presidents succeeding Mondlane, maintained the hope that boycotts, sanctions and perhaps British intervention were what was needed to bring down the racist Rhodesia government. 'The people of the Portuguese colonies,' he concluded, 'will not lay down their arms until Portugal has agreed to enter negotiations and to grant independence. This is the only condition for peaceful coexistence with Portugal.'

Mondlane himself seems to have been less of a reformist. In The Struggle for Mozambique,[100] *which was finished very few weeks before he was killed, he wrote:*

> *Whatever happens [to the war], whether we have to go on for ten or twenty years, fighting our way inch by inch down to Lourenço Marques [the capital], or whether the Portuguese give up and move out within the next few years, our problems will not end with independence. If the war has been long, however, these may be less acute. For the achievement of independence in itself does not change overnight the attitudes of the people. . . . People are beginning to realize that their future is now in their own hands. This is why we can view the long war ahead of us with reasonable calm.*

Agostinho Neto, MPLA's President, expressed somewhat the same thoughts when, in an interview in Algiers (Révolution Africaine,

1–7 May 1967) he said: 'The aims of the MPLA are not only political independence for the country, but also a basic transformation of the people. . . . The common struggle against Portuguese colonialism is already an important element in the formation of the national consciousness of our people.' In practical terms, what that consciousness achieves is perhaps best explained by Spartacus Monimambu, the military commander of the MPLA's eastern region—in the 1968 interview below (article I).

But by far the sharpest fighting ideologue in Portuguese Africa— and indeed in the whole continent—is Amilcar Cabral, head of the African Independence Party of Guinea and the Cape Verde Islands (PAIGC). Formed in September 1956 by Cabral and other 'petty-bourgeois intellectuals', as he says, the PAIGC focused on internal organization until 1959, then on political and propagandistic preparation for armed struggle until 1962. The first attack was launched during the night of 30 June–1 July of that year. By October 1969, despite 40,000 Portuguese troops using bombers, napalm, helicopters, and brutal pacification, the PAIGC had liberated two-thirds of the countryside, forcing the enemy to communicate between fortified towns through the air.

In the three passages below (article II), Cabral reveals one reason why the PAIGC has been so successful—his own power of analysis (he explains some of the other reasons). That analysis, of the objective conditions of his country, led him to junk most of the formal descriptions and prescriptions for revolution. For one thing, he discarded the notion of the peasantry as a revolutionary force. For another, he found that as there was no working class, to talk of the revolution led by the proletariat was absurd. He did accept the notion of a two-stage revolution, but only because the first would politicize the masses for the second. To Cabral, there was only one revolutionary 'motor'—the petty bourgeoisie. It alone could form the military vanguard and it alone was the political vanguard. As a nucleus (a political foco, to use a Guevarist term), the petty bourgeoisie could mount an effective armed offensive against Portuguese colonialism. But unless that offensive was transformed into a genuine war against domination and exploitation, that is against neo-colonialism (and, therefore, capitalism), it would not be a 'national liberation'.

Yet, Cabral understood that such a liberation must end up demanding that the petty bourgeoisie commit class suicide—when it could hope to rule and profit after political independence. Objectively, the petty bourgeoisie cannot so rule and profit unless it ties itself to neo-colonialism, which, in turn, would push it out of the foreground to make room for that bourgeoisie with the assets—not the petty (servicing, intellectual and bureaucratic) bourgeoisie, but the national bourgeoisie. Hence the winning motor force, the petty bourgeoisie, will have only this choice: class suicide, to die in order to be reborn with a proletariat mentality, or selling out.

The choice, says Cabral, is not dialectical. It is moral. It can and must be (and can only be) brought about by the petty bourgeoisie itself as it wages and leads the patriotic war—in which it finds the roots for the class struggle to follow. Cabral believes in man, in men, and that is surely one fundamental reason for the 'petty-bourgeois' PAIGC's revolutionary ('proletarian') success.

I Spartacus Monimambu: *In MPLA Liberated Areas*[101]

Q: *On 3 January, the MPLA announced that it was going to shift its headquarters from Brazzaville to Angola. How do you think this will affect the course of the struggle?*
A: This is very important for us. As you know, every revolutionary struggle must be carried out inside the country. And this cannot be done very well if the leaders themselves are not among the people. We are a mass organization, a popular movement, so we must be among the people. They must see that the leaders themselves are inside to direct and orient the struggle. This will give more courage to the people, and even to the guerrilla fighters. All of our political leaders, except for two or three, have now been trained militarily. So they can go inside and lead and help train the local leaders. What we need, what we want, is for local leaders to become conscious enough to lead their own people in the villages. The top leaders must bring these people to a high level of political consciousness and understanding.
Q: *Maybe you could now comment generally on the relationship within Angola between the military and political leadership.*

A: Our principle is to combine the military and the political. Everyone must be both, political and military together. We know that our basic problem is a political one, but it cannot be solved without violence. So, while the military aspect is secondary to the political, there is an interdependence between the two. The military and political actions must complement each other and develop parallel to one another. That is why we have both political and military leaders in the central committee. Here, both military and political people come together and lead the struggle together. But the people inside the country understand the necessity of representation outside, because without this there would be little chance of getting supplies or carrying out diplomatic activities.

Q: *Is the head of each zone a military leader, a political leader or a combination of both?*

A: In each of the five zones there is a military command, headed by a first commander who is himself both a military and political leader. Then in the whole of the Eastern Region, made up of these five zones, we have a regional command comprised of six or seven officers. Four of these, including myself, are on the Eastern Region Steering Committee. So we are both political and military officers. There is no difference between political and military leaders inside now. Every person holding a leadership position participates in both the military and political aspects of the struggle.

Q: *How does the popular militia function in relation to the MPLA's guerrilla forces?*

A: Without the militias the semi-regular forces of MPLA couldn't control this area. Moxico itself, you know, is four times larger than Portugal. So, to control this area, we need the help of the militia. This is why we are working hard to organize and train them. Their leaders have been trained by us inside, politically and militarily. And despite some difficulties with supplies they are able to patrol their area and help protect their people. You know there are people going to fish, to their gardens to cultivate, to the bush to collect honey from trees—they are still going everywhere. But each one has an important mission: to look after the place, to see who is coming in and who is going out.

Q: *How many people would you say are living in an average village in the semi-liberated area?*

A: It depends on the number of people who belong to such and such a chief. Sometimes there are fifty, sometimes eighty; and we have

decided that no more than a hundred can remain together in one place—with their houses close together but still a little separated. It depends on the bush. If it is not heavy, then not too many people will stay together. If it is heavy then they will be safe. All the houses will be well-camouflaged and can't be seen from planes.
Q: *Perhaps you could discuss the scale of MPLA's operations in the Eastern Region. How much territory and how many people are involved?*
A: The Eastern Front is about 500 miles long and some 310 miles deep. But these figures were calculated last year. Our people are still moving ahead. They are now in Bic and to the north we have already sent organizers and a guerrilla group into the Lunda district. So I can't tell you at this time exactly how far our zone of operation extends inside the country. As for the territories controlled or semi-controlled by us, they are Moxico and most of Cuando Cubango districts—with many enemy posts in between.

You can't find a single place in this area where people have remained in their traditional villages. They have already abandoned them. Or the Portuguese have caught them and brought them near their posts to live in concentration camp villages. Most have run away. But it is up to them to choose. They can either go to the Portuguese for help or to the freedom fighters. Most people come to the bush and live with us, some go with the Portuguese. But those who go with the Portuguese don't stay more than two or three months. After that they will die of hunger because they can't go into the bush to look after their crops. They are allowed to go there just one day a week, followed by Portuguese guards. But it is not enough for them; they feel they are in a prison, that they are not free there. So many of them run away and come to join us. Or when the freedom fighters go there they ask us to take them away from the place. There is not a very large population in these areas. Now we can say that there are more than 30,000 living with us in the semi-liberated areas. But not all of these have been politicized. We have sent organizers to many places to politicize the people, to mobilize them, organize them. We have found that those who quickly take our ideas to heart are the young chaps. The older ones, they just want to be safe, to avoid being killed, and they just continue doing their ordinary activities, that's all. It is very difficult to deal with the old people. I find it very difficult. But we know that you find people like that everywhere. They still need much help—with medicine, clothes, salt and soap. These are the most important needs of the people inside, because now many live without these things. They understand what our difficulties are in getting these things. We have already tried to do something about this. The problem is not completely solved but a part has been solved and we have given some satisfaction to the people.

Q: *Last June, at a meeting held in the Eastern Region, a number of new programmes were put forward. Perhaps you could comment generally on the progress that has been made. Let's take them one at a time, beginning with your efforts in the sphere of agricultural production.*

A: Agricultural production in the semi-liberated areas is increasing. In every zone the people are organized in sectors; a zone may have five or six sectors. In each sector there is a Revolutionary Committee of Action, a people's organization which concerns itself with the people's problems. They have a chairman, a secretary, a treasurer, etc. Committee members are elected by the people. There are about three hundred of them in an average sector. The people in each sector collectively cultivate what we call a people's plantation. All of them work together in one field. The products which come from their collective work are then used for the benefit of the people themselves. These people's plantations won't develop quickly in all zones. Where we have made the greatest progress in agriculture is in zones C and D. We already have thirty-five collectives in these zones. The important crops grown are rice, cassava, potatoes, manioc and maize. Apart from the collective each person has his own traditional garden where he can work. But on certain days everyone must work on the people's plantation, because on those days we use the militia to surround and protect the place. If they see a plane coming from very far away they will go into their trenches and camouflage themselves. They are safe there.

Q: *How many days a week do they work on the people's plantation?*

A: They work two days on the collective, then two days in their own gardens. The other days are for meetings, literacy classes, political education, etc. So they have two days of agricultural work on the collective, two days of personal work and two days of education; and then on Sundays they sing, dance, etc., because national culture is important also. We want to develop it, too.

Q: *In the area of education and cadre training you have set up*

Centres for Revolutionary Instruction (CIRs). How have these progressed?

A: These centres are very important to us. Before the end of 1967 we had already trained more than two thousand cadres outside, in many countries. But we find that it is more important to train them inside the country. We lack materials and have to do without many things—but these CIRs are very helpful to us now. Between August and February the first course was held and it was very successful. And many people's cadres, people trained educationally, militarily and politically, are now able to go and organize people, be active among the people. They also learned how to maintain themselves —to keep chickens, cultivate, sow, and so on. They were taught many things there. On 14 March we started the second course, the second part of the programme. Angola, you know, is a country with many illiterate, uninformed people who don't know how to read and write—probably worse than any other African country. The Portuguese have done it deliberately. Now it is up to us. We can't wait until we're free, but must begin now to educate our people, to teach them how to read and learn. The most important language is Luvale. But when one speaks Luvale, the Mbunda tribe can't understand it, the Chokwe tribe can't understand it. Now we have two languages: Luvale and Portuguese. But we also have people who translate from Portuguese to other local languages.

Q: *What is the basic content of the political education programme? Is it essentially nationalist in character or is it socialist and internationalist?*

A: Political education is, first of all, nationalist. The people must understand that we are all Angolans. But we know that tomorrow there will be many problems in Angola and that to solve them requires that we educate people in the ideological sphere. For us ideology is most important within the party because today we are a mass movement, a popular movement, and not yet a party with the structure of a party. But tomorrow there will be a party with its philosophy, its determined ideology and its structure. And to reach that level we must begin to prepare the way from today. That is why the MPLA is very interested in giving ideological education to our militants. For the people in general, at least for now, they need only nationalist education.

Q: *You mentioned national culture. What are you doing to make people aware of their Angolan national culture?*

A: Apart from Angolan traditional songs and dances, in our Centres for Revolutionary Instruction we are trying to give people a consciousness of themselves as Angolans. We put on theatrical performances showing the people what it was like before the Portuguese came in, and how our people resisted the Portuguese. Then, after that, how the struggle for our liberation began, and how it is progressing. This is what we're trying to organize, so that tomorrow we will have cultural unity throughout Angola. This is for the people to enjoy, but it is also very important educationally. If the people see what it was like before the Portuguese, after they came, during the early resistance and the present liberation struggle, it will be easier for them to see themselves as Angolans. We have some intellectuals in Angola, our own intellectuals within the revolution. And they are helping us with national culture. Some of these young chaps just coming from school are poets, like Dr Neto, and we are trying to use their poems to build our theatre, trying to execute them in theatrical form. That is another part of the effort we are making. In addition, there are now many revolutionary songs which we are teaching the people.

Q: *How do the people participate in decision-making at different levels? How do you engage them in the process of making new kinds of decisions?*

A: The action committees are related to MPLA's central committee. The instructions come from the central committee and are passed through the military command to the action committees. But it is not possible for the central committee to control everything directly. That is why we have created three regional steering committees whose members also serve on the central committee. They meet in various places, make their decisions, and if these decisions pertain to the people inside the country, they are sent through military command (for security reasons) to the action committees at the zone level. These action committees will then meet and transmit the information to the people through the committees at the sector and group levels. We have four levels, then: group, sector, zone and region. Within a sector there are many groups, which are residential units. There is only one chief in a sector, but he has responsibility for a large area within which there are smaller villages—which we now call groups—and these groups have their own organization. They, the people in each group, elect members to serve on their action committee.

Q: *Do you find that people in the groups and sectors tend to elect traditional leaders to the action committees? Or do they elect people with more progressive ideas?*

A: Today the traditional leaders are still respected. But if a traditional leader is not very interested in the struggle he will not have power, he will not be elected by the people. Someone else will be on top. The chief will remain chief but he will be without power. But if he is a good chief, a revolutionary one, it is better for him to lead his people.

Q: *So at the group level people elect their own action committee which sends representatives to the sector action committee.*

A: Yes. And then from the sector level they send their representatives to the zone action committee. In each zone there are some who are very intelligent and they represent their people on the regional committees. The central committee selects one or two from each zone who are militants, who are already politically educated, and they represent their zones on the regional committee. With the help of the military command these action committees keep registers of all marriages, births, deaths and so on. They also administer justice. Those traditional chiefs are well versed in local laws and customs, but we must take care with the traditional laws and habits which are not good, which are not adapted to the revolutionary conditions of today. So we must help them to settle some cases. In addition, they have their own police, recruited from the militia. The militia is paramilitary, but within a militia group they choose some to be police. They keep order in the villages, or groups, and in the sector.

Q: *You mentioned women's organizations. Perhaps you could discuss this question of the role of women in a little greater detail.*

A: For us the role of women in the struggle is very important, because in Angola, as everywhere in Africa, it is the women who have suffered most under colonial rule. Our organization of Angolan Women (OMA) is now fighting for the emancipation of the women of Angola. This organization is a part of the MPLA and shares our orientation. But inside the country they've got their own structures, programmes, etc., and represent the interests of the women through their organization. We find it is better if they have their own women leaders, who can lead them inside the country. They are now participating in the struggle without discrimination. When the OMA was formed, MPLA was located only in the northern region of

Angola; now we are in the east and south, so we must train their leaders—women leaders—both politically and militarily. We already have a number of women guerrillas and nurses, and we are training others to carry out political work among the women. In the guerrilla forces the women are not separated from the men; they serve right along with the men, under the same conditions.

Q: *Do women also serve on the action committees?*

A: They have their own OMA groups at every level, with their own elected officers and their women militia, too. Then in each zone the women have one representative who represents them on the zone action committee.

Q: *Have you also introduced democratic procedures within the military structure?*

A: Our movement is a democratic one and so our structures, both military and political, must also operate according to democratic principles. We have ranks within the military, but these ranks only separate the different areas of responsibility. There are no privileges which go with higher ranks. We all eat the same food and other rations are distributed equally.

Q: *Are there possibilities for the lower ranking freedom fighters to express their views or criticize the actions or decisions of the leadership at the various levels?*

A: Yes, of course. All militants have the right to criticize others, and also themselves, as in the party. In our political life we follow this principle of criticism and self-criticism. If someone or something is not going right in the party, politically, militarily, in production, etc., one has the right to say, 'This is not good for such and such reasons.' Anyone, whatever his rank—he may be a political or military leader, he may be in the central committee or the military commission, or a guerrilla or a member of the women's organization—if he is in the party he has a right to speak freely, to say whatever he wants. At all levels and for all ranks there exists criticism and self-criticism.

o

II Amilcar Cabral: *The Politics of Struggle*
i) Liberation and the Petty Bourgeoisie[102]

In the rural areas we have found it necessary to distinguish between two distinct groups: on the one hand, the group which we consider semi-feudal, represented by the Foulas, and, on the other hand, the group which we consider, so to speak, without any defined form of state organization, represented by the Balantes. There are a number of intermediary positions between those two extreme ethnic groups (as regards the social situation). I should like to point out straightaway that although in general the semi-feudal groups were Moslem and the groups without any form of state organization were animist, there is one ethnic group among the animists, the Mandjaks, which had forms of social relations which could be considered feudal at the time when the Portuguese came to Guinea.

I should now like to give you a rapid idea of the social stratification among the Foulas. We consider that the chiefs, the nobles and the religious figures form one group; after them come the artisans and the Dyulas, who are itinerant traders, and then after that come the peasants properly speaking. Although certain traditions concerning collective ownership of the land have been preserved, the chiefs and their entourages have retained considerable privileges as regards ownership of land and the utilization of other people's labour; this means that the peasants who depend on the chiefs are obliged to work for these chiefs for a certain period of the year. The artisans, whether blacksmiths (which is the lowest occupation) or leather-workers or what-not play an extremely important role in the socio-economic life of the Foulas and represent what you might call the embryo of industry. In general the peasants have no rights and they are the really exploited group in Foula society. Women take part in production but they do not own what they produce. Besides, polygamy is a highly respected institution and women are to a certain extent considered the property of their husbands.

Among the Balantes, which are at the opposite extreme, we find a society without any social stratification: there is just a council of old men in each village or group of villages who decide on the day-to-day problems. In the Balante group property and land are considered to belong to the village but each family receives the amount of land needed to ensure subsistence for itself. The means of production, or the instruments of production, are not collective but are owned by families or individuals. The Balantes still retain certain tendencies towards polygamy, although it is mostly a monogamous society. Balante women participate in production, but they own what they produce and this gives them a position which we consider privileged, as they are fairly free; the only point on which they are not free is that children belong to the head of the family, and the head of the family, the husband, always claims any children his wife may have; this is obviously to be explained by the actual economy of the group where a family's strength is ultimately represented by the number of arms there are to cultivate the earth.

In the rural areas I should mention the small African farm owners; this is a numerically small group but all the same it has a certain importance and has proved to be highly active in the national liberation struggle. In the town (I shall not talk about the presence of Europeans in the rural areas as there are none in Guinea) we must first distinguish between the Europeans and the Africans. The Europeans can easily be classified as they retain in Guinea the social stratification of Portugal (obviously depending on the function they exercise in Guinea). In the first place, there are the high officials and the managers of enterprises who form a stratum with practically no contact with the other European strata. After that there are the middle officials, the small European traders, the people employed in commerce and the members of the liberal professions. After that come the workers, who are mainly skilled workers.

Among the Africans we find the higher officials, the middle officials and the members of the liberal professions forming a group; then come the petty officials, those employed in commerce with a contract, who are to be distinguished from those employed in commerce without a contract, who can be fired at any moment. The small farm owners also fall into this group; by assimilation we call all these the African petty bourgeoisie (obviously, if we were to make a more thorough analysis, the higher African officials as well as the middle officials and the members of the liberal professions should also be included in the petty bourgeoisie). Next come the wage-earners (whom we define as those employed in commerce without any contract); among these are certain important sub-groups such as the dockworkers, the people employed on the boats carrying goods and agricultural produce; there are also the servants, who are mostly men in Guinea; there are the people working in repair shops and small factories; there are also the people who work in shops as porters and suchlike—these all come under the heading of wage-earners. You will notice that we are careful not to call these groups the proletariat or the working class.

There is another group of people whom we call the *déclassés*, in which there are two sub-groups to be distinguished. The first sub-group is easy to identify: what would be called the lumpen proletariat if there was a real proletariat: beggars, prostitutes and so on. The other group, not really *déclassé*, to which we have paid a lot of attention, has proved to be extremely important in the national liberation struggle: it is mostly made up of young people, connected to petty-bourgeois or workers' families, who have recently arrived from the rural areas and generally do not work; they thus have close relations with the rural areas, as well as with the towns (and even the Europeans). They sometimes live off one kind of work or another but they generally live at the expense of their families. Here I should just like to point out a difference between Europe and Africa; in Africa there is a tradition which requires that, for example, if I have an uncle living in the town, I can come in and live in his house without working and he will feed me and house me. This creates a certain stratum of people who experience urban life and who can, as we shall see, play a very important role.

Schematically, the methodological approach we have used has been as follows: first, the position of each group must be defined— to what extent and in what way does each group depend on the colonial regime? Next we have to see what position they adopt towards the national liberation struggle. Then we have to study their *nationalist* capacity and lastly, envisaging the post-independence period, their *revolutionary* capacity.

Among the Foulas, the chiefs and their entourages are tied to colonialism; particularly as in Guinea the Foulas were once conquerors (the Portuguese allied themselves with them in order to dominate Guinea at the beginning of the conquest). Thus the chiefs (and their authority as chiefs) are very closely tied to the Portuguese authorities. The artisans are extremely dependent on the chiefs; they live off what they make for the chiefs who are the only ones who can acquire their products so that there are some artisans who are simply content to follow the chiefs. The main point about the Dyula is that their permanent preoccupation is to protect their own personal interests; at least in Guinea, the Dyula are not settled in any one place, they are itinerant traders without any real roots anywhere and their fundamental aim is to get bigger and bigger profits. It is precisely the fact that they are almost permanently on the move which provided us with a most valuable element in the struggle. It goes without saying that there are some Dyula who have not supported our struggle, and there are some who have been used as agents against us by the Portuguese, but there are some whom we have been able to use to mobilize people, at least as far as spreading the initial ideas of the struggle was concerned—all we had to do was give them some reward, as they usually would not do anything without being paid.

Obviously, the group with the greatest interest in the struggle is the peasantry, given the nature of the various different societies in Guinea (feudal, semi-feudal, etc.) and the various degrees of exploitation to which they were subjected; but the question is not simply one of objective interest.

Foula peasants have a strong tendency to follow their chiefs. Thorough and intensive work was therefore needed to mobilize them. The Balantes and the groups without any defined form of state organization put up much more resistance against the Portuguese than the others and they have maintained their tradition of resistance to colonial penetration intact. This is the group that we found most ready to accept the idea of national liberation.

Does the peasantry represent the main revolutionary force, then? In Guinea, it must be said at once that *the peasantry is not a revolutionary force*—which may seem strange, particularly as we have based the whole of our armed struggle for liberation on the peasantry. A distinction must be drawn between a physical force and a revolutionary force; *physically,* the peasantry is a great force in Guinea : it is almost the whole of the population, it controls the nation's wealth; it is the peasantry which produces. But we know from experience what trouble we had convincing the peasantry to fight. It was not possible for our party militants and propaganda workers to find the same kind of welcome among the peasantry in Guinea for the idea of national liberation as the idea found in China.

The Europeans are, in general, hostile to the idea of national liberation; they are the human instruments of the colonial state in our country and they therefore reject *a priori* any idea of national liberation there. It has to be said that the Europeans most bitterly opposed to the idea of national liberation are the workers, while we have sometimes found considerable sympathy for our struggle among certain members of the European petty bourgeoisie.

As for the Africans, the petty bourgeoisie can be divided into three sub-groups as regards the national liberation struggle. First, there is the petty bourgeoisie which is heavily committed, and compromised with colonialism; this includes most of the higher officials and some members of the liberal professions. Second, there is the group which we perhaps incorrectly call the revolutionary petty bourgeoisie; this is the part of the petty bourgeoisie which is nationalist and which was the source of the idea of the national liberation struggle in Guinea. In the middle lies the part of the petty bourgeoisie which has never been able to make up its mind between the national liberation struggle and the Portuguese. Next come the wage-earners, which you can compare roughly with the proletariat in European societies, although they are not exactly the same thing; here, too, there is a majority committed to the struggle, but, again, many members of this group—wage-earners who had an extremely petty-bourgeois mentality and whose only aim was to defend the little they had already acquired—were not easy to mobilize.

Next come the *déclassés,* The really *déclassé* people, the permanent layabouts, the prostitutes and so on have been a great help to the Portuguese police for giving them information; this group has been outrightly against our struggle, perhaps unconsciously so, but nonetheless against our struggle. On the other hand, the group of mainly young people recently arrived from the rural areas with contracts in both the urban and the rural *milieux* has proved extremely dynamic in the struggle. Many of these people joined the struggle right from the beginning and it is among this group that we found many of the cadres whom we have since trained.

The importance of this urban experience lies in the fact that it allows *comparison:* this is the key stimulant required for a *prise de conscience.* It is interesting to note that Algerian nationalism largely sprang up among the émigré workers in France. As far as Guinea is concerned, the idea of the national liberation struggle was born not abroad but in our own country, in a *milieu* where people were subjected to close and incessant exploitation. Many people say that it is the peasants who carry the major burden of exploitation; this may be true, but so far as the struggle is concerned it must be realized that it is not the degree of suffering and hardship involved as such that matters: even extreme suffering in itself does not necessarily produce the *prise de conscience* required for the national liberation struggle. In Guinea the peasants are subjected to a kind of exploitation equivalent to slavery; but even if you try and explain to them that they are being exploited and robbed, it is difficult to convince them by means of an unlived explanation of a technico-economic kind that they are the most exploited people; whereas it is easier to convince the workers and the people employed in the towns who earn, say, ten escudos a day for a job in which a European earns between thirty and fifty, that they are being subjected to massive exploitation and injustice *because they can see it*. To take my own case as a member of the petty-bourgeois group which launched the struggle in Guinea, I was an agronomist working under a European whom everybody knew was one of the biggest idiots in Guinea; I could have taught him his job with my eyes shut but he was the boss: this is the *confrontation* which really matters.

It is our opinion that if we get rid of colonialism in Guinea the main contradiction remaining, the one which will then become the principal contradiction, is that between the ruling classes, the semi-feudal groups, and the members of the groups without any defined form of organization. The first thing to note is that the conquest carried out first by the Mandingues and then by the Foulas was a struggle between two opposite poles which was blocked by the very strong structure of the animist groups. There are other contradictions, such as that between the various feudal groups and those between the upper group and the lower. All this is extremely important for the future, and even while the struggle is still going on we must begin to exploit the contradiction between the Foula people and their chiefs, who are very close to the Portuguese. There is a further contradiction, particularly among the animists, between the collective ownership of the land and the private ownership of the means of production in agriculture. I am not trying to stretch alien concepts here; this is an observation that can be made on the spot: the land belongs to the village, but what is produced belongs to whoever produces it—usually the family or the head of the family.

There are other contradictions which we consider secondary. You may be surprised to know that we consider the contradictions between the tribes a secondary one; our struggle for national liberation and the work done by our party have shown that this contradiction is really not so important. The Portuguese counted on it, but as soon as we organized the liberation struggle properly the contradiction between the tribes proved to be a feeble, secondary contradiction; this does not mean that we do not need to pay attention to this contradiction; we reject both the positions which are to be found in Africa—one which says: there are no tribes, we are all the same, we are all one people in one terrible unity, our party comprises everybody; the other saying: tribes exist, we must base parties on tribes. Our position lies between the two; all structural, organizational and other measures must be taken to ensure that this contradiction does not explode and become a more important contradiction.

This has led us to the following conclusion: we must try and unite everybody in the national liberation struggle against the Portuguese colonialists. It is imperative to organize things so that we always have an instrument available which can solve all the other contradictions. This is what convinced us of the absolute necessity of creating a party during the national liberation struggle. There are some people who interpret our party as a front; perhaps our party is a front at the moment, but within the framework of this front there is our party which is directing the front, and there are no other parties in the front. For the circumstances of the struggle we maintain a general aspect, but within the framework of the struggle we know what our party is, we know where the party finishes and where the people who just rallied for the liberation struggle begin.

When we had made our analysis, we had some knowledge of other experiences and we knew that a struggle of the kind we hoped to lead—and win—has to be led by the working class. We looked for the working class in Guinea and did not find it. What then were we to do? We were just a group of petty bourgeois who were driven by the reality of life in Guinea, by the sufferings we had to endure, and also by the influence events in Africa and elsewhere had on us, in particular the experiences some of us acquired in Portugal and other countries in Europe.

And so this little group began. We first thought of a general movement of national liberation, but this immediately proved unfeasible. We decided to extend our activity to the workers in the towns, and we had some success with this; we launched moves for higher wages, better working conditions and so on. But we obviously did not have a proletariat. We quite clearly lacked revolutionary intellectuals, so we had to start searching, given that we—rightly—did not believe in the revolutionary capacity of the peasants.

One important group in the towns were the dockworkers; another important group were the people working in the boats carrying merchandise, who mostly live in Bissau itself and travel up and down the rivers. These people proved highly conscious of their position and of their economic importance and they took the initiative to launch strikes without any trade union leadership at all. We therefore decided to concentrate all our work on this group. This gave excellent results and this group soon came to form a kind of nucleus which influenced the attitudes of other wage-earning groups in the towns.

We also looked for intellectuals, but there were none, because the Portuguese did not educate people. In any case, what is an intellectual in our country? It would probably be someone who knew the general situation very well, who had some knowledge, not profound theoretical knowledge, but concrete knowledge of the country itself and of its life, as well as of our enemy. We, the people I have talked about, the engineers, doctors, bank clerks and so on, joined together to form a group.

There was also this other group of people in the towns, which we have been unable to classify precisely, which was still closely connected to the rural areas and contained people who spoke almost all the languages that are used in Guinea. They knew all the customs of the rural areas while at the same time possessing a solid knowledge of the European urban *milieux*. They also had a certain degree of self-confidence, they knew how to read and write (which makes a person an intellectual in our country) and so we concentrated our work on these people and immediately started giving them some preparatory training.

We were faced with another difficult problem: we realized that we needed to have people with a mentality which could transcend the context of the national liberation struggle, and so we prepared a number of cadres from the group I have just mentioned, some from the people employed in trade and other wage-earners, and even some peasants, so that they could acquire what you might call a working-class mentality. You may think this is absurd, that in order for there to be working-class mentality the material conditions of the working class should exist.

In fact we managed to inculcate these ideas into a large number of people—the kind of ideas, that is, there would be if there were a working class. We have trained about a thousand cadres at our party school in Conakry; in fact for about two years this was about all we did outside the country. When these cadres returned to the rural areas they inculcated a certain mentality into the peasants and it is among these cadres that we chose the people who are now leading the struggle. We are not a communist party or a Marxist–Leninist party but the people now leading the peasants in the struggle in Guinea are mostly from the urban *milieux* and connected with the urban wage-earning group. When I hear that only the peasantry can lead the struggle am I supposed to think we have made a mistake? All I can say is that at the moment our struggle is going well.

The concept of a party and the creation of parties did not occur spontaneously in Europe; they resulted from a long process of class struggle. When we in Africa think of creating a party now we find ourselves in very different conditions from those in which parties appeared as historico-social phenomena in Europe. This has a number of consequences, so that when you think 'party', 'single party', etc., you must connect all these things up with conditions in Africa, and with the history of the different societies.

A rigorous historical approach is similarly needed when examining another problem related to this—how can the underdeveloped countries evolve towards revolution, towards socialism? There is a preconception held by many people, even on the left, that imperialism made us enter history at the moment when it began its adventure in our countries: this preconception must be denounced. For somebody on the left, and for Marxists in particular, history obviously means the class struggle; our opinion is exactly the contrary. We consider that when imperialism arrived in Guinea it made us leave history—our history. We agree that history in our country is the result of class struggle, but we have our own struggles in our own country. The moment imperialism arrived, colonialism arrived. Obviously, we agree that the class struggle has continued, but it has continued in a very different way : our whole people is struggling against the ruling class of the imperialist countries, and this gives a completely different aspect to the historical evolution of our country. As we see it, in colonial conditions no one stratum can succeed in the struggle for national liberation on its own, and therefore it is all the strata of society which are the agents of history. This brings us to what should be a void—but in fact it is not. What commands history in colonial conditions is not the class struggle; I do not mean that the class struggle in Guinea stopped completely during the colonial period, it continued, but in a muted way. In the colonial period it is the colonial state which commands history.

Our problem is to see who is capable of taking control of the state apparatus when the colonial power is destroyed. In Guinea the peasants cannot read or write, they have almost no relations with the colonial forces during the colonial period except for paying taxes, which is done indirectly. The working class hardly exists as a defined class, it is just an embryo. There is no economically viable bourgeoisie because imperialism prevented it being created. What there is is a stratum of people in the service of imperialism who have learnt how to manipulate the apparatus of the state—the African petty bourgeoisie. This is the only stratum capable of controlling or even utilizing the instruments which the colonial state used against our people. So that we come to the conclusion that in colonial conditions it is the petty bourgeoisie which is the inheritor of state power (though I wish we could be wrong). The moment national liberation comes and the petty bourgeoisie takes power we enter, or rather we return, to history, and thus the internal contradictions of our social and economic conditions will break out again.

When this happens, and particularly as things are now, there will be powerful external contradictions conditioning the internal situation, and not just internal contradictions as before. What attitude can the petty bourgeoisie adopt? Obviously people on the left will call for the revolution; the right will call for the 'non-revolution,' i.e., a capitalist road or something like that. The petty bourgeoisie can either ally itself with imperialism and the reactionary strata in its own country to try and preserve itself as a petty bourgeoisie or ally itself with the workers and peasants, who must themselves take power or control power to make the revolution. We must be very clear exactly what we are asking the petty bourgeoisie to do. Are we asking it to commit suicide? Because if there is a revolution, then the petty bourgeoisie will have to abandon power to the workers and the peasants and cease to exist *qua* petty bourgeoisie. For a revolution to take place depends on the nature of the party (and its size), the character of the struggle which led up to liberation, if there was an armed struggle, what the nature of this armed struggle was and how it developed.

This connects with the problem of the real nature of the national liberation struggle. In Guinea, as in other countries, the implantation of imperialism by force and the presence of the colonial system considerably altered the historical conditions and aroused a response—the national liberation struggle—which is generally considered a revolutionary trend; but this is something which I think needs further examination. I should like to formulate this question: is the national liberation movement something which has simply emerged from within our country, is it a result of the internal contradictions created by the presence of colonialism, or are there external factors which have determined it? In fact I would even go so far as to ask whether, given the advance of socialism in the world, the national liberation movement is not an imperialist initiative. Is the juridical institution which serves as a reference for the right of all peoples to struggle to free themselves a product of the peoples who are trying to liberate themselves? Was it created by the socialist countries who are historical associates? Let us not forget that it was the imperialist countries who recognized the right of all people to national independence. Even Portugal, which is using napalm bombs against our people in Guinea, signed the declaration of the right of all peoples to independence. One may well ask oneself why they were so mad as to do something which goes against their own interests and whether or not it was partly forced on them. The real point is that they signed it. This is where we think there is something wrong with the simple interpretation of the national liberation movement as a revolutionary trend. The objective of the imperialist countries was to prevent the enlargement of the socialist camp, to liberate the reactionary forces in our countries which were being stifled by colonialism and to enable these forces to ally themselves with the international bourgeoisie. The fundamental objective was to create a bourgeoisie where one did not exist, in order specifically to strengthen the imperialist and the capitalist camp. The rise of the bourgeoisie in the new countries, far from being anything surprising, should be considered absolutely normal. It is something that has to be faced by all those struggling against imperialism. We are therefore faced with the problem of deciding whether to engage in an out-and-out struggle against the bourgeoisie right from the start or whether to try and make an alliance with the national bourgeoisie, to try to deepen the absolutely necessary contradiction between the national bourgeoisie and the international bourgeoisie which has promoted the national bourgeoisie to the position it holds.

What really interests us here is neo-colonialism. After the Second World War imperialism entered on a new phase: on the one hand, it worked out the new policy of aid, i.e., granted independence to the occupied countries plus 'aid', and, on the other hand, concentrated on preferential investment in the European countries. This was, above all, an attempt at rationalizing imperialism. Even if it has not yet provoked reactions of a nationalist kind in the European countries, we are convinced that it will do so soon. As we see it, neo-colonialism (which we may call rationalized imperialism) is more a defeat for the international working class than for the colonized peoples. Neo-colonialism is at work on two fronts—in Europe as well as in the underdeveloped countries. Its current framework in the underdeveloped countries is the policy of aid and one of the essential aims of this policy is to create a false bourgeoisie to put a brake on the revolution and to enlarge the possibilities of the petty bourgeoisie as a neutralizer of the revolution. At the same time it invests capital in France, Italy, England and so on. In our opinion the aim of this is to stimulate the growth of the workers' aristocracy, to enlarge the field of action of the petty bourgeoisie so as to block the revolution. In our opinion it is under this aspect that neo-colonialism and the relations between the international working-class movement and our movements must be analysed. *En passant*, I might point out that imperialism is quite prepared to change both its men and its tactics in order to perpetuate itself; it will make and destroy states and, as we have already seen, it will kill its own puppets when they no longer serve its purposes. If need be, it will even create a kind of socialism, which people may soon start calling 'neo-socialism'.

If there have been any doubts about the close relations between our struggle and the struggle of the international working-class movement, neo-colonialism has proved that there need not be any. Obviously I don't think it is possible to forge closer relations between the peasantry in Guinea and the working-class movement in Europe. What we must do first is try and forge closer links between the peasant movement and the wage-earners' movement in our country.

ii) Directives[103]

—In the liberated regions do everything possible to normalize the political life of the people. Section committees of the party (*tabanca* committees), zonal committees, regional committees, must be consolidated and function normally. Frequent meetings must be held to explain to the population what is happening with the struggle, what the party is endeavouring to do at any given moment, and what the criminal intentions of the enemy may be. In regions still occupied by the enemy, reinforce clandestine work, the mobilization and organization of the populations and the preparation of militants for action and support of our fighters.

—Develop political work in our armed forces, whether regular or guerrilla, wherever they may be. Hold frequent meetings. Demand serious political work from political commissars. Start political committees, formed by the political commissars and commander of each unit, in the regular army. Oppose tendencies to *militarism* and make each fighter an exemplary militant of our party.

—Educate ourselves, educate other people, the population in general, to fight fear and ignorance, to eliminate little by little the subjection to nature and natural forces which our economy has not yet mastered. Fight without useless violence against all the negative aspects, prejudicial to mankind, which are still part of our beliefs and traditions. Convince little by little, and in particular the militants of the party, that we shall end by conquering the fear of nature, and that man is the strongest force in nature.

—Demand from responsible party members that they dedicate themselves seriously to study, that they interest themselves in the things and problems of our daily life and struggle in their fundamental and essential aspect, and not simply in their appearance. Learn from life, from our people, learn from books, learn from the experience of others. Never stop learning.

—Responsible members must take life seriously, conscious of their responsibilities, thoughtful about carrying them out, and with a comradeship based on work and duty done. Nothing of this is incompatible with the joy of life, or with love for life and its amusements, or with confidence in the future and in our work.

—Reinforce political work and propaganda within the enemy's armed forces. Write posters, pamphlets, letters. Draw slogans on the roads. Establish cautious links with enemy personnel who want to contact us. Act audaciously and with great initiative in this way. Do everything possible to help enemy soldiers to desert. Assure them of security so as to encourage their desertion. Carry out political work among Africans who are still in enemy service, whether civilian or military. Persuade these brothers to change direction so as to serve the party within the enemy ranks or desert with arms and ammunition to our units.

— We must practise revolutionary democracy in every aspect of our party life. Every responsible member must have the courage of his responsibilities, exacting from others a proper respect for his work and properly respecting the work of others. Hide nothing from the masses of our people. Tell no lies. Expose lies whenever they are told. Mask no difficulties, mistakes, failures. Claim no easy victories.

iii) Ideology and Armed Struggle[104]

It is often said that national liberation is based on the right of all peoples freely to decide about their destinies and that the aim of this liberation is to obtain national independence. Although we do not disagree with this vague and subjective manner of expressing a complex reality, we prefer to be objective since, for us, the basis of national liberation, whatever the formula adopted by international law, lies in the inalienable right of each people to have its own history; and the aim of national liberation is the reconquest of this right usurped by imperialism, i.e., the freeing of the process of development of the national productive forces. For this reason, in our opinion, any national liberation movement which does not give due weight to this base and this aim may indeed fight against imperialism, but it will certainly not be fighting for national liberation.

This implies that, bearing in mind the essential features of the world economy of our time as well as of experiences already gained in the realm of anti-imperialist struggle, the main aspects of the struggle for national liberation is the struggle against neo-colonialism. Furthermore, if we consider that national liberation demands that a deep change should take place in the process of development of the productive forces, we see that the phenomenon of *national liberation* necessarily corresponds to a *revolution*. What matters is being aware of the objective and subjective conditions in which this revolution takes place and knowing the forms or form of struggle best suited to its realization.

We shall not here repeat that these conditions are frankly favourable at the present stage of the history of humanity; it is sufficient to recall that there also exist unfavourable factors, both on the international level and within each nation struggling for its liberation.

On the international plane, it seems to us that the following factors are at the very least unfavourable to the movement of national liberation: the neo-colonial situation of a large number of states achieving political independence being added to others having already achieved it; the progress made by neo-colonialism, particularly in Europe, where imperialism has recourse to preferential investment, encouraging the development of a privileged proletariat with the subsequent lowering of the revolutionary level of the labouring classes; the neo-colonial situation, whether overt or disguised, of some European states which, like Portugal, still possess colonies; the policy known as 'aid to the underdeveloped countries', practised by imperialism with the hope of creating or strengthening the autochthonous pseudo-bourgeoisies, necessarily enfeoffed to the international bourgeoisie, and thus blocking the path to revolution; the claustrophobic revolutionary timidity, which led several newly independent states with internal economic and political conditions favourable to revolution to accept compromise with the enemy or its agents; the growing contradictions beween anti-imperialist states; and, lastly, the threats, by imperialism, to world peace with atomic warfare. These factors contribute to reinforcing imperialism against the movements of national liberation.

Internally, we believe that the most important weaknesses or unfavourable factors lie in the socio-economic structure and in their evolutionary tendencies under imperial pressure or, to be more exact, in the little or complete lack of attention paid to the characteristics of this structure and these tendencies by the national liberation movements in the working out of the strategies of struggle.

This point of view does not claim to diminish the importance of other internal factors unfavourable to national liberation, such as economic underdevelopment, the social backwardness of the popular masses resulting from it and other less important discrepancies. But it should be pointed out that the existence of tribes does not emerge as an important anomaly except in terms of opportunistic attitudes, generally coming from detribalized individuals or groups within the national liberation movement. Contradictions between classes, even embryonic ones, are far more important than contradictions between tribes.

Although the colonial and neo-colonial situation are identical in essence, and though the main aspect of the struggle against imperialism is the neo-colonial aspect, we believe that it is vital to distinguish these two situations in practice. Indeed, the horizontal structure of autochthonous society, though more or less differentiated, and the absence of a political power composed of national elements, make possible the creation of a broad front of unity and struggle in the colonial situation, indispensable moreover to the success of the national liberation movement. But this possibility does not exempt us from rigorous analysis of the indigenous social structure, of the trends of its development and of the adoption in practice of appropriate measures to guarantee a real national liberation. Among these measures, we regard as indispensable the growth of a solidly united avant-garde, aware of the true meaning and aim of the national liberation struggle it must lead. This need is all the more pressing since we know that, with a few rare exceptions, the colonial situation does not allow or demand the significant existence of avant-garde classes (self-aware working classes and rural proletariat) which could ensure the vigilance of the popular masses with regard to the development of the liberation movement. Inversely, the generally embryonic character of the working classes and the economic, social and cultural situation of the most important physical force in the struggle for national liberation—the peasantry—do not enable the two main forces of the struggle to distinguish, on their own, true national independence from factitious political independence. Only a revolutionary avant-garde, generally an active minority, can be aware, from the start, of this difference and bring it, through struggle, to the notice of the popular masses. This explains the basically political character of the struggle for national independence and, to some degree, the importance of the form of struggle in the final result of the phenomenon of national liberation.

In the neo-colonial situation, the more or less accentuated vertical structuration of the indigenous society and the existence of a political power composed of autochthonous elements—national state—actually intensifies the contradictions within this society, and makes the creation of a front as broad as in the colonial case difficult, if not impossible. On the one hand, the material effects (mainly nationalization of the state bureaucracy and the increase of the economic initiative of the indigenous element, particularly on the commercial level) and psychological effects (pride of believing oneself led by one's own compatriots, exploitation of a religious or tribal solidarity between a few rulers and part of the popular masses) help to demobilize a considerable part of the nationalist forces. But the necessarily repressive character of the neo-colonial state *vis-à-vis* the forces of national liberation, the worsening of class discrepancies, the objective permanence of agents and signs of foreign domination (settlers who retain their privileges, armed forces, racial discrimination), the increasing pauperization of the peasantry and the more or less obvious influence of external interests, help to keep the flame of nationalism burning, progressively to sharpen the awareness of vast sectors of the people, and to rally the majority of the population to the ideal of national liberation as a way out of its neo-colonial frustration.

Furthermore, while the autochthonous ruling class is becoming progressively more bourgeois, the development of a working class composed of town workers and agricultural proletariat, all exploited by the indirect domination of imperialism, opens new vistas to the growth of national liberation. This working class, whatever its degree of political awareness (beyond a minimum limit, which is *awareness of its needs*) seems, in the case of neo-colonialism, to constitute the real popular avant-garde in the struggle for national liberation. But it will never be able completely to achieve its mission within the framework of this struggle (which does not end with the gaining of independence) if it does not join solidly with the other exploited classes, the peasants in general (farm workers, share-croppers, agricultural labourers, small farm-owners) and the nationalist petty bourgeoisie. The realization of this alliance demands the mobilization and organization of nationalist forces within the framework (or through the agency) of a strong and well-structured political organization.

Another important distinction between the colonial and neo-colonial situation is to be found in the perspectives of the struggle. The colonial case (where the *nation-class* is fighting against the repressive forces of the bourgeoisie of the colonizing country) may lead, at least apparently, to a nationalist solution (national revolution); the nation wins its independence and hypothetically adopts the economic structure which most suits it. The neo-colonial case (where the labouring classes and their allies are fighting simultaneously against the imperialist bourgeoisie and the autochthonous ruling class) is not resolved by a nationalist solution; it requires the destruction of the capitalist structure implanted by imperialism on the national territory, and postulates, precisely, a socialist solution. The distinction results mainly from the difference in level of the productive forces in the two cases and from the subsequent intensification of the class struggle.

It would not be difficult to show that, in the past, this distinction is barely apparent. One need only remember that in our present historical conditions—liquidation of imperialism which perpetuates its domination over our peoples by all possible means, and consolidation of socialism over a considerable part of the world—there are only two possible paths for an independent nation: to go back to imperial domination (neo-colonialism, capitalism, state capitalism) or the path of socialism. This option, on which compensation for the efforts and sacrifices of the popular masses during the struggle depends, is strongly influenced by the form of the fight and the degree of revolutionary awareness of those leading it.

Facts spare us from proving that the essential element of imperialism is violence. If we accept the principle *according to which the struggle for liberation is a revolution,* and that this ends only when the flag is hoisted and the national anthem sung, we shall see that there is not and cannot be national liberation without the use of liberating violence on the part of the nationalist forces, to counter the criminal violence of the agents of imperialism. No one doubts that, whatever may be the local characteristics, imperialism implies a state of permanent violence against the nationalist forces. No people on this earth having been subjected to the imperialist yoke (colonial or neo-colonial) has conquered its independence (nominal or actual) without victims. What matters is to determine what forms of violence may be used by the forces of national liberation, not only to counter the violence of imperialism, but also to guarantee, through struggle, the final victory of its cause: real national independence.

Past and present experiences of certain peoples, the current situation of the struggle for national liberation throughout the world (particularly in Vietnam, the Congo, and Zimbabwe) as well as the situation of permanent violence, or at least of discrepancies and uncertainties, of certain countries which have gained their independence by so-called pacific means, show us that not only are compromises with imperialism inoperative, but also that the normal path of national liberation, imposed upon the peoples by imperialist repression, is *armed struggle*.

It is evident, too, that both the effectiveness of this path and the stability of the situation to which it will lead after liberation depend not only on the characteristics of the organization of the struggle, but also on the political and moral awareness of those who, for historical reasons, are in a position to be the immediate heirs of the colonial or neo-colonial state. For the facts have shown that the only social sector capable of awareness of the reality of imperialist domination, and of running the state machinery inherited from this domination, is the autochthonous petty bourgeoisie. If we bear in mind the unpredictability, the complexity of the natural tendencies inherent in the economic situation of this social structure or class, we shall see that this specific inevitability of our situation constitutes one of the weaknesses of the national liberation movement.

The colonial situation which does not admit of the development of an autochthonous pseudo-bourgeoisie and in which the popular masses do not as a whole reach the necessary level of political awareness before the unleashing of the phenomenon of national liberation, offers the petty bourgeoisie the historical opportunity of running the struggle against foreign domination. Because of its objective and subjective situation—higher level of life than that of the masses, more frequent contacts with the agents of colonialism and hence more opportunities for humiliation, higher level of education and political culture, etc.—it is the stratum which most rapidly becomes aware of the need to free itself from foreign domination. This historical responsibility is taken on by the sector of the petty bourgeoisie that can, in the colonial context, be called revolutionary, while the other sectors ally themselves with colonialism to defend their social situation, however deludedly.

The neo-colonial situation, which demands the liquidation of the autochthonous pseudo-bourgeoisie for the achievement of national liberation, also gives the petty bourgeoisie the opportunity of fulfilling a front-rank, indeed decisive, role in the struggle for the liquidation of foreign domination. But, in this case, in virtue of the progress achieved in the social structure, the function of direction of

the struggle is shared (to a greater or lesser degree) by the more educated of the labouring classes and even with elements of the national
pseudo-bourgeoisie, imbued with patriotic feeling. The role of the
sector of the petty bourgeoisie which takes part in leading the
struggle is even more important, particularly since in the neo-
colonial situation itself it is more apt to take over these functions,
either because the working masses have economic and cultural limitations, or because of the complexes and limitations of an ideological nature which characterize the sector of the national pseudo-
bourgeoisie which is involved in the struggle. In this case, it is
important to note that the mission entrusted to it demands from
this sector of the petty bourgeoisie a great revolutionary conscience,
the ability to interpret the aims of the masses faithfully at each
phase of the struggle and to identify with them more and more.

But, however great the degree of revolutionary awareness of the
sector of the petty bourgeoisie called upon to fulfil this historical
function, it cannot free itself from this objective reality: the petty
bourgeoisie, as a service class (i.e., which is not directly involved in
the process of production), does not have at its disposal the economic bases which would guarantee it the assumption of power.
Indeed, history shows us that, whatever the role—sometimes important—played by individuals of the petty bourgeoisie in the
course of a revolution, this class has never been in possession of political power. And it could not be, because political power (state) is
based on the economic capacity of the ruling class and in the
conditions of colonial and neo-colonial society. This capacity is held
by only two entities : imperialist capital and the national labouring
classes.

To retain the power that national liberation puts into its hands,
the petty bourgeoisie has only one path: to give free rein to its
natural tendencies of embourgeoisement, allow the development of
a bureaucratic bourgeoisie—and of intermediaries—in the goods
cycle, in order to become a national pseudo-bourgeoisie, i.e., to betray the revolution and rally necessarily to imperialist capital. Now
all this corresponds to the neo-colonial situation, i.e., to the betrayal
of the objectives of national liberation. So as not to betray these
aims, the petty bourgeoisie has only one path: to strengthen its
revolutionary conscience, repudiate the temptations of embourgeoisement and the natural pressures of its class mentality, identify
with the labouring classes, not set itself up against the normal

development of the process of revolution. This means that the revolutionary petty bourgeoisie must be capable of class suicide, to come to life again as revolutionary workers. This shows us that though national liberation is essentially a political problem, the conditions of its development lend it certain characteristics which belong to the moral sphere.

NOTES

1 *Guerrilla Warfare: A Method*, in *Venceremos: The Speeches and Writings of Ernesto Che Guevara*, ed. John Gerassi (New York: Macmillan, and London: Weidenfeld and Nicolson, 1968), p. 279.

2 V. I. Lenin, *Selected Works*, three vols. (New York: International Publishers, 1967), Vol. 1, p. 200.

3 Letter to St Petersburg Social Democrats, cited in Brenda Jones, 'Lenin', *Sunday Times Magazine*, (London), 5 April 1970.

4 Lenin, *Selected Works, op. cit.* (1967), Vol. III, p. 91.

5 Lenin, *Selected Works, op. cit.* (1967), Vol. II, p. 427.

6 Lenin, *Guerrilla Warfare, Collected Works*, Vol. II (Moscow: Foreign Languages Publishing House, 1962).

7 Report of 25 November 1928, in *Selected Works of Mao Tsetung*, four vols. (Peking: Foreign Languages Press, 1965), Vol. I, p 73.

8 *ibid.*, pp. 97–8.

9 *ibid.*, pp. 123–4.

10 *ibid.*, pp. 165–7.

11 Mao, *Selected Works, op. cit.*, Vol. II, pp. 305–34, and included in the present volume as 'Revolution in Two Stages'.

12 *Time*, (New York), 10 March 1969.

13 Thakin Ba Thein Tin, 'Armed Struggle and Mao's Thought', in *Peking Review*, 25 August and 1 September 1967. The author was the CP's Vice-Chairman.

14 *Le Monde* (Paris), 8 May 1969.

15 See the article 'Liberated Areas', in *Communist International*, 5 March 1935, by a Chinese theoretician calling himself 'Li'.

16 See Cabral's analysis in the present volume, p. 386; also Gérard Chaliand, *Lutte Armée en Afrique* (Paris: Maspero, 1967); English ed. *Armed Struggle in Africa* (New York and

London: Monthly Review Press, 1969); and Basil Davidson, *The Liberation of Guinée* (London : Penguin, 1969).

17 Frantz Fanon, *The Wretched of the Earth* (New York: Grove Press, 1966), p. 33.

18 'Notre stratégie de la guérilla', in *Partisans* (Paris), January–February 1968.

19 From the French ed., *op. cit.*, p. 49.

20 See his *L'économie de l'Ouest-Africain* (Paris : Maspero, 1966); see also Ngouo Woungly Massaga (commander of ALNC's second front), 'Cameroon: A Watchword', in *Tricontinental* (Havana), January–April 1968.

21 Debray, *Revolution in the Revolution?* (New York : Grove Press, 1967), p. 24.

22 See Debray, *Essais sur l'Amérique Latine* (Paris : Maspero, 1967); English ed. *Strategy for Revolution,* ed. Robin Blackburn (London: Jonathan Cape, 1970); Ruben Vasques Diaz, *La Bolivia à l'heure de Che* (Paris: Maspero, 1968); Guevara, *Guerrilla Warfare* (New York : Monthly Review, 1961), and *Venceremos,* op. cit. (especially Chs 7, 9, 21, 35); Castro, *Aniversario del Triumfo de la Revolución Cubana* (Havana : Editora Política, 1967), and *'Criterios de Nuestra Revolución'*, in *Cuba Socialista* (Havana, September 1965), and the following speeches : 2 February 1962 ('Second Declaration of Havana'), 15 January 1966 (closing the Tricontinental Conference), 13 March 1967 (included herein in Vol. II), and 10 August 1967 (closing OLAS); Armando Hart, *Informe de la Delegación Cubana a la Primera Conferencia de la OLAS* (Havana : OLAS, July–August 1967, included herein in Vol. II); Carlos Romeo, 'Revolutionary Practice and Theory in Latin America', in *Latin American Radicalism,* ed. I. L. Horowitz, Josué de Castro and John Gerassi (New York : Random House, 1969); Miguel Arraes, *Le Brésil* (Paris : Maspero, 1969); Turcios Lima, untitled collection of writings, Institute del Libro, Havana, 1968; Hector Bejar Rivera, *Peru 1965: Apuntes Sobre una Experiencia Guerrillera* (Havana : Casa de las Americas, 1969); Carlos Marighela, *Pour la Libération du Brésil* (Paris : Seuil, 1970).

23 See Castro's OLAS speech, *op. cit.*

24 See John Gerassi, *The Great Fear in Latin America* (New York and London: Collier-Macmillan, 1965), pp. 327–9 and 443–6.

25 See *What is to be done?*, *Selected Works, op. cit.* (1967), Vol. I, pp. 97–257.

26 See his 'The Road of our Revolution', in *Arauco* (Santiago de Chile), February 1965.

27 *Colombie: Guérillas du Peuple* (Paris: Editions Sociales, 1969).

28 *Revolution in the Revolution?*, *op. cit.*, pp. 110–11.

29 *ibid.*, p. 113.

30 Textbook, originally entitled *The Chinese Revolution and the Chinese Communist Party*, written in Yenan in December 1939 (with help from other members of the Central Committee of the CCP) and used extensively in CP cadre-formation schools (pamphlet, English version, London: Foreign Languages Press, 1966).

31 The military section of a report given on 25 April 1945 (before the end of the Second World War) to the seventh Congress of the Chinese Communist Party, as reprinted in *The Battle Front of the Liberated Areas* (Peking: Foreign Languages Press, 1962).

32 Published in *Renmin Ribae* (People's Daily), China, 3 September 1965.

33 Mao, 'A Single Spark can Start a Prairie Fire', *Works, op. cit.*, Vol. I, p. 124.

34 Mao, 'Problems of Strategy in China's Revolutionary War', *Works, op. cit.*, Vol. I, p. 248.

35 V. I. Lenin, 'The Revolutionary Army and the Revolutionary Government', *Collected Works*, English ed. (Moscow: Foreign Languages Publishing House, 1962), Vol. VIII, p. 565.

36 The 'Four-Point Statement on China's Policy Towards the United States', in *Peking Review*, 13 May 1966.

37 Originally published in Bengali in *Katha o Kalam* (Siliguri, Darjeeling), October 1967; reproduced in English in *Liberation* (New Delhi), February 1968—the organ of India's Marxist–Leninist communists (Maoists).

38   See John Gerassi, *North Vietnam: A Documentary* (New York: Bobbs-Merrill, and London: Allen and Unwin, 1968).

39   Originally published in *Hoc Tap* (Study), September 1963, the theoretical organ of the Central Committee of the Vietnam Workers' Party (CP); English ed. (Peking: Foreign Languages Press, 1964).

40   Quoted in F. Engels, *Anti-Duhring* (Moscow : Foreign Languages Publishing House, 1959), p. 254.

41   Marx and Engels, 'Marx to L. Kugelman', *Selected Works* (Moscow: Foreign Languages Publishing House, 1955), Vol. II, p. 463.

42   Lenin, *Selected Works* (Moscow : Foreign Languages Publishing House, 1951), Vol. II Part I, pp. 246–7.

43   Lenin, *Selected Works* (London: Lawrence and Wishart, 1946), Vol. 10, p. 164.

44   Lenin, *Collected Works, op. cit.* (1962), Vol. II, p. 172.

45   Lenin, *Collected Works* (New York : International Publishers), Vol. XIX, p. 354.

46   *ibid.*, p. 366.

47   Lenin, *Collected Works, op. cit.* (1962), Vol. II, p. 173.

48   *ibid.*, p. 176.

49   Joseph Stalin, *Works* (Moscow: Foreign Languages Publishing House, 1953), Vol. 6, p. 121.

50   One of two articles published in pamphlet form 'on the occasion of the fiftieth anniversary of the October revolution', entitled *Forward Under the Glorious Banner of Revolution* (Hanoi: Foreign Languages Publishing House, 1967).

51   Published in *Vietnamese Studies* (Hanoi), No. 8, January 1966.

52   Speech celebrating the Thirtieth Anniversary of the Workers' Party of Korea (CP), delivered in Pyongyang on 10 October 1965 and published in Kim Il Sung, *Selected Works* (Pyongyang: Foreign Languages Publishing House, 1965), Vol. II.

53   Joan Robinson, *Monthly Review*, January–February 1965.

54   *op. cit.*

55   Written for the first issue of the organ of the Organization of Solidarity of Peoples in Africa, Asia and Latin America (OSPAAAL), printed in Havana, 12 August 1967, reprinted in *The People's Korea* (Tokyo), 23 August 1967.

56 From *Indonesian Society and Indonesian Revolution* (Jakarta: Jajasan Pembaruan and Demos, 1963).

57 From a speech delivered at the Fifth Congress of the Party of Labour of Albania at Tirana, November 1966; English version in *Indonesian Tribune* (Tirana), December 1966.

58 Article published in English by *World Outlook*, 16 September 1966; in three parts in *The Militant*, 3, 10 and 17 October 1966; and in pamphlet form (New York: Merit Publishers, 1966). All three are publications of the Fourth International.

59 *Constitution of the PKI* (Jakarta : Central Committee of the Partai Kommunis Indonesia, 1964).

60 M. H. Lukman, *About the Constitution* (Jakarta: Jajasan Pembaruan, 1959).

61 These statements were made to a Japanese correspondent. See *Asahi Shimbun* (Tokyo), 2 December 1965.

62 *ibid.*

63 *Granma* (Havana), English ed., 15 May 1966.

64 D. N. Aidit, *The Indonesian Revolution. Its Historical Background and Its Future* (Jakarta: Jajasan Pembaruan, 1964).

65 D. N. Aidit, *Forty Years of the PKI* (Jakarta : Jajasan Pembaruan, 1964).

66 Aidit, *The Indonesian Revolution, op. cit.*

67 *The Constitution of the PKI.*

68 Aidit, *Forty Years of the PKI, op. cit.*

69 D. N. Aidit, *Be a Good and Better Communist* (Jakarta: Jajasan Pembaruan, 1964).

70 D. N. Aidit, *In Defence of Pantja-Sila* (Jakarta: Jajasan Pembaruan, 1964).

71 Aidit, *The Indonesian Revolution, op. cit.*

72 Aidit, *Forty Years of the PKI, op. cit.*

73 D. N. Aidit, *The Peasants Crush the Village Devils* (Jakarta: Jajasan Pembaruan, 1964).

74 *World Marxist Review,* November 1965.

75 *Manila Chronicle,* 6 June 1964.

76 *The Economist* (London), 4 February 1967.

77 *ibid.*

78   *Philippine Herald,* 9 June 1966; and *Solidarity* (Manila), April–June 1966.

79   *Problems of Communism,* March–April 1967.

80   *The Economist, ibid.*

81   13 November 1967.

82   21 February 1969.

83   August 1950.

84   From Chs 21–5 of *Born of the People* (New York: International Publishers Co., 1953).

85   CBS, 11 June 1967.

86   Pamphlet in English, January 1968.

87   Theses (1) submitted for discussion to the Israeli Socialist Organization in August 1966 (later adopted) and published in English in pamphlet form by *Matzpen* (Compass), which is the ISO's Hebrew monthly journal (Tel-Aviv), July 1968; followed by declaration (2) by *Matzpen* from the same pamphlet.

88   Issued on 14 January by the Central Committee of Al-Fatah in all languages.

89   Pamphlet issued by the DPLF after August 1968 and translated by A. Shams.

90   Transcription of an unpublished taped interview by Bill Hillier of *Peace News* (London) of a top-ranking member of the DPFLP, in London on 16 May 1969.

91   Pamphlet issued in 1967. Translation from the Arabic by Fawwaz Trabulsi.

92   A series of notes written after the summer of 1960. The first set was published in *Révolution Africaine,* 14 December 1963; the second set, on the death of Lumumba, is from *Tricontinental,* July–August 1967. Both translations from the French by Juan Mechón.

93   Report presented at the Second African Peoples' Conference, 25–9 January 1960, in the name of Morocco's National Union of Popular Forces (UNFP), followed by the author's concluding remarks at the Afro-Asian Peoples' Solidarity Conference, Moshi, Tanganyika (Tanzania), February 1963. Translations by Judith Landry.

94 Programme of the National Liberation Front of Algeria, adopted by the National Revolutionary Council of the FLN in exile, at Tripoli, Libya, in June 1962. Published as a pamphlet in French by the FLN's Foreign Policy Department, and in English by the *Workers' Vanguard*, Toronto, Canada, in February 1963.

95 From various articles in *Legal Aspects of the UN Action in the Congo* (New York: Association of the Bar of New York City, 1962).

96 Lectures in French reproduced, with sample longhand photostats, by the Centre de Recherche et d'Information Socio-Politique (CRISP) of Brussels in their 'Travaux Africains du CRISP', Dossier documentaire no. 3, November 1965, in a booklet entitled *Les Cahiers de Gambona: Instructions Politiques et Militaires des Partisans Congolais (1964–1965)*. Translation by Martin Rossdale.

97 Statement made by the author during the 'Rivonia Trial' for sedition and sabotage, which ended, in June 1964, with his conviction.

98 Programme of the South African CP, adopted by its Fifth National Conference in 1962, and published by *The African Communist*, an official organ of the South African CP, in a pamphlet entitled *The Road to South African Freedom* (no date, but early 1963).

99 Report adopted by the Consultative Conference of the ANC held in Morogoro, Tanzania, from 25 April to 1 May 1969, and published in *Sechaba*, the official organ of the ANC, July 1969.

100 Penguin Books, 1969.

101 Interview by Don Barnett in Dar es Salaam on 21 March 1968, shortly before Monimambu, who had been wounded, returned to his command post, published in the *Guardian* (New York), 27 April, 7 and 11 May 1968.

102 From a series of speeches delivered at a seminar in Treviglio (Italy), 1–3 May 1964, convened by the Centro Frantz Fanon of Milan, and published in the *International Socialist Journal*, August 1964.

103 A series of directives issued by Cabral in 1965, translated by Basil Davidson and published in his *The Liberation of Guiné* (London : Penguin, 1969).

104   Speech delivered at the First Conference of the Organization of Solidarity of the Peoples of Asia, Africa and Latin America (OSPAAAL or Tricontinental Conference) held in Havana, 3–12 January 1966. Translation by Judith Landry.